THE LAW OF
TRAFFIC OFFENCES

Second Edition

by

Scott C. Hutchison, B.A., LL.B.
Crown Counsel
Crown Law Office — Criminal

Ministry of the Attorney General of Ontario

David S. Rose, B.A., LL.B.
Criminal Law Practitioner

Philip Downes, B.A., M.A., LL.B.
Crown Counsel
Crown Law Office — Criminal
Ministry of the Attorney General of Ontario

CARSWELL
Thomson Professional Publishing

The publisher is not engaged in rendering legal, accounting or other professional advice. If legal advice or other expert assistance is required, the services of a competent professional should be sought. The analysis contained herein represents the opinions of the authors and should in no way be construed as being either official or unofficial policy of any governmental body.

This work reproduces official English language versions of federal statutes and/or regulations. As this material also exists in official French language form, the reader is advised that reference to the official French language version may be warranted in appropriate circumstances.

The paper used in this publication meets the minimum requirements of the American National Standard for Information Sciences — Permanence of Paper for Printed Library Materials, ANSI Z39.48-1984.

Canadian Cataloguing in Publication Data

Hutchison, Scott C., 1962–
    The law of traffic offences

2nd ed.
Includes index.
ISBN 0-459-55345-3 (bound)
ISBN 0-459-55347-X (pbk.)

1. Traffic violations — Ontario.   I. Rose, David, 1961–   .
II. Downes, Philip, 1967–   .   III. Title.

KEO535.H87 1998   345.713'0247   C98-932427-3
KF2231.H87 1998

CARSWELL
Thomson Professional Publishing

One Corporate Plaza, 2075 Kennedy Road, Scarborough, Ontario M1T 3V4
Customer Service:
Toronto 1-416-609-3800
Elsewhere in Canada/U.S. 1-800-387-5164
Fax 1-800-298-5094

To Cathy, Neil and
their continuing work
SCH

To my wife Lisa, and my parents
DSR

To Dawne
PD

Acknowledgments

It has been almost ten years since the first edition of The Law of Traffic Offences appeared. Like any area of the law, the rules governing the prosecution and defence of traffic offences have changed over time. Some changes have been minor or incremental; others more substantial. Cumulatively, however, these minor and substantial changes mandated the preparation of a new edition.

The last ten years have also seen changes for the authors of the first edition. John Marko, a young lawyer freshly called in 1989, is now one of the most respected members of the criminal defence bar in Toronto. While the pressures of his practice ultimately prevented him from participating in the revision of the text, he continued with his customary courtesy to offer suggestions and guidance. We are indebted to him for the generosity and graciousness he has again demonstrated in dealing with a range of issues related to the text.

Two new authors have worked on this edition. David Rose is a lawyer in downtown Toronto with a busy litigation practice. Philip Downes is counsel in the Crown Law Office - Criminal, a branch of the Ministry of the Attorney General of Ontario.

Many people have offered us assistance in revising and improving the first edition and we are grateful to them all. A few require special mention. G. Paul Renwick provided expert advice on the issues presented in the chapter on "Common Offences". Brian Pregler brought to bear his excellent research skills identifying cases and statutes for updating. Phyllis Rose responded to computer crises by retyping chapter 7 on a Sunday. Phil and Scott are fortunate to work in the best criminal law office in Canada, the Crown Law Office - Criminal. We are grateful to our colleagues for their support and to our supervisors for the remarkable professional environment they foster.

Rachel Frances and Jilean Bell at Carswell have seen us through another project with their usual patience and professionalism.

David wishes to thank his wife, Lisa, for her patience during this project, and for surrendering the dining room table to stacks of cases during the writing of this edition.

Phil extends his gratitude to Dawne Way, for providing necessary perspective, and for tolerating his practical expertise on parking offences.

Scott offers his thanks to Catherine Bellinger, the bravest person he has ever met. (She knows a lot about driving. Really.)

While all of these people helped, none of them can be blamed for any deficiencies in the book. Those remain the responsibility of gremlins, pets and, if those excuses fail, computers.

The opinions expressed in this text are those of the authors alone, and do not necessarily reflect the opinions of the Ministry of the Attorney General.

We have tried to state the law as of August 15, 1998.

SCH
DSR
PD

Table of Contents

Table of Cases

1

General Matters

1. INTRODUCTION

The use of public highways in Canada is regulated by a number of different statutes and regulations enacted by the provincial and territorial levels of government.[1] In addition to these laws, federal legislation of general application governs certain aspects of the use of motor vehicles and highways throughout Canada. This text is directed at the most common offences which arise under the provincial and territorial schemes of regulation and the procedures related to them. Readers interested in the more serious *Criminal Code* offences are referred to *Criminal Code Driving Offences*[2] an excellent and exhaustive study of those offences.

---

1 The principal body of law governing the use of roadways is to be found at the provincial and territorial level. In Ontario, for example, there are a number of statutes which govern vehicles and the use of public and private roads, including: *Highway Traffic Act*, R.S.O. 1990, c. H.8; *Provincial Offences Act*, R.S.O. 1990, c. P.33; *Compulsory Automobile Insurance Act*, R.S.O. 1990, c. C.25; *Negligence Act*, R.S.O. 1990, c. N.1; *Motorized Snow Vehicles Act*, R.S.O. 1990, c. M.44; *Truck Transportation Act*, R.S.O. 1990, c. T.22; *Public Vehicles Act*, R.S.O. 1990, c. P.54; *Dangerous Goods Transportation Act*, R.S.O. 1990, c. D.1; *Off-Road Vehicles Act*, R.S.O. 1990, c. O.4. At the federal level the *Criminal Code of Canada*, R.S.C. 1985, c. C-46 creates a number of offences related to the use of motor vehicles both on and off public roadways which apply throughout Canada. These statutes are considered exhaustively in M. Segal's three volume *Manual of Motor Vehicle Law* (Carswell, Toronto: looseleaf 1982). As well, reference might be made to M. Segal & R. Libman *1997 Annotated Ontario Provincial Offences Act* (Carswell, Toronto: 1997).

2 McCleod, Takash & Segal, *Criminal Code Driving Offences* (Carswell, Toronto: 1987, looseleaf).

As noted, each province and territory has its own statute (or statutes) governing the use of vehicles and their use on public highway.[3] While each province or territory's statute includes provisions addressing matters unique to the particular jurisdiction, the general organisation and substance of these laws demonstrates a surprising measure of consistency.[4] Similarly, while the procedural regimes in place are based on different Acts, and each has a local 'flavour', there are elements in common which provide the basis for a discussion of issues which arise in any procedural regime. In this text we have attempted to deal with those similarities and themes in the context of a discussion of traffic offences. In some cases this is done through an examination of the key statutes in Ontario which are, in most respects, representative of the approaches taken elsewhere in the country.

2. CONSTITUTIONAL AUTHORITY IN RELATION TO HIGHWAY TRAFFIC

(a) Division of Power

The authority of the provinces to make laws creating highway traffic offences is found in their broad jurisdiction over "property and civil rights" under s. 92(13) of the *Constitution Act, 1867*. While the federal Parliament has exclusive authority to make Criminal Law, the provinces retain the power to enforce duly enacted regulatory schemes with fines or with a term of imprisonment of less than two years.[5]

There may be (indeed, there often is) some overlap between provincial and federal legislation. Consider, the provincial offence of "fail to remain at or return to the scene"[6] which is similar to the criminal offence of "fail to stop";[7] the conduct regulated is the same but both offences are within the constitutional jurisdiction of the enacting body.[8] This duplication or overlap of prohibitions does not render either statute invalid: only where it is impossible for the subject to obey the federal and provincial law at the same time will

---

3 The various provincial statutes and their key provisions are set out in Appendix A in table form.

4 See Appendix A which sets out in table form the various provincial statutes.

5 *R. v. Corry*, [1932] 1 W.W.R. 853 (Alta. C.A.); *Prince Edward Island (Provincial Secretary) v. Egan*, [1941] S.C.R. 396; *R. v. Mankow* (1959), 28 W.W.R. 433 (Alta. C.A.). This does not mean everything enacted under the guise of 'highway traffic' is constitutional. *Highway Traffic Act* provisions, which are in 'pith and substance' criminal law (e.g., street controls which are really anti-prostitution legislation), will fall outside provincial competence and be unconstitutional: *Westendorp v. R.* [1983] 1 S.C.R. 43.

6 Ontario *Highway Traffic Act*, R.S.O. 1990, c. H.8, s. 200; *Motor Vehicle Act*, R.S.B.C. 1996, c. 318, s. 62.

7 *Criminal Code*, s. 236.

8 *R. v. Stephens*, [1960] S.C.R. 823; *A.G. Québec v. Gagne*, [1969] R.L. 534; *R. v. Mankow, supra* note 5.

there be any conflict. In such a case, the federal legislation will govern and the provincial statute will yield.[9] The nature of traffic regulation, however, is such that, in most cases, there will be complementary (as opposed to conflicting) prohibitions.[10] For example, the provincially created offence of failing to stop for an officer when signalled to do so on a highway is a valid provincial offence even though it arguably overlaps with the federal *Criminal Code* offence of resisting or obstructing a peace officer. There is no constitutional inconsistency because it is possible (indeed, desirable) to comply with both the *Code* and the provincial statute.[11]

(b) Indian[12] Reserve Lands and Special Federal Jurisdiction

The extent to which provincial law applies to land such as Indian reserves or areas of special federal jurisdiction (such as airports and train stations) has been much litigated.

(i) *Indian Reserves*

With its judgment in *R. v. Francis*[13] the Supreme Court of Canada went a long way to resolving the question of whether provincial legislation (including traffic offences) applies to Indian reserve lands. The defendant had been convicted of failing to yield a right of way contrary to the New Brunswick *Motor Vehicle Act*.[14] He argued that he could only be convicted under the *Indian Reserve Traffic Regulations* (a federal statutory instrument) because of the federal government's exclusive jurisdiction to make laws which touched on "Indians".[15] The court rejected this, observing, "that, in the absence of conflicting federal legislation, provincial motor vehicle laws of general application apply *ex proprio vigore* on Indian reserves."[16] In other words, in general, provincial traffic laws apply to drivers and vehicles used on territory within Indian

---

9 *Multiple Access Ltd. v. McCutcheon* (1982), 138 D.L.R. (3d) 1 (S.C.C.); *Bank of Montreal v. Hall* (1990), 65 D.L.R. (4th) 361 (S.C.C.); Hogg, *Constitutional Law of Canada* (4th ed.) (Carswell, Toronto: 1997) ch. 16, pp. 423-441.

10 For a discussion of the procedural relationships between federal and provincial offences, either as included offences, or as giving rise to a plea based on 'double jeopardy' (or *autrefois*) principles, see Chapter Two: Procedural Issues in Traffic Offence Trials.

11 *R. v. Hisey* (1985), 12 O.A.C. 191 (Ont. C.A.). See also *R. v. Stephens*, [1960] C.C.S. 935 (S.C.C.). In *R. v. Ulysse* (1978), 44 C.C.C. (2d) 180 (Que. S.C.) we see a similar conclusion respecting overlapping prohibitions on driving while under a licence suspension.

12 The term "Indian" is regarded in some circles as disrespectful of First Nations people. It is used here as a legal term of art having its origin in, and taking its meaning from, s. 91 of the *Constitution Act, 1867* and the *Indian Act*, R.S.C. 1985, c. I-5, s. 1.

13 (1988), 41 C.C.C. (3d) 217 (S.C.C.).

14 R.S.N.B. 1973, c. M-17.

15 C.R.C. 1978, c. 959.

16 *Supra*, note 13 at p. 219-220.

reserves. The only limit on this general application of provincial laws is the possible existence of federal legislation which is *inconsistent* with the provincial statute which would otherwise apply. The issue in such cases becomes whether the provincial law is inconsistent with valid federal legislation and therefore inoperative under the doctrine of paramountcy. Where provincial regulation effectively compliments, rather than conflicts with, federal law, both can exist and apply of their own force.

(This does not mean that provincial traffic laws necessarily apply to all aspects of vehicle use on a reserve. The question of whether, for example, the law applies to a particular road or lot as a "highway" must be answered, as in any case. So, for example, if a roadway on a reserve was maintained, authorized and supervised by band members, and not accessible to the general public, it might not be considered to be a 'highway' for the purposes of those sections of the traffic legislation which only apply to vehicle use on a highway.[17])

(ii) *Federal Jurisdiction*

The federal government, in addition to its authority to criminalize serious vehicle misconduct, also has the power to make laws that are incidental to other federal heads of power.[18] For example, the federal government enjoys jurisdiction over aeronautics and airports. This jurisdiction gives the federal government the related authority to make laws respecting the use of vehicles on and around airports.[19] This authority does not, however, create a 'federal enclave' which ousts provincial jurisdiction.[20]

As well, the federal government has the authority to make laws dealing with traffic and parking issues in certain parts of Ottawa/Hull arising from the area's status as the National Capital Region.[21]

(iii) *Inter-jurisdictional Immunity*

The constitutional relationship between the provinces and the federal government includes a rule of interpretation creating a limited form of "inter-jurisdictional immunity". This in effect prevents one level of government from frustrating the efforts of the other.

---

17 *Galligos v. Louis* (1984), 33 M.V.R. 102 (B.C. S.C.), affirmed (1986), 46 M.V.R. 288 (B.C. C.A.). For other conclusions on different factual considerations, see *R. v. Wilson* (1990), 24 M.V.R. (2d) 284 (Man. Prov. Ct.), *R. v. Canute*, [1983] 5 W.W.R. 566 (B.C. Co. Ct.) and *R. v. Bellegarde* (1989), 80 Sask. R. 269 (Sask. Q.B.).

18 *R. v. Red Line Ltd.* (1930), 54 C.C.C. 271 (Ont. C.A.).

19 *R. v. Trabulsey* (1995), 97 C.C.C. (3d) 147 (Ont. C.A.), leave to appeal refused (1996), 104 C.C.C. (3d) vi (S.C.C.); *Desrosiers v. Thinel* (1962), 33 D.L.R. (2d) 715 (S.C.C.).

20 *R. v. Trabulsey, supra*; *R. v. Dick* (1985), 22 C.C.C. (3d) 129 (S.C.C.).

21 *R. v. Taggart*, [1966] 1 C.C.C. 137 (Ont. C.A.).

In *Greening*[22] Canada Post argued on behalf of two employees that provisions of the provincial traffic laws did not apply to drivers of Canada Post trucks. If the law interfered with the efficient collection and delivery of mail, as Canada Post claimed, then, according to the Canada Post argument, the law was unconstitutional:[23] the federal government has constitutional jurisdiction over "postal service"[24] and the provinces cannot interfere with that jurisdiction. This contention was rejected by the court. The doctrine of inter-jurisdictional immunity can only be invoked when the law being attacked interferes with some vital or integral part of the federal undertaking. The rules of the road which Canada Post was obliged to obey under provincial traffic laws only impacted on the periphery of the 'federal quality' of the delivery of the mail. No inter-jurisdictional immunity existed.

(iv) *Provincial Laws and Interprovincial Traffic*

While the principal authority over traffic offences rests with the provinces, the federal government does, as we have seen, retain authority in respect of some aspects of motor vehicle law. In addition to its ancillary authority in areas of Indian reserves and federal undertakings,[25] the federal government is responsible for the regulation of interprovincial traffic issues (e.g., the regulation of multi-province truck trips). As in other areas, the duplication or overlap of federal and provincial prohibitions does not render either government's law unconstitutional on a division of powers analysis.[26]

3. UNDERSTANDING THE LEGISLATION: THEMES AND DEVIATIONS

Most provinces have a collection of statutes to deal with various aspects of motor vehicle traffic and the regulation of issues associated with the use of the roads. One statute — usually either the *Highway Traffic Act*[27] or *Motor*

---

22 *R. v. Greening* (1993), 47 M.V.R. (2d) 167 (Ont. Prov. Div.) *per* Babe Prov. Div. J.; on appeal from (1992), 43 M.V.R. (2d) 53 (Ont. Prov. Div.) *per* Macdonnell Prov. Div. J. Canada Post also contended that the Ontario *Highway Traffic Act* did not bind the Crown. That argument was rejected also.

23 Canada Post argued, in effect, that it needed to break the laws related to interfering with the flow of traffic, parking and standing in order to be able to collect and deliver mail in a timely fashion.

24 *Constitution Act, 1867*, s. 91(5).

25 See the discussion immediately preceding this heading.

26 *R. v. Motorways* (1980) *Ltd.* (1989), 16 M.V.R. (2d) 38 (Ont. Prov. Ct.); *R. v. Kleysen Transport Ltd.* (1990), 31 M.V.R. (2d) 121 (Ont. Prov. Div.).

27 In Ontario the principal statute is the *Highway Traffic Act*, R.S.O. 1990 c. H.8. Other Ontario statutes include: *Compulsory Automobile Insurance Act*, R.S.O. 1990, c. C.25; *Negligence Act*, R.S.O. 1990, c. N.1; *Motorized Snow Vehicles Act*, R.S.O. 1990, c. M.44; *Truck Trans-*

Vehicle Act[28] — is the principal piece of legislation in the provincial sphere dealing with the use of motor vehicles. The Acts generally begin with definitional provisions setting out the meaning of certain terms used in the statute. To the extent that the defined words are used in offence-creating provisions, they become significant and ultimately form part of the definition of the offence which the Crown must prove.[29]

(a) "Highway"

In the absence of a statutory definition, the word 'highway' has been held to be a public road or way open to everyone for travel. In most jurisdictions the definition has been codified, and modified to capture most places where vehicles are used in a way that impacts on others who use such spaces as of right. This term is defined, for example, in the Ontario *Highway Traffic Act* to include;[30]

> ... a common and public highway, street, avenue, parkway, driveway, square, place, bridge, viaduct or trestle, any part of which is intended for or used by the general public for the passage of vehicles and includes the area between the lateral property lines thereof.

Many activities will attract prosecution only if they occur on a 'highway'. Where a section applies only to actions on a 'highway', it is important to first determine whether the location of the alleged offence falls within the legal definitions of that term.

In *R. v. Mansour*[31] the Supreme Court of Canada considered whether "a parking lot adjacent to an apartment building ... to which the public had access" was a "highway" under the province's legislation. After surveying the cases the court held that a parking lot is not a 'highway'. A similar issue was

---

portation Act, R.S.O. 1990, c. T.22; *Public Vehicles Act*, R.S.O. 1990, c. P.54; *Dangerous Goods Transportation Act*, R.S.O. 1990, c. D.1; *Off-Road Vehicles Act*, R.S.O. 1990, c. O.4.

28 *Highway Traffic Act*, R.S.A. 1980, c. H-7; *Motor Vehicle Act*, R.S.B.C. 1996, c. 318; *Highway Traffic Act*, S.M. 1985-86, c. 3; *Motor Vehicle Act*, R.S.N.B. 1973, c. M-17; *Highway Traffic Act*, R.S.N. 1990, c. H-3; *Motor Vehicles Act*, R.S.N.W.T. 1988, c. M-16; *Motor Vehicle Act*, R.S.N.S. 1989, c. 293; *Highway Traffic Act*, R.S.P.E.I. 1988, c. H-5; *Highway Traffic Act*, S.S. 1996, c. H-3.2; *Highway Safety Code*, R.S.Q. c. C-24.2; *Motor Vehicle Act*, R.S.Y. 1986, c. 118.

29 For example, if an offence must be committed on a "highway" then the Crown must prove beyond a reasonable doubt that the location of the offence was a highway.

30 *Highway Traffic Act*, R.S.O. 1990, c. H.8, s. 1(1) "highway". The same term is defined for the purpose of the *Criminal Code* (in s. 2 "highway") to mean "a road to which the public has the right of access, and includes bridges over which or tunnels through which a road passes". The definition in the British Columbia *Motor Vehicle Act*, R.S.B.C. 1996, c. 318 s. 1, is virtually identical.

31 (1979), 2 M.V.R. 1 (S.C.C.).

considered in *R. v. Douglas*[32] where the Ontario Court (Provincial Division), following a useful review of a number of cases, held that a paved roadway and parking lot of a privately owned apartment building, apparently used only by residents and guests, was not a highway. Similarly, a parking lot at a shopping mall is not a highway.[33]

A sidewalk was considered not to be a part of a highway in a case of careless driving,[34] though a bridge blocked at one end may be.[35]

A practical analysis was employed in *Cirillo v. R.*[36] where the court considered the case of a construction worker who operated a motor vehicle on a portion of highway which was temporarily closed to traffic for repairs. The definition, at least when applied in the context of a prosecution, should be strictly interpreted to give the benefit of any vagueness to the accused. Because the public was denied access at the time of the alleged offence the road had, at least for that time, ceased to be a highway.

In cases where the driving area is a road on an Indian reserve, close attention should be paid to whether, in fact, the road is "intended for or used by the general public for the passage of vehicles" (or other similar language in the statute).[37]

Cases dealing with definitions similar to that from the Ontario statute (quoted above) have variously held that service stations and car washes are not highways, though some parking lots might be.[38] The frozen surface of a lake used by the public on snowmobiles and light vehicles is not a highway[39] but the undedicated roadway/drive up to a federally owned airport is a highway.[40] A ferry employed in the business of carrying vehicles across

---

32 (1997), 35 O.R. (3d) 197 (Ont. Prov. Div.).

33 *Gill v. Elwood* (1970), 9 D.L.R. (3d) 681 (Ont. C.A.). On the question of parking lots and the definition of 'highway' see also: *Brinton v. Sieniewicz* (1969), 7 D.L.R. (3d) 545 (N.S. S.C.); *White v. Carter* (1973), 36 D.L.R. (3d) 315 (N.S. S.C.); *R. v. Love* (1994), 3 M.V.R. (3d) 266 (N.B. C.A.); *Gamache v. Basaraba* (1993), 43 M.V.R. (2d) 255 (Alta. Q.B.); *Sked v. Henry* (1991), 28 M.V.R. (2d) 234 (Ont. Gen. Div.); *Kidd v. George* (1973), 38 D.L.R. (3d) 278 (Alta. T.D.); *Morell v. McKenney* (1976), 73 D.L.R. (3d) 258 (P.E.I. S.C.).

34 *R. v. Wall* (1968), 11 Cr. L.Q. 223. But consider *Toronto (City) v. Consumers' Gas Co.*, [1941] O.R. 175 (C.A.), affirmed [1941] S.C.R. 584 which held that, at least in the civil context, the definition could embrace those parts of the roadway not intended for vehicles but open to public use, such as sidewalks.

35 *Wilson v. Piers* (1976), 22 N.S.R. (2d) 1 (N.S. S.C.).

36 (1981), 11 M.V.R. 16 (Ont. Co. Ct.).

37 *Supra*, note 17; *R. v. Thunderchild* (1995), 136 Sask. R. 295 (Sask. Q.B.).

38 *Woodbridge v. Bragg* (1956), 5 D.L.R. (2d) 413 (B.C. S.C.); *Lawson v. Watts* (1957), 7 D.L.R. (2d) 758 (B.C. S.C.) (service stations); *R. v. S. (No. 2)*, [1975] W.W.D. 57 (Man. Prov. Ct.) (car washes); *R. v. Carlberg* (1971), 3 C.C.C. (2d) 396 (Sask. Q.B.) (parking lots). See also *Penney v. Britt*, [1996] O.J. No. 2821 (Ont. Gen. Div.).

39 *Cleworth v. Zackariuk* (1985), 32 M.V.R. 23 (B.C. S.C.), affirmed 49 M.V.R. 275 (B.C. C.A.).

40 *R. v. Red Line Ltd.* (1930), 54 C.C.C. 271 (Ont. C.A.).

waterways can be a highway,[41] but light-rail train tracks over which the public is permitted to pass are not.[42]

(b) "Motor Vehicles"

The term "motor vehicle", when used within the Ontario *Highway Traffic Act* includes:[43]

> ... an automobile, motorcycle, motor assisted bicycle unless otherwise indicated in this Act, and any other vehicle propelled or driven otherwise than by muscular power, but does not include a street car, or other motor vehicles running only upon rails, or a motorized snow vehicle, traction engine, farm tractor, self-propelled implement of husbandry or road-building machine within the meaning of this Act.

The definition should be read in conjunction with the definitions of devices exempted from the definition: road building machine,[44] self-propelled implement of husbandry,[45] commercial motor vehicle,[46] farm tractor,[47] mobile home,[48] vehicle,[49] and wheelchair.[50] In general, provincial statutes exempt from the definition those devices which are share features with motor vehicles, but which have as their principal function some action other than transportation on public thoroughfares.

The most difficult cases arise where the vehicle driven is capable of being used for transportation but is designed as a piece of agricultural or construction equipment. In these cases the courts have followed the definitions closely, generally giving the benefit of any doubt to the defendant.[51]

---

41 *R. v. Wong* (1997), 29 M.V.R. (3d) 194 (B.C. S.C.).

42 *R. v. Luyben* (1991), 34 M.V.R. (2d) 203 (Alta. Prov. Ct.).

43 Ontario *Highway Traffic Act* s. 1(1) "motor vehicle". The definition of "motor vehicle" under the *Criminal Code* is much broader, and would capture vehicles not included in the *Highway Traffic Act* definition ("motor vehicle", means a vehicle that is drawn, propelled or driven by any means other than muscular power, but does not include railway equipment"). The difference can be important, especially with respect to the impact of criminal and provincial driving disqualification: *R. v. Swarychewski* (1957), 26 C.R. 176 (Man. C.A.) and *R. v. Shymanski*, [1992] S.J. No. 217 (Sask. Prov. Ct.).

44 Section 1(1) "road building machine".

45 Section 1(1) "self-propelled implement of husbandry".

46 Section 1(1) "commercial motor vehicle".

47 Section 1(1) "farm tractor".

48 Section 1(1) "mobile home".

49 Section 1(1) "vehicle".

50 Section 1(1) "wheelchair".

51 See *Bell Telephone Co. v. I.B. Purcell Ltd.*, [1962] O.W.N. 184 (Ont. Co. Ct.); *R. v. Marchand* (1968), 66 W.W.R. 761 (Sask. Dist. Ct.); *R. v. Vaisvyla* (1958), 29 C.R. 71 (Sask. Dist. Ct.).

A motorized 'go-kart' may be a motor vehicle,[52] so too a forklift, at least when in motion.[53] A vehicle which depends on another for propulsion (such as a towed vehicle) continues to be a "motor vehicle" if it possesses some independent control.[54]

(c) "Vehicles"

Some provisions are applicable to all "vehicles",[55] (generally a broader term) which includes all "motor vehicles", as well as any "trailer, traction engine, farm tractor, road-building machine and any vehicle drawn, propelled or driven by any kind of power, including muscular power, but does not include a motorized snow vehicle[56] or a street car.[57] A wheelchair is generally regarded as a vehicle as is a bicycle.[58] A transport trailer is a single vehicle rather than a combination of two vehicles for weight control even though it has two distinct parts.[59]

(d) "Standing" and "Stopping"

"Standing", when prohibited, means;[60]

> the halting of a vehicle, whether occupied or not, except for the purposes of and while actually engaged in receiving or discharging passengers.

"Stopping", when prohibited, means;[61]

> the halting of a vehicle, even momentarily, whether occupied or not, except when necessary to avoid conflict with other traffic or in compliance with the directions of a constable or other police officer or of a traffic control sign or signal.

To constitute a 'stop' all forward motion must cease.[62] In *R. v. Oliver*[63] a by-law prohibited stopping between 4 and 6 p.m. The defendant brought his vehicle

---

52 *Goldberg v. McKelvy*, [1975] 5 W.W.R. 517 (Man. C.A.).

53 *Jenkins v. Bowes Publishing Co.* (1991), 30 M.V.R. (2d) 212 (Ont. Gen. Div.).

54 *R. v. Morton* (1970), 75 W.W.R. 335 (B.C. Prov. Ct.); *Kavanagh v. Quinnsway Transport Ltd.* (1979), 23 Nfld. & P.E.I.R. 79 (Nfld. Dist. Ct.), reversed (1982), 40 Nfld. & P.E.I.R. 184 (Nfld. C.A.).

55 See, for example, s. 170 of the Ontario *Highway Traffic Act* which prohibits various stopping and parking of 'vehicles' on roadways.

56 But see *R. v. Bellanger* (1978), 1 M.V.R. 88 (Sask. Dist. Ct.).

57 Section 1(1) "bicycle".

58 *Carlson v. Chochinov* (1948), 56 Man. R. 179 (Man. C.A.) (wheelchairs); *R. v. Baggette*, [1975] 6 W.W.R. 464 (B.C. S.C.).

59 *R. v. Restigouche Transport Ltd.* (1980), 32 N.B.R. (2d) 493 (Q.B.).

60 Ontario *Highway Traffic Act* s. 1(1) para. 35.

61 *Ibid.*, section 1(1) para. 36.

62 *R. v. MacAdam* (1976), 22 N.S.R. (2d) 204 (N.S. Co. Ct.).

63 (1958), 119 C.C.C. 394 (B.C. S.C.); *R. v. MacAdam* (1976), 22 N.S.R. (2d) 204 (N.S. Co. Ct). But see *R. v. Holmes* (1939), 71 C.C.C. 358 (N.S. Co. Ct.).

to a halt at some time before 4 p.m. and parked it there. The court held that the no stopping by-law did not apply and quashed the conviction.

(e) "Driver"

The Ontario *Highway Traffic Act* defines driver as, "a person who drives a vehicle on a highway."[64] In *R. v. Miller*[65] the court found that someone exercising some control over a vehicle (in this case an army tank) being towed by another, was driving that vehicle. The two vehicles were separate units requiring two drivers.

In an English case, *R. v. Macdonagh*,[66] the accused was found pushing his vehicle with the driver's door open. He was using the steering wheel to direct the vehicle as he pushed it and both his feet were on the ground. The court held that a person is a driver if he or she is, "in a substantial sense controlling the movement and direction of the car."[67] 'Driving' is not 'pushing'. The fact that the defendant had his hand on the steering wheel is not determinative.

The Canadian test in the context of the *Criminal Code* rests on the conscious desire of the person to assume control over the vehicle. In *R. v. Belanger*[68] the accused was being taken to the station by police after being arrested. He took hold of the steering wheel in the police car and drove the car off the road. He was convicted of dangerous driving. This is apparently contrary to the position taken in the civil law context. In *Doiron v. Birdian*[69] the New Brunswick Court of Appeal held that a civil defendant who had grabbed the wheel was not a 'driver' under the statute. The court said:

> He did not assume actual physical control of the vehicle, he interfered with one aspect of control only, the steering. [The person in the driver's seat] was still in control of stopping and starting the car and of the speed of the car while in motion. The intent [of the section making the owner civilly liable for the actions of the 'driver' is to ...] make the owner responsible for the negligence of the person actually operating the vehicle not for actions of someone who interferes with the operation of the vehicle by the driver.

The owner was not liable for the actions of the person grabbing the steering wheel because that person was not a 'driver'.

---

64 Section 1(1). Other statutes have similar definitions – e.g. *Highway Traffic Act*, R.S.A. 1980, s. 1(f.1); *Highway Traffic Act*, S.M. 1985-86, c. 3, s. 1; *Motor Vehicle Act*, R.S.N.B. 1973, c. M-17, s. 1.

65 (1944), 82 C.C.C. 314 (Ont. Co. Ct.).

66 [1974] 1 Q.B. 448 (C.A.).

67 *Ibid.*, at p. 452.

68 [1970] S.C.R. 567.

69 (1980), 28 N.B.R. (2d) 520 (N.B. C.A.) at 527.

The Nova Scotia provision, which extends the definition to include a "person in charge of a vehicle", is limited to the person who is present on the scene and able to carry out the duties envisioned in the Act.[70]

A corporation cannot be a "driver".[71]

4. FEDERAL LEGISLATION RESPECTING HIGHWAY TRAFFIC OFFENCES

In addition to the provincial legislation governing the activities of drivers in almost all aspects of vehicle and highway use, there are a number of federal statutes which also regulate vehicles and drivers in particular circumstances. The *Government Property Traffic Act*[72] provides for the making of regulations creating offences related to vehicle use (including speeding etc.) on federal government property. The *Motor Vehicle Transport Act, 1987*[73] governs aspects of inter-provincial or 'extra-provincial' bus and truck undertakings.

The procedure governing the prosecution of certain federal offences is set out in the summary conviction portions of the *Criminal Code*[74] and the *Contraventions Act*.[75] The latter statute found its genesis in a series of statutes enacted with a view to simplifying procedure in minor, federally created, regulatory (and potentially criminal) offences. It permits the federal government to designate by regulation certain offences which will be prosecuted within what amounts to the same procedural stream as that provided for similar provincial offences in the province in which the charge is laid. By virtue of these regulations[76] a considerable number of offences — including most simple "traffic offences" under the *Government Property Traffic Act* — are made prosecutable within the provincial procedural stream. For example, if a charge were laid in Ontario, it would be prosecuted according to the *Provincial Offences Act*.[77] At this time, only Ontario has been identified in the regulations for this form of procedure. In all other provinces these offences are prosecuted using the more formal, cumbersome summary conviction procedure provided in the *Criminal Code*.

---

70 *R. v. Musolino* (1984), 63 N.S.R. (2d) 147 (N.S. C.A.).

71 *R. v. Dominion-U-Drive System Ltd.* (1954), 12 W.W.R. (N.S.) 708 (Alta. D.C.).

72 *Government Property Traffic Act*, R.S.C. 1985, c. G-6.

73 *Motor Vehicle Transport Act, 1987*, R.S.C. 1985, (3d Supp.), c. 29.

74 *Criminal Code* Part XXVII.

75 *Contraventions Act*, S.C. 1992, c. 47 as amended by S.C. 1993, c. 28; S.C. 1994 c. 22, c. 23, c. 26, c. 44; S.C. 1996, c. 7. See R. Libman, *Annotated Contraventions Act, 1997* (Carswell, Toronto: 1997).

76 SOR/96-312 and SOR 96-313.

77 *Provincial Offences Act*, R.S.O. 1990, c. P.33.

5. CLASSIFICATION OF HIGHWAY TRAFFIC OFFENCES

(a) **Introduction**

Canadian law places every criminal and quasi-criminal offence into one of three categories according to the mental element, or *mens rea*, which the Crown must prove.[78] The classic statement of the design and rationale of this system of classification is found in *R. v. Sault Ste. Marie (City)*,[79] in the judgment of Mr. Justice Dickson (as he then was). In that case the accused City had been charged with regulatory environmental offences. Examining the mental element of such 'public welfare' or regulatory offences, Mr. Justice Dickson concluded, on behalf of the majority, that such offences (which include virtually all traffic offences) fall into three classes:

> 1. Offences in which *mens rea*, consisting of *some positive state of mind* such as intent, knowledge, or recklessness, must be proved by the prosecution, either as an inference from the nature of the act committed or, by additional evidence.
> 2. Offences in which there is no necessity for the prosecution to prove the existence of *mens rea*; the doing of the prohibited act *prima facie* imports the offence, *leaving it open to the accused to avoid liability by proving that he took all reasonable care*. This involves consideration of what a reasonable man would have done in the circumstances. The defence will be available if the accused reasonably believed in a mistaken set of facts which, if true, would render the act or omission innocent, or if he took all reasonable steps to avoid the particular event. These offences may properly be called offences of strict liability ...
> 3. Offences of *absolute liability* where it is not open to the accused to exculpate himself by showing that he was free of fault. [Emphasis added]

Offences created by a province (by definition 'public welfare offences') are, in the absence of any explicit language to the contrary, presumed to fall into the second class of *strict liability* offences:[80]

> Offences which are criminal in the true sense fall in the first category. Public welfare offences would *prima facie* be in the second category. They are not subject to the presumption of full *mens rea*. An offence of this type would fall in the first category only if words such as "willfully", "with intent", "knowingly", or "intentionally" are contained in the statutory provision creating the offence. On the other hand, the principle that punishment should not be inflicted on those without fault applies. Offences of absolute liability would be those in respect of which the Legislature had made it clear that guilt would follow proof merely of the proscribed act. The overall regulatory pattern adopted by the legislation, the importance of the penalty, and the precision of the language used will be primary considerations in determining whether the offence falls into the third category.

---

78 For a discussion of the mental element in provincial offences generally, see Ontario Law Reform Commission, *The Basis for Liability for Provincial Offences* (Ontario: 1990).

79 [1978] 2 S.C.R. 1299 at pp. 1325-6 [hereafter *Sault Ste. Marie*.].

80 *Ibid.*, at pp. 1326.

The classification of the offence into one of these three catagories will determine what elements the Crown is obliged to prove and will determine whether certain defences are available to an accused.

(b) Absolute Liability

(i) *Generally*

Absolute liability offences allow for conviction upon proof of only the guilty actions or "*actus reus*" of the accused: if the Crown proves the guilty acts, and no applicable defence is raised, conviction follows. The subjective mental state or intention of the accused is not relevant. As such, defences which operate to negate the mental aspect of the offence (such as mistake of fact) have no application.

Defences which operate to defeat the guilty *act*, however, continue to operate to the benefit of the defendant.

Thus, for example, an act which is involuntary (in the sense of a thing done without any volition and therefore not truly the act of the defendant) is not guilty. A defence of involuntariness will succeed even where the offence charged is one of absolute liability.[81] A question remains, however, whether other 'defences' which justify or excuse the behaviour (rather than negating some essential element) are available.[82] Other defences which as a matter of doctrine operate to defeat the guilty act (and which therefore are valid defences to even an absolute liability offence) include automatism,[83] duress,[84] necessity,[85] insanity,[86] *de minimis non curat lex*,[87] self-defence,[88] and act of God.[89]

(ii) *Burden of Proof for General Defences*

Where a defendant raises one of the applicable general defences to an absolute liability offence, he or she needs only to raise a doubt in the mind

---

81 *R. v. Racimore* (1975), 25 C.C.C. (2d) 143 (Ont. H.C.).

82 Swaigen, John, *Regulatory Offences in Canada: Liability and Defences* (Toronto, Carswell: 1992), p. 27-8.

83 *R. v. Metro News Ltd.* (1986), 53 C.R. (3d) 289 (Ont. C.A.).

84 *R. v. Cancoil Thermal Corp.* (1986), 52 C.R. (3d) 108 (Ont. C.A.).

85 *R. v. Walker* (1979), 48 C.C.C. (2d) 126 (Ont. Co. Ct.); *R. v. Hales*, [1995] O.J. No. 735; *R. v. Morris*, [1994] B.C.J. No. 1253.

86 *Hill v. Baxter*, [1958] 1 All E.R. 193 (C.A.).

87 See below Chapter 7, Common Defences, and the discussion under heading 3.

88 *R. v. Breau* (1959), 32 C.R. 13 (N.B. S.C.).

89 *R. v. Springbank Sand & Gravel* (1975), 25 C.C.C. (2d) 535 (Ont. C.A.).

of the court. If the court has a doubt about whether a defence on the merits[90] is made out, the defendant is entitled to an acquittal.[91]

(iii) *Constitutional Limits on Absolute Liability*

Section 7 of the *Charter of Rights* provides that, "Everyone has the right to life, liberty and security of the person and the right not to be deprived thereof except in accordance with the principles of fundamental justice." In *Ref Re Section 94(2) British Columbia Motor Vehicle Act*,[92] the Supreme Court of Canada considered the limits on government in imposing punishment without proof of any morally wrongful act, or without any mental element. In that case the British Columbia statute governing motor vehicle use provided a minimum seven day jail term for repeated driving while under suspension. It made the offence of driving while suspended an absolute liability offence. Striking the section down, and setting constitutional limits on the availability of absolute liability offences, Mr. Justice Lamer (as he then was) wrote:[93]

> In my view it is because absolute liability offends the principles of fundamental justice that this Court created presumptions against legislatures having intended to enact offences of a regulatory nature falling within that category. This is not to say, however, and to that extent I am in agreement with the Court of Appeal, that, as a result, absolute liability per se offends s. 7 of the *Charter.* ...
> I am therefore of the view that the combination of imprisonment and absolute liability violates s. 7 of the Charter and can only be salvaged if the authorities demonstrate under s. 1 that such a deprivation of liberty in breach of those principles of fundamental justice is, in a free and democratic society, under the circumstances, a justified reasonable limit to one's rights under s. 7.

An absolute liability offence cannot carry a potential sentence of imprisonment.

It should be noted that when justifying an absolute liability offence for which imprisonment is a potential sentence, the state cannot rely on mere "administrative expediency".[94] Something more must be shown. This rule operates to give added strength to the limits on absolute liability. Legislation which imposes absolute liability on any offence will be carefully scrutinised. Further, the rule gives constitutional status to the presumption against such liability where imprisonment is a possible sentence: legislatures are presumed to have enacted laws which are not unconstitutional.

---

90 As opposed to a procedural defence, such as an allegation of abuse of process, where the accused may bear the burden of proof on a balance of probabilities. See *R. v. O'Connor* (1996), 103 C.C.C. (3d) 1 (S.C.C.).

91 *R. v. Oakes*, [1986] 1 S.C.R. 103 (S.C.C.); see also *R. v. Walker, supra* note 85.

92 [1985] 1 S.C.R. 486.

93 *Ibid.*, at 515-6.

94 *Ibid.*, at 518.

(iv) *Prison as a Fine Enforcement Tool*

An important issue arises with respect to regimes which create the possibility of imprisonment only to enforce the payment of monetary penalties. If an absolute liability offence is punishable only by a *monetary penalty*, no violence is done to the principle of fundamental justice that no person should be imprisoned for an absolute liability offence. However, if the fine is in turn enforceable by imprisonment, does the statute run afoul of the rule in *Ref. re s. 94(2) British Columbia Motor Vehicle Act*? To put it another way, if a person can be imprisoned for non-payment of a fine imposed for an absolute liability offence, is that offence 'punishable' by imprisonment?

The question is not a moot one. In its 1990 report on *The Basis of Liability for Provincial Offences*, the Ontario Law Reform Commission noted that almost 30% of offenders in custody were there for defaulted fines.[95] The issue awaits a definitive determination.[96]

(c) Strict Liability

Most offences under provincial traffic legislation fall into this category. This "half-way house" between full *mens rea* and absolute liability was created by the court in the *Sault Ste. Marie* case.[97]

This category of offence imposes a burden on the defendant to prove that she took all reasonable steps to prevent the occurrence of the offence. While the prosecution does not need to prove that the defendant acted with a guilty mind, the defendant may escape conviction if she can demonstrate an innocent mental state. An innocent mental state is one which manifests "due diligence" on the part of the defendant. "Due diligence" is a reasonable, good faith effort by the defendant to bring her actions within that allowed under a regulatory scheme. Thus a defence of due diligence is made out where a person takes all reasonable steps to avoid doing the act prohibited. Most defences to strict liability offences are really forms of this "due diligence/non-negligence" standard. For example, the defence of officially induced error of law requires the defendant to establish that she did all that a reasonable person would do to discover the law and then took all reasonable steps to bring her behaviour within the law.

---

95 Ontario Law Reform Commission, *The Basis of Liability for Provincial Offences* (Ontario, 1990), p. 16. See also *R. v. Nickel City Transport* (1993), 42 M.V.R. (2d) 20 (Ont. C.A.), *per* Arbour J.A., concurring in the result.

96 In *R. v. Richard*, [1996] 3 S.C.R. 525 the Supreme Court of Canada considered the general constitutionality of the procedure provided under New Brunswick's *Provincial Offences Procedure Act*, S.N.B. 1989, c. P-22.1 and noted before upholding the law that because no one could be put in prison for breach of a motor vehicle offence under the New Brunswick regime — even for non-payment of a fine — then s. 7 was not engaged (see ¶31 of the judgment).

97 *Supra*, note 79.

(d) The Process of Categorization

There is, in effect, a presumption that a regulatory offence — virtually all provincially created offences and almost all federally created offences outside the *Criminal Code* — will be classified as strict liability:[98] the party seeking to have the court interpret the offence as either absolute liability or full *mens rea* bears the burden of persuasion. In determining whether an offence ought to be interpreted as one of absolute liability (rather than strict liability), the courts will examine:[99]

- the overall regulatory pattern adopted by the Legislature;
- the subject matter of the legislation;
- the importance (or severity) of the penalty; and
- the precise language used [in the statute creating the offence].

In addition, the court must consider the constitutional limits imposed on the creation of offences of absolute liability in a number of cases (discussed below).

In examining the **overall regulatory pattern**, the court will consider whether "the language of the provision is direct and the issue of compliance is simple and straightforward". If the language would seem to invite no possible exception to enforcement this will speak in favour of a finding of absolute liability. One further consideration is the impact of classification on the effective enforcement of the statute creating the offence: if it is impossible, or impracticable, to enforce the prohibition if the offence is classified as strict liability, then the courts will be inclined to accept the prosecutor's contention that it is properly considered to be an offence of absolute liability.[100] If, however, the statute is complex and on its face permits exceptions (however

---

98 D. Stuart, *Canadian Criminal Law* (3d ed.) (Carswell, Toronto; 1995), p. 173.

99 *R. v. Nickel City Transport* (1992), 47 M.V.R. (2d) 20 (Ont. C.A.).

100 See *R. v. Chapin*, [1979] 2 S.C.R. 121 at 132 where Dickson J. observed (in the context of a regulatory offence related to hunting licences):

> The best the Crown can do to shift this offence into the category of absolute liability is to suggest that the availability of defence of reasonable care would considerably weaken enforcement of the legislation. This may be true, but as Weatherston J.A. observed, the problems that may be encountered in the administration of a statute or regulation are a very unsure guide to its proper interpretation. Difficulty of enforcement is hardly enough to dislodge the offence from the category of strict liability, particularly when regard is had to the penalties that may ensue from conviction. I do not think that the public interest, as expressed in the Convention, requires that s. 14 of the Regulations be interpreted so that an innocent person should be convicted and fined and also suffer the mandatory loss of his hunting permit and the possible forfeiture of his hunting equipment, merely in order to facilitate prosecution.

narrowly defined) the court may be inclined to conclude that the limited defence available for strict liability offences attaches to the offence.[101]

The **subject matter** of the legislation involves an examination of the area of activity regulated and the role of the offence in that regulation. If universal compliance is essential or important to the proper operation of the regulatory regime in question, then the court will be more inclined to conclude that the offence is one of absolute liability. Similarly, as the penalty scale increases the courts become less likely to find an intention to create an absolute liability offence. As noted earlier, if imprisonment is legally available as a direct penalty (and perhaps if it is available to enforce payment of fines) the offence cannot be classified as one of absolute liability.

The **language used** is also relevant. Clearly language explicitly stating that an offence is one of absolute liability will suffice in any statutory interpretation exercise. It is not enough, however, that the legislation say "no one shall" — while such language is apparently "absolute" in its framing, it is, standing alone, little more than the standard language of prohibition in Canadian law.

Some commentators have criticised the *Sault Ste. Marie* three-class approach. They argue that it is difficult to apply the test and that it unfairly leaves the accused to prove their defence. Further, it is often difficult to understand or justify why some 'morally serious' offences (for example, environmental violations) are subject to the *Sault Ste. Marie* analysis while conduct which is generally less stigmatized, but which is technically *criminal* (for example), is considered always to be full *mens rea*.[102]

(e) The Classification of Various Offences

(i) *Absolute Liability Traffic Offences*

The following offences have been held by various courts to be offences of absolute liability (as in other areas, reference should be had to the offence creating provision in any particular province or territory):

- Failing to stop at a red light;[103]

- Offence of operating a motor vehicle with a muffler which did not operate properly;[104]

---

101 This presumption is effectively included in the British Columbia *Offence Act*, R.S.B.C. 1996, c. 338 s. 6, which provides that no person can be imprisoned for an absolute liability offence.

102 D. Stuart, *Canadian Criminal Law* (3d ed.) (Carswell, Toronto: 1995) at pp. 172-181.

103 *R. v. Kurtzman* (1991), 4 O.R. (3d) 417 (Ont. C.A.), citing *R. v. Brennan* (1989), 18 M.V.R. (2d) 161 (Ont. C.A.). See also *R. v. Hammond* (1978), 1 M.V.R. 210 (Ont. Co. Ct.). See "Obey traffic signs" under the next heading.

104 *R. v. Petrie* (1993), 44 M.V.R. (2d) 311 (Alta. Q.B.).

- Speeding (but see below under "Strict Liability");[105]
- Vehicle Equipment Rules;[106] and
- Driving while suspended.[107]

(ii) *Strict Liability Traffic Offences*

These offences have been held to be strict liability offences. Such offences invite conviction without proof of any *mens rea*, but permit an accused to escape conviction by demonstrating the defence of "due diligence". These offences include:

- Weight distribution rules for trucks;[108]
- Unsafe combination of vehicles;[109]
- Failing to yield right of way to pedestrian on crosswalk;[110]
- Driving while suspended;[111]
- Failing to remain;[112]
- Speeding (but see above under "Absolute Liability");[113]

---

105 *R. v. Hickey* (1976), 29 C.C.C. (2d) 23 (Ont. Div. Ct.), reversed (1976), 13 O.R. (2d) 228 (C.A.); *R. v. Cunningham* (1979), 1 M.V.R. 223 (Ont. Div. Ct.); *R. v. Lemieux* (1978), 41 C.C.C. (2d) 33 (Que. C.A.); *R. v. Greening* (1991), 98 Nfld. & P.E.I.R. 267 (Nfld. T.D.) and *R. v. King* (1985), 54 Nfld. & P.E.I.R. 286 (Nfld. Dist. Ct.) dealing with *Highway Traffic Act*, R.S.N. 1970, c. 152, ss. 131(1), 131(2); *R. v. Harper* (1985), 45 C.R. (3d) 186 (B.C. Co. Ct.).

106 See also *R. v. Kehoe* (1990), 21 M.V.R. (2d) 24 (Ont. Prov. Div.) (noise levels) and perhaps *R. v. Petrie*, [1993] A.J. No. 1069.

107 *R. v. Courchene* (1986), 45 M.V.R. 84 (Man. Prov. Ct.).

108 *R. v. Nickel City Transport, supra*, note 99; see also in *R. v. Mannion Transportation Ltd.* (1985), 31 M.V.R. 246 (Sask. Q.B.); *R. v. Donline Haulage Inc.* (1980), 4 M.V.R. 241 (Ont. Co. Ct.); *R. v. Boyde* (1987), 4 M.V.R. (2d) 113 (B.C. Prov. Ct.) and *R. v. Spacemaker Products Ltd.* (1980), 7 M.V.R. 265 (Ont. Co. Ct.). Earlier cases suggested that these offences might be absolute liability, but this position has been overtaken in later authorities: *R. v. Allen* (1979), 79 C.C.C. (2d) 563 (Ont. Dist. Ct.).

109 *R. v. Robbins* (1996), 26 M.V.R. (3d) 184 (Ont. Prov. Div.).

110 *R. v. Davis* (1996), 21 M.V.R. (3d) 65 (N.S. C.A.).

111 *R. v. MacDougall*, [1982] 2 S.C.R. 605, 18 M.V.R. 180, 142 D.L.R. (3d) 216; *R. v. Bellomo* (1996), 14 M.V.R. (3d) 63 (Ont. Prov. Div.); *R. v. Coleman* (1985), 31 M.V.R. 258 (Man. Q.B.).

112 *R. v. Weir* (1992), 36 M.V.R. (2d) 118 (Ont. Prov. Div.).

113 The trend in provincial authority would suggest that speeding is an absolute liability offence — see the previous heading. However, at least in Nova Scotia, there is a body of authority favouring a classification of strict liability: *R. v. Williams* (1992), 39 M.V.R. (2d) 315 (N.S. C.A.); *R. v. Hicks* (1990), 35 M.V.R. (2d) 311 (N.S. Co. Ct.) though this would seem to have been heavily influenced by the authority in that province suggesting that imprisonment in default of a fine engaged the constitutional prohibition against absolute liability where imprisonment was a possible penalty (*Reference re s. 94(2) of the Motor Vehicle Act (British*

- Depositing a filthy substance on a highway;[114]
- Making an unsafe turn (and other turning offences);[115]
- Operating a motor vehicle without fastening load;[116]
- Operating a motor vehicle not equipped with proper brakes;[117]
- Owner liability for 'photo radar' speeding charge;[118]
- Driving without insurance;[119]
- Driving while suspended, disqualified or unlicensed;[120]
- Maintenance of Brakes and Safety Equipment;[121]
- Maintain Odometer;[122]
- Obeying traffic signs;[123]
- Careless Driving or Driving without Due Care and Attention;[124]
- Failing to wear seatbelts;[125]
- Driving without insurance;[126]
- Crossing solid line on roadway;[127] and

Columbia), *supra*, note 92. For a slightly different approach, see *R. v. Parsons* (1981), 11 M.V.R. 39 (N.S. Co. Ct.) which suggests a modified form of due diligence really amounting to involuntariness. See also *R. v. Cook*, [1993] N.S.J. No. 588 and *Morris*, unrep. May 27, 1994 (B.C. S.C.); QL [1994] B.C.J. No. 1253.

114 *R. v. Barker*, [1992] Y.J. No. 74 (Yukon Terr. Ct.) contrary to Yukon's *Highways Act*, S.Y. 1991, c. 7, s. 32(j).

115 *R. v. L. (M.V.)* (1988), 90 A.R. 164 (Alta. Prov. Ct.) contrary to *Highway Traffic Act*, R.S.A. 1980, c. H-7, s. 95(2).

116 *R. v. Burge* (1988), 72 Nfld. & P.E.I.R. 158 (P.E.I. S.C.) contrary to *Highway Traffic Act*, R.S.P.E.I. 1974, c. H-6, s. 207(2).

117 *R. v. Wallace* (1983), 19 M.V.R. 302 (Nfld. Dist. Ct.) contrary to *Highway Traffic Act*, R.S.N. 1970, c. 152, *Highway Traffic, Licence and Equipment Regulations*, s. 8(1)(a).

118 *R. v. Tilden Car Rental Inc.* (1991), 85 Alta. L.R. (2d) 345 (Alta. Prov. Ct.), *R. v. Free* (1990), 103 A.R. 138, 72 Alta. L.R. (2d) 167 (Alta. Prov. Ct.).

119 *R. v. Carter* (1985), 53 Nfld. & P.E.I.R. 145 (Nfld. Dist. Ct.).

120 *R. v. MacDougall* (1981), 60 C.C.C. (2d) 137 (N.S. C.A.); *R. v. Richard* (1979), 14 C.R. (3d) 165 (Que. S.C.) contrary to Quebec's *Highway Code*, R.S.Q. 1977, c. C-24, s. 85. Contrast this to the full *mens rea* offence created by the *Criminal Code*: *R. v. Williams* (1976), 11 Nfld. & P.E.I.R. 164 (Nfld. Dist. Ct.).

121 *R. v. McDorman* (1984), 27 M.V.R. 37 (B.C. Co. Ct.); *R. v. Wallace* (1983), 19 M.V.R. 302 (Nfld. Dist. Ct.) (brakes).

122 *R. v. Sherman*, [1991] A.J. No. 411 (Alta. Prov. Ct.).

123 *R. v. Higgins* (1981), 60 C.C.C. (2d) 246 (N.S. C.A.), but see "failing to stop at a red light" in the previous heading. See also *R. v. Bolland*, [1993] N.S.J. No. 582 (N.S. Prov. Ct.).

124 *R. v. Kozun*, [1997] S.J. No. 98 (Sask. Q.B.).

125 *R. c. Shahrabani*, [1996] Q.J. No. 1126 (Que. Sup. Ct.(Cr. Div.)); *R. v. Gallant* unrep. October 21, 1988 (Ont. Prov. Ct.) Info.No. 0780378.

126 *R. v. Blackburn* (1981), 57 C.C.C. (2d) 7 (B.C. C.A.); *R. v. Gallagher* (1985), 55 Nfld. & P.E.I.R. 109 (Nfld. Dist. Ct.); *R. v. Carter* (1985), 53 Nfld. & P.E.I.R. 145 (Nfld. Dist. Ct.).

127 *R. v. White* (1984), 49 Nfld. & P.E.I.R. 139 (Nfld. Dist. Ct.).

- Failing to obey traffic signs and signals.[128]

(iii) *Full Mens Rea Traffic Offences*

The least common form of traffic offence on the *Sault Ste. Marie* three-category classification system is the 'full *mens rea*' offence. The mental element of these offences most closely resembles that required in traditional criminal prohibitions. These offences have been held to include:

1. Willfully avoiding police officer.[129]
2. Failing to stop on signalling by police officer.[130]

Other offences which, by their language, seem inclined to a classification as full *mens rea* offences include:

3. Defacing or removing highway notices.[131]

(f) Special Mental Elements in Strict Liability Offences?

There may be some room for special mental elements in strict liability offences. In *Strasser v. Roberge*[132] the Supreme Court of Canada appeared to put a gloss on the rule in *Sault Ste. Marie*, saying that there may be a mental quality required in some offences, or at least that the defendant could escape liability if he or she could demonstrate the absence of such a special mental state. In Strasser the defendant was charged with a regulatory offence, participating in an illegal strike. Beetz J. writes:[133]

> [T]he fact that an offence may contain an intentional element does not prevent it from being classified in the categories of strict liability or absolute liability offences: what was held in *R. v. Sault Ste. Marie* ... as I understand that decision, was not that strict liability and absolute liability offences do not contain intentional elements; rather, it was that the prosecution is not required to prove that element in order to obtain a verdict of guilty.

It is possible then to have a strict liability offence with a mental element. This 'reverse onus' configuration of such offences may be of questionable constitutionality in light of constitutional entrenchment of the presumption of innocence.[134]

---

128 *R. v. Higgins* (1981), 46 N.S.R. (2d) 80 (N.S. C.A.).
129 Offence created in s. 216(3) of Ontario *Highway Traffic Act*; see *R. v. Dilorenzo* (1984), 26 M.V.R. 259 (Ont. C.A.) and *R. v. Parker* (1992), 41 M.V.R. (2d) 257 (Ont. Gen. Div.); *R. v. Traves* (1986), 43 M.V.R. 188 (Ont. Dist. Ct.).
130 *R. v. Dilorenzo* (1984), 2 O.A.C. 62 (Ont. C.A.).
131 *Highway Traffic Act*, R.S.O. 1990, c. H.8, s. 184.
132 [1970] 2 S.C.R. 953.
133 *Ibid.*, at p. 979.
134 See Morton & Hutchison, *The Presumption of Innocence* (Carswell, Toronto: 1987) at pp. 24-27, 99-102.

6. COMMON ISSUES IN TRAFFIC OFFENCE CASES

(a) Corporate, Employer and Owner Liability

The nature of regulatory legislation is such that it often engages issues related to the liability of business entities. In the context of traffic offences, the question of whether the charged defendant is responsible in law may require a consideration of issues surrounding **corporate, employer** and **owner** liability.

A *corporation* is a person for most legal purposes, and can be liable to regulatory and criminal prosecution in much the same way as an individual. The acts of the employees of the corporation, when undertaken within the scope of their employment by the corporation, are in law the acts of the corporation.[135] The mental element of the offence, whether as an affirmative element to be proven by the prosecution, or in the form of a defence of due diligence, are determined by looking at the 'directing mind' of the corporation. This legal notion looks to the senior managers, directors and executives of a corporation and derives from them the practical "directing mind, will centre, brain area or ego"[136] In order to provide a defence to the corporation as employer the evidence must show, on a balance of probabilities, that the corporate accused took all reasonable steps to prevent the commission of the offence as a corporate entity.[137] In *Sault Ste. Marie*[138] the Supreme Court of Canada observed that:

> One comment on the defence of reasonable care in … [the] context [of employers and corporate liability] should be added. Since the issue is whether the defendant is guilty of an offence, the doctrine of *respondeat superior* has no application. The due diligence which must be established is that of the accused alone. Where an employer is charged in respect of an act committed by an employee acting in the course of employment, the question will be whether the act took place without the accused's direction or approval, thus negating wilful involvement of the accused, and whether the accused exercised all reasonable care by establishing a proper system to prevent commission of the offence and by taking reasonable steps to ensure the effective operation of the system. *The availability of the defence to a corporation will depend on whether such due diligence was taken by those who are the directing mind and will of the corporation, whose acts are therefore in law the acts of the corporation itself.* … [Emphasis added]

---

135 *R. v. Canadian Dredge & Dock Co. Ltd.* (1985), 19 C.C.C. (3d) 1 (S.C.C.). In this sense, the corporation is not 'vicariously liable', but rather is directly responsible as though it were an individual who had acted directly. Some exceptions may exist to this general rule. For example, some authorities have held that specific offences are directed at individuals engaged in particular activities, like driving, even if they act as employees. Thus, where an offence is directed at "drivers" corporations may not be chargeable: *R. v. Dominion-U-Drive System Ltd., supra*, note 71. See also D. Saxe, *Environmental Offences: Corporate Responsibility and Executive Liability* (Canada Law Book, Aurora: 1990) pp. 90-102, 112-123.

136 *R. v. Canadian Dredge & Dock Co. Ltd., supra*, note 135.

137 *R. v. Spacemaker Products Ltd., supra* note 108.

138 *Supra* note 79 at p. 1331.

Some offences are worded in such a way that a corporation cannot be accused. For example, most offences which are directed at "drivers" will not engage corporations, because such entities cannot be 'drivers'.[139]

(b) Emergency Vehicles

Emergency vehicles are given special rights of way to permit them to perform their important duties in a timely way.[140] In the absence of a specific statutory exemption from the operation of the legislation, or some applicable defence, emergency vehicles are expected to adhere to the rules of the road like any other user of the highway.[141] This requirement is important because of the need for predictable and consistent behaviour by all vehicles.

Thus, for example, where the driver of an ambulance failed to activate the siren until just before entering an intersection without yielding, he was guilty of the offence of failing to yield the right of way. The statutory preconditions for entering the intersection with the right of way did not exist and the driver's conduct was therefore culpable.[142]

7. THE ROLE OF PARALEGALS OR AGENTS IN THE PROSECUTION AND DEFENCE OF TRAFFIC OFFENCES

The position of paralegals (sometimes called "agents")[143] in the prosecution and defence of traffic offences remains unsettled notwithstanding that the issue has been around for some time.[144] A debate continues respecting the appropriate range of services which paralegals should be allowed to offer.

---

139 *Supra* note 71.

140 For example, the *Highway Traffic Act*, R.S.O. 1990, c. H.8, s. 128(13) exempts fire department vehicles, vehicles used by persons in the performance of their duties as police officers, and ambulances, provided certain preconditions are met.

141 But see *R. v. Redshaw* (1975), 31 C.R.N.S. 255 (Ont. Co. Ct.).

142 *R. v. Jones* (1985), 42 Alta. L.R. (2d) 41 (Alta. Prov. Ct.).

143 The term "paralegals" has no fixed meaning at law, but is used here to refer to anyone who acts as agent or legal advisor to one of the parties in a traffic offence prosecution for remuneration and who is not a lawyer, articling student or law student. The term 'agents' is used in s. 800 of the *Criminal Code*, and is sometimes confused with the idea of a paralegal. Agents include any person appearing to speak on behalf of another, including relatives, or individuals appearing to represent a corporate accused.

144 In *R. v. Lemonides* (1997), 10 C.R. (5th) 135 (Ont. Gen. Div.), a summary conviction prosecution where the interpretation of s. 800 of the *Criminal Code* was in issue Madam Justice Wein observed at p. 141-142:

> Ten years ago, in *R. v. Lawrie & Points Ltd.* (1987), 59 O.R. (2d) 161, 32 C.C.C. (3d) 549 (C.A.), a case dealing with the appearance of agents on provincial offence matters, the Court of Appeal politely invited the Legislature to remedy the underlying problems concerning the legislation relating to the status of agents and other paralegals (at 23):
>
> > It is ironic that there is a lack of clarity in the statutes governing the legal profession and their application to the respondents. I commend for the Legislature's attention

Advocates for paralegals argue that they serve an important public function by ensuring that low and middle income earners have access to straightforward legal services. Moreover, the nature of the charges defended by paralegals in the area of traffic offences is such that there is little likelihood a person of modest means would obtain legal aid, or would, in any event, be in a position to retain counsel privately. The concern of those who urge caution is, of course, that the public will be "taken in" by unscrupulous or simply untrained individuals acting as paralegals.[145] Such persons face no meaningful regulation — anyone can call themself a paralegal without any prior qualification, ongoing supervision or professional discipline.[146]

Many members of the general public feel there is a demand for affordable legal services which currently is not being satisfied by the legal profession. However, lawyers have been either unwilling or unable to find a satisfactory way of servicing, on a large scale, members of the public who desire representation in respect of simple traffic offences. In Ontario, where paralegals have been lawful for more than a decade, the result has been the creation of a fairly large paralegal force. Trouble has arisen, however, owing to the significant differences in the quality of representation provided by this group.

Whether paralegals or paid agents can represent persons charged with traffic offences is determined by reference to the legislation governing the practice of law generally, and any special procedural statute governing provincial and traffic offences. Typically, provincial statutes make it an offence to practice law, or act as a barrister, without the sanction of the local law society.[147] If, however, the statute governing a particular area of activity authorizes "agents" to appear on behalf of those charged with traffic offences, some courts have interpreted this as an exception to the general prohibition.[148] In Ontario, for example, the *Provincial Offences Act*[149] authorizes "agents" to appear for defendants and the *Crown Attorney Act*[150] authorizes paralegals to

---

the clarification of this legislation and also the status of agents and other paralegals which is now a matter of considerable public discussion.

Since that time nothing concrete has been done by the legislature, despite various task force reports and recommendations. Now the courts of this Province face increased pressure from the paralegal community, who have begun to appear in provincial courts in order to represent the accused charged in *Criminal Code* matters.

145 For an egregious example of the allegations of paralegal misconduct, see *R. v. Lemonides ibid.*

146 For a look at the history of this continuing issue, see S. Thom, "What to do About Paralegals" (1993), XXVII L.Soc. Gaz. 1:34. See as well the *Report of the Task Force on Paralegals* (Ontario Ministry of the Attorney General, Toronto: 1988) (the *Ianni Report*) which had recommended an overhaul of the regulation of paralegals in Ontario.

147 See, for example, the *Law Society Act*, R.S.O. 1990, c. L.8, s. 50.

148 *R. v. Lawrie & Points Ltd.* (1987), 59 O.R. (2d) 161 (Ont. C.A.).

149 R.S.O. 1990, c. P.33, s. 82.

150 R.S.O. 1990, c. C.49, s. 6(2).

appear for the prosecution and this has been held to authorize agents to appear for a fee.

In the first of a series of cases dealing with this issue in different provinces, the Ontario Court of Appeal[151] concluded that it was legal for agents in that province to act for a fee for individuals charged with provincial offences. While the absence of any governmental or quasi-professional control was of concern to the court, it could not be said to make the practice illegal. A similar result was reached in Newfoundland.[152] In later cases, however, courts in other jurisdictions (Manitoba[153] and British Columbia[154]) have reached the opposite result on the basis of similar statutes. In these provinces, the activities of paid paralegal agents remains illegal.

---

151 *Supra,* note 148.
152 *Law Society of Newfoundland v. Nixon* (1992), 94 D.L.R. (4th) 464 (Nfld. C.A.).
153 *Law Society of Manitoba v. Lawrie* (1989), 61 D.L.R. (4th) 259 (Man. Q.B.).
154 *Law Society of British Columbia v. Lawrie* (1991), 84 D.L.R. (4th) 540 (B.C. C.A.).

2

Procedural Issues in Traffic Offence Trials

1. INTRODUCTION

The prosecution of provincially created offences has, over the last 20 years, undergone a substantial overhaul intended to balance administrative efficiency, public convenience and the mandates of natural justice. Ontario lead the way with its procedural statute, the *Provincial Offences Act* in 1979.[1] As one author has observed:[2]

> An examination of the *Provincial Offences Act* clearly illustrates its primary objective of providing a comprehensive code of procedure which reflects the nature and gravity of the conduct sought to be regulated. The disproportionately stringent rules for criminal procedure are replaced by a procedure which emphasizes convenience, efficiency and simplicity at every stage of the proceedings.

Most other provinces have since established, in one form or another, their own procedural statutes.[3] In some cases these procedural statutes only provide a mechanism for 'ticketing' minor offences; in others, like Ontario, they create a complete procedural regime intended to deal with all procedural issues related to the prosecution of provincially created offences.

---

1 *Provincial Offences Act*, S.O. 1979, c. 4, now R.S.O. 1990, c. P.33. See M. Segal and R. Libman, *The 1998 Annotated Ontario Provincial Offences Act* (Carswell, Toronto: 1998) and S. Stewart and J. Macey, *Provincial Offences Procedure in Ontario* (Earlescourt Press: Toronto, 1998).

2 R. Kelly, "The *Provincial Offences Act*: An Overview", proceedings Canadian Bar Association, *Provincial Offences Court: Practice and Procedure* (May 9, 1992).

3 Perhaps the most comprehensive is the British Columbia *Offences Act*, R.S.B.C. 1996, c. 336. See as well the Alberta *Provincial Offences Procedure Act*, R.S.A. 1988, c. P-21.5 and the New Brunswick *Provincial Offences Procedure Act*, S.N.B. 1987, c. P-22.1.

2. CONSTITUTIONAL ISSUES

The *Provincial Offences Act* in Ontario provides a comprehensive code for procedure in prosecutions based on provincial statutes. The Act, first passed in 1979,[4] was intended to remove many of the unnecessary formalities which originated in the context of criminal prosecutions from the procedure used in regulatory cases. This is not to suggest that a modern procedural statute is a licence for sharp or unfair practice by government officials. The principles of natural justice, the right to be heard and to have an impartial hearing, survive the Act, but often in a modified form. This was noted early in the life of the *Provincial Offences Act* by Associate Chief Justice Mackinnon in *R. v. Jamieson*[5] when he observed:

> The Provincial Offences Act is not intended as a trap for the unskilled or unwary but rather ... as an inexpensive and efficient way of dealing with, for the most part, minor offences. The way in which the proceedings were conducted by the Provincial Court Judge [in this case] may have resulted in a denial of natural justice.

The strictures of the criminal law were seen as a burden to the efficient enforcement of quasi-civil offences such as those found in traffic legislation: the new scheme is intended to remove these strictures where they serve no function while preserving valuable procedures which contribute to the fair administration of quasi-criminal, regulatory legislation.[6]

The *Charter* extends to provide basic procedural protection to persons charged with traffic offences.[7] This does not mean, however, that every procedure traditionally associated with the administration of criminal justice is guaranteed. Rather, it ensures that legislative measures which operate to 'streamline' the prosecution of such cases are fundamentally fair.

One important aspect of these streamlined procedural statutes is the provision for convictions where a defendant fails to take some step required by the statutory scheme to request a trial. These "default convictions" represent a significant departure from criminal procedure which requires the prosecution to prove its case even if the accused is not present. In *R. v. Richard*[8] the Supreme Court of Canada considered this aspect of the New Brunswick regime

---

4 S.O. 1979, c. 4.

5 (1981), 64 C.C.C. (2d) 550 at 552 (Ont. C.A.). See also *R. v. Carson* (1983), 34 C.R. (3d) 86 (Ont. C.A.).

6 Even the older system of Summary Convictions Acts was recognized as existing as a discrete procedural regime with a relaxed attitude when compared with the *Criminal Code*, see *R. v. Sporring* (1978), 42 C.C.C. (2d) 246 (Ont. Div. Ct.).

7 *R. v. Richard*, [1996] 3 S.C.R. 525 and *R. v. Wigglesworth*, [1987] 2 S.C.R. 541.

8 See *Richard, ibid.* See also *R. v. Grant* (1986), 28 C.C.C. (3d) 32 (B.C. S.C.) (justifying summary procedures in traffic cases) and *R. v. Greckol* (1991), 64 C.C.C. (3d) 430 (Alta. Q.B.) (upholding procedure for dealing with "fail to respond" tickets under *Provincial Offences Procedure Act* in Alberta).

and found it to be constitutionally sound. The entire scheme under the New Brunswick statute (like all such statutes) attempted to ensure that a person who wanted a trial got one by providing complete information (through the ticket) respecting how to request a trial and providing adequate mechanisms to allow an accused to obtain a trial in the event of an erroneous conviction without trial. As such it amounted to a mechanism for, in effect, a defaulted "waiver" of any right the accused had for a trial: the scheme simply provided that the justice system would interpret a failure to request a trial as a waiver of one's right to require such a procedure.

3. THE ONTARIO PROVINCIAL OFFENCES ACT AND REFORMED PROCEDURAL STATUTES

These modern procedural statutes generally attempt to tailor the procedural formality to the seriousness of the particular offence charged and the particular transaction. In Ontario, the Act establishes three procedural streams with varying degrees of formal protections. The streams are distinguished from the outset by the original charging document. As the consequences of a prosecution become more serious, the number of procedural protections for the accused increases, until, in the most serious procedural stream, the procedural protections closely mirror those available in summary conviction prosecutions using the procedure in Part XXVII of the *Criminal Code*.

(a) The Ontario *Provincial Offences Act*, Part I: *Simple Traffic Violations*

Prosecutions falling into the first procedural stream are instituted by the filing of a *Certificate of Offence* in the court office. This procedure is used when the violation alleged is of a relatively minor nature. In the vast majority of cases, it allows for the expeditious resolution of truly regulatory violations without a court appearance. Most traffic prosecutions take place within this procedural stream.

(b) The Ontario *Provincial Offences Act*, Part II, *Parking Violations*

This, the simplest procedure, is established in Part II of the Act, and is set in motion by the issuance of a *Notice of Parking Infraction* and the filing with the court of a *Certificate of Parking Infraction.*[9] As the name suggests, this scheme is limited to parking offences and applies whether the offence flows from provincial statute or municipal by-law. Because this system depends on a revised system of licence registration, it was necessary to delay the proclamation into force of these provisions. Prior to this, the prosecution of parking offences was governed by the cumbersome *Summary Convictions*

---

9 *Parking Infractions Statute Law Amendment Act, 1992*, S.O. 1992, c. 20.

Act.[10] With the proclamation of Part II the prosecution of all parking offences in Ontario falls under the *Provincial Offences Act*.

In Ontario, with amendments to the Act in 1992[11] municipalities were assigned principal responsibility for the administration of the regime established under this Part. They also enjoy the fine revenue from such prosecutions. The initiation of a prosecution is simplified by permitting the *Notice of Parking Infraction* to be served by putting it on the driver's windshield.[12]

(c) The Ontario *Provincial Offences Act*, Part III, *Serious Traffic Violations*

The third procedural stream deals with more serious traffic and other provincial offences. Of the three procedural streams, this procedure most closely resembles the traditional criminal process and is instituted by the laying of an information before a Justice of the Peace. The attendance of the defendant is achieved by the issuances of a summons, or, in rare cases, a warrant of arrest.

(d) Certificate of Offence ("Ticketed") Prosecutions in Ontario

(i) *Generally*

The modified procedure used in Part I or Certificate of Offence prosecutions under the Ontario *Provincial Offences Act* offers a useful structure to consider issues common to many special procedural statutes. While the discussion that follows draws on the Ontario procedure, the issues recur in the context of other provincial regimes.

The procedure for simple certificate prosecutions is set out in Part I of the Act. Provincial Offences Officers (police officers as well as designated public officers or individuals) are issued multipart form packages which each contain a Certificate of Offence, Summons and Offence Notice. There is a carbon free copy made of the different forms with the documents drafted in such a way that the officer prepares all three at the same time, discarding those he does not use.[13]

The prosecution is formally initiated by the officer filing with the court office a Certificate of Offence in which the officer certifies that he believes

---

10 R.S.O. 1970, c. 450.

11 The *Streamlining of Administration of Provincial Offences, 1998*, S.O. 1998, c. 4, added provisions to the *Provincial Offences Act* to authorize the Ministry of the Attorney General to enter into agreements to have municipal entities perform courts administration and prosecution functions in respect of *Provincial Offences Act* charges, and court administration functions in respect of *Contraventions Act* charges. The new provisions provide a regime to have fine revenue from provincial offences (less victim fine surcharges and other identified amounts) paid to the municipal entity that is responsible for these functions.

12 The *Notice* may be served by leaving it "in a conspicuous place" on the vehicle at the time of the infraction. Ontario *Provincial Offences Act* s. 15(4).

13 See Appendix B for these forms.

the person named on the Certificate of Offence has committed the offence described. If the officer personally served the defendant with an Offence Notice or Summons (as will usually be the case) then he will also certify that fact. It should be remembered that in the Part I procedure the Certificate of Offence takes the place of an information and is therefore the formal charge which the accused person is called upon to answer. As such it must meet certain legal standards. The Certificate must provide the court with sufficient information to give it jurisdiction over the charge and must give the accused enough information to allow him to make a knowledgeable plea and defence.[14]

(ii) *Limits of Part I Prosecutions*

Besides providing both the defence and the prosecution with a number of procedural simplifications, the decision to proceed by way of a Part I prosecution severely limits the potential penalties which may be imposed on a defendant. By virtue of s. 12(1) of the *Provincial Offences Act*, the maximum penalty for any offence is reduced to $500. A court hearing a trial under this Part cannot impose any harsher sentence and no term of imprisonment is available.[15] If the accused is informed of the charge by Offence Notice (as opposed to a Summons) the accused is further insulated by s. 12(2) of the Act which prohibits any other penalty including forfeiture. Only demerit points and licence suspensions continue to operate.[16]

Whenever considering the constitutionality of the diminished procedural protections under Part I, it is important to remember the limited penalties available and the absence of imprisonment as a direct penalty.[17]

(e) **Procedural "Shortcuts": Offence Notices**

Before filing the Certificate of Offence (the formal charge), the officer will have served (or, if the charge comes some time after the events giving rise to the officer's belief that an offence has occurred, perhaps arranged for another officer to serve) on the accused either an Offence Notice (or perhaps a Summons) setting out essentially the same information as is found in the

---

14 See the discussion below under heading 4, "Attacking the Charging Document".

15 At least not as a direct sentence. Payment of a monetary penalty imposed under Part I may, in an extreme case, be enforced by imprisonment using the procedure in s. 69, but this is very rare in Ontario now. The procedure in s. 69 is set up to provide a defendant with every opportunity to avoid imprisonment.

16 Further, except for the purposes of demerit points or licence suspensions, no other loss may result from the conviction. Specifically, nothing seized may be forfeited. (s. 12(2)).

17 *R. v. Richard*, [1996] 3 S.C.R. 525. But *quaere* whether imprisonment as a means to enforce a fine will engage s. 7 concerns? See the comments of Mr. Justice Laforest in *Richard* at ¶31, and the discussion above in ch. 1 in section 5(b)(iv) "Prison as a Fine Enforcement Tool."

Certificate of Offence. Where the officer issues a Summons, the matter should proceed in an expeditious manner and is akin to a more serious Part III information-based prosecution. The defendant who has been served with a summons must attend at court even if he wishes to plead guilty and there must be a public airing of the case. If, however, the officer serves the accused with an Offence Notice a number of procedural "short-cuts" come into play.

(i) Plead Guilty Without an Appearance

The Offence Notice will indicate a "set fine" for the offence. Because the officer must indicate on the Offence Notice what the set fine for the offence is, this procedure is only available where a set fine has been promulgated for that offence.[18] Where this has been done and the officer has initiated the process by way of the Notice, the accused is given a number of options. The accused may simply plead guilty to the offence stated in the Offence Notice by signing the back of the Offence Notice in the appropriate place and paying the set fine. There is no need for a court appearance by the accused. Once the court office accepts the payment of the fine and endorses the certificate (filed there by the officer) by noting that the fine has been paid, the plea is considered to have been formally accepted and the fine imposed.[19] (The importance of this provision is that it prevents the accused from being recharged with the same offence under the more serious provisions of Part III.) The matter is closed as far as the provincial charge is concerned.

(ii) Guilty with an Explanation

If the accused has no defence to the charge but feels that some circumstance related to the offence or to her personal situation argues against the full set fine (e.g., the full fine would cause financial hardship), or if the accused needs an extended time to pay the fine, then she may plead guilty and make

---

18 See *Highway Traffic Act*, s. 1(1)(j) and s. 6 of the *Rules of Provincial Offences Court*, R.R.O. 1980, Reg. 809. The Chief Judge of the Provincial Offences Court is responsible for setting and publishing the set fines under the regulations.

19 The Ontario *Highway Traffic Act*, s. 8 provides that:

> 8.(1) Where an offence notice is served on a defendant and he does not wish to dispute the charge, he may sign the plea of guilty on the offence notice and deliver the offence notice and amount of the set fine to the office of the court specified in the notice.
>
> (2) Acceptance by the court office of payment under subsection 1 constitutes a plea of guilty whether or not the plea is signed and endorsement of payment on the certificate of offence constitutes the conviction and imposition of a fine in the amount of the set fine for the offence.

> This section takes on some importance where police later attempt to charge a more serious offence. The fact of the plea and acceptance of the fine create the possibility of a later plea of autrefois convict (a form of double jeopardy) for the accused. See also *R. v. J.W.* (1990), 89 Sask. R. 103 (Sask. Q.B.).

submissions as to the sentence. This is commonly called "pleading guilty with an explanation".[20]

It should be understood that this plea constitutes an admission of the offence and any submissions should go only to the amount of the monetary penalty. The accused cannot avoid a finding of guilt or the demerit points or other administrative sanctions which necessarily follow under this procedure. It is also worth mentioning that this procedure can only be used where the accused wishes to plead guilty to the very offence with which she is charged. This cannot be used to plead guilty to a 'lesser offence'. That can only be done pursuant to s. 45(4) with the consent of the prosecutor in open court.[21] An accused may plead guilty and make submissions through an agent or counsel, but if this course of action is followed the accused should sign the guilty plea on the back of the Offence Notice as evidence of her intent. (In Ontario, some justices are understandably reluctant to take pleas from agents or even counsel. Signing prevents the possibility of the Justice requiring a second appearance by the representative.)

The situation has arisen where the accused invoking this less formal procedure pleads guilty and seeks a lesser penalty and, in the course of doing so, she puts forward an explanation which, if believed, would constitute a defence to the charge. In such a case, the justice hearing the submissions can and should strike the plea and make it clear to the accused that she is entitled to a trial on the merits.[22] (If the accused wishes to change her plea it is then up to the accused to present the Offence Notice properly indicating her desire to plead not guilty. Such a case should be treated as though the accused had never pleaded guilty and will proceed as scheduled by the court office. The accused may also again plead guilty, this time in open court, with representations as to penalty, relying on matters besides those going to a possible defence.)

If the court decides that, in the circumstances, it is appropriate to reduce the penalty to less than the set fine or to less than the minimum fine, it shall endorse the certificate to that effect and give reasons.[23]

The Justice hearing representations with respect to sentence has no power to amend or quash the certificate.[24]

It is not unusual for an officer to wait a day or two before filing his Certificate of Offence with the court office. This may be especially so in more remote areas. Because the Certificate of Offence is the formal charging document and

---

20 *Ibid.*, s. 7(1).
21 See the discussion below in section 10 under the heading "Included Offence".
22 *R. v. Adgey* (1973), 23 C.R.N.S. 298 (S.C.C.).
23 Section 19, *Rules of the Provincial Offences Court, supra.* This is similar to the procedure now provided in s. 726.2 of the *Criminal Code*.
24 Section 14, *Rules of the Provincial Offences Court, supra.*

the only record of the offence at the court office, the Justice cannot take a plea with submissions unless he has the Certificate of Offence.[25]

(iii) *Indicate an Intention to Appear and Plead — Modified Procedures*

The final option for an accused is to indicate an intention to appear and plead not guilty by signing the third box on the Offence Notice, delivering it to the court office indicated and awaiting a trial date. The accused, by filing the properly endorsed Offence Notice with the court, sets in motion the trial process. The burden of getting the Offence Notice to the court within the prescribed time is on the accused. The Clerk of the Court is then required to, as soon as is practicable, give the accused notice of the time and place of the trial.[26]

Prior to 1993, this process in Ontario saw the accused actually plead not guilty and request a trial by mail. A trial date was set and a notice sent to the accused. The charging officer and other witnesses were notified and required to attend. Even if the accused did not attend, the Crown was obliged to call evidence and prove the charge.[27] Much court time was wasted on 'show trials' in cases where the accused did not attend. These trials *in absentia* did little to advance the sound administration of justice and consumed valuable court time.

In 1993, the *Provincial Offences Act* was amended[28] to modify this method of proceeding in a small but significant way. The Act now looks to the accused to request a trial and requires that the accused attend at court and enter a plea of not guilty in open court before the prosecution is obliged to call evidence. An accused who requests a trial but who does not attend is treated in a manner similar to an accused who has not responded to the Offence Notice at all (see below).[29]

The 1993 amendments also prescribed a special procedure for "first appearance courts" intended to provide an early procedural opportunity to

---

25 *Ibid.*

26 It is also possible for an accused to make written submissions if the address listed for him on the Certificate of Offence is outside the territorial jurisdiction of the court. The address listed on the Certificate will probably be the address listed on the accused's driver's licence. The accused who wishes to use this procedure should sign the offence notice not guilty and include his written dispute. If the Justice feels that the dispute raises a valid point he should direct a hearing of the witnesses to determine the legitimacy of the accused's point. If, after a full hearing, the Justice is convinced that the accused is guilty he may so find and convict the accused. However, he is limited to imposing the set fine. For a good analysis of this process and the dangers, see Drinkwalter and Ewart, *Ontario Provincial Offences Procedure* pp. 55-58.

27 This is a trial *in absentia*. See *Provincial Offences Act*, R.S.O. 1990, c. P.33, s. 6(2) (as it stood prior to 1993 amendments.)

28 *Provincial Offences Statute Law Amendment Act*, S.O. 1993, c. 31.

29 *Provincial Offences Act*, R.S.O. 1990, c. P.33, s. 9.1, as amended.

resolve cases, and to provide for the better scheduling of trials. In jurisdictions designated in the province, the normal "write in trial request" is set aside and a system of first appearance courts is established. An accused who wishes to plead not guilty in these locations (most large cities in the province) must attend at court on any day during designated hours to appear before a justice, request a trial date, and set that date. In practice, the prosecutor and a police officer are present and can deal with issues which permit a resolution of the charge.[30]

(iv) *Challenging the Charging Officer's Evidence*

One further change occasioned by the 1993 statute provides that where an accused intends to challenge the evidence of the charging officer that the accused will so indicate at the time of requesting a trial. Where an accused does not so request, the certified statements of the charging officer contained in the Certificate of Offence are proof, in the absence of evidence to the contrary, of the facts certified in the Certificate of Offence.[31] This procedure is intended to eliminate the need for a police officer to attend in those cases where the officer had little or no real evidence to give on the issues engaged by the defence.

(v) *Did Not Respond*

If the accused does not respond within fifteen days of receiving the Offence Notice he will automatically be convicted. Under s. 9 of the Act a Justice of the Peace will review the Certificate of Offence filed in the court and determine if it is valid on its face. If it is, that is, if it charges an offence known to law and is otherwise regular, the Justice of the Peace is required to convict the accused and impose the set fine. If there is something wrong with the Certificate of Offence, if it is not "complete and regular on its face" the proceeding shall be quashed, as though the document was never issued.

(vi) *Failure to Attend for Trial*

As noted, the 1993 amendments removed the need for the prosecution to prove the charge in a trial *in absentia* where the accused failed to attend on the date fixed for trial. Where the accused fails to attend, the charge is dealt with as though it were a case where the accused had not responded to the Offence Notice and, if the charge is regular on its face, a conviction is entered. This approach improves case flow and bolsters public confidence in the administration of justice. This process is constitutional.[32]

---

30 *Ibid.*, s. 5.1, as amended.
31 *Ibid.*, ss. 5.1, 48; *R. v. Panchal*, [1995] O.J. No. 3149 (Ont. Prov. Div.).
32 *R. v. Pilipovic*, [1996] O.J. No. 3139.

(f) Fail-safe Provisions

This system of "automatic convictions" has the potential to operate unfairly. The party named in the Certificate of Offence may have a perfectly good reason for not responding to the charge or failing to attend the trial. It may have been impossible for the defendant to respond because of health reasons or the defendant may have taken reasonable steps to assure delivery of the Notice which was lost in the mail. The defendant may have been wrongly identified and never have received the notice in the first place, or may have simply never received the trial notice in the mail for no reason within the control of the defendant. In such a case, in the Ontario regime, the accused may look to s. 11 which provides that:

> **11.** (1) If a defendant who has been convicted without a hearing attends at the court office during regular office hours within fifteen days of becoming aware of the conviction and appears before a justice requesting that the conviction be struck out, the justice shall strike out the conviction if he or she is satisfied by affidavit of the defendant that, through no fault of the defendant, the defendant was unable to appear for a hearing or a notice or document relating to the offence was not delivered.
>
> (2) If the justice strikes out the conviction, he or she shall give the defendant and the prosecutor a notice of trial or proceed under section 7.
>
> (3) If a notice of trial is given, the defendant shall indicate on the notice of intention to appear or offence notice if the defendant intends to challenge the evidence of the provincial offences officer who completed the certificate of offence.
>
> (4) If the defendant indicates an intention to challenge the officer's evidence, the clerk of the court shall notify the officer.
>
> (5) A justice who strikes out a conviction under subsection (1) shall give the defendant a certificate of the fact in prescribed form.

To be eligible for the saving provision of this section, the accused must have failed to deliver his notice (or failed to receive a notice) "through no fault of his own". This suggests that some due diligence standard may be applied to the actions of an accused under this section.[33] Whether using some agent to deliver the notice (friend, messenger or post office) or failing to give notice of a change of address qualifies a defendant for the protection of the section will depend on the facts of each case. It is our opinion, however, that in most cases arising under s. 11, the Justice should accept the defendant's explanation if it is at all reasonable. It must be remembered that the result, after all, of granting the relief sought is to see the matter tried on its merits, and that is the ultimate purpose of any code of procedure.

---

33 The courts have been fairly generous in their interpretation of this provision: *Newfoundland (A.G.) v. Baldwin* (1986), 59 Nfld. & P.E.I.R. 148 (Nfld. T.D.).

An application under s. 11 (or s. 19, which is to the same effect in the case of a parking violation prosecuted under Part II) shall be in form 102 as set out in the regulations.[34]

As might be expected, this default conviction scheme has come under *Charter* scrutiny. In the early case of *R. v. Carson*,[35] the accused was convicted after failing to respond to an Offence Notice which charged him with driving without a proper headlight. He claimed that the provision in s. 9 allowing for default convictions without a trial violated his right to be presumed innocent until proven guilty. The Ontario Court of Appeal dismissed the appeal. The court took the view that, while the section appeared on its face to violate s. 11(d) of the *Charter*, it was saved by s. 1 as a reasonable limit on the *Charter* right. Looking at the overall scheme, the volume of work done by the Provincial Offences Court, the various mechanisms in place for the accused to deal with the charge without excessive technical difficulties, the minimal penalties, and the "fail-safe" provisions in s. 11, the court found that the relatively minor infringement of the *Charter* right was justified.

The same result was reached in *Richard*[36] by the Supreme Court of Canada which held that the overall organization of the provisions in the New Brunswick procedural statute[37] amounted to a scheme to determine when and how an accused might waive his or her right to a trial.

(g) Part III Prosecutions: Charges on Information

(i) *Initiating Proceedings*

As noted above, Part III prosecutions are initiated by the laying of an information before a Justice of the Peace. The procedure employed in such a prosecution is similar to that employed in *Criminal Code* prosecutions and is generally more complex and cumbersome than that found in Part I, Certificate prosecutions. To issue the charging document the person who wishes to charge the accused must lay before a Justice a sworn statement alleging facts which would constitute an offence under provincial legislation. While a Certificate may only be issued by a Provincial Offences Officer, anyone may initiate a Part III prosecution by laying a sworn information before a Justice of the Peace.[38]

---

34 R.R.O. 1990, Reg. 200, see Appendix D.

35 (1983), 20 M.V.R. 54 (Ont. C.A.).

36 *Supra*, note 7.

37 *Provincial Offences Procedure Act*, S.N.B. 1987, c. P-22.1.

38 Section 3(2) of the *Provincial Offences Act* only empowers "a provincial offences officer" to issue a certificate of offence. Any private citizen wishing to lay a charge under a provincial Act *must* look to Part III. The purpose of requiring individuals to use this more complex procedure is to limit abuses by private complainants. By requiring a private citizen to convince a Justice of the Peace on evidence given under oath that there is good reason to believe

Where an officer finds someone in the act of violating some provision of a provincial law which is deserving of a Part III prosecution, he may issue a summons before laying the information.[39] If the Justice of the Peace refuses to issue process (i.e., accepts the charging document, but declines to issue any formal document requiring the accused person to attend and answer the charge), the Justice shall cancel the summons so issued and give notice of the cancellation to the defendant. It should be noted that the summons is not the charging document and as such is not subject to the same legal scrutiny as the information.

There is no requirement that the Justice and the defendant reside in the same jurisdiction or even that the Justice be assigned to the jurisdiction where the offence is to be tried, so long as the information is returnable in the proper jurisdiction.[40]

When the Justice issues process on an information he confirms any summons issued by the officer. Some authors have suggested that there is nothing to prevent an officer from presenting a single information to a series of Justices, each fulfilling a separate function (the first accepting the information and confirming the summons and the second actually issuing process).[41]

Section 25 sets out the statutory requirements of an information.[42]

(ii) *Why Proceed under Part III?*

There are three principal reasons that a Provincial Offences Officer might choose to swear a Part III information (rather than a Certificate of Offence). Firstly, he might simply want to ensure that it will be open to the prosecution to seek the more serious penalties available under Part III. Secondly, the expiration of the thirty-day limitation period for service of a Notice[43] may have expired since the date of the offence, leaving no option. Finally, it is possible that, in rare cases, the authorities would want the Justice to issue a province-wide warrant for the arrest of the accused. Under s. 24 such a power is available in limited cases.[44]

---

that an offence has been committed, this provision operates to prevent frivolous complaints. The streamlined procedure under Part I might become the vehicle for injustice if it could be set in motion by anyone who was upset with his or her neighbour.

39 See s. 23. This is similar to s. 451 of the *Criminal Code* which allows an officer to issue an appearance notice to an accused before process issues.

40 Section 23(2).

41 Drinkwalter and Ewart, *supra* note 26, at 92.

42 See below under heading "Attacking the Charging Document."

43 See s. 3(3).

44 For a helpful discussion of the advantages of proceeding under Part III, see Drinkwalter and Ewart, *supra* note 26, at 79-84.

4. ATTACKING THE CHARGING DOCUMENT: 'GETTI' TECHNICALITIES UNDER THE ONTARIO *PROVIN(* *ACT*

(a) Introduction

It is important to remember that the central purpose of the modern procedural statutes like the *Provincial Offences Act*[45] has been to eliminate unnecessary procedural 'technicalities' from regulatory prosecutions.[46] It was not intended that a purely formal defect should be fatal to a charging document. The main consideration in these cases is to be the effect of the defect on the parties and their rights under the procedures available under the Act. Even a substantive error may be allowed if it is possible for the court to correct the error without depriving the defendant of his right to know and defend the charge against him.

Most such statutes provide broad powers to amend a charge to cure defects which are merely formal in nature. For example, under the *Provincial Offences Act* the Justice has a broad discretion to amend the charging document to cure defects and to bring it in line with evidence. The court may amend the Certificate or Information in certain circumstances set out in s. 34:

> **34.** (1) The court may, at any stage of the proceeding, amend the information or certificate as may be necessary if it appears that the information or certificate,
>
> > (a) fails to state or states defectively anything that is requisite to charge the offence;
> >
> > (b) does not negative an exception that should be negatived; or
> >
> > (c) is in any way defective in substance or in form.
>
> (2) The court may, during the trial, amend the information or certificate as may be necessary if the matters to be alleged in the proposed amendment are disclosed by the evidence taken at the trial.
>
> (3) A variance between the information or certificate and the evidence taken on the trial is not material with respect to,
>
> > (a) the time when the offence is alleged to have been committed, if it is proved that the information was laid or certificate issued within the prescribed period of limitation; or
> >
> > (b) the place where the subject-matter of the proceedings is alleged to have arisen, except in an issue as to the jurisdiction of the court.

---

45 R.S.O. 1990, c. P.33.

46 For an example of the sort of trivial defect that might have been fatal in an earlier age, see *R. v. Sullivan* (1968), 3 C.R. (N.S.) 132 (Ont. S.C.) which held that a checkmark in a box on a ticket invalidated it because the statute referred to marking the box with an "X". See also *Toronto (Metropolitan) v. Beck* (1990), 23 M.V.R. (2d) 61 (Ont. H.C.J.) criticizing the "overly technical" approach of the trial court to *Provincial Offences Act* issues.

(4) The court shall, in considering whether or not an amendment should be made, consider,

>   (a) the evidence taken on the trial, if any;

>   (b) the circumstances of the case;

>   (c) whether, having regard to the merits of the case, the proposed amendment can be made without injustice being done.

(5) The question whether an order to amend an information or certificate should be granted or refused is a question of law ...

The key passage in understanding this power is s. 34(4)(c). If the court cannot make the amendment without depriving the accused of some right, then it should not use its power to repair the document. In fact, if it is impossible to amend without depriving the accused to some right, the Justice probably has no jurisdiction to make the amendment.

Section 34 provides that particulars may be ordered before or during trial if necessary to ensure a fair trial for the defendant. Particulars should describe the alleged violation in more detail than is found in the charging document in order to make it possible for the defendant to put forward a full answer and defence to the charge. An order for particulars should not, however, be made if it would simply serve to bind the prosecution to prove unnecessary facts.[47]

(b) Duplicitous Charging Documents

Section 33 provides:

33. (1) A defendant may at any stage of the proceeding apply to the court to amend or divide a court that,

>   (a) charges in the alternative different matters, acts or omissions that are stated in the alternative in the enactment that creates or describes the offence; or

>   (b) is double or multifarious,

on the ground that, as framed, it prejudices him in his defence.

This provision would be used where the charge in the Certificate or Information as worded is broadly enough to include two possible offences. In such a case, the accused is really called upon to answer two charges at once. Further, if the accused is later charged in respect of the same wrongful act he or she may be prevented from pleading a previous conviction because, on the face of the Certificate, it is impossible to say for certain what the charge was.

---

47 In the criminal context, see *R. v. Govedarov* (1975), 3 O.R. (2d) 23 (Ont. C.A.), affirmed on other grounds (*sub nom. R. v. Popovic*) [1976] 2 S.C.R. 308 (S.C.C.).

Challenges based on this complaint are often based on an interpretation of the section giving rise to the allegation — does it create one offence or two?[48] For example, the language creating the common offence of 'careless driving' normally prohibits driving "without due care or attention" or "without reasonable consideration for others using the highway". Is this one offence or two?[49] If the section creates one offence that can be committed in several ways, then generic charging language is permissible — if it creates two offences, then the charge must be worded to identify which is alleged. While an amendment to cure such a defect is common, it has, for the accused, the advantage of focusing the allegation by the prosecutor and thereby may provide a defence.

(c) The Misspelled Name

A frequently cited error is a misspelled name. Often a defendant will seek to quash a charging document because the name on the document is not spelled correctly. The test in such cases is whether typical reasonable defendant, reading the misspelled name would say "This is not me" or "This is me, but there is a mistake in the spelling of my name".[50]

(d) Objections at Trial

An objection to a defect on the face of the document should be taken before the plea. If an amendment is allowed by the court and an adjournment is necessary, the court has a limited power to order costs in favour of the accused.[51]

It is important to raise an objection at trial to a defect in a charging document. If a defendant fails to object to the wording of the document at trial he will be deemed to have accepted the form of the charge and cannot appeal on the ground that it was somehow defective.[52]

When challenging the charging document, it is important to remember the circumstances under which it is usually presented to the accused. Normally,

---

48 See, for example, *R. v. Timplaru* (1987), 47 M.V.R. 41 (Sask. Q.B.).

49 See ch. 6, "Careless Driving," below.

50 This problem is thoroughly canvased in J.D. Ewart, "Appellation non Controlée: The Misspelling of the Defendant's Name in Informations or Certificates of Offence" (1981), 23 Crim. L.Q. 492.

51 See ss. 37 and 60 of the Ontario *Provincial Offences Act.*

52 Section 124 provides:

> 124 (1) Judgment shall not be given in favour of an appellant based on any alleged defect in the substance or form of an information, certificate or process or any variance between the information, certificate or process and the evidence adduced at trial unless it is shown that objection was taken at the trial and that, in the case of a variance, an adjournment of the trial was refused notwithstanding that the variance had misled the appellant.

the officer has served an Offence Notice on the accused immediately after the incident giving rise to the charge. The circumstances will usually be such that the defendant will have actual knowledge of the transaction alleged in the charging document.[53] If this is not the case and the defendant intends to challenge the charging document, the defendant should make it clear to the court that the charge was not communicated to him until some time after the event giving rise to the charge or that the confusing nature of the events giving rise to the charge deprives the defendant of any special advantage in understanding the charge.

(e) Short Forms in the Regulations

Most statutes provide that certain pre-approved short form language can be used to charge common traffic offences. For example, s. 13(2) of the *Provincial Offences Act* provides:

> **13.** (2) The use on a [Offence Notice or Summons] of any word or expression authorized by the regulations to designate an offence *is sufficient for all purposes* to describe the offence designated by such word or expression. [Emphasis added.]

The regulations made under this section create official short forms to describe offences. They generally provide a fair, common sense description of the offence alleged.[54] If the officer preparing the Offence Notice or summons does not know the official short form, or in cases where there is no such short form for the offence alleged, any words adequately describing the offence are allowed.[55] A document using the officially approved short form cannot be challenged as failing to give sufficient information about the offence charged.[56]

If something other than the official short form is used, the charging document will nonetheless be sufficient if it clearly:[57]

1. Identifies the offence alleged (i.e., the statutory breach that is alleged);

2. Gives reasonable information with respect to the act or omission to be proved; and

3. Identifies the transaction referred to.

---

53 *R. v. Sporring, supra,* note 6.

54 The short forms for the relevant offences are reproduced in the appendix.

55 *R. v. Myers* (1975), 23 C.C.C. (2d) 50 (B.C. C.A.) and *R. v. Delfing* (1982), 17 Man. R. (2d) 343 (Man. Co. Ct.), approving the use of the expression "possess a radar detector in a motor vehicle" to describe the offence created by *Highway Traffic Act,* R.S.M. 1970, c. H-60, s. 223(4)(a)(iii).

56 *R. v. Sporring, supra,* note 6. See also *Charlottetown (City) v. MacKinnon* (1991), 32 M.V.R. (2d) 1 (P.E.I. C.A.).

57 See Ewart & Drinkwalter, *supra* note 26 at 67-70 and 99-102.

It is not necessary for a charge to be exhaustive in its description of the trans-action alleged to be sufficient to survive challenge. In some cases, where the charge is legally sufficient, the accused may nonetheless desire or require addi-tional details to know the charge against him or her. In such cases the accused can move for particulars, which amount to a more detailed factual allegation about the conduct of the accused alleged to constitute an offence.[58]

(f) Defects not affecting the validity of a charging document or which may be amended[59]

Given the nature of charging documents under modified procedural statutes, and the broad flexibility shown in respect of defects in such docu-ments, it is not surprising that a number of 'defects' have been held not to go to the substance of the charge. It is equally unremarkable that few facial defects in charging documents alleging traffic offences result in the document being quashed. Between the latitude shown to such defects, the relative ease of preparing such charging documents, and the training provided to officers, few, if any, fatal defects should arise.

The following errors in charging documents have been held to be either no defect, or subject to amendment by the court at the request of the prosecutor:

- Failure of an officer to sign a Notice or Summons;[60]
- Failure to state the district and court in which the offence notice is to be returnable;[61]
- Use of unofficial short forms (e.g., H.T.A.) provided the document is otherwise sufficient;[62]
- Charging "speeding" without proper statutory references;[63]
- Failure to name the victim of the offence;[64]
- Failure to specify the means of carrying out the offence;[65]

---

58 *R. v. Devereaux* (1975), 22 C.C.C. (2d) 568 (Ont. H.C.J.) and *R. v. Gauthier* (1977), 36 C.C.C. (2d) 420 (Ont. H.C.J.).

59 For a complete list of the statutory terms of an information or certificate in Ontario, see s. 25 of the Ontario *Provincial Offences Act*.

60 *R. v. Elliot* (1981), 12 M.V.R. 35 (Ont. C.A.).

61 *R. v. Callahan* (1981), 21 M.V.R. 127 (Ont. C.A.); *R. v. Arnold* (1982), 17 M.V.R. 61 (Ont. H.C.J.); *R. v. Greenspan* (1982), 17 M.V.R. 57 (Ont. Prov. Ct.).

62 *R. v. Lemieux* (1980), 15 M.V.R. 126 (Ont. C.A.). See also *R. v. Vaughan* (1978), 1 M.V.R. 32 (Ont. Dist. Ct.) dealing with proceedings under the old *Summary Convictions Act*, R.S.O. 1970, c. 450, s. 7(5).

63 *R. v. Kartna* (1979), 2 M.V.R. 259 (Ont. H.C.J.); *R. v. Lemieux* (1978), 1 M.V.R. 27 (Ont. Dist. Ct.).

64 Section 25(7)(a).

65 Section 25(7)(f).

- Omitting the word "limited" in a corporate name;[66]
- Using the word "operate" instead of "drive";[67]
- Use of incorrect section number or failure to state a section number where the offence is adequately described in words;[68] and
- Minor deviations in the form used for the ticket, or minor departures from approved forms.[69]

(g) Defects for which amendments have been refused or which have been held to render the charging document a nullity

These defects, which will be rare, would seem to render a charging document a nullity:

- Missing signature on the information (either the Justice or the informant);[70]
- No date of the offence;
- No name for the defendant;[71]
- No name for the charging officer;[72]
- No location given for the offence;
- No offence indicated or none known to law;
- Information sworn after the end of the limitation date; and
- Failing to properly identify offence that accused (as owner) stood charged with.[73]

5. THE TRIAL

(a) Procedural Details

Courtrooms used in traffic cases are usually arranged in one of two patterns:

---

66   *Re R. and J. F. Brennan & Associates Ltd.* (1981), 61 C.C.C. (2d) 1 (Ont. H.C.).

67   *R. v. West* (1982), 35 O.R. (2d) 179.

68   *R. ex rel. James v. Joy Oil Co. Ltd.* (1959), 123 C.C.C. 370 (Ont. C.A.). See also *R. v. Jamieson* (Oct. 25, 1985, B.C. Co. Ct.) summarized at 15 W.C.B. 143.

69   *R. v. Schepens* (1989), 16 M.V.R. (2d) 198 (Alta. Q.B.); *R. v. Scott*, [1995] O.J. No. 4282. See also the applicable interpretation statute, such as the Ontario *Interpretation Act*, R.S.O. 1990, c. I.1-1, s. 28(d), which permits deviations from prescribed forms, generally if they do not alter the substance of the form, and are not calculated to mislead.

70   *R. v. Kapoor* (1989), 52 C.C.C. (3d) 41 (Ont. H.C.).

71   *Supra*, note 50.

72   *R. v. Bertolucci et al.*, [1995] O.J. No. 4283 (Ont. Prov. Div.).

73   *R. v. Schepens*, *supra*, note 69; *R. v. Oakcrest Food Stores (1976) Ltd.* (1982), 17 M.V.R. 103 (B.C. S.C.).

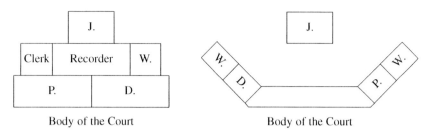

J. = Judge or Justice of the Peace
W. = Witness Box
D. = Defendant or Defendant's Representative
P. = Prosecution

The cases to be heard at the sittings of the court for that day will usually be listed on a docket outside the courtroom. The list may be called in any order and, while the judge or justice presiding retains control over the proceedings, as a practical matter, the prosecutor usually arranges the order in which the list is to be called. Ordinarily matters are called in the order which will allow the quickest cases to be dealt with first. Shorter cases (adjournments on consent, guilty pleas) with counsel are called first, and then pleas without counsel are called. Finally, matters involving trials are called, usually with an eye to the anticipated length of the particular matter, and its procedural history.

Where an accused has indicated an intention to plead not guilty after receiving an Offence Notice or where a Summons has been issued in a Part I prosecution or in any Part III prosecution, the Clerk of the Court will set the case down for trial. As a matter of practice, the court will usually co-ordinate with the officer preparing the Certificate, setting the case for that officer's next "court day".

6. DISCLOSURE

The prosecution in criminal and quasi-criminal cases (such as traffic offences) has a general duty to disclose to the defendant the nature of the evidence which will be lead by the prosecution at trial, as well as any other exculpatory evidence, or information, in the hands of the prosecution which might be helpful for the defence. For example, if the defendant made a statement at the time of the incident giving rise to the charges, the defence has a right to know what was taken down and under what circumstances.

In the leading case dealing with disclosure, *R. v. Stinchcombe*,[74] the Supreme Court of Canada left open the question of whether the duty on the prosecution to make disclosure in summary matters (and provincial offences) was the same as the very demanding duty imposed in more serious indictable

---

74 (1991), 68 C.C.C. (3d) 1 (S.C.C.).

cases.[75] There is no principled reason to invite a different rule in summary or provincial offences, but obviously the resources devoted to disclosure in a modest traffic offence cannot be the same as that in a more serious matter. The form or manner of disclosure for a traffic offence will not be identical, therefore, to that in more serious criminal cases. In Ontario the issue of disclosure was canvassed by a special committee convened to assist the Attorney General on matters related to disclosure generally. The committee report (taking the name of the chair and known as the Martin Report) noted:[76]

> In summary conviction and *Provincial Offences Act* prosecutions, proper disclosure will, as suggested by Sopinka J. in *Stinchcombe* [(1991), 68 C.C.C. (3d) 1 (S.C.C.)] no doubt will vary with the nature of the statute defining the offence, and the circumstances of the prosecution. Accordingly, the detailed recommendations with respect to disclosure that follow may have varying degrees of applicability and/or importance. In most summary conviction prosecutions and prosecutions under the *Provincial Offences Act*, the disclosure will be simple and brief. On the other hand, certain matters, for example, some prosecutions under [environmental protection legislation] may be highly complex, and may involve very serious allegations with grave consequences. In such cases, full disclosure may be more lengthy and complex, and its significance may be heightened.

Disclosure of material in the possession of the prosecutor in traffic offences is usually simple enough to arrange.[77] Often, all that is in the pos-

---

75 *R. v. Stinchcombe, ibid.*, at p. 13, where Mr. Justice Sopinka for the court said:
    The general principles referred to herein arise in the context of indictable offenses. While it may be argued that the duty of disclosure extends to all offenses, many of the factors which I have canvassed may not apply at all or may apply with less impact in summary conviction offences. Moreover, the content of the right to make full answer and defence entrenched in s. 7 of the *Charter* may be of a more limited nature. A decision as to the extent to which the general principles of disclosure extend to summary conviction offences should be left to a case in which the issue arises in such proceedings. In view of the number and variety of statutes which create such offences, consideration would have to be given as to where to draw the line.

76 The *Report of the Attorney General's Committee on Charge Screening, Disclosure and Resolution Discussions* (Ontario Ministry of the Attorney General, Toronto; 1993) (the *"Martin Report"*) at p. 186. The Report recommended (recommendation 36, found at p. 184 of the report) that "the nature and extent of disclosure should not vary based on whether the charge was prosecuted by way of indictment, summary conviction procedure, or prosecuted under the *Provincial Offences Act*". See also *R. v. Fineline Circuits Ltd.* (1991), 10 C.R. (4th 241 (Ont. Prov. Div.).

77 In Ontario the *Crown Policy Manual*, (the manual for Ontario Crown Attorneys and prosecutors) policy D-1 "Disclosure" provides:
    In Provincial Offence prosecutions, upon request, the defendant in a minor part one [ticket traffic offence] will be provided with a copy of the certificate of offence and a copy of the notes of the police officer and witnesses if any.
    For more serious part one [traffic ticket] offences, upon request, the defendant will be provided with the above plus a copy of any accident reports or other documents to be utilized by the prosecution.
    For part three offences [charged on an Information with more serious penalties] the defendant will be provided with a copy of the Information, police officer or witness notes and any documents to be utilized in the prosecution.

session of the prosecutor, however, is a prosecution sheet or summary prepared by the investigator. This should be obtained through the prosecutor's office. In addition though, there is nothing to prevent the defendant or the defendant's representative from contacting the officer responsible and asking to see his or her notes.

Of course there is no duty on the defence to give up the theory or evidence that it intends to rely upon.[78]

It is not unheard of, however, for the representative of the defendant or the defendant to wait until the trial date to ask to see the file on the accused. This is too late. While the prosecutor may give disclosure at this time if possible, there is no duty to do so. The only obligation on the prosecution is to give disclosure in response to a reasonable and timely request. If the defence has sought disclosure from the prosecution and been refused, the defendant may make a motion to have the charge dismissed.[79]

If a defendant has been diligent in seeking reasonable disclosure from the prosecution and such has not been forthcoming, the trial court can order that disclosure be made in a reasonable manner before the case proceeds.[80] The defence must show that the material that it seeks is at least potentially relevant to an issue in the case before the court will order disclosure. As well, material in the possession of the Crown may be withheld based on recognized legal privilege.[81]

7. COSTS

The term "costs" connotes two forms of expense incurred by an accused. Firstly, there is the cost of retaining a representative to defend the charge. Secondly, there are out of pocket expenses associated with having witnesses attend and give evidence. In general, there is no authority in a traffic court to award

---

For photo-radar offences, the defendant will be provided with a copy of the certificate of offence, a copy of the notes of any police officer and an opportunity to view the photograph. If the defendant wishes a copy of the photograph, he or she can make arrangements with the police authority to secure a copy at the defendant's cost.

Any additional material such as the radar manual should be the subject of an application to court.

See also *R. v. Shannon* (1992), 42 M.V.R. (2d) 128 (Ont. C.A.) where the Court held that an accused has no right to obtain a copy of the operating manual for a mere investigative aid or tool such as a "radar-detector" (which identified cars possibly using radar detection equipment).

78 With the exception of business records which must be served by whatever party intends to produce them at trial at least 5 days before trial. Ontario *Evidence Act*, R.S.O. 1990, c. E.23, s. 35(3).

79 But see Ewaschuk, *Criminal Pleadings & Practice in Canada* (2nd ed.) (Canada Law Book, Aurora: 1987, looseleaf) §31: 8390 and the cases cited therein.

80 *R. v. Stinchcombe*, *supra*, note 74.

81 *R. v. Shannon*, *supra*, note 77.

'costs' in the form of lawyer or agent fees to a defendant.[82] There is, however, a very limited power to make an order of costs to defray the expenses associated with the attendance of witnesses.[83]

8. MOTIONS PRIOR TO PLEA

Before entering a plea to the charge, the accused should bring any challenges to the charging document. A failure to do so will usually constitute an acceptance of the document as valid on its face. While the court continues to have jurisdiction to amend the document, the plea can be read as curing any defect going to the accused person's understanding of the offence charged (for example the date or the section number).

(a) **Adjournments**

(i) *Generally*

It may sometimes happen that either the defence or prosecution is unable to proceed on the date which has been set for trial. (In prosecutions where the process of setting a date takes place in writing this is more likely because, once the defendant indicates an intention to plead not guilty, he or she is not necessarily consulted as to the date to be set for trial.)[84] In such a case, either side may seek an adjournment. A witness for the prosecution or the defence may be sick or travelling and therefore unable to attend on the date set for trial. Some valid reason may prevent the defendant from coming to court to answer the charge.

A motion for an adjournment should normally be made as soon as the need for an adjournment comes to the party's attention (in most cases on at least three days notice). The party seeking the adjournment should file a notice of motion with the court three days before the day when the motion is proposed to be heard. The notice of motion should include an affidavit indicating the facts upon which the moving party relies in the application for the adjournment.

The trial court in Ontario also has a general power under s. 49(1) to grant adjournments in such circumstances. When the defendant or his representative seeks an adjournment, it is important to explain exactly why the trial should

---

82 *R. v. 974649 Ontario Inc.* (1995), 101 C.C.C. (3d) 48 (Ont. Gen. Div.); *R. v. Lem* (1993), 45 M.V.R. (2d) 322 (Ont. C.A.); *R. v. Anachemia Solvents Ltd.* (1994), 14 C.E.L.R. (N.S.) 110 (Ont. Prov. Div.). There is a limited power to award costs on appeal: see Ontario *Provincial Offences Act*, s. 138(3).

83 See s. 60 of the Ontario *Provincial Offences Act* and the regulations made thereunder: R.R.O. 1990, Reg.945 (as amended by O. Regs. 678/92, 501/93, 493/94).

84 In some parts of Ontario a 'first attendance court' procedure is used to require those who want a trial to attend in person to set a date: Ontario *Provincial Offences Act*, s. 5.1. This provision facilitates pre-trial discussions between defendants and prosecutors as well as ensuring that when a date is set for a trial, the accused has some input.

not proceed as scheduled. Both sides should be allowed to make representations to the court. If, for example, a witness has gone away on holidays, the
defendant should be ready to explain to the court in general terms what the
witness will give evidence about and when they are expected to return. If the
defendant has waited to the last minute to raise the need for an adjournment,
the prosecution will point out that it has its civilian witnesses in court and
is ready to proceed.

While it is not unusual for a court to grant an adjournment if the defendant
has a good reason on the first appearance, there is no rule requiring that an
adjournment be granted. When the defendant sends some representative
(lawyer, agent, friend or relative) to explain why the defendant cannot attend,
that person should be ready to proceed to trial and make submissions as to
sentence just in case the adjournment is denied and the trial goes ahead.

In deciding whether to allow an adjournment of a trial because a witness
is not available, the court will consider:[85]

1. whether the absent witnesses are material witnesses in the case;
2. whether the party applying has been guilty of delay or neglect in omitting
   to endeavour to procure the attendance of these witnesses; and
3. whether there is a reasonable expectation that the witness can be procured
   at the future time to which it is sought to put off the trial.

(b) Adjournment to Obtain Representation

The *Provincial Offences Act* recognizes the basic right of the defendant
to be represented by counsel or an agent of his choice (though the agent may
be rejected by the trial judge).[86] The cases have held that this important right
requires that every reasonable adjournment to retain representation should be
granted.[87] This is, however, no absolute right to an adjournment. If a defendant
is responsible for the fact that his representative has not appeared (either by
firing him or failing to inform him of the court date), he may be forced to
proceed.[88]

9. PLEAS

The document filed in the court office after receiving the Offence Notice
indicating an intention to proceed to trial (i.e., to plead not guilty) does not

---

85 *R. v. Darville* (1956), 116 C.C.C. 113 (S.C.C.); *R. v. Barrette* (1977), 29 C.C.C. (2d) 189
   (S.C.C.).
86 See also *R. v. Lawrie and Points Ltd.* (1987), 59 O.R. (2d) 161 (Ont. C.A.). See also
   R. v. Lemonides (1997), 10 C.R. (5th) 135 (Ont. Gen. Div.).
87 *Barrett v. the Queen* (1976), 29 C.C.C. (2d) 189 (S.C.C.).
88 *R. v. Harrison and Alonzo* (1982), 67 C.C.C. (2d) 401 (Alta. C.A.).

bind the accused to plead not guilty at the time of the trial. The accused may plead guilty to the offence charged and he will be allowed to make submissions as to the proper sentence. The prosecutor will also be allowed to make submissions as to what sentence should be imposed.

(a) Lesser Included Offences

The accused may also plead guilty to any other offence and if the prosecutor consents the court may accept this plea, amend the charging document and convict the accused of this offence.[89] This is of course different from the idea of pleading guilty to a lesser included offence under the *Criminal Code*. The offence to which the accused pleads guilty need not fall within the narrow technical definition of an "included offence", as that term is understood in the *Criminal Code*. This flexible procedure is representative of the informality available under the Act.

(b) Special Pleas

It is a basic principle that a person is not to be tried twice for the same offence. Under the *Criminal Code*, a claim by an accused that the charge in issue has already been dealt with is to be tried under a special plea. An accused must plead a previous conviction ("autrefois convict"), acquittal ("autrefois acquit") or an issue already determined ("issue estoppel" or "res judicata") before entering a plea of guilty or not guilty on the charge.[90] Consistent with its move to less complex procedure, the *Provincial Offences Act* removes the need for such special pleas.[91]

For example, in a case of a charge of speeding, a defendant may argue that he was previously acquitted of a charge of careless driving arising at the same time on the finding of the earlier Justice that he was not the driver. The prosecution, having failed once to prove that the defendant was the driver, cannot retry that issue by charging a second offence.[92]

It is, of course, open to the defendant to frame his or her argument in terms of s. 7 or s. 11(h) of the *Charter*.

---

89 Section 45(4) of the Ontario *Provincial Offences Act* provides that:
   > **45.** (4) Where the defendant pleads not guilty to the offence charged but guilty to any other offence, whether or not it is an included offence, the court may, with the consent of the prosecutor, accept such plea of guilty and accordingly amend the information to substitute the offence to which the defendant pleads guilty.

90 *Criminal Code*, R.S.C. 1970, c. C-34, s. 535 as amended.

91 See ss. 44 and 45.

92 For a review of the law relating to defences based on an earlier finding ("autrefois acquit", "autrefois convict", and "res judicata"), consult *Keinapple v. the Queen* (1975), 15 C.C.C. (2d) 524 (S.C.C.). For an example of the principle in the context of traffic offences, see *R. v. Brisson* (1986), 13 O.A.C. 27 (C.A.).

10. THE CRIMINAL CODE AND "INCLUDED" TRAFFIC OFFENCES

Criminal charges often include other "lesser offences" within the definition of one charge, such that an accused, who faces an allegation of the more serious charge, might also be found guilty of the lesser offence as well. As well, an accused charged with a criminal offence can plead not guilty to the offence charged, but guilty to a lesser included offence, and with the consent of the prosecution the court can accept that plea and proceed to sentence the accused. In the true criminal sphere, the notion of a "lesser included offence" is based on the principles of pleading by the prosecution and is governed by the Code.[93]

The relationship between *Criminal Code* offences and provincial offences, for the purposes of the rules related to included offences, arises in two instances. Firstly, can an accused facing a *Criminal Code* driving offence plead guilty to a "lesser included" offence created under a provincial highway statute (e.g., "dangerous driving" down to "careless")? And, secondly, can a court which acquits an accused on a *Criminal Code* driving charge (e.g., impaired driving) nonetheless convict on a "lesser included" offence created under provincial highway statutes?

As to the first question, the weight of authority would seem to suggest that an accused facing a *Criminal Code* charge may plead guilty to an "included" offence under a provincial statute. Two Alberta cases in particular point in this direction. In *R. v. Lauweryssen*[94] and *R. v. Stewart*,[95] the courts examined the provincial procedural statute[96] and the provisions of the *Criminal Code* which govern pleas to lesser offences in the context of summary conviction matters.[97] The courts concluded that an accused could invoke the provisions of the *Criminal Code* and plead not guilty to the *Code* offence, but guilty to a provincial offence that was 'included' (in the sense that the facts supporting the charge were clearly included in the facts alleged to support the criminal charge).

On the second question, it is less clear that an accused facing a *Criminal Code* charge might be convicted of a "lesser included" traffic charge after a trial.[98]

---

93 *Criminal Code*, ss. 606, 662.
94 (1992), 41 M.V.R. (2d) 305 (Alta. Q.B.); *mandamus* application by Crown from (1992), 124 A.R. 381 (Alta. Prov. Ct.).
95 (1992), 78 C.C.C. (3d) 158 (Alta. Q.B.); See also *R. v. Hunt*, unrep. Feb. 16, 1989, Pepler P.C.J. (Alta. Prov. Ct.) summarized at [1989] A.W.L.D. 412 for the same proposition and *R. v. Kowch*, unrep. Feb. 10, 1992 (Alta. Prov. Ct.). For the contrary view, see *R. v. Albert*, [1993] AJ. No.86.
96 The Alberta *Provincial Offences Procedure Act* [S.A. 1988, c. P-21.5] incorporated the provisions of the *Criminal Code*.
97 *Criminal Code*, ss. 606, 662(1).
98 *R. v. Stewart*, unrep. Nov. 18, 1992 (Alta. Prov. Ct.) summarized at 18 W.C.B. (2d) 76; *R. v. Anthony (No. 2)*, unrep. July 13, 1982 (N.S. C.A.) summarized at 8 W.C.B. 153; *R. v. Fisher*, unrep. Oct. 15, 1997, Ont. Prov. Div., summarized at 36 W.C.B. (2d) 246.

Similarly, it would seem that the Crown cannot include *Criminal Code* and provincial traffic charges on the same charging document. While some of the language in the Code might appear to permit such a procedure, it puts the accused in the position of answering too broad an allegation.[99]

It would appear that there is no jurisdiction for a court trying an accused on a *Criminal Code* charge of dangerous driving to find the accused guilty of careless driving under the *Highway Traffic Act* as an included offence.[100]

11. THE PROPER ROLE OF THE JUDGE

The judicial officer presiding at a traffic trial, whether judge or justice of the peace, should allow the defendant or his agent or counsel to present the case for the defence fully and without interference. Both sides must be allowed to call and cross-examine witnesses.[101] While the court has a duty to assist an unrepresented accused to ensure a fair trial, it is wrong for the judge to become an advocate for such an accused:[102]

> While it is undoubtedly true that a trial judge has a duty to see that an unrepresented accused person is not denied a fair trial because he is not familiar with court procedure, the duty must necessarily be circumscribed by what is reasonable. Clearly it cannot and does not extend to his providing the accused at each stage of his trial the kind of advice that counsel could be expected to provide if the accused were represented by counsel. *If it did the trial judge would quickly find himself in the impossible position of being both advocate and impartial arbiter at one and the same time.* [Emphasis added]

Lay justices of the peace, that is justices without formal legal training, are perfectly capable of discharging the judicial duties associated with the fair trial of traffic offences.[103] They enjoy specialized training and the supervision of more senior members of the judiciary, usually through the provincial court bench.

Both the prosecution and the defence are entitled to a hearing free from any reasonable apprehension of bias.[104]

---

99 *Re R. and S.* (1986), 26 C.C.C. (3d) 30 (Alta. Q.B.), But see case of *R. v. Spratt* (1964) 1 O.R. 77 (Ont. Co. Ct.).

100 *R. v. Stewart* (1992), 18 W.C.B. (2d) 76 (Alta. Prov. Ct.). Although it would appear that the practice of accepting a plea to careless driving where an accused is initially charged with the *Criminal Code* offence of impaired driving, is in place in some jurisdictions. Whether there is indeed jurisdiction for a Court to do it is still an open question: *R. v. Fisher*, [1997] O.J. 4424 (Ont. Prov. Div.); *R. v. Garnett* (1995), 15 M.V.R. (3d) 198 (B.C. Prov. Ct.); *R. v. Martinez* (1996), 89 O.A.C. 152 (C.A.).

101 *R. v. Jamieson* (1981), 64 C.C.C. (2d) 550 (Ont. C.A.).

102 *R. v. Taubler* (1987), 20 O.A.C. 64 (Ont. C.A.).

103 *R. v. Davies* (1990), 56 C.C.C. (3d) 321 (Ont. Prov. Div.); *R. v. Heagle* (1983), 23 M.V.R. 20 (Sask. Q.B.) (whether justices are legally competent to deal with traffic cases under *Traffic Safety Court of Saskatchewan Act* R.S.S. 1978, c. T-19 (replaced by S.S. 1988-89, c. T-19.1)).

104 *R. v. Stuart* (1983), 54 A.R. 157 (Alta. Q.B.).

The duty to be fair and even-handed extends throughout the proceedings, including proceedings on sentencing, and an appellate court may consider a reasonable apprehension of bias arising as a result of proceedings on sentence.[105]

12. REPRESENTATION

A defendant may appear and act personally or by agent or counsel.[106] Where the defendant is a corporation, the corporation must appear and act by agent or counsel.[107] However, the court retains the power to bar any agent if the agent is incompetent to advise the party represented or if they fail to understand and comply with the duties and responsibilities of an agent. This power should be exercised sparingly; a defendant should be allowed to have whatever representative he or she wants, as long as that person is able to fulfill the basic duties of an agent. This section confirms the right of a defendant to have a lawyer present to argue the case in court or to appear in the place of the defendant. The right is extended to agents who are not lawyers.[108] While there is a right to have counsel if one so desires, there is no right to state funded counsel.[109] Nor is there any obligation on the court to inform an accused facing a traffic offence of his right to retain counsel before considering the charge.[110]

In some cases it may be necessary to have the defendant present in court. In these instances, the court retains the power to summons the defendant to appear.[111]

Where the defendant has been convicted, the court must give the defendant, or his counsel or agent, an opportunity to make submissions as to sentence.[112]

13. ROLE OF THE PROSECUTOR

In Canada the prosecutor occupies a quasi-judicial role, whether prosecuting criminal or regulatory offences. This imposes on prosecuting counsel, or a prosecuting agent, a general duty of fairness. Under this regime a prose-

---

105 *R. v. McKinnon*, [1997] B.C.J. No. 736 (B.C. S.C.).

106 On the question of whether a paralegal agent can appear for a fee, see the discussion at the end of Chapter 1, under heading 7 "The Role of Paralegals or Agents in the Prosecution and Defence of Traffic Offences".

107 Section 50 of *Provincial Offences Act*, R.S.O. 1990, c. P-33. This is also stated in s. 82 which provides that, "A defendant may act by counsel or agent".

108 See note 86 above.

109 *R. v. Rowbotham* (1988), 41 C.C.C. (3d) 1; *R. v. Matheson*, [1994] 3 S.C.R. 328.

110 *R. v. Asfaw*, [1996] O.J. No. 2036.

111 See note 107 above.

112 Section 57(1), and see below, ch. 9 "Sentencing and Administrative Sanctions in Traffic Cases".

cutor's duty is not simply to seek conviction but to act as a minister of justice.[113]

One issue peculiar to traffic offences is the role of the police prosecutor. In some locales, police officers act as prosecutor in provincially created traffic offences. This practice is criticised on the basis that the prosecutor should be independent.[114] So long as the particular prosecutor is not also a witness to, or the charging officer in, the offence being tried, there would appear to be no constitutional impediment to the case proceeding with that officer as prosecutor.[115]

14. PART II: PARKING INFRACTIONS

This procedure is, as the name implies, intended to cover violations of parking regulations whether they appear in federal or provincial legislation or municipal by-laws (though the vast majority of the offences are municipally created). The scheme removes many of the unnecessary procedural hurdles which existed under the cumbersome *Summary Convictions Act*,[116] which, until the proclamation of the Part II provisions, governed the prosecution of parking offences.

The Part II procedure relies on a revised system of vehicle permits and a new presumption of regularity in the preparation and service of documents. This is a more effective system than that which it replaces. The old *Summary Convictions Act* scheme was based on a presumption of irregularity, which required notice and proof at every turn. Issues related to the preparation and treatment of documents related to such regimes should be considered with this in mind.[117]

(a) The New System

The new system assumes that the plates on a vehicle properly identify the owner/operator of the vehicle in question, and that the placing of a Notice of Parking Infraction on the vehicle will make the responsible party aware of the alleged violation.[118]

---

113 This notion of the Crown or prosecutor as a minister of justice, and not a mere advocate for conviction, has been subject to extensive comment: see, for example, *R. v. Boucher* (1954), 110 C.C.C. 263 (S.C.C.); *R. v. Bain* (1992), 69 C.C.C. (3d) 481 (S.C.C.).

114 F. Armstrong & K. Chase, "The Right to an Independent Prosecutor" (1975) 28 C.R.N.S. 160.

115 *R. v. Randall* (1989), 49 C.R.R. 368 (B.C. S.C.).

116 R.S.O. 1970, c. 450.

117 *Toronto (Metropolitan) v. Beck, supra*, note 46.

118 See Drinkwalter and Ewart, *supra* note 26, at 71-73.

Further, as a result of amendments in 1992[119] the Ontario statute shifted the administration (and fine revenue) for parking infractions to municipalities. This shift included a new step in the procedure to minimize the number of cases of disputed tickets not contested at trial. The new process sees a Certificate of Impending Conviction sent to the registered owner of the vehicle, inviting the owner to respond if he or she desires to contest the Infraction Notice. If no response is received to the Notice of Impending Conviction the municipality (through a person designated in regulations) prepares a Certificate Requesting a Conviction. The Clerk of the Court is obliged to enter a conviction upon receiving a properly prepared certificate requesting the same, and the set fine and costs recorded.[120]

The defendant will then have fifteen days in which to file a not guilty plea in a manner similar to that in Part I prosecutions.[121] Alternatively, the defendant may not wish to dispute the charge, in which case he or she will simply pay the set fine to the place shown on the Notice of Parking Infraction.

(b) Abbreviated Wording That May be Used in the Charging Document

As with Certificate prosecutions under Part I, the legislation provides that the government can make regulations allowing for "official" short forms to describe offences.[122]

(i) *Limits on Issuing Authority*

The issuance of notices under Part II is limited to Provincial Offences Officers. It is further limited by the requirement that the officer issuing the ticket have *personal knowledge* that the parking infraction has been committed. That is, the officer must personally see the vehicle illegally parked, and cannot rely on the reports of others.[123] This should limit the number of purely clerical errors which can flow from hearsay passing on of licence numbers and street locations.[124]

(ii) *Failsafe Provisions*

Section 20 (dealing with defaults under the Part II procedure) allows a defendant to reopen a matter arising from a parking infraction within fifteen

---

119 S.O. 1992, c. 20.

120 This process is detailed in what is now ss. 18 to 18.6.

121 *Ontario Provincial Offences Act*, s. 17(1).

122 Section 21. See Appendix C for the regulations setting out the short forms passed by the provincial government.

123 Section 16(2). See also, Drinkwalter and Ewart, *supra*, note 26, at 74.

124 *Ibid.*

days of learning of the default conviction. The procedure in such a case is similar to that under s. 11.[125]

(iii) *Trial, etc.*

Trials of parking infraction are governed by the same law as the other two forms of proceeding.

15. TIME LIMITATIONS ON THE PROSECUTION AND THE DEFENCE

(a) Counting Days

When calculating the expiration of limitation periods or notice periods, one does not count the day on which the first event took place but does count the day on which the last event took place. For example, if the offence took place on March 1, then March 2 would be the first day and so on to March 31, which would be the thirtieth day. If the Offence Notice or Summons was served on March 31, it would be within the limitation period. Service on April 1 would be too late. If the time period to be calculated is six days or less and the last date on which the step could be taken is a Saturday, Sunday or statutory holiday, the last day is moved to the next following juridical day. Thus if March 31 was a Saturday, Sunday or statutory holiday, the following juridical or "business day" would become the last day.[126]

(b) Time Limits on the Prosecution

Section 3(3) of the *Provincial Offences Act* requires that an Offence Notice or a Summons shall be served within 30 days of the events giving rise to the alleged offence. Failure to serve the accused with either a Summons or an Offence Notice in this time is an absolute bar to a Part I prosecution. The prosecutor must choose between using the more serious Part III procedure or abandoning the prosecution.

---

125 Section 20, provides:

> **20.** Where the defendant has not had an opportunity to dispute the charge or appear or represented at a hearing for the reason that, through no fault of his own, the delivery of a necessary notice or document failed to occur in fact, and where not more than fifteen days have elapsed since the conviction first came to the attention of the defendant, the defendant may attend at the court office during regular office hours and may appear before a justice and the justice, upon being satisfied by affidavit in the prescribed form of such facts, shall strike out the conviction [... and the matter will be set down for trial].

> See above at notes 34 and 35 and surrounding text for a discussion of s. 11. (and see Appendix B for the forms to be used on a s. 11 or s. 20 application).

126 *Rules of Practice and Procedure of the Provincial Offences Courts*, R.R.O. 1980, Reg. 809, s. 4.

Also, the Certificate must be filed with the Clerk of the Court within seven days of it being served on the defendant. Failure to meet this time limit is fatal. Similarly, the Clerk must stamp the date of filing on the Certificate, or the prosecution is barred.[127]

Even if the prosecution proceeds under Part III, a six-month limitation still applies.[128] The prosecution must be commenced within a six-month period. This requirement is satisfied by laying an information within this time. An accused need not be informed of the charge within the six-month period, but clearly the *Charter of Rights* requires that the accused be informed promptly and have a trial within a reasonable time. This is, of course, further subject to any specific limitation which might exist in the statute creating the offence.[129] It should be noted that the expiration of a limitation period does not affect prosecutions under some other authority unless it may be considered as an abuse of process. Just as the prosecution may use the Part III procedure if it has missed the thirty-day period for Part I service, the Crown may decide that, for example, a *Criminal Code* prosecution, unaffected by the particular delay, is warranted by the circumstances of the offence.

The time limit for initiating any proceedings may be waived by the Justice with the consent of the accused.[130] The purpose of this provision is to allow the accused to plead guilty to an offence for which the limitation has passed. Thus, if an accused is charged with dangerous driving under the *Criminal Code*, and some time after the six-month time limit has expired, an agreement is reached with the Crown's office that it would be proper to accept a plea of guilty to the less serious provincial offence of careless driving, the accused may waive the limitation period, and plead guilty to the less serious offence.

(c) Post Office Strikes

In the event of postal disruption, the court may extend the time for the service of notices or documents.[131] If the defendant does not receive some document or in good faith mails some document which is not received, and as a result is denied a chance to appear or be represented, the defendant may, if convicted, appear before a Justice of the Peace and, under s. 11, apply to have the conviction set aside.[132]

There is a rebuttable presumption that a notice mailed to someone at their last known address was received.[133]

---

127 *Ibid.*, ss. 9 and 10.
128 *Provincial Offences Act*, R.S.O. 1990, c. P-33, s. 76(1).
129 See Drinkwalter and Ewart, *supra* note 26, at 253.
130 *Provincial Offences Act*, s. 76(2).
131 The Provincial Offences Court is given this power by O. Reg. 816.
132 See above under heading (ii) Fail-Safe Provision.
133 *Provincial Offences Act*, *supra* note 128 at s.87(2).

16. YOUNG TRAFFIC OFFENDERS

With the introduction of the *Young Offenders Act*[134] and repeal of the *Juvenile Delinquents Act*,[135] Ontario was required to amend its *Provincial Offences Act* to provide separate proceedings for young people.[136] The amendments create Part VI of the Act. This Part sets out a code of procedure for young people between the ages of 12 and 16. No person under 12 years of age can be convicted of a provincial offence.[137] The idea behind the amendments is to modify the offences procedure to take into account the special needs of young people in conflict with the law, keeping in mind always the broad range of offences covered by provincial regulation.

(a) Notice to Parents

While the Part I form of proceeding is available for young people, an Offence Notice process allowing for a plea of guilty without an appearance is not permitted: the young person must be dealt with through a summons and an open airing of the charge in court. As soon as possible after issuing the summons, the officer (or in the case of a young person released on a recognizance, the officer in charge) shall give notice to the parents of the youth by delivering a copy of the summons (or recognizance) to the parents.

Parent is defined as including "an adult with whom the young person ordinarily resides".[138] This requirement would, therefore, appear to be satisfied by notice to an older brother, sister, other relative or even potentially a roommate, as well as the natural parents.

Failure to give notice to a parent is not fatal, but if no parent attends with the young person the court has a discretion to either dispense with the notice or adjourn the proceedings to allow notice.

(b) Lower Maximum Penalties

Where a young person is found guilty of the offence, a slightly different penalty structure applies. The court may order a fine which is not to exceed the set fine, the maximum fine for the offence, or $300, whichever is the *least*. In the alternative, the court may suspend the passing of sentence and place

---

134 R.S.C. 1985, c. Y-1.

135 R.S.C. 1970, c. J-3.

136 *Provincial Offences Statute Law Amendment Act*, S.O. 1983, c. 80.

137 *Provincial Offences Act*, s. 94.

138 Section 93 defines this term, and "young person", and makes it clear that the Part looks to the age of the person at the time of the offence, and not the time of the prosecution, for its application.

the young person on probation, or discharge the young offender absolutely.[139] Similarly, where the prosecution is by information, the court is limited to a fine of the maximum for the offence, or $1000, whichever is less, but may suspend sentence or discharge the young person.[140]

(c) No *Ex Parte* Convictions

A young person cannot be convicted *ex parte*.[141] Rather, if the young person does not attend, a procedure is provided to compel their attendance.

(d) Appeals in Young Offender Cases

An appeal from proceedings dealing with a young person is taken to the District Court, but is dealt with as though it were an appeal to the Provincial Court (Criminal Division).[142]

---

139 *Provincial Offences Act*, supra note 128 at s. 97; however, s. 12(2) (maximum penalties on Part I (ticket) offences) applies to the young offender so that regardless of the penalty the demerit points and other regulatory ramifications follow the finding of guilt.
140 Section 101.
141 Section 98.
142 Section 105.

3

Procedural Issues in Traffic Offence Appeals

1. INTRODUCTION: THE STRUCTURE OF "CORRECTION" IN TRAFFIC OFFENCES

Appeals in all legal proceedings are a product of statute. There is no common law procedure which provides for an appeal. There are two forms of 'correction' which can exist at law. The first is the relatively well-known process of an appeal from the decision of a trial court. An appeal is a review of the record at trial to determine whether there has been a legal error which causes the court to question the result of the trial.[1] A less well-known form of review, however, is provided through the ancient "prerogative writs" which permit a very limited form of review to determine if there has been jurisdictional error by the trial court. This latter form of review is relatively narrow and governed by a number of highly technical rules.

As in our discussion of procedural issues at trial, we have looked to the Ontario *Provincial Offences Act* as a basis for our discussion, but many if not all, of these issues arise under any provincial regime.

---

1 *R. v. Francisty*, [1997] O.J. No. 2118 (Ont. Prov. Div.), where the court observed:

> An appellate court acting under s. 136(2) of the *Provincial Offences Act* is to conduct the appeal by means of a review, that is a reconsideration of the trial proceedings. This provision reflects the informal nature of appeals in respect of Part I and II proceedings. Put another way, this form of appeal was clearly intended by the Legislature to be very broad: appellate relief is available as of right and there are no restrictions on the sorts of issues which may be raised:

citing as further authority: *R. v. Stephenson* (1984), 13 C.C.C. (3d) 112 (Ont. C.A.); *R. v. Murray* (1983), 22 M.V.R. 66 (Ont. H.C.); *R. v. Anderson* (November 28, 1985), Doc. 2716/85 (Ont. S.C.).

2. STATUTORY FRAMEWORK FOR APPEALS IN ONTARIO

Part VII of the *Provincial Offences Act* establishes a statutory code governing appeals and reviews of decisions made in the course of provincial offence prosecutions. As with other procedural regimes, the *Provincial Offences Act* understands two forms of review: prerogative remedies and appeals. Appellate review again looks to the three procedural streams and attempts to treat less serious offences, Part I and II prosecutions, in a more summary fashion. Part III offence appeals are only slightly different. The procedure for secondary review in the Court of Appeal for Ontario is almost identical in the case of all offences.

Prerogative remedies address jurisdictional errors which might occur in any step in the prosecution. There is no distinction made between Part I, II and III offences for the purposes of jurisdictional review.

Section 116 of the *Provincial Offences Act* allows the defendant, prosecutor or the Attorney General by way of intervention to appeal from a conviction or dismissal or from a finding as to ability, because of mental disorder, to conduct a defence or as to sentence. Section 99 relates to proceedings commenced by information under Part III of the *Provincial Offences Act* only. Section 118(1) permits a defendant or the prosecutor or the Attorney General by way of intervention to appeal an acquittal, conviction or sentence in a proceeding commenced by Certificate of Offence or Traffic Violation under Part I or II of the *Provincial Offences Act.* The appeal is to the Provincial Court (Criminal Division) of the county or district in which the adjudication was made unless it was a Provincial Court Judge who presided in the first instance in which case the appeal is to the District Court.

3. PREROGATIVE RELIEF

(a) Introduction

Prerogative relief, in the form of an order in lieu of one of the traditional writs,[2] will issue to remedy jurisdictional errors. Under the Ontario statute, s. 140(1) gives statutory voice to authority of the province's superior court, the Ontario Court (General Division), to grant such relief in the form of at least three of the writs, *mandamus*, prohibition, and *certiorari*. Section 140(2) addresses the question of notice, making it clear that notice should be given to all parties, the decision maker and the Attorney General. Questions related to the form of the application, the nature of the materials to be filed in support, etc. fall under the *Rules of Civil Procedure*:[3] Rules 14 (commencement of proceedings) and 38 (applications-jurisdiction and procedure).

---

2   The traditional writs are *mandamus*, prohibition, *certiorari, habeas corpus ad subjiciendum*, and *procedendo.*

3   It is important to keep in mind that, while they are quasi-criminal in nature, provincial offences are not criminal and do not look to the criminal rules.

Prerogative relief will ordinarily be refused if there is any other remedy available to the party seeking to invoke this power. As well, the court enjoys a discretion to refuse to grant prerogative relief, and this discretion will be exercised where the true merits of the case do not warrant intervention, even if some technical error is present.[4]

(b) *Certiorari*

Perhaps the most common of the prerogative remedies, *certiorari* calls upon the reviewed decision maker or actor to present the record to a superior court so that it might be reviewed. It will remedy jurisdictional errors by inferior courts in those circumstances where no appeal is otherwise available. It will, for example, issue to quash a search warrant which was granted without jurisdiction. Applications for other prerogative remedies often include a request for "*certiorari*-in-aid" of the principal relief. In these cases, the request for *certiorari* is intended to insure that the record is fully before the reviewing court. Thus, for example, a notice might seek an order for "*mandamus* with certiorari-in-aid".

(c) **Prohibition**

Prohibition is employed to prevent an inferior tribunal from exercising, or attempting to exercise, a jurisdiction which it does not possess or which it has exceeded. For example, where the court is proceeding under a statute which is alleged to be *ultra vires* or where there is bias or a demonstrated reasonable apprehension of bias from a tribunal, prohibition may issue.

(d) *Mandamus*

This remedy is used where a court refuses to do that which it is required by law to do or where a court refuses or declines to exercise a jurisdiction that it enjoys. It is a remedy used more by the prosecution than the defence, though it is available to both.

(e) *Habeas Corpus ad Subjiciendum*[5]

Often called the 'great writ', *habeas corpus* has a rich history. In Ontario it continues to look to pre-Confederation statutes and the common law to understand this remedy.[6] The writ issues to remedy deprivations of liberty

---

4 *R. v. Gronka*, [1996] O.J. No. 1936.

5 Section 142 of the *Provincial Offences Act* speaks to the particulars of this relief in provincial offence prosecutions or decisions made on the authority of the Act.

6 *Habeas Corpus Act* (1866), Stat.U.C. 29-30 Vict. (1866), chap. XLV; consolidated as *Habeas Corpus Act*, R.S.O. 1990, c. H-1.

which are said to be without legal justification. Often *certiorari* will issue in aid of *habeas corpus*. While cases of deprivations of liberty are comparatively rare in provincial offences, they are not unknown and this remedy remains important.[7]

(f) Procedendo

Even less common is the writ of *procedendo*. By this remedy, a superior court returns a matter to an inferior tribunal in cases where the record has been removed to the superior court to review the jurisdiction of that tribunal[8] or where the court has declined to proceed out of deference to the review pending in the superior court. For example, a defendant might seek to bring an application for prohibition on the basis of an allegation of bias and then allow that application to linger in the superior court while the trial was delayed. The superior court has a jurisdiction to require the inferior court to resume its consideration of the matter and to return the record to that court for that purpose.

(g) Stays of Proceedings

Given the strict rule stated in s. 141(3), it is important for appellate counsel to ensure that no appeal is available before seeking to obtain prerogative relief. Recently the question has arisen whether the prosecutor can appeal from a pre-trial stay of proceedings entered as remedy under s. 11(b) of the *Charter*. Section 141(3) prevents prerogative relief if an appeal is available. Sections 116(1) and 135(1) give the prosecutor the right to appeal from a "dismissal" or an "acquittal" respectively. The question is whether a permanent stay of proceedings imposed judicially is tantamount to a dismissal or an acquittal such that the prosecutor can appeal as of right.

Several recent cases seem to put this issue to rest, in favour of a right of appeal. In *R. ex rel. John Holmes v. Regal Park Homes Inc.*,[9] a complex *Building Code* prosecution was stayed by the presiding justice of the peace on the basis of unreasonable delay. The prosecutor had first pursued prerogative relief in the General Division only to have the application dismissed on the authority of s. 141(3). The prosecutor then sought an extension of time to file an appeal to the Provincial Division (from the original order), having missed the limitation date while seeking a remedy under s. 140(1). In his reasons for judgment on the motion to extend time to the prosecutor, Judge

---

7 See, for example, *R. v. Hill* (1991), 1 O.R. (3d) 62 (Ont. Gen. Div.).

8 See generally, *Frankel v. The Queen* (1968), 68 W.W.R. 201 (Alta. C.A.); *Dick v. The Queen* (1978), 40 C.C.C. (2d) 270 (Ont. H.C.J.) and *R. v. Batchelor* (1980), 56 C.C.C. (2d) 20 (Ont. H.C.J.) for examples of the writ being used in the criminal context.

9 Unreported, February 4, 1992, Ont. Ct. (Prov. Div.), Fairgrieve Prov. J.

Fairgrieve of the Provincial Division makes it clear that an order staying proceedings under s. 11(b) of the *Charter* is tantamount to a "dismissal" or an "acquittal" and that the prosecutor does enjoy a right of appeal. Since *R. v. Beason*[10] it has been clear, in Ontario at least, that a stay entered under s. 11(b) was tantamount to dismissal or acquittal and that the necessary appellate avenues were opened by such a disposition.[11]

4. RELEASE PENDING APPEAL

(a) Introduction

Release from custody pending appeal is provided for in ss. 110 and 132 of the Act. Those sections provide that a judge may order a person's release upon any of the conditions set out in s. 150(2). Section 150 is contained in the portion of the *Provincial Offences Act* which deals with bail pending trial. It is curious that unlike the *Criminal Code*, continued detention pending appeal (or trial for that matter) may only be premised on a concern that the defendant will fail to attend court. There is no secondary ground which would permit a person to be detained if it was in the public interest or for the protection of the public. The person having custody of an appellant who was ordered detained pending the hearing of the appeal, where the appeal has not commenced within 30 days from the day on which notice of the appeal was given, must apply to a judge to fix a date for the hearing of the appeal pursuant to s. 113(1). Subsection (2) provides that upon receiving an application under subsection (1), the judge shall, after giving the prosecutor a reasonable oppor-

---

10 (1983), 7 C.C.C. (3d) 20 (Ont. C.A.). If there were any doubt on this matter one would have thought that it was addressed by the judgment of the Supreme Court in *R. v. Kalanj* (1989), 48 C.C.C. (3d) 459 (S.C.C.) where the court held that such a stay was tantamount to an acquittal for the purposes of considering whether it gave rise to a right of appeal to that court.

11 In *R. v. Clintar Limited, Cliff Barker & Terry Nicholson*, unreported endorsement, April 27, 1992, Ont. C.A. in chambers, Mr. Justice Griffiths seems to have accepted this analysis. In denying leave on this point his Lordship said:

> The Applicants seek leave to appeal from the judgment of Murphy J. dated March 5th, 1992, on 2 grounds:
> [...].
> 2. There was no right of appeal from a stay of proceedings. The Provincial Offences Act authorizing an appeal only where there was a "conviction" or an "acquittal".
> Murphy J. in a very carefully reasoned judgment with which I agree, dealt with both issues. He properly considered that the second issue had been disposed of by the Supreme Court of Canada in *R. v. Jewitt* (1985) 21 C.C.C. (3d) 7 where the Court held that a stay was tantamount to a dismissal. [...].
> One of the decisions, that of Locke J. in *City of Toronto v. Brian Smith* (November 1, 1991), has been cited, arriving at the same result. There does not appear to be any divergency of opinion on the issue at the level of the Ontario General Division.
> Accordingly, I dismiss the application for leave to appeal.

tunity to be heard, fix a date for the hearing of the appeal and give such directions as he thinks appropriate for expediting the hearing of the appeal. An appellant or respondent who is in custody as a result of the decision appealed from is entitled to be present at the hearing of the appeal.[12]

(b) Payment of Fines Pending Appeal

A person does not waive his right of appeal by reason only that he pays the fine or complies with any order imposed upon conviction.[13] A very important provision is s. 111 of the Ontario Act. It states in subsection (1) that a notice of appeal by a defendant shall not be accepted for filing if the defendant has not paid in full the fine imposed by the decision appealed from. Subsection (2), however, provides that a judge may waive compliance with subsection (1) and order that the appellant enter into a recognizance to appear on the appeal. (Similar provisions exist in other procedural statutes to ensure that appeals are not engaged to avoid fine payments.) As part of the recognizance, the judge may require the appellant to pay an amount as a bond or may make the appellant produce a number of people who are prepared to pledge a sum of money or a piece of property to secure the appellant's future co-operation with officials. Section 112 states that the filing of a Notice of Appeal does not stay the conviction unless a judge so orders. These provisions, taken as a whole, ensure that a person cannot use the appeal process as a delaying tactic to avoid the penalty imposed unless good cause is shown why the punishment should not be meted out pending the hearing of the appeal.

5. INITIATING AN APPEAL

The first step in any appeal where a fine was imposed is to attend at the Provincial Offences Court Office located at the court where the conviction was entered and pay the fine imposed upon conviction. One should remember, however, that an application may be brought, as outlined above, to a judge of the court where the appeal is to be heard for an order pursuant to s. 94(2) waiving the requirement that the fine be paid before the Notice of Appeal can be filed. A person should not be prevented from filing an appeal because he is financially unable to pay the fine before the time in which a notice of appeal is to be filed. The court office will usually be able to provide the form to be used as the Notice of Appeal (Form 302 for Part III appeals and Form 201 for Part I appeals). The form itself is fairly straightforward. An appellant should be careful to include a mailing address and telephone number and set out the grounds or reasons for appeal. If there is insufficient space on the form, a separate piece of paper may be attached to Form 302 where the grounds of appeal

---

12 Section 118(2).
13 Section 135.

can be set out. An appeal lies to the Provincial Court (Criminal Division) of the county or district in which the adjudication was made if the appeal is from the decision of a Justice of the Peace. If the appeal is from the decision of a Provincial Judge, it is heard by a judge of the District Court of the district in which the adjudication was made.[14]

An appellant will require three copies of a Notice of Appeal. One should be kept for the appellant's use. The other two should be served on the provincial prosecutor (or Crown Attorney's office where the Crown prosecutes such offences). That office will keep a copy and make a note on the other admitting service. The original is then filed with the Clerk of the Court in which the appeal is to be heard.[15]

6. TIME LIMITS

(a) Common Time Limits

If the proceedings were commenced by information, the appeal is pursuant to s. 116 of the Act, and the rules provide that the Notice of Appeal must be filed no later than 30 days after the date of the decision sought to be appealed from.[16] If the proceedings were commenced by Certificate, an appeal is pursuant to s. 135. Section 135 states that the Notice of Appeal must be filed within 15 days after the making of the decision appealed from, in accordance with the rules.[17] Appeal notices are not accepted after this date without a judge's order permitting late filing.

(b) Power to Extend Time to Appeal or Take Other Step

An appeal court normally enjoys a broad discretion to extend the time within which an accused or defendant can take the steps of appealing. While this power is normally exercised generously, it does not excuse every delay by an appellant. If, for example, the appellant has allowed an extended period of time to pass and the original charge would be difficult or impossible to re-prosecute, the court will refuse an extension, even if the appellant has been unaware of the earlier proceedings.[18]

---

14 See ss. 132(2)(a) and (b).
15 See s. 135(2).
16 See O. Reg. 723/94, s. 5(3).
17 See O. Reg. 722/94, s. 6(5).
18 *R. v. Ho*, [1997] B.C.J. No. 1030 (B.C. S.C.). See as well the discussion below in section 9 "Extensions of Time."

7. TRANSCRIPTS

Having filed the Notice of Appeal, an appellant should also arrange to have three copies of the transcripts of the trial proceedings prepared by the court reporter. The usual practice is for court reporters to request that people outside the legal profession ordering transcripts make full payment of the estimated costs at this time, and, indeed, lawyers are frequently asked to provide a deposit prior to the transcript being prepared. In any event, a reporter's certificate indicating that the transcripts have been ordered is then completed by the reporter and given to the appellant. In some jurisdictions, transcripts are frequently not ordered, and instead, at the hearing of the appeal, a tape of the trial proceedings is played. This practice is permitted in Ontario for appeals under Parts I and II by virtue of s. 136. It is, however, not a practice to be encouraged, as the tape recordings are often of a poor quality. Some court offices will not accept a Notice of Appeal for filing unless it is accompanied by a court reporter's certificate.

Upon completion of the transcript, one must attend court and obtain the three copies. As with the Notice of Appeal, one copy is for the appellant and one copy is delivered to the provincial prosecutor's office or the Crown's office. The prosecutor admits service on the final copy and this copy is then filed with the court. The last step in the ordinary course of events is for the clerk to assign a date for the hearing of the appeal.[19] Keep in mind that pursuant to s. 127 the court may order, upon application by either the appellant or respondent, the appeal to proceed by way of trial *de novo*. This is usually ordered because the condition of the record from the court below is poor (both the documentary evidence and the transcript), but it may be ordered for any other reason. In such cases, the evidence of any witness taken before the trial court may be read if that evidence has been authenticated or if the appellant and respondent consent to the reading in of the earlier testimony. Further, the court must be satisfied that either the attendance of the witness cannot reasonably be obtained or by reason of the formal nature of the evidence or otherwise, the court is satisfied that the opposite party will not be prejudiced. When this procedure is adopted, the evidence read in has the same legal force and effect as if the witness had given the evidence before the court.[20]

If transcripts are not available, and no reasonable reconstruction of the events at trial is possible, it may be necessary to order a new trial.[21] Thus, for example, where both the transcript and the judge's notes of the trial were

---

19 See s. 135(3).

20 Section 127. For example, if the only issue was identification and there was only a civilian witness to the incident, the evidence of the attending officer (establishing the location, etc.) might be so entered.

21 *R. v. Wells* (1985), 54 Nfld. & P.E.I.R. 251 (Nfld. T.D.).

unavailable in an appeal from a speeding conviction, the court held that a new trial was required.[22]

8. APPEALS BY WAY OF NEW TRIAL — PART III

Section 127 invites the court considering an appeal from a Part III prosecution to deal with the appeal by way of a new trial or trial *de novo*.

The most common reason for an appeal by way of a new trial is a deficiency in the record,[23] but s. 127 is clearly not limited to only such circumstances. There must be a good reason for an appeal to proceed under this provision.[24] In the context of a criminal prosecution, an accused is thought to have the right to have an appeal determined on a true record of the proceedings below and a significant deficiency in that record will be a legitimate, and sometimes successful, ground of appeal.[25] This is not the case where an appeal by way of new trial is available and the judge will be in error if she orders a new trial on the basis of the submissions made respecting defects in the record.[26]

Where an application has been made to have the appeal heard by way of a new trial under s. 127, or where the notice of appeal indicates an intention to make such an application, the appeal will not be listed until after that application has been considered.[27]

It may be that the Crown is constitutionally barred from an appeal by way of a new trial.[28]

9. EXTENSIONS OF TIME

It is not unusual for an appellant to be caught by the severe time limits established for the launching of an appeal to the Court of Appeal (or to the court of first appeal for that matter). The Act provides for the extension of time in appropriate circumstances. The law with regard to the extension of

---

22 *R. v. Gaba*, [1978] 4 W.W.R. 119 (Man. Co. Ct.); see also *Re Cameron* (1978), 39 C.C.C. (2d) 427 (Ont. H.C.) and *R. v. Vogel* (1976), 1 A.R. 365 (C.A.).

23 *R. v. Greymac Mortgage Corp.* unreported, January 29, 1981 (summarized at [1981] Ont. D. Crim. Conv. 5085-01.) (Ont. Dist. Ct.).

24 See the comments in *R. v. Faulkner* (1977), 37 C.C.C. (2d) 26 (N.S. Co. Ct.) suggesting that a trial *de novo* might be appropriate where the first trial was tainted by bias or where there had been an adjournment refused or the case was otherwise such that, notwithstanding that the record was physically intact, it was wanting.

25 *R. v. Calvery* (1956), 18 W.W.R. 623 (Man. C.A.); *R. v. Horvat* (1977), 34 C.C.C. (2d) 73 (B.C. C.A.).

26 *R. v. Steinmiller* (1979), 47 C.C.C. (2d) 151 (Ont. C.A.); *R. v. Patrick Sheridan*, unreported endorsement, March 17, 1992 (Ont. C.A.).

27 Rule 18(3).

28 *Thibault v. Corporation Professionelles des Medecins du Québec* (1989), 49 C.C.C. (3d) 1 (S.C.C.).

time to file a Notice of Appeal (or an application for leave to appeal) is well settled. In *R. ex rel. John Holmes v. Regal Park Homes Inc.*,[29] Judge Fairgrieve of the Ontario Court (Provincial Division) sets out considerations on an application for an extension of time to file a Notice:

> In determining whether an extension of time should be granted, a number of factors need to be considered. In Drinkwalter and Ewart, *Ontario Provincial Offences Procedure* (1980), at p. 307, the authors refer to the "well defined and reasonably strict" criteria gleaned from the cases, referring specifically to judgments of the Ontario Court of Appeal in *R. v. Gruener* (1979), 46 C.C.C.(2d) 88 (Thorson J.A., in chambers) and *R. v. Scheller* (No.2) (1976), 37 C.R.N.S. 349 (Lacourcière J.A., in chambers). The requirements include:
>
> > 1. That the applicant has shown an intention to appeal within the time limited;
> >
> > 2. That there is sufficient merit to the appeal;
> >
> > 3. That the applicant exercised due diligence or has a reasonable excuse for not having instituted the appeal within the appeal period;
> >
> > 4. That the refusal of the application would amount to a denial of justice.
>
> In *R. v. Greeley* (Nfld. C.A.), January 19, 1990), an unreported decision of Goodridge C.J.N. [...] his Lordship added to the list consideration of whether an important question of law was in issue (which may not be particularly relevant to P.O.A. appeals to this Court), and also whether there would be prejudice to the other party due to the delay in instituting the appeal.

While His Honour has put the four considerations as 'requirements' they are probably better thought of as factors to be examined: it can hardly be that an application would be refused if it would amount to a denial of justice simply because there was no proof of due diligence.[30]

An application to extend time will often be the subject of consent. Where the motion is contested, an affidavit from the client or the lawyer with carriage of launching the appeal should be included setting out the merits of the appeal, the formulation of the intention to appeal, and the efforts by the appellant to act within time.

10. ATTENDING AT THE APPEAL

Occasionally, people do not wish to attend the appeal hearing in person or by counsel, but still wish the appeal to proceed. If it is at all possible, an appellant should be represented at the hearing, either in person or by counsel. The arguments to be advanced simply cannot be made as forcefully when presented in written form only, without the benefit of oral argument. Of course,

---

29 *Supra* note 9, at p. 2.

30 It may be that intention to appeal within time may be an absolute requirement.

there is no need for an appellant to attend if represented by counsel,[31] although the power of a court to impose sentence may be exercised notwithstanding that the appellant or respondent is not present.[32] If it is impossible for the appellant to attend in person or by counsel, a written notice of this intention, together with a statement of the issues and arguments the appellant wishes to advance, should be served on the prosecutor and filed with the court.[33] Indeed, even if the appellant intends to appear in person or by counsel at the hearing of the appeal, it is always helpful to buttress oral arguments with clear written submissions.

With respect to the appeal court receiving the full record that was before the Provincial Offences Court, s. 115 of the *Provincial Offences Act* provides:[34]

> Where a notice of appeal has been filed, the clerk of the provincial offences court appealed from of the appeal and, upon receipt of the notification, the clerk of the provincial offences court shall transmit the order appealed from and transmit or transfer custody of all other material in his possession or control to the clerk of the appeal court to be kept with the records of the appeal court.

If, for whatever reason, the appellant decides not to proceed with the appeal, a Notice of Abandonment should be filed. This may well avoid an order of costs, which can be awarded against an appellant[35] and will serve to advise the prosecutor and court that there is no need to prepare for the hearing of the appeal. Note, however, that once a transcript has been ordered, it still must be paid for, regardless of whether or not the appeal proceeds. The court may dismiss an appeal where the appellant fails to pursue it with all due vigour. It may also dismiss an appeal where the appellant has failed to comply with any order made under s. 110 or 111 or with the conditions of any recognizance entered into under either of those sections.[36]

11. SUBSEQUENT APPEALS

Section 114 of the *Provincial Offences Act* allows a defendant or the prosecutor or the Attorney General by way of intervention to appeal from the judgment of a court sitting on appeal from a decision of the Provincial Offences Court. This may only be done, however, with leave of a justice of appeal on special grounds, upon any question of law alone or as to sentence in accordance

---

31 Section 118(1).
32 Section 118(3).
33 Section 119.
34 See section 133 which is to the same effect but which deals with the Court of Appeal.
35 Section 129.
36 See ss. 111 and 120.

with the rules made under s. 123.[37] Section 123 provides that the Lieutenant Governor in Council may make rules of court not inconsistent with this or any other Act for the conduct of and governing practices and procedures on appeals in the provincial courts (criminal division), the county and district courts and the Court of Appeal under this Act, and respecting any matter arising from or incidental to such appeals.

The right to appeal beyond the first level of review is "severely restricted".[38] The standard for the granting of leave to appeal has been described as a "very high threshold".[39] There are at least three elements which must be present before leave can be granted:

1. The Appellant must state "special grounds" upon which the appeal is to be argued (leave is not granted at large);

2. The appeal must be on a question of "law alone";

3. It must be, in the particular circumstances of the case,

    (i) "essential in the public interest" or

    (ii) "essential ... for the due administration of justice"

that leave be granted.

The first two elements are relatively simple to explain. "Special grounds" simply limits the granting of leave to the grounds stated in the proposed notice of appeal or to a ground or grounds stated by the judge granting leave.

Just what is a "question of law alone" is less readily distilled into a simple statement. One author offers the following as examples of matters which might be considered to be questions of law alone:[40]

1. admissibility of evidence (but not where dependant on proof of predicate fact);

2. construction or interpretation of a statute;

3. meaning of a word in an indictment or information;

---

37 With respect to proceedings commenced by certificate under Parts I or II of the *Provincial Offences Act*, an appeal lies from the judgment of the provincial court (criminal division) to the Court of Appeal, with leave of a justice of appeal, on special grounds, upon any question of law alone, in accordance with the rules made under s. 123 — see s. 122(1). Section 122(2) does not allow for leave to appeal to be granted under subsection (1), unless the justice of appeal considers that in the particular circumstances of the case it is essential in the public interest or for the due administration of justice that leave be granted. Pursuant to subsection (3), upon an appeal under this section, the Court of Appeal may make any order with respect to costs that it considers just and reasonable. Subsection (4) states that no appeal or review lies from a decision on a motion for leave to appeal under subsection (1).

38 Segal & Libman, *Annotated Rules of Criminal Practice*, 1999 (Carswell: Toronto, 1998).

39 *R. v. Zakarow* (1990), 74 O.R. (3d) 621 at 625 (Ont. C.A. [In chambers]).

40 See Ewaschuck, *Criminal Pleadings and Practice in Canada* (2nd ed.), (Canada Law Book: Aurora, 1987, looseleaf), at 23:1000.

4. legal construction of a written document;

5. the meaning of a word;

6. the legal effect of a finding of fact (including *Charter* violations);

7. impermissible 'speculation' by a trier of fact;

8. quashing or refusing to quash an information;

9. granting of a directed verdict of acquittal;

10. a finding of fact based on no evidence;

11. availability of plea of *autrefois* acquit or *autrefois* convict;

12. compliance with statutory procedural requirement;

13. amendment of information;

14. jurisdiction of the court;

15. a failure to exercise a discretion judicially.

This list is intended only to provide examples of the sort of questions that have been accepted by the courts as posing issues of law alone.

The most difficult hurdle in a motion for leave to appeal is the requirement that the granting of leave be "essential in the public interest or for the due administration of justice."[41] This requirement is the most common stumbling block between an appellant and the court of appeal. In *R. v. Zakarow*[42] Mr. Justice Carthy considered the question of whether leave should be granted to the Crown to pursue an appeal from an acquittal entered by a judge of the Provincial Court (Criminal Division). After observing that the judgment appealed from was in his opinion wrong in law and that the conviction should not have been interfered with, Mr. Justice Carthy wrote:[43]

> However, s. [139] of the *Provincial Offences Act* sets a very high threshold for granting of leave to appeal. There must be special grounds on a question of law and it must be essential to the public interest or for the due administration of justice that leave be granted. No matter how wrong the judgment under appeal may be, these other criteria must be met. The section was clearly drafted to eliminate all but appeals on the most significant issues. The *Consumer Reporting Act* [the statute creating the offence in issue] provides significant protection to the privacy of individuals and its interpretation has significance, but the statute does not have such a pervasive influence in our daily lives to attract language such as "essential in the public interest" or "due administration of justice".

---

41 Section 131(2) and 139(2).

42 (1991), 1 O.R. (3d) 621 (Ont. C.A. [In chambers]).

43 *Ibid.*, at 625-6.

The question was considered by Mr. Justice Lacourcière in *R. v. Krukowski*[44] where his Lordship seems to have taken a slightly more relaxed approach to the standard:[45]

> As a general rule, decisions made by the Ontario Court (Provincial Division) in its appellate capacity are intended to be final. They can only be reviewed in exceptional cases where the resolution of a question of law alone may have an impact on the jurisprudence in a way that is of interest to the public or to a broad segment of the public. Needless to say, a question of law has to be a pure question of law, not a question of fact or one of mixed fact and law, the latter being of importance to the parties only. …
>
> Although I agree that the section contemplates that leave will be granted to resolve only the most significant issues, I do not think that the words "essential in the public interest" should be so narrowly interpreted as to prevent leave to appeal being granted where the interpretation of a statute raises a question of public importance.
>
> If the adjective "essential" is interpreted as meaning "indispensable requisite", the threshold requirement will bar leave to appeal in all but the most exceptional circumstances. However, if "essential" in the context of s.[131] is taken to mean "material, important", adopting another definition set out in the *Shorter Oxford Dictionary*, then the interpretation comports with the contextual language, particularly the words "on special grounds" and "in the particular circumstances of the case". The latter interpretation does not fetter the discretion intended to be given to the justice of appeal in his consideration of each application; the narrow interpretation would tend to render s. [131] nugatory.

His Lordship granted leave.[46]

The rule is generally applied more strictly in cases in which the Crown seeks leave to appeal to the Court of Appeal.[47]

12. POWERS OF APPEAL COURT

(a) Appeals Under Parts I and II

On an appeal, the court may affirm, reverse or vary the decision appealed from or where, in the opinion of the court, it is necessary to do so to satisfy the ends of justice, direct a new trial. Where the court directs a new trial, it is held in the provincial offences court presided over by a justice other than the justice who tried the defendant in the first instance. The appeal court may, however, with the consent of the parties to the appeal, direct that the new trial

---

44 (1991), 2 O.R. (3d) 155 (Ont. C.A. [In chambers]).

45 *Ibid.*, at 159-60.

46 Examples of cases where leave has been granted offer some guidance as to the sort of issue which might properly go forward: *R. v. Triumbari* (1988), 42 C.C.C. (3d) 481 (Ont. C.A. [In chambers]); *R. v. Lawrie* (1987), 48 M.V.R. 189 (Ont. C.A., [In chambers]); *R. v. Valente* (1982), 2 C.C.C. (3d) 7 (Ont. C.A. [In chambers]); *R. v. Jamieson* (1982), 64 C.C.C. (2d) 550 (Ont. C.A. [In chambers]); *R. v. Memorial Gardens* (1991), 2 O.R. (3d) 417 (Ont. C.A. [In chambers]).

47 *R. v. Hovila and Tasanko Trucking Ltd.*, [1995] O.J. No. 50.

be held before the justice who tried the defendant in the first instance or before the judge who directs the new trial.

The court is required to give the parties an opportunity to be heard for the purpose of determining the issues, and may, where circumstances warrant, make such inquiries as are necessary to ensure that the issues are fully and effectively defined.

Section 136 states:

> (3) In determining a review, the court may,
>
>> (a) hear or rehear the recorded evidence or any part thereof and may require any party to provide a transcript of the evidence, or any part thereof, or to produce any further exhibit;
>>
>> (b) receive the evidence of any witness whether or not the witness gave evidence at trial;
>>
>> (c) require the justice presiding at the trial to report in writing on any matter specified in the request; or
>>
>> (d) receive and act upon statements of agreed facts or admissions.

(b) Powers of the Appeal Court in Appeals From Part III Prosecutions

On the hearing of an appeal against conviction, the court may allow the appeal where it is of the opinion that a factual finding should be set aside on the ground that it is unreasonable or cannot be supported by the evidence. It may also allow the appeal where it is of the opinion that the judgment of the trial court should be set aside on the ground of a wrong decision on a question of law or on any ground where the court is of the opinion there was a miscarriage of justice.[48] The court may dismiss the appeal where it is of the opinion that the appellant, although he was not properly convicted on a count or part of an information, was properly convicted on another count or part of the information. The appeal may also be dismissed where no substantial wrong or miscarriage of justice has occurred.[49]

(c) New Trials

In allowing the appeal, the court may direct a finding of acquittal or order a new trial. New trials are to be held in a provincial offences court presided over by a justice other than the justice who tried the defendant in the first instance, unless the appeal court otherwise directs that the new trial be held before the justice who tried the defendant in the first instance.[50] Where the

---

48 See s. 120.

49 See s. 120. This, of course, is parallel to the provisions in s. 686 of the *Criminal Code*.

50 See s. 126.

court dismisses an appeal it may substitute the decision that in its opinion should have been made and affirm the sentence passed by the trial court or impose a sentence that is warranted in law.[51] Where an appeal is from an acquittal, the court may by order, dismiss the appeal, order a new trial or enter a finding of guilt with respect to the offence of which, in its opinion, the accused should have been found guilty, and pass a sentence that is warranted in law.[52]

(d) Sentence Appeals

Where an appeal is taken against sentence, the court shall consider the fitness of the sentence appealed from and may hear fresh evidence. It may then either dismiss the appeal or vary the sentence within the limits prescribed by law for the offence of which the defendant was convicted. The court has the power to impose any sentence it considers fit in the circumstances. Any time spent in custody by the defendant on the charge before the court may be considered.[53]

(e) Appeals Based on Defects in the Charging Document

Appeals premised on a defective process, Certificate or information, to be successful, must show that the objection was taken at trial and in the case of a variance, that an adjournment of the trial was refused notwithstanding that the variance had misled the appellant.[54] Defects in a conviction or order, if appealed, will lead only to an order curing the defect.[55]

Any writing, exhibit or other thing relevant to the appeal may be ordered produced, and any witness who was compellable at trial but who was not called may be ordered to attend and be examined.[56] The right to cross-examine is, of course, preserved.[57]

Consistent with its approach to this summary form of appeal, s. 138 of the Act broadly describes the powers of the court hearing an appeal from a Part I or II matter. The court may "affirm, reverse or vary the decision appealed from or where, in the opinion of the court, it is necessary to do so to satisfy

---

51 See ss. 120(2) and (3).

52 See s. 121.

53 See s. 122.

54 See s. 124(1).

55 See s. 124(2). That is, the court will amend the document to properly reflect the offence of which the defendant was convicted. This may be important if, for example, in a subsequent proceeding based on the same circumstances, the defendant wished to plead the previous conviction.

56 See s. 117(1).

57 See s. 117(2).

the ends of justice, direct a new trial".[58] If a new trial is ordered, it will be before a different justice than the one who presided originally, unless the parties consent otherwise. The court can, with the consent of the parties, direct that the justice to hear the new trial will be the Provincial Judge who heard the appeal.[59] Costs can be awarded.[60]

(f) Costs in Appeals

In an appeal from a decision made under Part III, where an appeal is abandoned or is heard and dismissed, the court may make any order with respect to costs that it considers just and reasonable. Where an appellant or respondent is ordered to pay costs, they are to be paid to the clerk of the trial court, in turn to be paid by the clerk to the person entitled to them. The court's order should fix the period within which the costs shall be paid. Costs which the court orders to be paid are deemed to be fines for the purpose of enforcing payment (unless the person is a prosecutor acting on behalf of the Crown).[61]

With respect to appeals under Parts I and II of the Act, s. 138(3) reads as follows:

> (3) Upon an appeal, the court may make an order under section 60 for the payment of costs incurred on the appeal, and subsection (3) thereof applies to the order in the same manner as to an order of a provincial offences court.

Section 60 reads:

> **60.** (1) Upon conviction, the defendant is liable to pay to the court an amount by way of costs that is fixed by the regulations.
>
> (2) The court may, in its discretion, order costs towards fees and expenses reasonably incurred by or on behalf of witnesses in amount not exceeding the maximum fixed by the regulations, to be paid,
>
>> (a) to the court or prosecutor by the defendant; or
>>
>> (b) to the defendant by the person who laid the information or issued the certificate, as the case may be
>
> but where the proceedings is commenced by means of a certificate, the total of such costs shall not exceed $100.
>
> (3) Costs payable under this section shall be deemed to be a fine for the purpose of enforcing payment.

---

58 The language here is clearly biased in favour of having the court dispose of the matter rather than ordering a new trial. This is, of course, consistent with the general approach of the *Provincial Offences Act.*

59 Section 138(2).

60 Section 138(3).

61 Section 129. This is curious because it suggests that while costs may be ordered against a prosecutor, there is no way of enforcing payment. See also *R. v. Moodie* (1984), 13 C.C.C. (3d) 264 (Ont. H.C.J.).

Only in extraordinary circumstances are witnesses ever heard on an appeal, and therefore subsection (2) is of very limited application. This is unfortunate as it seems only fair that both the prosecutor and the defendant should be able to claim costs from the other where circumstances merit. As it reads now, only the prosecutor may claim costs.

(g) Reopening Appeals

Normally, once a court has adjudicated on a case it ceases to have jurisdiction to consider the matter further. The court is said to be *functus officio*. One exception to this general rule is the power of an appellate court to 'reopen' an appeal where the case has not been dealt with or concluded on its merits. If an appeal is dismissed because the appellant failed to attend the hearing or because materials were not filed in a timely way, the court continues to have the power to entertain an application to reopen the appeal. This avenue is often preferred to the course of attempting to appeal the decision dismissing the appeal.

In one case[62] the accused had failed to attend the date set for his appeal because he was ill and the appeal was dismissed in his absence. When he later appeared before the same judge seeking to explain what had happened and to "have his day in court", the appellate court judge explained that, having dismissed the case on the earlier date, he had no power to further consider the matter. The defendant appealed further to the British Columbia Court of Appeal which held that the judge hearing the first level of appeal had the authority to re-open the appeal because the case had not been determined on the merits and the interests of justice required it (the appellant had a legitimate reason for not appearing).[63]

13. CHART SHOWING PROGRESS OF TRAFFIC CASE

On the following page you will find a chart indicating the progress of a charge through the procedure established in the *Provincial Offences Act*.

---

62 *R. v. Wigmore*, [1997] B.C.J. No. 1505 (B.C. C.A.).

63 The appellant in *Wigmore* had been ill and had contacted the court office on the day of his first appeal to inform them of this. On the subject of reopening appeals, see also *R. v. Audy (No. 1)* (1977), 34 C.C.C. (2d) 228 (Ont. C.A.); *R. v. Dunbrook* (1978), 44 C.C.C. (2d) 264 (Ont. C.A.); *R. v. Blaker* (1983), 6 C.C.C. (3d) 385 (B.C. C.A.); *R. v. Jansen* (1996), 77 B.C. A.C. 236 (C.A.).

Appellate Review
Under Part III of the *Provincial Offences Act*

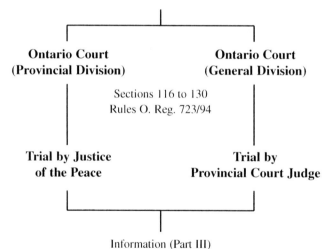

Supreme Court of Canada

[With leave, question of national importance, law alone:
Supreme Court Act R.S.C. 1985, c. S.26, s. 40(1)]

Court of Appeal for Ontario

[With leave, law alone or special grounds, or sentence:
Provincial Offences Act s. 131]

**Ontario Court
(Provincial Division)**

**Ontario Court
(General Division)**

Sections 116 to 130
Rules O. Reg. 723/94

**Trial by Justice
of the Peace**

**Trial by
Provincial Court Judge**

Information (Part III)

**Appellate Review
Under Part I & II of the *Provincial Offences Act***

R.S.O. 1990, c. P-33

Supreme Court of Canada

↑

[With leave, question of public importance, law alone:
Supreme Court Act R.S.C. 1985, c. S.26, s. 40(1)]

↑

COURT OF APPEAL FOR ONTARIO

↑

[With leave, on special grounds, essential in public interest
or for due administration of justice question of law alone:
Provincial Offences Act s. 139]

↑

ONTARIO COURT (PROVINCIAL DIVISION)

↑

[Appeal to Ontario Court (Provincial Division) presided over by
Provincial Judge whether trial before Provincial Judge or justice of the peace:
Provincial Offences Act ss. 135 to 139, Rules O. Reg. 722/94]

↑

Trial in ONTARIO COURT (PROVINCIAL DIVISION)
presided over by "JUSTICE"

(Note that *Provincial Offences Act*, s. 1, defines "Justice" to include
Provincial Judge and justice of the peace)
[Prosecution initiated by *Certificate of Offence* (Part I)
or *Certicate of Parking Infraction* (Part II)]

**Appellate Review
Under Part I & II of the *Provincial Offences Act***

R.S.O. 1990, c. P-33
WHERE DEFENDANT IS A "YOUNG PERSON"

SUPREME COURT OF CANADA

↑

[With leave, question of public importance, law alone:
Supreme Court Act R.S.C. 1985, c. S.26, s. 40(1)]

↑

COURT OF APPEAL FOR ONTARIO

↑

[With leave, on special grounds, essential in public interest
or for due administration of justice question of law alone:
Provincial Offences Act s. 139]

↑

ONTARIO COURT (GENERAL DIVISION)

↑

Trial in **ONTARIO COURT (PROVINCIAL DIVISION)**
presided over by
Provincial Offences Act s. 108
[Prosecution initiated by *Certificate of Offence*
or *Certificate of Parking Infraction*]

4

Evidence and Traffic Offences

1. INTRODUCTION: EVIDENCE IN CONTEXT

The Supreme Court of Canada recently provided the following useful overview of the role and purpose of evidence in any trial:[1]

> The ultimate aim of any trial, criminal or civil, must be to seek and to ascertain the truth. In a criminal trial the search for truth is undertaken to determine whether the accused before the court is, beyond a reasonable doubt, guilty of the crime with which he is charged. The evidence adduced must be relevant and admissible. That is to say, it must be logically probative and legally receivable. The evidence may be that of eyewitnesses, or it may be circumstantial, including the production of physical evidence which is often termed "real evidence". In every criminal case, if there is to be conviction, the evidence must be sufficiently convincing that the trier of fact is satisfied beyond a reasonable doubt of the guilt of the accused.

Whether charged with a parking offence or with first degree murder, an individual can only be convicted if a judge or justice is satisfied to the requisite degree of proof that the evidence presented by the prosecutor demonstrates the defendant's guilt. The Court is bound by the factual portrayal of the events in question: conjecture, speculation, myth, or stereotype can play no part in a finding of guilt. Similarly, if the accused person presents a version of events to the court that casts doubt on the claims advanced by the prosecution, then the accused should be found not guilty.

The proper, thoughtful and comprehensive presentation of evidence plays a fundamental role in the outcome of any dispute. Without sufficient and proper evidence, a prosecutor cannot be expected to take a case to trial, and, while

---

1 *R. v. Nikolovski*, [1996] 3 S.C.R. 1197 at 1206.

many accused persons are acquitted without calling any evidence, effective presentation of defence evidence will often secure an acquittal in the face of a compelling case for the prosecution.[2] It is not the role of the trier of fact, however, to search for the facts him or herself, but to adjudicate on the basis of the evidence put before the Court, to supervise the presentation of that evidence, and to ensure that all parties are given a fair opportunity to present their case. The adversarial context for this evidence is a fundamental principle of Canadian justice.[3] In short:

> Our mode of trial procedure is based upon the adversary system in which the contestants seek to establish through relevant supporting evidence, before an impartial trier of facts, those events or happenings which form the bases of their allegations. This procedure assumes that the litigants, assisted by their counsel, will fully and diligently present all the material facts which have evidentiary value in support of their respective positions and that these disputed facts will receive from a trial judge a dispassionate and impartial consideration in order to arrive at the truth of the matters in controversy.[4]

The presentation of evidence, however, is not simply a lining up of anything and everything that may inform the issue. Both effective tactics, and the myriad of rules governing the admissibility of evidence will influence the unraveling of a case. An understanding of the fundamental laws of evidence is central to effective advocacy and thus satisfactory adjudication in any level of court. While it is beyond the scope of this text to explore in detail all the evidentiary decisions which may comprise trials in the context of traffic offences, it is hoped that an outline of some of the more common evidentiary issues that arise will assist those who appear and adjudicate in these cases.

While the formalities of the rules of evidence may not always be strictly enforced in the trial of provincial traffic offences,[5] particularly where the accused is unrepresented, some basic principles still apply, and some more complex evidentiary problems arise fairly frequently.

---

2 Consistent with the terminology of the *Provincial Offences Act*, s. 1, the terms "prosecutor" and "prosecution" rather than "Crown" are used here, since trials of traffic offences include those conducted by private and/or Municipal prosecutors, who are not agents of the Attorney General (and thus the Sovereign) but are agents for the Municipality, and hence referring to them as "Crowns" is improper.

3 *Borowski v. Canada (Attorney General)* (1989), 47 C.C.C. (3d) 1 at 13 (S.C.C.); *R. v. Swain* (1991), 63 C.C.C. (3d) 481 at 504 (S.C.C.). See also Weiler, "Two Models of Judicial Decision Making" (1968), 46 *Can. Bar Rev.* 406 at 412.

4 *Phillips et al. v. Ford Motor Co. Of Canada Ltd. et al.*, [1971] 2 O.R. 637 (Ont. C.A. per Evans J.A.).

5 One of the philosophies of the *Provincial Offences Act* is to eliminate excessive technicalities that sometimes punctuate trials of more serious offences: *R. v. Discovery Place Ltd.*, [1996] O.J. No. 690, affirmed [1997] O.J. No. 1887 (Ont. C.A.); *Toronto (Metropolitan) v. Beck* (1990), 23 M.V.R. (2d) 61 (Ont. H.C.).

2. THE BURDEN AND STANDARD OF PROOF

(a) The Presumption of Innocence

Perhaps the best known principle of the law of evidence is the presumption of innocence. That principle underlies the concepts of the burden and standard of proof. An accused person is presumed to be innocent until the prosecution proves that he or she committed the offence with which he or she is charged. In other words, the burden of proving the case falls on the prosecution, and there is no burden on the defendant to prove innocence. If the prosecution cannot meet the burden of proving guilt, then the accused must be found not guilty, whether or not he or she has called any evidence. The presumption of innocence also requires that the evidence be convincing beyond a reasonable doubt. This is known as the standard of proof. The most famous statement of this rule is found in *Woolmington's Case*,[6] where Viscount Sankey L.C. said:

> ... [T]hroughout the web of the English Criminal Law one golden thread is always to be seen, that is the duty of the prosecution to prove the prisoner's guilt ... If, at the end of and on the whole of the case, there is a reasonable doubt ... the prosecution has not made out the case and the prisoner is entitled to an acquittal.

Both the presumption of innocence and the requirement of proof beyond a reasonable doubt are accorded constitutional status by virtue of ss. 7 and 11(d) of the *Canadian Charter of Rights and Freedoms*.[7] Section 11(d) reads:

> **11.** Any person charged with an offence has the right ...
>
> (d) to be presumed innocent until proven guilty according to law in a fair and public hearing by an independent and impartial inquiry.

A person "charged with an offence" includes someone charged with a quasi-criminal offence such as those found in provincial highway traffic acts, since they are in their very nature criminal offences, some carrying penal consequences.[8] For our purposes, it is sufficient to say that the presumption of innocence is a constitutional rule requiring that the prosecution prove every element of a provincial offence beyond reasonable doubt before the defendant may

---

6 [1935] A.C. 462 at 481 (H.L.).

7 *Canadian Charter of Rights and Freedoms* (Part I of the *Constitution Act*, 1982, being Schedule B to the *Canada Act 1982* (U.K.), 1982, c. 11).

8 *Wigglesworth v. The Queen* (1987), 37 C.C.C. (3d) 385 (S.C.C.); *R. v. Richard*, [1998] 3 S.C.R. 525. Procedurally, however, it may be that a person is not "charged with an offence" at the time of issuance of the certificate of offence. These certificates have been held only to be administrative documents which are preliminary to the actual charging: *Re Mccutcheon and City of Toronto et al.* (1983), 41 O.R. (2d) 652 (Ont. H.C.). But see *Saint-Lambert (Ville) v. Dries* (1991), 31 W.C.B. (2d) 254 (Que. S.C.). See Chapter 2 on procedure in trials of traffic offences.

be convicted.[9] The presumption of innocence has some particular relevance in the regulation of highway traffic. For example, many provinces have passed legislation which incorporates a "reverse onus" with the concomitant aim of protecting the public. School bus stopping offences are an example.[10]

It should be remembered too that any piece of evidence in and of itself is not a fact until the Judge or Justice accepts it as such. Additionally, while the elements of the offence must be proven beyond a reasonable doubt, it is not every single piece of evidence which is subject to the criminal standard of proof, rather the Judge "must consider the evidence as a whole and determine whether guilt is established beyond a reasonable doubt."[11]

(b) The Standard of Reasonable Doubt

Notoriously difficult to define and explain, the nebulous concept of reasonable doubt is nevertheless at the heart of our trial process. As the Ontario Court of Appeal has recently stated:[12]

> The reasonable doubt standard imports our society's value judgment that it is better to let the guilty go free than to convict the innocent. And it infuses our criminal law with the moral force needed to command the respect and confidence of the community.

Although the presumption of innocence requires that the prosecution present proof of guilt beyond a reasonable doubt, it is not easy to articulate exactly what amounts to such proof. As the noted legal author Wigmore observed:[13]

> The truth is that no one has yet invented or discovered a mode of measurement for the intensity of human belief. Hence there can be yet no successful method of communicating intelligibly to a jury a sound method of self-analysis for one's belief.

The Supreme Court of Canada has recently entrenched the following fundamental elements of the concept of reasonable doubt:[14]

- a reasonable doubt is not a doubt based upon sympathy or prejudice;

---

9 In so far as the elements of the offence are concerned, it is important to keep in mind the special status of strict liability offences and the absence of any mental element in the definition of the offence. While the prosecution need not prove any mental state, the accused is allowed to escape a conviction if he or she can prove that there was an innocent mental state. See generally Chapter One. See J. C. Morton & S. C. Hutchison, *The Presumption of Innocence*, (Carswell, Toronto: 1987) at pp. 93-95.

10 *R. v. Wilson* (1997), 31 M.V.R. (3d) 238 (N.B. C.A.).

11 *R. v. Morin* (1988), 44 C.C.C. (3d) 193 at 211 *per* Sopinka J. (S.C.C.).

12 *R. v. Jenkins* (1996), 107 C.C.C. (3d) 440 at 459 (Ont. C.A.).

13 4 *Wigmore on Evidence* (3d ed., Chad. Rev.), para. 2497.

14 *R. v. Lifchus* [1997] 3 S.C.R. 320. The Court described reasonable doubt as a term which has "come echoing down the centuries in words of deceptive simplicity." See also *R. v. B.*, [1998] 1 S.C.R. 306.

- rather, it is based upon reason and common sense;
- it is logically connected to the evidence or absence of evidence;
- it does not involve proof to an absolute certainty;
- it is not proof beyond any doubt nor is it an imaginary or frivolous doubt;
- more is required than proof that the accused is probably guilty — a conclusion only that the accused is probably guilty must result in acquittal;
- it is not simply an ordinary expression, but has a special meaning in the criminal law context;
- equating reasonable doubt to a "moral certainty" is not appropriate;

While the burden of proof falls on the prosecution in proving all the elements of an offence, that burden is legally reversed in certain instances, both in true crimes and in regulatory statutes.

In traffic offences this reversal is particularly germane, as many offences provide for an exception or exemption which, if shown to operate in favour of the accused will provide a full defence to the charge. Section 47(3) of the *Provincial Offences Act*, for example, states that:

> [T]he burden of proving that an authorization, exception, exemption or qualification prescribed by law operates in favour of the defendant is on the defendant, and the prosecutor is not required, except by way of rebuttal, to prove that the authorization, exception, exemption or qualification does not operate in favour of the defendant, whether or not it is set out in the information.

The evidentiary burden on the defendant is on a balance of probabilities. The section has been upheld as not being in violation of s. 11(d) of the *Charter* as it creates an exception rather than an presumption.[15]

(c) Evidence Statutes

Both the federal and provincial governments have enacted evidence acts to deal with certain evidentiary issues.[16] In traffic cases, the Ontario statute applies.

There are many potentially applicable sections of the *Evidence Act*, particularly relating to the admissibility of public documents.[17] The most important

---

15 *R. v. Schwartz*, [1988] 2 S.C.R. 443; *R. v. Lee's Poultry Ltd.* (1985), 17 C.C.C. (3d) 539 (Ont. C.A.).

16 Federally, see the *Canada Evidence Act*, R.S.C. 1985, c. C-5; Alberta *Evidence Act*, R.S.A. 1980, c. A-21; British Columbia *Evidence Act*, R.S.B.C. 1997, c. 52; Manitoba *Evidence Act*, R.S.M. 1987, c. E150; New Brunswick *Evidence Act*, R.S.N.B. 1973, c. E-11; Newfoundland *Evidence Act*, R.S.N. 1990, c. E-16; Northwest Territories *Evidence Act*, R.S.N.W.T. 1974, c. E-4; Nova Scotia *Evidence Act*, R.S.N.S. 1989, c. 154; Ontario *Evidence Act*, R.S.O. 1990, c. E.23; Prince Edward Island *Evidence Act*, R.S.P.E.I. 1988, c. E-11; Saskatchewan *Evidence Act*, R.S.S. 1978, c. S-16; Yukon Territory *Evidence Act*, R.S.Y.T. 1986, c. 57.

17 Sections 24-29, 31-35.

question dealt with under the Ontario legislation is proof by way of a business record.[18] Section 35 provides:

(1) In this section,

(a) "business" includes every kind of business, profession, occupation, calling, operation or activity, whether carried on for profit or otherwise;

(b) "record" includes any information that is recorded or stored by any means.

(2) Any writing or record made of any act, transaction, occurrence or event is admissible as evidence of such act, transaction, occurrence or event if made in the usual and ordinary course of any business and if it was in the usual and ordinary course of such business to make such writing or record at the time of such act, transaction, occurrence or event or within a reasonable time thereafter.

(3) Subsection (2) does not apply unless the party tendering the writing or record has given at least seven days notice of his intention to all other parties in the action, and any party to the action is entitled to obtain from the person who has possession thereof production for inspection of the writing or record within five days after giving notice to produce the same.

(4) The circumstances of the making of such a writing or record, including lack of personal knowledge by the maker, may be shown to affect its weight, but such circumstances do not affect its admissibility.

(5) Nothing in this section affects the admissibility of any evidence that would be admissible apart from this section or makes admissible any writing or record that is privileged.

If otherwise admissible, there is no need to serve the document in accordance with subsection (3).[19]

Of course Parts IV and V of the *Provincial Offences Act* itself contain a number of provisions which speak to evidentiary issues, such as general trial procedure on a not guilty plea,[20] the Court's authority to receive and consider evidence on a different charge,[21] and the recording of evidence.[22] Regulations are in place respecting electronic documents, providing for, *inter alia*, the proper certification and filing of electronic documents in court.[23]

---

18 For example, proof by an invoice book to establish the value of damage done to a vehicle, or a work time sheet to establish a defence of alibi.

19 *R. v. Bredin*, [1993] O.J. No. 854 (Ont. Prov. Div.).

20 Section 46.

21 Section 47(1).

22 Section 83.

23 O. Reg. 499/94 under the *Highway Traffic Act*.

3. SOME BASIC EVIDENTIARY RULES

(a) Relevance and Materiality

The first principle of the law of evidence is that all relevant evidence is admissible unless rendered inadmissible by virtue of some exclusionary rule. The general rule states that evidence will only be relevant if it is logically connected to a material fact in the case. In other words, relevance:[24]

> ... requires a determination of whether as a matter of human experience and logic the existence of "Fact A" makes the existence or non-existence of "Fact B" more probable than it would be without the existence of "Fact A." If it does then "Fact A" is relevant to "Fact B." As long as "Fact B" is itself a material fact in issue or is relevant to a material fact in issue in the litigation then "Fact A" is relevant and *prima facie* admissible.

Relevance will be determined according to this general principle on a case by case basis, since the ultimate determination is obviously dependent on what issues are material to the case at hand. Thus, the weather conditions at the time of the alleged offence will likely be irrelevant to a charge of driving while suspended, but may be highly relevant to a charge of careless driving. The importance of relevance is often overlooked in favour of other more 'complicated' objections.[25]

(b) Probative Value vs. Prejudicial Effect

Regardless of how relevant a piece of evidence may be, it will nevertheless be subject to exclusion if its probative value is outweighed by its prejudicial effect. In other words, the significance and expedience of the evidence in establishing the proposition in question will be weighed against the potential for the evidence to improperly distort the reasoning process of the trier of fact in reaching a just conclusion. Typically such prejudice will arise from viewing inflammatory photographs or hearing inflammatory comments, which often amount to comments on the accused's character or past conduct which, while strictly speaking relevant to the charge, run the risk of leading the trier of fact into an impermissible chain of reasoning in reaching a verdict. Defence counsel will wish to consider this line of objection in assessing photographs of an accident scene or the potential evidence of any eye witnesses.

---

24 *R. v. Watson* (1996), 108 C.C.C. (3d) 310 at pp. 323 to 324 (Ont. C.A.).

25 Hearsay is a classic example. The classic response to a hearsay objection is that the statement is not being offered for the truth of its contents but for the fact of the statement having been made. The fact of the statement having been made must of course be relevant. See Hon. Mr. Justice David Watt, "Hearsay, or not Hearsay? C'est la Question." February 1995 *Canadian Bar Association – Ontario 1995 Institute of Continuing Legal Education - Recent Issues and Developments in Criminal Law*.

(c) Circumstantial Evidence

Often there will be no one who saw the accident or the alleged violation. Rather, there will be evidence which we are able to use to come to a conclusion because of our knowledge of how the world works. The former type of evidence is known as direct evidence, while the latter is usually referred to as indirect or circumstantial evidence. It is evidence of surrounding circumstances to an alleged offence from which logical inferences can be drawn. For example, if someone tells us that they looked outside and saw it snowing, we have direct evidence that it snowed. If, however, we go to bed with the ground bare and then, upon awakening the next morning, we see the ground covered in snow, we have indirect or 'circumstantial' evidence that it snowed. It is a common misunderstanding that a conviction cannot result from evidence which is entirely circumstantial. Often, circumstantial evidence is all that is available, and will offer compelling indication as to what occurred. Because of the potential remoteness of this type of evidence, however, there is a protective rule in place to help guard against the danger of a miscarriage of justice.

(d) The Rule in *Hodge's Case*

In most cases there will be both circumstantial and direct evidence. However, if there is only circumstantial evidence, this rule (which takes its name from an old English case)[26] ensures the operation of the presumption of innocence. The rule requires that, where the evidence against the accused person on any element of the offence is entirely circumstantial, the court must be satisfied that the evidence defeats any reasonable explanation. That is, the circumstantial evidence must be such as to leave no reasonable explanation but that which indicates the guilt of the accused.[27] Before the court can find the defendant guilty, it must be satisfied, not only that the circumstances have been proved beyond reasonable doubt and that they are consistent with the defendant having committed the offence, but also that the facts are such as to be inconsistent with any other rational conclusion than that the defendant is guilty.[28]

---

26 *Re Hodge's Case* (1838), 168 E.R. 1136.

27 This rule sees its most common traffic application in careless driving cases, where the police rely on the final resting places of the automobiles to prove that a driver was careless. See below, Chapter 6, "Careless Driving". Consider also *R. v. Ouseley*, [1973] 1 O.R. 729 (Ont. C.A.) for a discussion of the issue in the context of 'follow too closely.'

28 *R. v. Cooper*, [1978] 1 S.C.R. 860 at 873; *R. v. Charemski* (1998), 1 S.C.R. 679; Tanovich, D., "Upping the Ante in Directed Verdict Cases were the Evidence is Circumstantial" (1998) 15 C.A. (5th) 21.

(e) Judicial Notice

While, as we have said, it is a fundamental principle that a court is allowed
to consider only the facts which have been proven by admissible evidence
actually before it when deciding a case, some facts are so obvious that it would
be foolish to require proof of their existence. For example, it would be absurd
to dismiss a traffic case because a prosecutor failed to present evidence that
the intersection of Queen and Bay in Toronto is a built up area or that February
is a winter month in Canada. The concept of judicial notice allows the
acceptance by a Court of a factual matter without the requirement of proof.
While the concept of judicial notice has expanded beyond its original meaning,
and encompasses more than one form,[29] for our purposes the rule is stated
simply and accurately by O'Hearn Co. Ct. J. in *R. v. Bennet*:[30]

> Courts will take judicial notice of what is considered by reasonable men [and
> women] of that time and place to be indisputable either by resort to common
> knowledge or to sources of indisputable accuracy easily accessible to men [or
> women] in the situation of members of that court.

Thus, there is no need to call evidence of a fact which is known to be true.
Courts will usually take judicial notice of facts such as dates and times (for
example, the fact that a particular day was a Monday or a public holiday)[31]
or well-known geographical features (for example, the general division of the
counties of the province,[32] that Toronto is in Canada,[33] that a certain town
is within the local judicial region,[34] or that one cannot drive from Dartmouth
to a point outside of Nova Scotia in under twenty minutes),[35] the location and
configuration of major roads in the area where the case is being tried,[36] or

---

29 See David. M. Paciocco, "Judicial Notice in Criminal Cases: Potential and Pitfalls" (1997),
40 C.L.Q. 35.

30 (1971), 4 C.C.C. (2d) 55 at 66 (N.S. Co. Ct.). See also *R. v. Paul* (1998), 124 C.C.C. (3d)
1 (N.B. C.A.); *R. v. Bélanger* (1991), 43 Q.A.C. 208 (Que. C.A.).

31 Where an offence can only be committed during certain times and days (for example, no
stopping during rush hour Monday to Friday), the Court will usually take judicial notice
of a calendar whether or not the officer has one in his or her possession, or whether the
officer is able to testify as to the specific day in question. In fact, it is probably sufficient
for the officer to simply testify that the ticket was issued on one of the specified days without
having to say which particular day of the week it was, and the evidence is open to challenge
on cross-examination or by defence evidence in chief.

32 *R. v. Mcgregory* (1895), 2 C.C.C. 410 (Ont. H.C.J.).

33 *R. v. Cerniuk* (1948), 91 C.C.C. 56 (B.C. C.A.).

34 *R. v. Discovery Place Ltd.*, *supra*, note 5.

35 *R. v. Porter* (1961), 130 C.C.C. 116 (N.S. S.C.); *R. v. Goodwin*, [1965] 2 C.C.C. 127 (B.C.
C.A.); *Harnden v. Kosir* (February 13, 1995), Doc. 393724/90 (Ont. Gen. Div.).

36 *R. v. Dawson*, [1994] B.C.J. No. 678 (Prov. Ct.); *R. v. Gardiner*, [1990] O.J. No. 2370 (Gen.
Div.); *R. v. Yachmin*, [1995] O.J. No. 1304 (Prov. Div.). These and other examples of forms
of judicial notice are cited in Paciocco, *supra* note 29 at 38-39.

that the sun sets in the west, not the north-west.[37] In one case the court took judicial notice of the fact that a "Dodge" is a motor vehicle within the meaning of the legislation.[38] While in many instances the judicially noticed facts are indisputable, and the court then is required to notice them, there is some authority for the view that a trial judge retains the discretion not to take judicial notice.[39] It should be remembered that one of the purposes of judicial notice is to increase the efficiency of the trial process.

The common law position that the Court is required to judicially notice domestic, common and statute law is entrenched by legislation, including, in Ontario, the *Interpretation Act*:

> **7.** (1) Every Act shall be judicially noticed by judges, justices of the peace and others without being specially pleaded.
>
> (2) Every proclamation shall be judicially noticed by judges, justices of the peace and others without being specifically pleaded.

An "Act" includes an "enactment."[40] However, delegated legislation such as that passed by municipalities to regulate parking under the authority of the *Municipal Act* will often not be familiar or accessible enough to be judicially noticed, and will need to be proved as a fact, and it would appear that the *Interpretation Act* does not apply to municipal by-laws, proof of which are governed by the *Municipal Act* itself.[41] Thus, in trials of parking offences the prosecutor will enter the pertinent by-law as an exhibit (even though a separate copy of the by-law need not be filed as an exhibit for each case — a certified copy of the by-law present in the court is sufficient).[42] The Ontario *Evidence Act* requires courts to take judicial notice of the signature of any Canadian judge appended to a judgment, order, certificate, etc.[43]

Matters which should not be the subject of judicial notice include scientific issues, or the effect of medication on an individual's impairment.[44] Nor should judicial notice be taken of the fact that the standard written demand for a screening device that was usually read out contained the express words

---

37   *MacNeil Estate v. Gillis* (1994), 128 N.S.R. (2d) 305 (N.S. S.C.).

38   *R. v. Smith* (1957), 119 C.C.C. 227 (N.S. S.C.).

39   *R. v. Zundel* (1987), 31 C.C.C. (3d) 97 (Ont. C.A.), leave to appeal to S.C.C. refused (1987), 56 C.R. (3d) xviii. See also *R. v. S. (R.D.)*, [1997] 3 S.C.R. 484, where L'Heureux Dubé J. stated in dissent that a judge could take judicial notice of the prevalence of racism in an area.

40   *Interpretation Act*, R.S.O. 1990, c. I.11.

41   See *Peterborough (City) v. Lockyer* (1992), 12 O.R. (3d) 214 (Ont. Prov. Div.) and the critique of the holding in that case by Martin Teplitsky, "Proof of By-Law is Governed by Legislation, Not Judicial Notice" (1993), 15 *Advocates' Q.* 380. See also *Grand Central Ottawa Ltd. v. Ottawa (City)* (1997), 39 O.R. (3d) 47 (Ont. Prov. Div.).

42   *R. v. Margetis* (1988), 9 M.V.R. (2d) 19 (Ont. H.C.J.).

43   Section 36(1).

44   *R. v. Van Groen* (1997), 34 W.C.B. (2d) 510 (B.C. S.C.).

that the sample of breath be provided "forthwith".[45] The workings of sophisticated equipment (for example, radar or breathalyzers) cannot be judicially
noticed,[46] although it is not necessary for the prosecution to call expert
evidence as to the inner workings of such devices. To the extent that a court
is satisfied that the officer operating the radar device for example, has received
adequate training, can operate the instrument competently, and that the
readings obtained are an accurate reflection of the facts, then judicial notice
is in effect taken of the fact that the device is generally known to be a reliable
instrument for measuring speeds, so that radar evidence will establish a *prima
facie* case for the Crown.[47] The issue was considered in *R. v. Joudrey*[48] where
it was held that radar devices have provided reliable and accurate evidence
in many cases:

> ... even though it is not clear such accuracy is "within the knowledge of persons
> generally". But it is within the knowledge of judges and the law.
>
> When matters are relevant to a particular issue, as here the possibilities of inac-
> curacy in the radar readings, and there has been a full disclosure at trial, as in
> this case, so that the information, coming apparently from an accurate source,
> is not received "behind the back of counsel" ... it seems a judge may take judicial
> notice of them

Based in part on passages from a textbook on speeding and radar, the trial
judge in that case went on to take judicial notice that:[49]

- a radar instrument reading is *prima facie* evidence of speed;

- it is not, however, infallible;

- exterior factors, be they atmospheric or environmental, such as clouds, snow,
  rain, fog, wind or glass, may affect the accuracy of its reading.

This rule of evidence also allows the court to look to readily available and
reliable sources to get information. Two acceptable sources of information
under this rule are dictionaries[50] and recently published maps.[51]

The court should not take judicial notice of a matter which is central to
the dispute, even if it seems to be a matter which is not open to argument.
A common example in traffic cases is the qualifications of an officer to operate

---

45 *R. v. Phelan* (1997), 35 W.C.B. (2d) 175 (Nfld. C.A.).

46 *R. v. Waschuk* (1970), 1 C.C.C. (2d) 463 (Sask. Q. B.). See also *R. v. Bland* (1974), 20 C.C.C.
    (2d) 332 (Ont. C.A.).

47 *D'Astous v. Baie-Comeau* (Ville) (1992), 74 C.C.C. (3d) 73 (Que. C.A.).

48 (1992), 39 M.V.R. (2d) 235 at 244 (N.S. Prov. Ct.).

49 *Ibid.*, at p. 245.

50 See *R. v. Quinn* (1975), 27 C.C.C. (2d) 543 (Alta. S.C.); *R. v. Scaynetti* (1915), 25 C.C.C.
    40 (Ont. H.C.J.).

51 *R. v. Jameson and others* [1896] 2 Q.B. 425. Judicial notice should also be taken of a calendar
    where one is available, if the charge is limited to certain days (e.g., stopping in a posted
    no stopping zone during rush hour Monday to Friday).

a radar device properly, or that the particular device was operating properly at the particular time.[52] Courts should not take judicial notice of such matters. In certain circumstances, doing so will in effect create a "judicial reverse onus", contrary to s. 11(d) of the *Charter*.[53] The rule which allows judicial notice is intended to make it possible for the court to avoid endless streams of evidence on obvious points. It is not intended to relieve the duty on the prosecution to prove disputed points. In *R. v. Eagles*,[54] the court refused to take judicial notice of the actual boundaries of a municipality. There the trial court had taken judicial notice of the fact that Lakeshore Road is within the City of Sarnia. The charge was speeding, under what is now s. 128(1)(b), and proof that the area was "built up" was essential to a conviction. If the defendant disputed the fact of location and the prosecution failed to prove it by evidence, the trial court could not properly take judicial notice of so central a matter. This rule should rarely work any hardship on the prosecution; if the issue is genuinely within the ambit of normal judicial notice (that is, if it is truly obvious), it should be simple to prove.

While this position is probably correct (that is, that even the obvious must be proved if the defendant disputes it), cases have repeatedly held that where the location of the offence is so well-known as to be notorious, the court may take judicial notice of the place. Thus in one case, the court took notice of the fact that the location of a speeding charge was on property of the National Capital Commission.[55] See also *R. v. Redlick*,[56] where the court said:

> It is clear that the location is an essential ingredient of this offence. The court must be satisfied in order to convict that the offence occurred in a city, town, police village or other built-up area. Normally this would require evidence, especially if there is a dispute as to this matter, but I do not believe that evidence must be given in all cases, especially where it is so obvious to everyone that the offence has occurred within such an area. One should not be required to prove the patently obvious. It is only where there is some dispute or some possible disagreement about whether the location is within such an area or whether it is not [that evidence must be lead].

(f) Facts Proved In Other Cases

Some issues of fact are repeatedly before the courts. There is a great temptation to dispense with full proof of such factual matters and simply get on with the trial. It is improper, however, to use evidence or findings of fact from

---

52   Manraj & Haines, *The Law on Speeding and Radar*, (2nd ed.) (Butterworths: Markham, 1991) at p. 26.

53   *R. v. Stewart* (1997), 30 M.V.R. (3d) 305 (N.B. Q.B.).

54   (1976), 31 C.C.C. (2d) 417 (Ont. H.C.J.).

55   *R. v. Potts* (1982), 66 O.R. (2d) 219 (Ont. C.A.), leave to appeal to S.C.C. refused, May 17, 1982).

56   (1978), 41 C.C.C. (2d) 358 at p.359(Ont. H.C.J.).

previous trials to convict in a later case. Thus, for example, it was an error for a trial court to dispense with proof of the scientific accuracy of a breathalyzer simply because the matter had been proved in cases already heard.[57] It is submitted that this rule prevents trial courts from accepting evidence derived from radar or other technical equipment without proof of the reliability of this type of equipment as a part of the body of evidence presented in the trial in which such evidence is offered.

The damaging effects of drinking and driving are a well-known and indisputable fact such that they have been held to properly be the subject of judicial notice.[58] The presumption of regularity that the Ministry had properly designated a construction zone was not within the ambit of judicial notice.[59]

(g) Refreshing Memory

The evidence of a police or provincial offences officer will almost invariably commence with the "qualification" of the officer's notes.[60] Typically, the following sequence of questions and answers occurs:

> Q: On [date of offence] I understand you were employed as a [police/provincial offences officer]?
> A: Yes.
> Q: Did you make any notes regarding the matter before the court?
> A: Yes.
> Q: When did you make these notes?
> A: At the time of [or immediately following] the offence.
> Q: Have you made any additions, deletions or alterations to these notes?
> A: No.
> Q: Why do you wish to refer to these notes?
> A: In order to refresh my memory of the events in question.

The prosecutor will then ask for the Court's permission for the officer to refer to the notes in order to refresh his or her memory of the events in question. Defence counsel will sometimes wish to address questions of their own with respect to the notebooks, but should be limited at this time to questions which go to the currency of the notes, and the nature of any alterations or additions that may have been made. The issue of refreshing memory, while usually *pro forma* in criminal trials, is not always straightforward. Particularly in traffic offences, where an officer may issue dozens of tickets in a given week, or even day, the reality is that the officer's memory may not be refreshed, and he or she may have no memory of the individual ticket at all. In practice, many

---

57 *R. v. Skelton*, [1968] 3 C.C.C. 35 (B.C. S.C.).

58 *R. v. Tremblay* (1995), 30 W.C.B. (2d) 317.

59 *R. v. Friedlan* (1993), 48 M.V.R. (2d) 64 (Ont. Prov. Div.).

60 The "note" is usually nothing more than the officer's copy of certificate of infraction, occasionally supplemented by some notes in the officer's memo book or, in the case of parking infractions, notes made at the bottom of the officer's copy itself.

trials of traffic matters are perfunctory and, particularly where an accused is unrepresented, it is usually immaterial as to whether the officer really remembers the incident in question.

Strictly speaking, the rule on refreshing memory falls into two categories, in Wigmore's terminology a "present memory revived" and a "past recollection recorded". The former occurs when the reviewing of a note "jogs" the memory such that the event as it happened is recalled to memory. The latter occurs when the witness is unable, notwithstanding a memory aid, to recall the event in question, but is able to say that on an earlier occasion he or she had a perfect recollection of the incident, and at that time truly recorded the same. At common law this latter evidence was admissible, but it presents problems for the cross-examiner who can only examine as to the usual practice of the witness, not his or her conduct on the particular occasion in question. Hence the contemporaneity requirement, and the requirement that the witness be able to vouch for the accuracy of the recording of his or her recollection.[61] The situation is encapsulated in this excerpt from what is still the leading case in this area:

> The witness could not, from memory alone, testify to an inspection made shortly before the accident; it would hardly be possible that he could; it was then proposed to put into his hand a report, signed by him in the usual course of his work, shewing that the car had been examined at that time; but, upon such objection, that was prevented. If looking at the report, the witness could have said, "that is my report, it refers to the car in question, and shews that it was examined at the time, and, though I cannot from memory say that it was then examined, I can now swear that it was, because I signed no report that was untrue, and at the time I signed this report I knew that it was true." That would, of course, be very good evidence.[62]

The witness in this situation is not "refreshing his memory", but the procedure has nevertheless been mislabeled as such through the years. In such cases, it is the document that constitutes the evidence, and theoretically should be received as an exhibit for the truth of its contents, the officer having no capacity to testify to the events he or she no longer recalls. The rule is, in essence, simply an exception to the hearsay rule on the basis that the statement was made in circumstances that guarantee its reliability. Further, the occasions on which an officer will not be allowed to testify will be few, since it would seem that the memory loss must be total for the rule to be triggered.[63] Thus in

---

61 In the former category of cases, contemporaneity is not an essential requirement. See also *R. v. B. (K.G.)* (May 4, 1998), (Ont. C.A.); *R. v. Shergill* (1997), 13 C.R. (5th) 160 (Ont. Gen. Div.) for a review of the law in this area, as well as a useful review of the procedure to be followed when refreshing a witness' memory.

62 *Fleming v. Toronto Railway Co.* (1911), 25 O.L.R. 317 at 325 (Ont. C.A.).

63 *C.(J.) v. College of Physicians and Surgeons of British Columbia*, [1990] 2 W.W.R. 673 (B.C. C.A.).

practice the categories of recollection are not so distinct, the strict rule probably often honoured in the breach, and officers will routinely testify notwithstanding that their recollection of the events in question is not perfect.[64] Further, there is nothing to prevent an officer from "refreshing" his or her memory from notes prior to testifying. In any event, where the witness purports to recall the events, the veracity of that recollection and the accuracy of the events related can of course be tested under cross-examination.[65]

(h) Statements and Admissions made by the Accused

Where the prosecution tenders evidence of a statement made by the accused to a police officer, the statement should normally be subject to a *voir dire* to determine its voluntariness, which the Crown must prove beyond a reasonable doubt. Unless a sufficient explanation can be given for not doing so, the prosecution will generally be required to call at the voluntariness *voir dire* any and all officers present during the giving of the statement.[66] Typically, in highway traffic matters this will be a statement made by the accused at the time the ticket was issued. The following standard questions are usually put to an officer testifying on the *voir dire*:

1. When you approached the accused were you with anyone else?

2. Were you in uniform?

3. Did you have a conversation with the accused?

4. Where did this conversation take place?

5. Did you have any physical contact with the accused?

6. Did you promise any favours or threaten the accused in any way?

7. Did the accused appear to have an understanding of the English language?

8. Did the accused appear to be under the influence of alcohol or drugs?

9. Was the accused under arrest at the time?

Of course if the answer to the last question is yes, then the officer will have been obliged to advise the accused of his or her *Charter* rights to counsel and to remain silent. Defence counsel will rarely call the accused to testify on a voluntariness *voir dire*. As a general rule, the accused's statement should be adduced as part of the prosecution's case in chief.[67] If the prosecution attempts to lead the statement in cross-examination it is open to the accusation of

---

64 This will be particularly so in trials alleging a breach of parking by-laws.

65 See also *R. v. Meddoui* (1990), 61 C.C.C. (3d) 345 (Alta. C.A.), leave to appeal to S.C.C. quashed for want of jurisdiction 69 C.C.C. (3d) iii (note) (S.C.C.).

66 *Thiffault v. The King* (1933), 60 C.C.C. 97 (S.C.C.).

67 *R. v. Briden* (1960), 127 C.C.C. 154 (Ont. C.A.).

splitting its case. The prosecution is not permitted to introduce the statement for the first time in rebuttal.[68]

An accused cannot of course be compelled to give a statement, and where voluntariness is not established, the statement will not be admissible. However, most provincial statutory regimes include a requirement that the driver of a vehicle involved in a traffic collision give a statement to a police officer, or other person in authority. For example, s. 199(1) of the *Highway Traffic Act* in Ontario obliges the operator of a vehicle involved in an accident which results in a prescribed amount of damages to report the accident forthwith.[69] Subsection (3) further requires that:

> A police officer receiving a report of an accident, as required by this section, shall secure from the person making the report, or by other inquiries where necessary, the particulars of the accident, the persons involved, the extent of the personal injuries or property damage, if any, and the other information as may be necessary to complete a written report concerning the accident and shall forward the report to the Registrar within ten days of the accident.

The section does not relieve the prosecution of the need to prove the voluntariness of any statement thus made, however, the statutorily compelled nature of the statement may render it inadmissible against the maker where it is given in compliance with the statute.[70] Some provincial legislation prohibits the use of such statements at trial, and it is submitted that even where such a statutory prohibition does not exist, where an accused knowingly gives a statutorily compelled statement, that statement should be *prima facie* inadmissible as a violation of the accused's right to protection from self-incrimination.[71]

(i) Prior Statements

As a general principle, a witness who gives evidence inconsistent with a statement previously made, can have the contradiction put to him or her. If the witness does not adopt the prior statement, then the trier of fact can only use the prior statement to assess the credibility of the witness. It cannot be used for its truth unless it meets the criteria of necessity and reliability as set out by the Supreme Court of Canada in *R. v. B. (K.G.)*.[72] The procedural

---

68 *Ibid.*

69 See Chapter 8, "Common Offences."

70 *R. v. Sarkonak* (1990), 23 M.V.R. (2d) 45 (Man. Q.B.); *R. v. Tveter* (1997), 25 M.V.R. (3d) 228 (Alta. Q.B.). But see also *R. v. White* (1998), 32 M.V.R. (3d) 161, leave to appeal to S.C.C. granted Sept. 17, 1998; and *R. v. Spyker* (1990), 29 M.V.R. (2d) 41 (B.C. S.C.).

71 However, see *R. v. Fitzpatrick*, [1995] 4 S.C.R. 154 for a consideration of this issue in the context of provincial fisheries legislation. It would seem well-reasoned that such a statement should be inadmissible in the trial of a *Criminal Code* offence: *R. v. White, supra*, note 70.

72 (1993), 79 C.C.C. (3d) 257 (S.C.C.). See also *R. v. U. (F.J.)* (1995), 101 C.C.C. (3d) 97 (S.C.C.).

requirements of adducing evidence of prior statements are governed by ss. 20 and 21 of the Ontario *Evidence Act*.[73]

It is also generally inadmissible for an accused person to lead evidence that he or she on an earlier occasion had given an exculpatory statement consistent with his or her evidence at trial. The policy reason for the rule is that such a statement is generally seen as being of little assistance to the trier of fact. It unnecessarily expands the scope of the trial,[74] and is inherently unreliable due to the potential for fabrication.[75] Prior consistent statements are admissible under certain circumstances. They are generally inapplicable to trials of traffic offences, but are generally not admissible to prove the truth of their contents.[76]

4. A PRIMER ON HEARSAY

(a) Introduction

The basic rule against hearsay evidence is frequently misunderstood. The general principle says that an out of court statement made to the witness is not admissible through the mouth of the witness to prove the truth of that statement. In other words, in a prosecution for careless driving, witness X cannot testify that accused A told her that she was driving without her lights on. The prosecution would clearly want to rely on that statement to prove that A was indeed driving without her lights on, and as such would fall foul of the prohibition. The common law rule has undergone substantial change in recent years, such that it can reasonably be said that the rule now operates on a general principle that where *prima facie* hearsay evidence is otherwise necessary (in that it is evidence otherwise unavailable) and reliable (the circumstances surrounding the making of the statement satisfy certain criteria of trustworthiness) then the evidence will be admitted and can be used for the truth of its contents.

Unrepresented accused will regularly proffer hearsay evidence, and the prosecutor is often placed in the awkward position of having to object to evidence which the accused sees as being wholly relevant to their defence. Unless the evidence is clearly not harmful to the prosecution, it is nevertheless important that the objection be registered.

---

73 R.S.O. 1990, c. E-23, ss. 20, 21.

74 *R. v. Beland* (1987), 36 C.C.C. (3d) 481 at 489-90 (S.C.C.); *R. v. Toten* (1993), 83 C.C.C. (3d) 5 (Ont. C.A.).

75 Sopinka, Lederman & Bryant, *The Law of Evidence in Canada* (Butterworths: Markham, 1992) at 307-308.

76 *R. v. Lajoie* (1993), 64 O.A.C. 63; *R. v. J.A.* (1996), 95 O.A.C. 383 (Ont. C.A.).

(b) Multinova Photo-Radar Evidence of Speed As Hearsay Evidence[77]

Photographic evidence of speed in the form of "photo radar" has been held to be admissible hearsay evidence since it possesses a sufficient circumstantial degree of trustworthiness and accuracy.[78]

Certain statutory provisions allow for the reception of hearsay evidence, most notably where evidence is provided by way of a certificate purporting to verify the content of some official record, most often vehicle and plate ownership, and the driving history of a defendant.[79] While in practice it is rarely an issue, s. 47(2) of the *Provincial Offences Act* allows a Court to decide whether or not the defendant is the person referred to in the document on the basis of "credible or trustworthy" information, including hearsay.[80] The Ontario *Evidence Act* also stipulates that there is no requirement to prove the handwriting or official position of anyone certifying to the truth of "any matter or thing as to which he or she is by law authorized or required to certify."[81]

5. *VIVA VOCE* EVIDENCE

Our system of proof places great emphasis on oral or *viva voce* (literally, 'living voice') evidence. The bulk of the evidence presented in any case will come in the form of sworn oral testimony given by witnesses appearing in the courtroom. The rules which govern the way such evidence is to be introduced are intricate, and the art of extracting just the right evidence is one that is difficult for even the most experienced counsel. This short chapter is no place to learn either the art or law of questioning witnesses. We intend only to highlight the principal issues and to relate them to the law dealing with traffic offences. Anyone wishing a more thorough discussion of the art or law of examining witnesses is referred to Earl Levy's leading text, *The Examination of Witnesses in Criminal Cases.*[82]

(a) Preparing Witnesses

It is entirely proper for the party calling a witness to prepare that person to give evidence. This should not, however, go to the point of coaching the witness by encouraging or signalling the witness as to the nature of the

---

77 Photo radar is now no longer in use in Ontario as a result of a change in government policy in 1995.

78 *R. v. Chow* (1991), 68 C.C.C. (3d) 190 (Alta. C.A.). See the general principles of this exception to the rule against the admission of hearsay evidence, *R. v. Khan*, [1990] 2 S.C.R. 531; *R. v. Smith*, [1992] 2 S.C.R. 915.

79 *Highway Traffic Act* s. 210(7); *Provincial Offences Act* s. 47(2), s. 48.1, s. 57(4) *R. v. Vlajkovic* (1994), 5 M.V.R. (3d) 219 (Ont. C.A.).

80 See also *Provincial Offences Act* s. 104.

81 Section 37.

82 3rd Edtn., Carswell, 1994.

evidence that the counsel or agent wants given. Rather the witness should be made aware of the case the party needs to make and the area upon which that party intends to question the witness. There is no property in a witness, and either side is entitled to speak to any witness prior to trial. A witness is not, of course, obliged to talk to counsel.[83]

There is no duty on the defence to call witnesses whose evidence might help the prosecution, though the prosecutor has a duty to present all helpful evidence to the court.[84]

A witness should be told where to stand and how to address the court ("your worship" for a Justice of the Peace, or "your honour" for a judge). The role of counsel or agent should be made clear and the forms of examination in chief, cross-examination and re-examination explained. A witness should be told to speak loud enough to be heard and to address his or her answers to the judge or to counsel asking the question. A witness being cross-examined should never look to counsel who called the witness for the answer.

If language is a problem this is the time (and not the day of trial) to decide whether an interpreter is needed, although the requirement for an interpreter is often taken care of by virtue of the first appearance process.

(b) Exclusion of Witnesses

Before any evidence is tendered, counsel is entitled to ask, and a judge has the authority to exclude from the courtroom any prospective witness.[85] The reason for this rule is to prevent subsequent witnesses from knowing the evidence which has already been given, thus minimizing the danger of a witness shaping his or her evidence to conform with the theory of one side of the case. This is a common law rule stemming from the Court's inherent authority to control its own process, and differs in that sense from s. 52 of the *Provincial Offences Act* which grants a judge authority to exclude the accused and members of the public under certain limited circumstances. While a witness who disobeys such an order may be in contempt of court, the evidence of that witness should still be allowed. The fact that the witness has heard earlier witnesses only affects the weight of his or her evidence.[86] As a rule an order excluding a witness will be granted as a matter of course.[87] Normally, the investigating officer is allowed to remain in the courtroom to instruct the prosecutor. The defendant can only be excluded from the courtroom under very limited and rarely invoked situations.

---

83 For a discussion of prosecutorial considerations when interviewing witnesses, see *The Commission on Proceedings Involving Guy Paul Morin*, Fred Kaufman C.M., Q.L., Commissioner (1990), Vol. 2, p. 1221.

84 *Wu (alias Wu Chuck) v. R.* (1934), 62 C.C.C. 90 (S.C.C.).

85 *R. v. Hoyt* (1943), 93 C.C.C. 306 (N.B. S.C., App. Div.).

86 *R. v. Dobberthien*, [1975] 2 S.C.R. 560.

87 *R. v. Learn* (1981), 63 C.C.C. (2d) 191 (Ont. H.C.).

Where expert opinion evidence is to be led, the court will normally allow an expert to stay in the courtroom to hear the background which will form the basis of his or her opinion.[88]

(c) Other Matters Relating to Oral Evidence

Some jurisdictions permit the informant officer to appear as the prosecutor, testifying on his own behalf, and cross-examining witnesses. For most minor offences, particularly parking violations, this is merely a matter of administrative expediency where the charge presents little or no issues of legal complexity and most trials are *pro forma*. The practice has been upheld as a justified infringement of an accused's s. 11(d) right under the *Charter* to be tried by an independent tribunal.[89]

Section 39(1) of the *Provincial Offences Act* empowers the Court to issue a summons to any witness who is able to give material evidence in a proceeding under that Act.

With the consent of all parties, the court may consider evidence against an accused on more than one charge.[90] This will be common in charges arising from the *Highway Traffic Act* where a defendant is often charged with two or more offences arising out of a single incident. An accused's consent is not required, however, for two offences contained in the same information to be tried together. In other words, s. 38(2) of the *Provincial Offences Act* allows for severance where it is determined that "the ends of justice" require it. The general rule is that offences under the *Highway Traffic Act* arising out of the same circumstances should be tried together.[91] A defendant may be convicted of an offence, even though that offence is not charged, where all the elements have been proven and it is included in the offence charged.[92]

While to all intents and purposes rendered superfluous by the *Canadian Charter of Rights and Freedoms*, the basic principles of the conduct of a trial are statutorily defined in the *Provincial Offences Act*:

46. (2) The defendant is entitled to make full answer and defence.

(3) The prosecutor or defendant, as the case may be, may examine and cross-examine witnesses.

(4) The court may receive and act upon any facts agreed upon by the defendant and prosecutor without proof or evidence.

(5) Despite section 8 of the *Evidence Act*, the defendant is not a compellable witness for the prosecution.

---

88 *Bleta v. R.* [1964] S.C.R. 561.

89 *R. v. Randall* (1989) 8 W.C.B. (2d) 15 (B.C. Co. Ct.); *R. v. 397273 Ontario Ltd.*, [1993] O.J. No. 3417 (Ont. Prov. Div.); *R. v. Kennedy*, [1997] O.J. No. 2717 (Ont. Gen. Div.).

90 *Provincial Offences Act* s. 47(1); *R. v. Clunas*, [1992] 1 S.C.R. 595.

91 *R. v. Vlajkovic*, *supra* note 79.

92 *Provincial Offences Act* s. 55.

Evidence in proceedings under the *Provincial Offences Act* must be recorded,[93] and this invariably means by audio tape recording which can later be transcribed if required for further proceedings.

(d) Examination-in-chief

Sometimes called 'direct examination' (the American expression), examination-in-chief occurs when the party calling the witness elicits evidence by asking the witness questions. As a general rule, a witness may not be asked a leading question in examination-in-chief. The reason for this rule is self-evident:[94]

> Some of the reasons given for this prohibition are the danger that a witness who is nervous will simply assent to a question or give the easiest answer and accordingly give evidence which he did not intend to give or which he does not believe. Further, leading questions are objectionable because of the possibility of pre-arrangement between examiner and the witness as well as the impropriety of suggesting the existence of facts which are not in evidence.

> To this one can only add the danger of a witness who innocently desires to please the party who has put him or her in the box and is therefore open to suggestion from that party.

(e) Leading Questions

A leading question is one which improperly suggests to the witness the answer which the questioner expects to be given. As Levy observes:[95]

> A leading question is one that suggests the desired answer to the witness. Where the questioner wishes to elicit from the witness a description of a hat that the witness observed, the witness should not be asked: "Was Mr. Jones wearing a white straw hat?" The witness should be guided through a series of questions of this nature: "Did Mr. Jones have anything on his head? What was it? What was the hat made of? What colour was the hat?" A question is also leading if it assumes a fact in dispute which has been given in evidence so that the witness has ostensibly to admit the fact in order to answer the question.

Leading questions are proper when the topic is one which is not in dispute. Thus it is often proper for a witness to be lead through evidence as to background (address, occupation, etc.) and even lead up to the time and place of the events in issue.

---

93 *Provincial Offences Act* s. 83. Mechanical failure causing an incomplete record will invariably lead to a new trial being ordered if an appeal is taken: *R. v. Harbour View* (1984), 13 W.C.B. 319 (Ont. Prov. Ct.).

94 Bruce Long, *The Prosecutor's Handbook*, 1987, Ministry of the Attorney General, p. B11-1. See also *R. v. Deacon* (1947), 87 C.C.C. 271 (Man. C.A.); *R. v. Williams* (1982), 66 C.C.C. (2d) 234 (Ont. C.A.).

95 *Supra* note 82.

(f) Cross-Examination

Cross-examination is the *sine qua non* of our adversarial system. It is essential in testing the strength or frailty of the opposing party's case. Probably because of its central importance, it is the subject of many rules and practices. Good cross-examination only comes with experience, but it is important to know some of the more fundamental rules.

As a matter of procedure, in Part I and II infractions, the defendant's opportunity to challenge the evidence of the officer who issued the ticket is specifically drawn to the charged person's attention, and the defendant is required to indicate at the time of requesting trial whether he or she intends to challenge the officer's evidence.[96]

The rules respecting proper cross-examination are many.[97] In general, a party is given wide latitude in cross-examination, but the prosecution is more restricted in its approach than the accused. Some of the more frequently encountered prohibitions on cross-examination are the following:

- the prosecutor cannot cross-examine the accused as to "bad character" unless the accused first puts his or her character in issue;[98]
- It is improper to ask the accused (or any witness) why another witness would be lying.[99] The credibility or veracity of a witness is something for the judge to assess;
- It is improper, both ethically and legally for counsel to ask questions which are known to be inadmissible. Thus counsel should not examine documents or other evidence which he or she is not entitled to put into evidence,[100] particularly after the evidence has already been ruled inadmissible;[101]
- But counsel may put unproven facts to a witness, although where the witness denies the fact counsel will be stuck with the answer.[102] Such hypotheticals should not amount to prejudicial or abusive examination, and the judge retains the discretion to prevent questioning along this line;[103]

---

96 *Provincial Offences Act* s. 5.2(1), 18.1.2. It would seem that in practice this option is rarely exercised, either because it is not specifically explained to the attention of the defendant at the time of requesting trial, or, more likely, because the defendant can then rely on the prosecution inevitably withdrawing the charge if the officer fails to attend on the trial date. This is perhaps unfortunate, as many defendants indicate that they wish to challenge the officer's evidence and then plead guilty with an explanation, thus defeating the purpose of the section, that of administrative efficiency. See, however, *R. v. Chatterton* (February 10, 1995) (Ont. Prov. Div.) for comments on this section.

97 For a thorough consideration of the limits of proper cross-examination, see Peter M. Brauti, "Improper Cross-Examination," (1997), 40 C.L.Q. 69.

98 *R. v. McNamara (No. 1)* (1981), 56 C.C.C. (2d) 193 (Ont. C.A.), affirmed 19 C.C.C. (3d) 1 (S.C.C.), *sub nom. R. v. Canadian Dredge & Dock Co.*

99 *R. v. Vandenberghe* (1995), 96 C.C.C. (3d) 371 (Ont. C.A.); *R. v. F. (A.)* (1996), 1 C.R. (5th) 382 (Ont. C.A.).

100 *R. v. Howard* (1989), 48 C.C.C. (3d) 38 (S.C.C.).

101 *R. v. Calder* (1996), 105 C.C.C. (3d) 1 (S.C.C.).

102 *Fox v. General Medical Council*, [1960] 1 W.L.R. 1017 (P.C.).

103 *R. v. F. (J.E.)* (1993), 85 C.C.C. (3d) 457 (Ont. C.A.).

- Overly aggressive cross-examination will not be permitted. The judge is duty bound to protect a witness from abusive or harassing cross-examination.[104] Constantly repeating questions which have already been answered is improper.[112]

(g) Rebuttal Evidence

The prosecution is obliged to call all the evidence required to prove its case in chief, and the judge should exercise his or her discretion to allow the prosecution to reopen its case judicially.[106] It is not proper to 'hold back' evidence in order to surprise the accused. Where evidence is only marginally relevant to the prosecution's case in chief, or where the evidence is only made relevant by virtue of evidence led by the defence, then the prosecution will be entitled to call that evidence in reply.[107]

6. INTERPRETERS

It is not unusual for a witness or a defendant to require someone to interpret the court proceedings into a language other than English or French. In larger metropolitan areas, this is more common and courts have translators readily available within the building. As pointed out already, the first appearance process has assisted in the efficient assignment of interpreters where required. Where the request for trial form indicates that the accused has requested an interpreter, and the interpreter has not been assigned to the court, the prosecution may request an adjournment. It is submitted, however, that the prosecution should only do so where it is not in the public interest to withdraw the charge. If, however, an accused is capable of proceeding in the language of the court, then the prosecution is entitled to ask that the trial proceed.

Section 84 of the *Provincial Offences Act* authorizes the use of interpreters in proceedings under the Act. There is nothing, however, requiring an 'official' interpreter: anyone who is proficient in both the language of the trial (English or French) and the language spoken by the witness or defendant may act as an interpreter.[108] Where a defendant does not speak the language of the proceedings, he or she is allowed to have an interpreter sit at the defence table and translate the proceedings. An interpreter sworn under s. 84(1) of the *Provincial Offences Act* should be sworn in the following manner:[109]

---

104 *R. v. Varga* (1994), 90 C.C.C. (3d) 484 (Ont. C.A.).

112
  R. v. Fanjoy (1985), 21 C.C.C. (3d) 312 (S.C.C.).

106 *R. v. G. (S.G.)*, [1997] 2 S.C.R. 716.

107 *R. v. Ostell* (1992), 15 W.C.B. (2d) 427 (Ont. Gen. Div.).

108 *Provincial Offences Act* s. 84(2).

109 Rules in Provincial Offences Proceedings, R.R.O. 1990, Reg. 200, subrule 27(2). The oath to be given to an interpreter sworn under the less formal authority of subsection 84(2) is contained in subrule 27(2).

I, ... do swear (or solemnly affirm) that I am capable of translating and will translate to the best of my skill and ability from . . . . (language) to . . . . (language of proceedings) and from . . . . (language of proceedings) to . . . . (language) in this proceeding.

SO HELP ME GOD (Omit this last line in an affirmation).

Pursuant to s. 126(1) of the *Courts of Justice Act*, R.S.O. 1990, c. C.43, an accused who speaks French has the right to require that the proceedings be bilingual. However, it would seem that it is no violation of the accused's rights if the prosecutor is not bilingual as long as there is an interpreter present.[110] Section 14 of the *Charter of Rights* provides that "a party or witness in any proceedings who does not understand or speak the language in which the proceedings are conducted or who is deaf has the right to the assistance of an interpreter". The right to an interpreter is also a component of the constitutional right of an accused to make full answer and defence.

7. DEMONSTRATIVE EVIDENCE

(a) Photographs[111]

Often the best way to demonstrate some point in court is to present photographs. For example, in a case where the charge is one of failing to obey a traffic sign, the defence might present photographs showing that it is impossible to see the sign from the driver's position because of foliage. In such a case, a photograph can dramatically and conclusively bring home the point to the court.

The rule of photographic evidence in traffic offence trials has become particularly important since the introduction of "photo radar" evidence in speeding cases.[112]

Before a photograph may be admitted the party offering it must establish, by oral evidence, that it is a fair and accurate depiction of the scene or thing shown and is relevant to some issue at trial.[113] In most cases, it will be important to establish that the photograph was taken at or very near to the time of the alleged offence. Usually this will be done by calling the photographer, but anyone familiar with the true appearance of the scene may

---

110 *R. v. Chevrier* Ont. C.A. Charron J.A., application for leave to appeal refused August 7, 1997.

111 The discussion here relates to photographic evidence of surrounding circumstances as opposed to establishing identity where a judge is called on to make an evidentiary assessment of the photograph: *R. v. Nikolovski, supra,* note 1.

112 See *R. v. Tsang* (April 22, 1998), (B.C. Prov. Ct.); *R. v. Bosworth* (August 27, 1998) (B.C. Prov. Ct.).

113 *Dilabbio v. R.* (1965), 46 C.R. 131 (Ont. C.A.).

confirm the accuracy of the photograph[114] (although Levy[115] suggests that *Charette v. R.*[116] holds that these factors are now only applicable to weight, and not admissibility).

As a practical matter, where photographs are made an exhibit, they or any other exhibit can be returned to the defendant immediately following the trial on the consent of both parties, otherwise it is held with the court until the expiry of any appeal periods.[117]

(b) Videotapes or Films

Videotapes can provide cogent and convincing evidence. Their use as viable, real and testimonial pieces of evidence has been recognized in a variety of contexts over the years.[118] The Supreme Court of Canada recently had this to say about videotapes in the context of evidence of identity:[119]

> The video camera on the other hand is never subject to stress. Through tumultuous events it continues to record accurately and dispassionately all that comes before it. Although silent, it remains a constant, unbiased witness with instant and total recall of all that it observed. The trier of fact may review the evidence of this silent witness as often as desired. The tape may be stopped and studied at a critical juncture.

Generally speaking, evidence in the form of videotape may be admissible on the same terms as a photograph. In summary:[120]

> Once it is established that a videotape has not been altered or changed, and that it depicts the scene of a crime, then it becomes admissible and relevant evidence. Not only is the tape (or photograph) real evidence in the sense that that term has been used in earlier cases, but it is to a certain extent, testimonial evidence as well. It can and should be used by a trier of fact in determining whether a crime has been committed and whether the accused before the court committed the crime. It may indeed be a silent, trustworthy, unemotional, unbiased and accurate witness who has complete and instant recall of events. It may provide such strong and convincing evidence that of itself it will demonstrate clearly either the innocence or guilt of the accused.

---

114 *R. v. Wildman* (1981), 60 C.C.C. (2d) 289 reversed on other grounds, [1984] 2 S.C.R. 311; *R. v. Creemer and Cormier* (1968), 1 C.R.N.S. 146 (N.S. S.C., A.D.).

115 Levy, *supra*, note 82, p. 34.

116 (1980), 51 C.C.C. (2d) 350 (S.C.C.).

117 *Provincial Offences Act* s. 48.

118 *R. v. Pleich* (1980), 55 C.C.C. (2d) 13; *R. v. Rowbotham* (1988), 41 C.C.C. (3d) 1; *R. v. Leaney*, [1989] 2 S.C.R. 393; *R. v. L. (D.O.)*, [1993] 4 S.C.R. 419; *R. v. B. (K.G.)*, *supra* note 72; *R. v. Nikolovski*, *supra* note 1.

119 *R. v. Nikolovski*, *supra* note 1 at 1210. In *R. v. Maloney (No. 2)* (1976), 29 C.C.C. (2d) 431 (Ont. Co. Ct.), however, evidence in the form of a videotape of a hockey fight was excluded because it was in slow motion and therefore not a true representation of what had happened.

120 *R. v. Nikolovski*, *supra* note 1 at 1215.

> The weight to be accorded that evidence can be assessed from a viewing of the videotape. The degree of clarity and quality of the tape, and to a lesser extent the length of time during which the accused appears on the videotape, will all go towards establishing the weight which a trier of fact may properly place upon the evidence.

The trier of fact assesses the weight that should be accorded the evidence of the videotape in the same manner as he or she assesses the weight of the evidence given by *viva voce* testimony.[121]

8. COLLISION RECONSTRUCTIONS

Reconstruction evidence traditionally consists of police evidence concerning road measurements, tire marks, distances between cars, etc. The potential exists, however, for a party to introduce accident reconstructions through the use of computerized images. This form of evidence is very new (indeed may only have been used in the United States), and its admissibility will undoubtedly be challenged. It is submitted that it will be subject to the rules relating to expert evidence (see below).

9. EXPERT EVIDENCE

(a) The Normal Rule Against Opinion Evidence

As a general rule, courts are interested in fact, not opinion. Thus a witness is prohibited from expressing an opinion on a matter in issue. There are two exceptions to this rule. First, a witness may give an opinion on a matter about which he or she is qualified to testify as an expert. Secondly, any witness can offer an opinion about particular matters deemed to be within the realm of everyone's knowledge, and which thus require no special expertise.[122] For example, any witness could testify as to their estimate of how fast a car was travelling,[123] but only a properly qualified expert could give an opinion on how fast a vehicle would have had to have been travelling to make a given set of skid marks.

Speeding is of course the most common offence which will involve expert testimony at trial, that testimony invariably coming from the police officer who operated the specialized equipment used to detect speeding vehicles. But the scope of expert evidence is considerable. Experts may even testify on matters which would not at first blush be susceptible to that kind of analysis. Thus they have testified to the circumstances consistent with classic signs of a driver

---

121 *Ibid.*
122 *R. v. Fisher*, [1961] O.W.N. 94 (Ont. C.A.).
123 *R. v. German* (1949), 89 C.C.C. 90 (Ont. C.A.); *R. ex rel. Neely v. Tait*, [1965] 1 C.C.C. 16 (N.B. Co. Ct.).

falling asleep or displaying a lack of attention, suddenly awakening or regaining awareness, and taking evasive action.[124]

The Ontario *Evidence Act* limits to three the number of experts each side may call without leave of the judge.[125] In practice, however, it would seem that this limitation would apply to each issue rather than constituting an overall cap.

(b) Matters Where Expertise is not Required

While the law relating to expert evidence has undergone some changes in recent years, the fundamental test for when an expert is necessary has remained the same:

> An expert's opinion is admissible to furnish the Court with scientific information which is likely to be outside the experience and knowledge of a judge or jury. If on the proven facts a judge or jury can form their own conclusions without help, then the opinion of the expert is unnecessary.[126]

As already suggested, there are some areas in which everyone is an expert. That is, there is no need for special skill before a court will listen to an opinion without a special qualification. These include:

- estimates of a vehicle's speed;
- whether a person is intoxicated;[127]
- handwriting;[128]
- age;[129]
- identity of a person.[130]

(c) The Criteria for Admissibility of Expert Evidence

Expert evidence will be received if:[131]

- it is relevant to a fact in issue;[132]
- the expert is properly qualified;
- the expert evidence is of assistance to the trier of fact; and

---

124 *R. v. Kozun* (1996), 31 W.C.B. (2d) 433 (Sask. Prov. Ct.) (Appeal allowed on other grounds).

125 Section 12.

126 *R. v. Abbey* (1982), 29 C.R. (3d) 193 at 210 (S.C.C.).

127 *Graat v. R.*, [1982] 2 S.C.R. 819.

128 *Petre v. R.*, [1933] S.C.R. 69.

129 *R. v. Cox*, [1898] 1 Q.B. 179.

130 *R. v. Lanigan* (1983), 53 N.B.R. (2d) 388 (N.B. C.A.).

131 *R. v. Mohan* (1994), 89 C.C.C. (3d) 402 (S.C.C.).

132 See "Relevance and Materiality" above.

- the evidence is not subject to some rule of exclusion.

Where the evidence offered relates to a novel scientific technique or area of knowledge, then it must meet a threshold test of reliability which takes into account the validity or *bona fide* nature of the subject matter.[133]

Even if the expert evidence satisfies all other criteria with respect to admissibility, it will still be excluded if it contravenes an exclusionary rule apart from the rule against opinion evidence itself.[134] The most likely rule of exclusion to which the evidence may succumb is that which forbids evidence going only to the disposition of the accused person to commit the crime. It is particularly important to ensure that this criteria is adhered to when it is the prosecution which seeks to tender the evidence. If it is established that the expert evidence is relevant to an issue other than simply disposition, such as the identity of the perpetrator, then the probative value of the evidence in relation to that issue must be weighed against its prejudicial effect on the accused. Expert testimony will also sometimes appear to fall foul of the rule against hearsay evidence. However, it is well-established in Canadian courts that, "there is an acceptable hearsay component in the make-up of every expert's knowledge which is drawn upon in formulating the opinion."[135]

Expert evidence is to be weighed by the trier of fact in the same manner as any other evidence. When faced with conflicting expert opinions on a crucial point, the trier of fact can only act on the basis of the prosecution's expert evidence if he or she feels sure that it was correct.[136]

(d) Qualifying the Expert

The proper qualification of an expert demands two requirements: first, the expert must possess a sufficient level of competence or qualification in the area in which he or she is to testify. Second, the expert should testify *only* with respect to the areas of expertise in which he or she has been qualified. In other words, the expert should not stray beyond the bounds of his or her properly qualified knowledge. In *Mohan, supra*, Sopinka J. put it this way:[137]

> the evidence must be given by a witness who is shown to have acquired special or peculiar knowledge through study or experience in respect of the matters on which he or she undertakes to testify.

---

133 *R. v. Melaragni* (1992), 73 C.C.C. (3d) 348 (Ont. Gen. Div.). See also D. Paciocco, "Evaluating Expert Opinion Evidence for the Purpose of Determining Admissibility: Lessons From the Law of Evidence" (1994), 27 C.R. (4th) 302.

134 *R. v. Morin* (1988), 44 C.C.C. (3d) 193 (S.C.C.).

135 *Supra*, note 75 at p. 547.

136 *R. v. Bourguignon* (1997), 118 C.C.C. (3d) 43 (Ont. C.A.); *R. v. Molnar* (1990), 55 C.C.C. (3d) 446 at 447 (Ont. C.A.).

137 *Supra* note 131 at p. 414.

As long as the court is satisfied that the expert possesses knowledge that will assist the trier of fact, the extent or depth of the witness' qualifications is a matter of weight for the jury.[138] A determination as to the adequacy of the witness' qualifications can be reflected in many factors including *inter alia*, academic qualifications, practical experience, length of time in their chosen profession, publications and pedagogical record. Before a court will listen to the opinion of a witness on some point, the party tendering the witness as an expert must satisfy the court that the witness has some special knowledge or skill which will allow him or her to help the court understand the evidence.

There is no requirement, however, that an expert's knowledge be supported by any formal course of training. Indeed, it is often the case that one would want to have someone with practical experience rather than 'book-learning'.[139] For example, where a defence of unavoidable mechanical breakdown is offered, there is no reason to believe that a local automobile mechanic will be any less credible or helpful to the court than a university educated engineer.

When qualifying an expert for the court, it is acceptable to lead the witness. In cases where the witness' qualifications are extensive, it is appropriate to file the witness' resumé with the court as an exhibit. When the witness' various qualifications (whether they come from a course of study or from experience) have been put before the court, the party offering the expert should ask that the witness be accepted by the court as an expert in the appropriate area. Defence counsel may cross-examine with respect to the validity of the witness' qualifications. Unless the area of proposed expertise is particularly novel, however, this is usually done in the course of normal cross-examination, and the extent of the witness' expertise is a matter of weight.

(e) Experts and Radar

Radar evidence, when properly proven, establishes a *prima facie* case[140] and, unchallenged, is convincing beyond a reasonable doubt. It must be remembered, however, that radar is simply a tool and that, like any tool, it can malfunction or be improperly used. Until the court is convinced beyond a reasonable doubt that the radar was in good working order and properly operated, evidence of a reading is useless.

As Manraj and Haines observe,[141] modern radar devices are "deceptively simple" to use. It must nonetheless be remembered that the instrument is a sophisticated scientific device which is subject to alteration by the slightest

---

138 *R. v. Marquard* (1993), 85 C.C.C. (3d) 193 at 224 (S.C.C.) *per* McLachlin J.

139 *Rice v. Sockett* (1912), 8 D.L.R. 84 (Ont. Div. Ct.); *R. v. Dugadzic* (1981), 57 C.C.C. (2d) 517 (Ont. C.A.).

140 *R. v. Ayler* Unreported August 20 1981 (Prov. Off. Appeal Court).

141 *Supra*, note 52.

upset. For example, a surface scratch of only 1/20,000 of a centimetre on a tuning fork used in calibrating a radar device can lead to an inaccurate reading of up to eight kilometres per hour.[142]

As explained above, before anyone, whether police officer or civilian witness, is allowed to give opinion evidence on the functioning or operation of a radar unit that person should be qualified as an expert in the operation of radar devices (though a witness need not have an understanding of the scientific principles which support the working of the instrument).

(f) A Prosecution Checklist[143]

The proper operation of the radar on the day in question should be proven. The prosecution should prove that:

- the radar vehicle was properly stationed;
- the radar speed control unit was working (no false readings, fluctuations);
- the radar was properly calibrated (either by a proven tuning fork or by running a car with a proven speedometer through the beam before and after the shift);
- the conditions under which the vehicle entered the beam;
- the reading and notation of the speed from the unit.

In proving the expertise of the operator, the prosecutor should put before the court:

- formal training programmes the officer has taken;
- years of experience;
- types of units used; and
- the techniques used in this case (stationary vehicle, moving same direction, moving opposite direction).

The police officer witness will generally give this information as a matter of course without even being asked these specific questions by the prosecutor. Thus counsel should pay careful attention to the officer's evidence in order to ensure that its *pro forma* appearance does not leave out or misstate any important information.

The use of laser speed detectors by police officers is now commonplace. Their validity is still being established in the courts, but will undoubtedly soon reach a status similar to that of traditional radar. Currently, an officer will often testify that he or she tested the laser device by passing it through a traditional radar.

---

142 *Ibid.*, at pp. 26-32.
143 *Ibid.*

(g) Questioning the Expert

An expert is presented to give an opinion to the judge or justice to assist him or her in understanding the significance of evidence already before the court. The proper form of questioning, then, is to present the facts as established by the evidence (or as the evidence at least suggests) to the expert as a hypothetical and then to ask his or her opinion on that scenario.

For example, if, in a radar case, there is evidence that there was an electrical storm, an international airport, and a large neon sign near the officer's radar unit, the witness should be asked what affect, in his or her opinion, these factors might have on the accuracy of the reading.[144] "If there had been an electrical storm on the scene would that, in your opinion, affect the reading?" "What if there was an international airport within two miles of the place where the reading was taken?" "Would your opinion change if I suggested that there was a large neon sign less than fifty feet from the line of sight where the officer's radar reading was taken?"[145] The expert's answers to these questions will allow the judge to understand the significance of the evidence led on these issues.

(h) Laying the Basis

The expert's function is to interpret evidence for the court and so it is important to be sure that there is something for the expert to interpret. This is called laying the basis for the expert's opinion. Continuing our radar example, if there was no evidence suggesting that there was an airport near the location of the radar unit, it would be improper to ask the expert how that would change his or her opinion. Without some evidence before the court suggesting that there was an airport, such a question is irrelevant.

(i) A Defence Checklist for Radar

- Jurisdiction must be established;
- The officer visually observed the target vehicle and formed the opinion that it appeared to be speeding. This observation was then corroborated by the radar reading;
- The instrument must be operated by someone trained in its operation. He or she need not have knowledge of the electronics or mechanism of the device but must be thoroughly familiar with its use. That, it is submitted, means that she actually has knowledge of the specific radar instrument she is using and not merely a general knowledge of how radar instruments should be operated. In short, the training must be adequate;

---

144 The examples are drawn from Manraj and Haines *supra*, note 52 at pp. 66-7.
145 See generally Levy, *supra* note 82, chapter 12.

- Evidence relating to the testing of the instrument should include the following:

  (i)   The operator must give evidence that he or she conducted an approved test of the instrument. The officer may establish this by showing that he or she read the manual which relates to the specific device operated, and which indicated that certain tests should be performed in a specific manner. Otherwise, the officer may indicate that he or she was trained with respect to the particular device being operated, certain tests are required to be performed. Generally speaking, this will entail an automatic internal calibration test and a calibrated tuning fork test being performed;

  (ii) Following *R. v. Bourque, supra*, there may be a requirement that the accuracy of the tuning fork be proven beyond a reasonable doubt. This requirement may, however, be limited to jurisdictions which have legislation requiring a certificate of accuracy relating to the tuning fork used be tendered into evidence. It may be argued that such a requirement is advisable in light of the fact that an accused motorist is denied the opportunity to substantiate the radar reading. Radar is today accepted as a technological wonder which is thought to be virtually infallible. A requirement that the tuning forks used to test the device are themselves accurate simply provides an additional safeguard against human and mechanical errors;[146]

  (iii) Time of tests must be noted before and after occurrence. Obviously, they should be performed before and after the speed of the accused motorist has been captured by the instrument. Tests performed after the motorist is targeted should be performed in the same manner as they were prior to his being pulled over. In the usual course of events, an officer will test the device at the beginning and end of the time spent at any one location. The cases do not establish that it is absolutely necessary but it is preferable if a patrol car travelling at a pre-determined speed is run through the radar field in order to ensure that the device is truly capable of accurately measuring speeds;

  (iv) The tests performed should have satisfied the officer that the instrument was operating properly and was capable of accurately

---

146 This, of course, imposes an additional burden on the prosecution. The argument is made that, ultimately, such safeguards lead to an absurd result. Do we then require the prosecution to show that the device which established the tuning forks to be accurate, itself is accurate? And what about the device that established this device was accurate? Moreover, tuning forks are calibrated to a certain reading and are usually then stamped or engraved with that reading. If the radar device being tested produces the exact reading as that indicated by the tuning fork, it defies reason to suggest that there is an exact corresponding inaccuracy in the device being tested.

registering speeds. Moreover, the officer should be sure that the device operated properly in reference to the motorist's vehicle;

(v) The range of the instrument should be established, as should the fact that the instrument was capable of accurately registering speeds across this entire range. Some cases indicate this requirement is not essential, however, the radar operator should be able to establish that the target vehicle was within the operational area of the beam at the time the reading was displayed;

• The officer may be challenged by suggesting that he or she flagged down an allegedly speeding vehicle whose speed is attributable to the speed of another vehicle within the range of this unit.[147] Also, the device should have been used in an area where road conditions are such that there is minimum possibility of distortion;

• Identity of the driver must be established, usually by the driver having produced for the officer a valid driver's licence;

• Like any evidence, radar readings may be rebutted on cross-examination. A reasonable doubt may be raised either by matters elicited in examination-in-chief or cross-examination of defence evidence. For example, while the failure to show the radar reading to the defendant is not fatal where the reading has been locked in, it would probably go to credibility that an officer refused to show the motorist the radar reading upon request. Often, police officers do not make any notes when they charge a person with speeding, and they may flag down a great many speeders on any given day. Their inability to recall specifics relating to the charge may enable the defence to raise a reasonable doubt as to the accuracy of the radar reading.

---

147 Laser speed detectors purport to overcome this problem.

5

Speeding

1. INTRODUCTION

Speeding is easily defined as driving a motor vehicle at a rate of speed in excess of that permitted by statute, which can be municipal, provincial, or in some cases even federal.[1] Speeding under provincial traffic legislation is a regulatory offence, and it should not be considered a crime. It seems inevitable that, at some point, all drivers will speed, but as Manraj and Haines observe,

> [s]ome get caught and some do not and there is nothing in a speeding conviction that in any way compromises a citizen's honesty and integrity and uprightness or render's him less worthy in society's eyes.[2]

Of course, if in a given instance, speeding indicates something more, such as negligence or recklessness, the driving may support more serious charges such as careless driving, or even dangerous driving under the *Criminal Code*.

2. THE STATUTORY PROVISIONS

Rate of speed is found in the following sections of the provincial traffic legislation.

---

1 *Hargett v. Civil Service Commission*, 49 Ill. App. 3d 856 (1977); *People v. Nasella*, 155 N.Y.S. 2d 4633 (Magistrates Ct. 1956); *Thompson v. State*, 453 P. 2d 314 (Okla., 1969). For an example of federal law regulating speeding, see *R. v. Potts* (1982), 14 M.V.R. 72 (Ont. C.A.), leave to appeal refused (1982), 66 C.C.C. (2d) 219n (S.C.C.).

2 Manraj and Haines, *The Law of Speeding and Radar* (2nd ed.) (Markham: Butterworth & Co., 1991) at p. 2.

Province	*Sections*
Alberta	69 – 75[3]
British Columbia	145 – 147[4]
Manitoba	95 – 105[5]
New Brunswick	140 – 146[6]
Newfoundland	110 – 111[7]
Nova Scotia	100 – 106[8]
Ontario	128 – 130, 132[9]
Prince Edward Island	176 – 177[10]
Saskatchewan	36 – 41[11]
Yukon Territories	117, 131 – 133[12]
N.W.T.	169 – 180[13]

3. THE MENTAL ELEMENT OF THE OFFENCE

(a) Absolute Liability

In *R. v. Sault Ste. Marie (City)*,[14] Dickson J. articulated three categories of criminal and quasi-criminal offences: full *mens rea* offences; strict liability; and absolute liability.[15] Speeding is generally understood to be an absolute liability offence, that is, one

> … in respect of which the Legislature had made it clear that guilt would follow proof merely of the proscribed act.[16]

To obtain a conviction, the prosecution need not show that the defendant intended to speed. Intention is, *prima facie*, irrelevant to the offence. Nor may the defendant raise the defence of due diligence in speeding. In other words, it is equally irrelevant that the defendant took all reasonable steps to avoid speeding.

There is ample authority supporting the proposition that speeding is an offence of absolute liability. In *R. v. Gillis*,[17] it was held that *mens rea* is not an essential element of the offence of speeding. Therefore, the defendant was

---

3 R.S.A. 1980, c. H-7.

4 *Motor Vehicle Act*, R.S.B.C. 1996, c. 318.

5 S.M. 1985-86, c. 3.

6 *Motor Vehicle Act*, R.S.N.B. c. M-17.

7 R.S.N. 1990, c. H-3.

8 *Motor Vehicle Act*, R.S.N.S. 1989, c. 293.

9 *Highway Traffic Act*, R.S.O. 1990, c. H.8.

10 *Highway Traffic Act*, R.S.P.E.I. 1988, c. H-5.

11 *Higway Traffic Act*, S.S. 1996, c. H-3.2.

12 *Motor Vehicles Act*, R.S.Y. 1980, c. 118.

13 *Motor Vehicles Act*, R.S.N.W.T. 1988, c. M-16.

14 [1978] 2 S.C.R. 1299 (S.C.C.).

15 See Chapter 1 (*supra*) for a complete discussion of this issue.

properly convicted despite his belief, based on a defective speedometer, that he was driving within the speed limit.

In *R. v. Hickey*,[18] the defence argued that a defective speedometer caused the defendant to honestly believe that he was not speeding. The investigating officer tested the speedometer at the scene and confirmed that it was not working properly. The Ontario Court of Appeal, however, ultimately held that the offence was one of absolute liability. The defendant's defence was of no application, and did not prevent a conviction.

The British Columbia Court of Appeal reached a similar conclusion in *R. v. Harper*,[19] and *R. v. Geraghty*,[20] as did the Quebec Court of Appeal in *R. v. Lemieux*.[21]

(b) Strict Liability

Since the first edition of this text, however, cases have emerged which hold to the contrary from *Hickey* and *Gillis*, *viz.* that speeding is in fact an offence of strict liability, and as such carries with it the due diligence defence.

For instance, in *R. v. Hicks*,[22] Hall J. held that, if speeding under the Nova Scotia *Motor Vehicle Act* is one of absolute liability, then it offends the *Charter*. Rather than strike down the legislation as offensive to the *Charter*, His Honour saved the legislation from such a fate by declaring that it was one of strict liability. On that basis, the defences of reasonable mistake of fact, and due diligence are available.

A similar result occurred in *R. v. Williams*,[23] where the defendant was charged with speeding under s. 106(2) of the Nova Scotia *Motor Vehicle Act*.[24] At trial he was convicted, it being held that speeding is an offence of absolute liability. In the Court of Appeal, however, this was overturned and a new trial

---

16 *Supra* note 14, at 1326.
17 (1974), 18 C.C.C. (2d) 190 (N.S. C.A.).
18 (1976), 30 C.C.C. (2d) 416 (Ont. C.A.).
19 (1986), 44 M.V.R. 313 (B.C. C.A.).
20 (1990), 22 M.V.R. (2d) 57 (B.C. C.A.).
21 (1978), 41 C.C.C. (2d) 33 (Que. C.A.).
22 (1991), 35 M.V.R.(2d) 311 (N.S. Co. Ct.).
23 (1992), 39 M.V.R. (2d) 315 (N.S. C.A.).
24 R.S.N.S. 1989, c. 293, s. 106(1).

> 106(1) Notwithstanding any other provision of this Act, but subject to subsection (2) and Section 109, no person shall drive a motor vehicle at a speed in excess of eighty kilometres per hour on any highway at any time.
>
> (2) The Minister or the Provincial Traffic Authority may fix rates of speed in excess of eighty kilometres per hour, but not in excess of one hundred and ten kilometres per hour, for certain highways and may erect and maintain signs containing notification of such rate of speed, and the driver of a motor vehicle who exceeds the rate of speed so fixed shall be guilty of an offence.

ordered. Section 106(2) was held to create an offence of strict and not absolute liability.[25]

This line of reasoning is not isolated to Nova Scotia. In *R. v. Morris*[26] the defendant was charged with speeding, but testified that she increased her speed in order to change lanes. This was done to avoid collision with a truck fast approaching from behind. She was convicted at trial, the trial judge holding that the defence of necessity had no effect in an offence of absolute liability, in this case speeding. This ruling was overturned. Necessity is indeed a defence to speeding. Although the court is not explicit in its language, it is implicit in the ruling that speeding is not categorized as an offence of absolute liability.

4. THE DEFENCE OF NECESSITY

It is clear that, insofar as necessity is a defence to the charge of speeding, it is inconsistent with the above authority that the offence is one of absolute liability. Again, there is no defence to absolute liability offences other than that the act itself did not occur.

In *R. v. Kennedy*,[27] the defendant was travelling 64 m.p.h. in a 40 m.p.h. zone. He testified that he could not slow down because he was being followed too closely. O'Hearn Co. Ct. J. said,

> In the instant case, I have no doubt that the preservation of the life of the defendant or his wife or even of a valuable piece of property such as his motor vehicle might justify exceeding a speed limit but I have a problem as to whether the course he took was necessary.[28]

A similar result was arrived at in *R. v. Paul*.[29] As Anderson Co. Ct. J. outlined the facts,

> The respondent (defendant) in this matter, Lawrence Frederick Paul, stated his occupation to be Director of Programmes for Alcoholism and Drug Abuse for all Indian People in Nova Scotia, employed by the union of Nova Scotia Indians.

> On the morning of August 9, 1972, Mr. Paul took three patients in to the Nova Scotia Hospital Alcoholism Clinic. While there he attended a group therapy session to speak to the Indian people in Micmac. Mr. Paul related that while there he received a telephone call from Truro which made it necessary for him to immediately return to Truro to meet with two young people with whom he had made an arrangement. This arrangement, according to Mr. Paul, was that these two young people, boys, were to buy marijuana from a person who was selling it on the reserves, hand the marijuana over to Mr. Paul, who, in turn, was to hand it over to a member of the R.C.M.P. Drug Squad in Sydney. Mr. Paul indicated that this was the only way that he could get the Band Council of the reserves to exclude

---

25 See also *R. v. Cook*, [1993] N.S.J. No. 588 (N.S.Co.Ct.) for similar authority.

26 (1994), 5 M.V.R. (3d) 110 (B.C. S.C.).

27 (1972), 7 C.C.C. (2d) 42 (N.S. Co. Ct.).

28 *Ibid.*, at p. 44.

29 (1973), 12 C.C.C. (2d) 497 at p. 497-498 (N.S. Co. Ct.).

persons he knew as traffickers from the reservations. He was of the opinion that the R.C.M.P. could not, or would not, take any action against the drug offenders on the different reserves. Mr. Paul did not leave the hospital immediately, but had to make arrangements for someone to take over the group therapy session, and then left Dartmouth via the Micmac Rotary, Nova Scotia Highway 118, to the No. 102 towards Truro. The accused said that he was exceeding the posted speed limit, however, felt that the boys were afraid and would not stay in the motel. Earlier, Mr. Paul had made reservations with the manager of a motel in Truro to give the boys a room when and if they needed it. The boys were in this motel waiting for Mr. Paul.

It was at this time that the defendant was caught speeding. Anderson Co. Ct. J. allowed the appeal, holding that, while the defence of necessity is available, it is only available in the most exceptional circumstances, and this case was not one of them.

In *R. v. Greening*,[30] the difficulty with allowing the defence of necessity to speeding infractions is most apparent. The defendant had been clocked on radar at 119 k.m.h. in a posted 90 k.m.h. zone. He had testified that he was forced to move into a passing lane and accelerate his vehicle in order to avoid collision with a group of slow moving antique vehicles. The trial court accepted this explanation and acquitted him on the basis that his action was necessary to avoid collision.

On appeal, Mr. Justice Barry said that,

> [I]t is not a defence for the respondent to offer proof of innocent intention. Applying the rule in the *Sault Ste. Marie* case to this case, I find that the offence of speeding under s. 109(3)(c) of the *Highway Traffic Act* is an absolute liability offence, and that the intention of the respondent, however innocent would not justify his admitted act of driving his motor vehicle at a speed in excess of the legal limit.

If the appeal court had left the matter at that, the appeal would have been justifiably dismissed, and the absolute liability offence would have been safe from the defence of necessity. Unfortunately, His Honour continued by saying that,

> Even if the defence of necessity were open to the respondent in the present case, the burden of proof would lay upon him to satisfy the court that his action in driving his car at a speed in excess of the limit was the only means open to him of avoiding an accident. ... However, the evidence adduced at trial does not support such a finding.[31]

This leaves the application of the defence of necessity in speeding infractions open to question. If absolute liability offences render the defendants intention irrelevant, then necessity should have no place in the prosecution of speeding offences. On the other hand, courts seem reluctant to completely abandon this defence for this charge.[32]

---

30 (1992), 40 M.V.R. (2d) 81 (Nfld. T.D.).

31 *Ibid.*, at p. 83, 84.

32 See, for example, *R. v. Rizzetto* (1997), 34 W.C.B. (2d) 308 (N.S. S.C.).

5. POSTED SPEED LIMITS

(a) General

In *R. v. Clark*,[33] the Ontario Court of Appeal considered the issue of whether or not formal proof of a by-law prescribing a speed limit was required in order to convict. Jessop J.A. pointed out that although the relevant by-law was not placed in evidence,[34] there had been evidence of a speed limit sign given. He therefore held the conviction to be proper. Compliance with the regulations under the *Highway Traffic Act* is proven upon evidence of the erection of speed limit signs at the appropriate place, and there is no need to prove directly the existence of the by-law. In reaching its decision the court made reference to the English case of *Gibbins v. Skinner*,[35] where Lord Goddard held that s. 1(7) of the *Road Traffic Act*, 1934 required traffic signs to be erected in order that motorists would have adequate information concerning whether or not directions were in force with regard to a length of road deemed to be in a built-up area. On this point Lord Goddard said,

> The fact that it was proved or admitted that appropriate signs had been erected was, in my opinion, *prima facie* proof that the necessary directions and steps had been taken to direct that the road be deemed to be in a built up area.[36]

The same issue arose again in *R. v. McLaren*,[37] where the defendant had been charged with failing to yield to a pedestrian at a pedestrian cross-over. The issue for the court to decide was whether the prosecution was required to prove the existence of the by-law designating the cross-over as a pedestrian cross-over within the meaning of the *Highway Traffic Act*, and if so, did the Provincial court Judge err in law in failing to hold that evidence of signs at the cross-over was evidence of the existence of the designating by-law? The Court of Appeal accepted the reasoning of *Clark*, concluding that it governed the disposition of this question, and therefore evidence adduced that a sign was posted constituted sufficient proof of the relevant by-law.

In *R. v. Keenan*,[38] the defendant appealed his conviction for speeding on several grounds, one of which was lack of proof of the municipal by-law limiting the speed. Selbie J. dismissed these arguments saying firstly, that judicial notice of the by-law must be taken, and secondly that the signage itself

---

33 (1974), 18 C.C.C. (2d) 52 (Ont. C.A.).
34 See *Peterborough (City) v. Lockyer* (1992), 12 O.R. (3d) 214 (Ont. Prov. Div.) where Prov. Ct. J. Collins ruled that the Court can take judicial notice of a municipal by-law under the *Interpretation Act*. R.S.O. 1990, c. I.11, and so proof of a municipal by-law is unnecessary. For *contra*, see *R. v. Stewart* (1997), 34 W.C.B. (2d) 65.
35 [1951] 1 All E.R. Rep. 1049 (U.K. K.B.).
36 *Ibid.*, at 1052.
37 (1981), 10 M.V.R. 42 (Ont. C.A.).
38 (1994), 3 M.V.R. (3d) 21 (B.C. S.C.).

is evidence of the by-law.[39] On the first point, the court noted that, according to s. 10 of the *Interpretation Act*,[40]

(1) Judicial Notice shall be taken of a regulation made under an Act of the Province;[41]

(2) No order or conviction shall be quashed or set aside, and no defendant shall be discharged, by reason only that evidence has not been given of any of the matters referred to in subsection (1).

Since, according to s. 1 of the *Interpretation Act*, a "regulation" includes a "by-law", the appeal cannot succeed on this argument.

6. CONSPICUOUSLY POSTED SPEED LIMITS

Section 128 of the *Highway Traffic Act*[42] grants to municipalities the power to prescribe lower rates of speed for motor vehicles passing through its jurisdiction.[43] This applies to speeds in public parks[44] and over bridges.[45] Other jurisdictions have similar provisions.[46] In Ontario, as in Manitoba, such lower rate of speed "… shall not be less than 10 kilometres per hour and signs indicating the maximum rate of speed shall be posted in a conspicuous place at each approach to the bridge". Other jurisdictions, such as Alberta[47] and Saskatchewan,[48] merely refer to such signage being posted on the highway.

What constitutes a conspicuous place may well be the subject of some dispute. In *R. v. Redden*,[49] the defendant was in the last of three vehicles in line that passed a speed limit sign indicating a prescribed maximum speed of 90 k.m.h. Behind the defendant followed a police car that clocked him at a steady speed of 113 k.m.h. The location where he was stopped was approximately 5 kilometres after the posted speed sign. It was held that while proof of a speed limit sign having been posted must be shown in evidence, there is no requirement that a sign be at the exact same spot as where the offence occurred. If that were the case, a continuous line of speed signs would be necessary, which obviously was not the Legislature's intention.

---

39 Citing, with approval, *R. v. Clark, supra* note 33.
40 R.S.B.C. 1979, c. 206.
41 See also *R. v. Friedlan*, [1993] O.J. No. 720.
42 R.S.O. 1990, c. H.8.
43 *Ibid.*, at s. 128(2).
44 *Ibid.*, at s. 128(4).
45 *Ibid.*, at s. 128(6).
46 See, for example, *Highway Traffic Act* (Manitoba) s. 98(4), *Motor Vehicle Act* (Yukon) s. 117(4) and *Motor Vehicle Act* (B.C.), s. 146(7).
47 *Highway Traffic Act* s. 70(3).
48 *Highway Traffic Act* s. 38.
49 (1978), 1 M.V.R. 119 (N.S. C.A.).

R. v. Cunningham[50] stands for the proposition that where a defendant misreads a posted speed limit sign it is a mistake of law, and not a valid defence. The appellant was convicted of driving at a speed in excess of 30 m.p.h. in a 30 m.p.h. zone. He entered the highway in an area where the speed limit was 30 m.p.h. and while driving he saw a sign up ahead that read "45 m.p.h. begins". He innocently failed to see the word "begins" at the bottom of the sign, and thought the sign applied to the zone in which he was driving. He therefore accelerated, and was caught speeding. The court rejected the defence and convicted.

In *R. v. Comeau*,[51] the defendant was charged with exceeding the *prima facie* limit contrary to s. 96(1) of Nova Scotia's *Motor Vehicle Act*. Evidence was adduced that he travelled 102 k.m.h. in a 90 k.m.h. posted zone. At the close of the Crown's case, a motion for dismissal was granted on two grounds. Firstly, there was no evidence that the signs were posted. Secondly, it was submitted that the signs did not conform to the regulation because underneath the sign was an appendage indicating "k.m.h.". The Crown's appeal to the County Court was dismissed and it sought leave to appeal from the Court of Appeal. The judgment of that Court was delivered by Jones J., who allowed the appeal. He held that there is no need to prove the posting of signs in view of s. 96(1), which makes it an offence to drive over 80 k.m.h. on any highway at any time. It was nonetheless open to the Court to find that the sign did not comply with the relevant regulation because it was not clear that the appendage actually formed part of the sign. Indeed, the appendage may have constituted a separate sign immediately below the sign posted by regulation. These letters were added for informational purposes, and even as part of a sign would not invalidate it if it otherwise conformed to the regulations. This is because the reference to kilometres (which is the stipulation for speed required by law) is reasonable. To hold otherwise would be contrary to the express intent of the Legislature.

Similarly, in *R. v. Salami*[52] the respondent had been acquitted of speeding because there was no evidence lead as to the speed limit on the municipal road in question. This verdict was quashed on appeal. Curtis J. was of the view that in this circumstance the general speed limit was an issue to be displaced by the defendant[53]

---

50 (1979), 1 M.V.R. 223 (Ont. Div. Ct.).
51 (1980), 9 M.V.R. 308 (N.S. C.A.).
52 (1997), 27 M.V.R. (3d) 26 (B.C. S.C.).
53 Following *R. v. Cook* (1994), 2 M.V.R. (3d) 281, 130 N.S.R. (2d) 115, 367 A.P.R. 115 (N.S. S.C.).

(a) Maintaining Signs

In *R. v. Rutledge*,[54] O'Hearn Co. Ct. J. considered what interpretation is to be given to the word "maintain" in s. 79(2) of the Nova Scotia *Motor Vehicle Act*.[55] Section 79(2) reads:

> (2) The fact that the sign or signal has been erected and maintained shall be *prima facie* evidence that the sign or signal is erected in compliance with this Act and that the matter stated or represented on the sign complies with that determined by the Minister.

His Honour held that even though the word "maintain" may well include an element of violation on the part of the Minister or the traffic authority, it does not, within the ordinary meaning of "maintain", necessarily involve any activity on their part. That would arise only if the sign were damaged or otherwise changed so as to require active intervention. If the sign remains standing and clearly visible without change in its ability to communicate its message, that constitutes sufficient maintenance within the meaning of "maintained" in the section.

(b) Proving the case

R. v. Dubé[56] dealt with s. 143(3)(a) of the New Brunswick *Motor Vehicle Act*.[57] That section created a presumption whereby the existing speed limit on a highway was proved when evidence had been lead of a sign that was passed by the defendant and where it was shown that no other sign existed up until the point of stopping. At trial, the case was dismissed because the Crown had failed to show there "was no other sign then erected indicating any other speed limit between the first mentioned sign and the place of the alleged offence". An essential ingredient of the offence had not been proven.

On appeal, Daigle J. held that the trial judge had misdirected himself when he ruled that s. 143(3)(a) must be complied with in order to support a conviction. The trial judge further misdirected himself in disregarding the whole of the evidence introduced at trial. The existence of any signs indicating a speed limit had a probative force independent of any statutory presumption. Common sense suggests, in the absence of evidence to the contrary, that signs erected on the roadway are the result of the ordinary and proper operation of governmental authority. Upon the police officer's testimony, and without the presumption, it could not be said that there was sufficient evidence for a conviction to be recorded, and therefore the Crown's appeal was dismissed.

---

54 (1981), 62 C.C.C. (2d) 314 (N.S. Co. Ct.).
55 R.S.N.S. 1967, c. 191, see now R.S.N.S. 1989, c. 293, s. 88(2).
56 (1983), 21 M.V.R. 244, 47 N.B.R. (2d) 411, 124 A.P.R. 411 (N.B. Q.B.).
57 R.S.N.B. 1973, c. M-17.

(c) Erection of Speed Limit Signs and the Presumption of Regularity

In *R. v. Coad*,[58] the defendant had driven past a traffic sign located on the right side of the highway. This sign measured 18 inches by 24 inches and was positioned five feet from the ground. The sign plainly read, "Speed Limit 25" and was illuminated. At trial, the defendant was convicted. On appeal, ultimately to the Court of Appeal, the conviction was upheld, with the Court of Appeal being divided on the issue.

The portion of the highway where the excessive speed occurred was a limited-speed area under the Order-in-Council passed pursuant to s. 42(a) of the *Vehicles and Highway Traffic Act*,[59] which stated that "the Minister of Highways shall erect such signs along the highway or portion thereof as he deems adequate to notify any person driving a vehicle theron of the maximum speed limit fixed".

The appellant argued that the sign in question was not erected by the Minister of Highways, and so it could not be said that he deemed it adequate for the purpose of notifying persons driving vehicles of the maximum speed limit. Ford J., with O'Connor C.J.A. concurring, held that the facts with respect to the sign are *prima facie* evidence that it was erected and deemed adequate by the Minister pursuant to the Order-in-Council. His Lordship therefore upheld the conviction. Porter J.A., with whom Johnson J.A. wrote a separate but concurring opinion, would have allowed the appeal. He held that there was no evidence from which it could be inferred that the Minister performed his statutory function and published the order by erecting a sign along the highway or portion thereof "which he deemed adequate to notify any person thereon of the maximum speed limit" fixed by the Governor's order. A road foreman had testified that he thought he moved the sign near the portion of the highway designated in the Minister's order but that he was not sure when he did it, although he thought it was in the month of December 1954, which was before the order was gazetted. Porter J.A. held that unless reliance was placed on his faulty memory, there was no evidence at all from which the court could infer the time at which a sign was moved there. If the court accepted the "doubting statement", the sign was moved before the order became effective. "No sign, therefore, can be said to have been 'erected by the Minister', let alone deemed adequate by him" according to Porter J.A.[60]

In *R. v. Tsumura*,[61] the defendant brought an application by way of stated case in respect of his conviction for driving a motor vehicle "at a greater rate of speed than that indicated on a sign, to wit: 30 m.p.h. which the Minister of Highways had caused to be erected on the said Highway". The issue was

---

58 (1956), 115 C.C.C. 61 (Alta. C.A.).

59 R.S.A. 1955, c. 356.

60 *Supra*, note 58 at p. 268.

61 (1960), 128 C.C.C. 280 (B.C. C.A.).

whether the Crown was required to lead evidence at trial to demonstrate that the Minister of Highways or some other competent authority had authorized a speed limit of 30 m.p.h. imposed on the portion of the highway upon which the defendant was then driving.

The only evidence that had been adduced by the Crown concerning the geographical location of the alleged offence and the fact of the defendant being the driver of the vehicle in question was the presence of a sign on the highway indicating this area was a 30 m.p.h. zone and that the defendant had exceeded the speed limit.

In arriving at his decision, Mcinnes J. made reference to then s. 184[62] of the British Columbia *Motor Vehicle Act*:

> The existence of a sign permitted by this Act and purporting to regulate the use of the highway in any manner shall be prima facie evidence that the sign was duly erected and maintained by the proper authority under this Act or the regulations and in accordance therewith.[63]

His Lordship held that, in light of this section, and in absence of any evidence to the contrary, the Magistrate was entitled to draw the inference from the existence of the sign that it had been erected and maintained by the proper authority. Pursuant to s. 133(2) of the *Motor Vehicle Act*, this was permitted. The appeal was therefore dismissed.

Whether or not signs are posted may well be a problem in photoradar cases. In *R. v. Simpson*,[64] the defendant was charged with speeding. The Crown sought to tender proof of the offence by way of photoradar certificate. At trial the defendant had testified that he had not seen any posted speed limit in the vicinity of the photoradar van. Furthermore, the signage on the highway in question was frequently changed because of ongoing construction. J.P. Makhdoom acquitted saying:

> During trials involving the non-photoradar cases arising out of s. 151(3) or for that matter any other sections of the Motor Vehicle Act respecting the signs such as s. 151(4), 151(7), 152 or 202 witnesses for the Crown, in order for them to present prima facie evidence with respect to the signs being disobeyed, clearly and at times painstakingly present their sworn or affirmed evidence as to the location of such signs whether or not these were clear and unobstructed on the day and time of the commission of an alleged offence. Presentation of evidence with respect to location, clarity and unobstructiveness of the regulatory signs is one such standard which helps the triers arrive at the truth. I see no reason to compromise this standard when dealing with matters pursuant to s. 76.1(2) of the Motor Vehicle Act.[65]

---

62 Now s. 201.

63 *Ibid.*, at p. 281; *Motor Vehicle Act*, 1957 (B.C.), c. 39, s. 184.

64 [1997] B.C.J. No. 3050.

65 ie. The photoradar provisions. See also *R. v. Etherington*, [1997] B.C.J. No. 3042.

7. LIMITS SET BY THE GEOGRAPHIC BUILD-UP OF AN AREA

(a) General

In *R. v. Graves*,[66] the defendant was acquitted of speeding in a "residential area" contrary to s. 92(2)(a) of the *Motor Vehicle Act*[67] on the basis that more explicit proof than was given was required to show that the speeding took place in a "residence district" as defined in the Act.

The definitions of "residence district" and "business district" given in s. 1(bc) and (c) of the Act were:

> (bc) "residence district" means the territory contiguous to a highway not com-
> prising a business district when the frontage on the highway for a distance of
> 100 metres or more is mainly occupied by dwellings or by dwellings and business
> premises and includes any section of a highway so designated by the traffic
> authority by the erection of appropriate signs; ...

> (c) "business district" means a territory contiguous to a highway upon which fifty
> per cent or more of the frontage for a distance of not less than 100 metres is
> occupied by business premises and includes a section of a highway so designated
> by the traffic authority by the erection of appropriate signs. ...

A police officer testified that:

> "The area is definitely a residential area. There's houses all over the area". On
> being asked about posted traffic signs, he said, "I don't believe there is any on
> that street. It's just strictly a residential area." Asked about the distance that the
> defendant was clocked he said, "I believe it would be about a tenth of a kilo-
> metre ...[68]

Judge O'Hearn held that the dismissal was premature in light of the recent trend in the law to require trial courts to use their common knowledge of the meaning of language.[69] There was evidence given by the police officer from which the court could conclude that the part of the road in question was not a business district and was a residence district within the meaning of the Act. Hence the appeal was allowed and a new trial ordered.

In *R. v. Moore*,[70] the Prince Edward Island Supreme Court considered an appeal by a defendant convicted of speeding in a "business district" contrary to s. 163(2) of the province's *Highway Traffic Act*.[71]

The sole Crown witness, a police officer, gave evidence that the appellant was operating a motor vehicle in the area at a rate of 50 m.p.h. and that this

---

66 (1980), 6 M.V.R. 113 (N.S. Co. Ct.).

67 R.S.N.S. 1967, c. 191.

68 *Supra*, note 66 at p. 114.

69 See *R. v. Schaefer* (1989), 22 M.V.R. (2d) 256 (B.C. Co. Ct.) which stands for the proposition
that when the signage refers to a playground, evidence of a park will not suffice in the absence
of evidence that this is a playground for children.

70 (1973), 12 C.C.C. (2d) 393 (P.E.I. S.C.).

71 R.S.P.E.I. 1974, c. H-6.

area was marked with signs facing the appellant which read "Maximum 40". This evidence was accepted.

A regulation passed pursuant to the *Highway Traffic Act* (P.E.I.) defines "business district" as follows:

> That section of the highway wherein a maximum speed limit of forty (40) miles per hour is indicated by the erection of a sign at each end of such section of the highway is designated as a business district. [72]

The regulation, however, does not stand alone. Section 152 of the *Highway Traffic Act* states:

> **152.** (1) Subject to sub-section (2) of Section 163, signs to indicate the highway or part of a highway wherein the driving of a vehicle in excess of a certain maximum speed is prohibited may be erected in accordance with sub-section (2) of this Section.
>
> (2) The highway or part of a highway wherein any special maximum speed limit applies shall be indicated by the erection of a sign at each end of the highway or part of the highway to which the maximum speed limit applies and facing the stream of traffic entering the highway or part highway, the signs having inscribed thereon the words "SPEED LIMIT" or "MAXIMUM SPEED" and the maximum speed limit.
>
> (3) Each sign in the form prescribed by sub-section (2) of this Section may be varied by the insertion on the sign of such figures as may be prescribed by the Minister or traffic authority for the place where the sign is erected.
>
> (4) Signs to indicate that the end of the highway or part of the highway to which the maximum speed limit applies has been reached may be erected at each such end, the signs having inscribed thereon the words "END ZONE" or "END M.P.H. ZONE" and the figures indicating the speed. [73]

As it provided that "any special maximum speed limit ... shall be indicated by the erection of a sign...having inscribed thereon the words 'SPEED LIMIT' or 'MAXIMUM SPEED' and the maximum speed limit", the signs as described in the evidence did not comply with the mandatory requirements of the *Highway Traffic Act* and were inadequate to determining the area in question as a business district.

(b) Proving Location Where Location Establishes the Speed Limit Applicable

In *R. v. Eagles*,[74] the defendant had been stopped for the offence of speeding contrary to s. 82(1)(b) of the *Highway Traffic Act*,[75] while entering

---

72 Designation of Urban and Business Districts Regulations, E.C. 225/65 (am. 1039/77).

73 *Highway Traffic Act*, 1964 (P.E.I.), c. 14.

74 (1976), 31 C.C.C. (2d) 417 (Ont. H.C.).

75 R.S.O. 1970, c. 202.

the city of Sarnia. The defendant had been clocked by radar at a speed of 48 m.p.h. There was no evidence that the point where the defendant allegedly committed the offence was within the limits of the city of Sarnia, nor was there any evidence concerning the speed limit at that place. The Justice of the Peace, however, took judicial notice of the fact that the particular place was within the city and by virtue of the then s. 82(1)(b) of the *Highway Traffic Act* the speed limit in a city was 30 m.p.h.

Robins J. (as he then was) held that unlike cases where the offence occurred is relevant only to establish the territorial jurisdiction of the Court, the offence being an offence wherever committed. The location in this case was an essential element of the offence and judicial notice ought not to have been resorted to, so as to relieve the Crown of its obligation to produce evidence to support the material allegation of the charge. Furthermore, it cannot be said that the actual boundaries of a municipality are sufficiently notorious that they are entitled to judicial recognition.

In *R. v. Redlick*,[76] the defendant was charged with travelling 58 m.p.h. in a 50 m.p.h. zone, contrary to the then s. 82(1)(b) of the *Highway Traffic Act*[77] This section establishes (as does the current s. 109) a general speed limit for the entire province that applies to cities, towns, villages, police villages and other built-up areas. Linden J. held that while it is clear that location is an essential element of the offence, where there is no dispute as to this matter then such evidence need not be given in every case, especially where it is so obvious to everybody that the offence has occurred within such an area. Here, everyone involved in the trial was fully aware of the location of the offence on Linday Street south near the Kentucky Fried Chicken shop. The defendant had lived in the area for some 20 years and was familiar with it as were the prosecutor and the trial judge. In these circumstances, therefore, Linden J. held it proper for the trial judge to take judicial notice that this offence took place in a city, town, police village or other built-up area. The conviction was therefore affirmed.[78]

8. DETECTING SPEED

(a) Photoradar

There are presently two provinces, Alberta and British Columbia,[79] utilizing photoradar devices to prove the offence of speeding.[80] In Ontario, the

---

76 (1978), 41 C.C.C. (2d) 358 (Ont. H.C.).

77 Amended 1977, c. 19, s. 3(1)(b).

78 See also the discussion of Judicial Notice in Chapter 4.

79 *Motor Vehicle Act*, R.S.B.C. 1996, c. 318.

80 For more information on photoradar, see the internet sites: http://www.sense.bc.ca, http://users.cyberbeach.net~/mtrenout/photo2.htm/, http://www.inforamp.net/~dma /photorad.html and http://www.klatu.com/sds/photo.html.

devices were operated for a brief period of time but their use was discontinued in 1995. Quebec used the devices in the 1970's but has long since abandoned them.[81] Although precise figures are elusive, it would appear that the enforcement of speeding laws by the use of photoradar devices has a noticeable effect in reducing the overall traffic speed of those routes subject to photoradar monitoring. If a reduction in speed is an obvious and simple method of making roads safer, then photoradar is one of traffic safety's best kept secrets. Given the prospect of such a simple and effective method of enforcing speeding laws, it is puzzling why more provinces do not use photoradar.[82] It has been noted that, in the case of Calgary, "Th[e] autobahn attitude is slowly changing with the introduction of photo radar".[83]

The most common photoradar device in use is the Swiss-made Multanova 6f.[84] This device clocks, records and photographs the speed of a motor vehicle. It is self testing, and can be used to measure the velocity of traffic coming toward, or moving away from the unit. It is accurate to plus or minus 3 per cent at 100 k.m.h.[85] The Multanova then produces a digital picture of the vehicle indicating its velocity, location and time. The Multanova can work at night, taking its pictures via a high-powered flash light. Evidence is presented in court in the form of a picture displaying the vehicle at the time of offence, the velocity, the speed limit and the registered owner of the vehicle.[86]

In *R. v. Tsang*[87] the poor quality of a photoradar image was the basis of an acquittal. In that case the picture as put into evidence contained not only the defendant's vehicle, but an additional set of yellowish lights, possibly that of a motorcycle passing the defendants vehicle. J.P. Hayes said that,

> In previous cases where it is possible to determine positively that another vehicle was present in the photograph travelling in the same direction as the accused, the Crown has usually entered a "stay of proceedings". While Mr. Tsang's vehicle is clearly present in the photograph receding from the speed monitoring device, the lack of definition in the photographic evidence precludes any positive explanation to account for the presence of the additional lights. Mr. Tsang is speculating that these lights may represent an additional vehicle (motorcycle) proceeding in the same direction as his own receding from the speed monitoring device. *R. v. Nikolovski* allows the trier of fact to take a view of the photograph, and that view finds evidence which supports Mr. Tsang's speculation. ...[88]

---

81 In the United States, photoradar devices are presently in use in Arizona, California, Colorado, District of Columbia, Michigan, Missouri, Oregon, and Utah.

82 For a contrary view, see the website at www.sence.bc.com.

83 *Forensics, Policing and the Law* Vol. 1, No. 6, Fall 1993.

84 This device is used widely in Alberta. British Columbia uses the American Traffic Systems "Autopatrol PR - 100/200". For U.S. Appellate authority upholding a finding that the PR 100 has not been shown to be reliable, see *Municipality of Anchorage v. Baxley et al.* unreported (Alaska C.A.).

85 *R. v. Hedayat* (1992), 41 M.V.R. (2d) 218 (Alta. Q.B.).

86 *Ibid.*, at p. 221.

87 [1998] B.C.J. No. 1216.

88 *Ibid.*, at paras. 37-39.

His worship thus held that the poor quality of the photograph could not displace the possibility that another vehicle had been responsible for the photoradar image being triggered. The crown could not therefore prove the charge beyond a reasonable doubt.

(b) Challenges to the Admissibility of Photoradar evidence

Notwithstanding the apparent reliability and accuracy of the device, there have been challenges to the admissibility of photoradar evidence. They have met with limited success.

In *R. v. Winder*,[89] the defendant argued that he should have been notified that he was under surveillance when being photographed by photoradar. Signage, it was argued, ought to have been posted within 150 feet of the photoradar location disclosing the presence of the photoradar device. Without such a sign, the defendant's rights under s. 11(d) of the *Charter* had been violated because he had not been advised promptly of his infraction. To this, the Court of Appeal said:

> We do not agree that the failure to place a sign to this effect at a photo radar location infringes s. 11(d). There is nothing in that section of the *Charter* which speaks to a timing requirement in terms of notification of the commission of an offence and reading one into this section of the *Charter* could lead to absurd and impractical results. Indeed we note that by the appellant's own expert's evidence, the value of the sign would itself be questionable. For these reasons, therefore, we dismiss the appeal.[90]

In *R. v. Macdonald*,[91] the defendant challenged the evidence obtained by the Multanova. He attempted to raise a reasonable doubt about the accuracy of the device. Laven P.C.J. acquitted the defendant saying:

> The multanova device is no doubt a "state of the arts" device. It is complicated in its inner workings and mechanisms including digital computers and radar and camera facility. It has not legislative sanction or authority ...
>
> The Multanova device — without more — can only be a "prima facie" proof — always susceptible to rebuttal or the raising of a reasonable doubt raised by matters elicited on examination or by Crown or defence evidence. There is no "back up" evidence which could be construed as a corroboration to the findings of the machine. There must be proper and meaningful visual observation by the operator of the offending vehicle coupled with meaningful notes or memoranda therof made at the time or shortly thereafter.
>
> Therefore ... I find that the Multanova device is not by itself, or as operated by the Calgary Police Service, a technically fit and proper device (at all times and without fail) capable of accurately measuring and recording the speed of a motor

---

89 (1995), 174 A.R. 170 (Alta. C.A.).

90 *Ibid.*, at 171.

91 (1990), 108 A.R. 245 (Alta. Prov. Ct.).

vehicle — all for the purposes for which it is used and in the manner in which it is operated.[92]

In Alaska, that Court of Appeal has adopted similar reasoning, *viz* that there must be some corroboration of the photoradar device, absent which there is a reasonable doubt as to the accuracy of the readings.[93]

Macdonald, however, was effectively overturned in *R. v. Chow*.[94] In *Chow*, the trial judge refused to admit the photoradar image into evidence. He took the view that this evidence was hearsay which could not be solved by the testimony of the Multanova operator, and there was no legislative sanction to provide for the admission of such hearsay evidence. Ultimately, the Alberta Court of Appeal held that, while the measurements obtained by the Multanova device is hearsay evidence, it is sufficiently reliable and trustworthy to be legally admissible as evidence. The photograph itself is not evidence, it is only the measurements recorded thereon which is the primary evidence. The court noted that the evidence:

> may still be receivable if the surroundings reveal that the evidence is both accurate and enjoys circumstantial guarantees of trustworthiness.

> The record we have compels the conclusion that the Multanova, aptly described as a marriage between radar and photography, provided and recorded accurate information and what it recorded was admissible in evidence.[95]

This raises the question, if the photograph is not evidence, then how does the prosecutor prove that the defendants vehicle was the one speeding? Notwithstanding this difficulty, *Chow* is the most authoritative decision regarding the admission of photoradar evidence.

In *R. v. Halliday*,[96] the Crown had called no evidence attesting to the reliability of the Multanova device other than the device being turned on and performing its usual self diagnostic. The defendant then argued that there was evidence as to the accuracy and reliability of the device. The Court remarked that:

> Lacking such independent or external testing, or even any evidence why it was not done, the Crown asks this Court, in essence, to accept the accuracy of the readings of speed established by the Multinova [sic] simply because the instrument has tested itself and "says" they are. There is no evidence that the Multinova [sic] in use on December 17, 1994 had been tested against any other known constant or even the estimates of Comm. Zdunich to demonstrate its relia-

---

92 *Ibid.*, at p. 247-248.

93 See *Municipality of Anchorage v. Clyde Baxley, Linda Weatherhold, Jeff Ullom and Heather Siegel.* Unreported [No. 1552 - October 16, 1997].

94 (1991), 33 M.V.R. (2d) 171 (Alta. C.A.). See also "RADAR CAMERA EVIDENCE" Case Comment on *R. v. Chow* By Roger Harris at 37 M.V.R. (2d) 122. For a contra holding to *Chow*, see *Re Broadway*, [1994] B.C.J. No. 3299.

95 *Chow, supra,* note 94 at p. 172.

96 (1995), 19 M.V.R. (3d) 7 (Alta. Prov. Ct.).

bility. In my view this "self test" is not sufficient to satisfy the circumstantial guarantees of trustworthiness required by the cases, nor are Comm. Zdunich's visual observations in this case sufficient to supply that guarantee and this "self-test" alone does not allow me to conclude beyond a reasonable doubt that the Multinova [sic] was able to accurately measure speeds at the time of the offence alleged.

I am not satisfied that the Crown has met its onus of establishing a prima facie case of speeding against the Defendant and, accordingly, the charge against Mr. Halliday is dismissed.[97]

In *R. v. Guinn*,[98] the defendant successfully argued at trial that the photoradar picture did not sufficiently identify his licence plate number or jurisdiction. The trial judge agreed, excluded the photoradar evidence, and acquitted. On appeal, Madam Justice Levine said:

I agree with Crown counsel's submissions in this case that the Justice of the Peace erred in excluding the certificate on the grounds that it was inadmissible. The legislature did not say that the judge hearing a dispute must be able to read the photograph and that judge must be able to make out the license plate and the jurisdiction. What the legislature says is that an enforcement officer, in order to use a certificate as evidence, must be in a position to sign and complete a certificate setting out the information required in the prescribed form. The certificate requires that the enforcement officer state that she has determined the license plate number and that it is issued in the particular jurisdiction. In my view, the procedure provided by the statute not only provides for the Crown to provide evidence on an expedited basis, it avoids the kind of debate that took place in this case about the subjective ability of a particular person to read or not read the license plate or the jurisdiction on the photograph. If the defendant person wishes to adduce evidence to the contrary, including by cross-examining the enforcement officer as to how he made the determination that she did, the opportunity is available to do that.
I find that the certificate should have been admitted pursuant to the statutory provisions and allow the Crown's appeal.[99]

In the prosecution of speeding cases using photoradar evidence, there is a gap in time between the time the vehicle was photographed and the time the summons is served on the registered vehicle owner. This gap in time has been the subject of court challenge. In *R. v. Hedayat*,[100] the defendant was acquitted at trial on the basis that it took 25 days between the time of offence and the delivery of his summons. Without hearing any evidence from the defendant, the trial judge entered a stay of proceedings on the basis that such delay impaired the ability to make full answer and defence. On appeal, Chrumka J. overturned the acquittal and ordered a new trial. He commented that:

---

97 *Ibid.*, at p. 11-12.

98 (1997) Doc. No. CC970321 Vancouver Registry (B.C. S.C.).

99 *Ibid.*

100 (1991), 34 M.V.R. (2d) 12 (Alta. Prov. Ct.), reversed (1992), 41 M.V.R. (2d) 218 (Alta. Q.B.).

The trial judge, before hearing any testimony on the question of delay, appeared to assume that because of the passage of 25 days from the date of the alleged offence to the date of notice thereof being given, that no accused could or would likely remember sufficient details to properly defend him or herself. In my view this is a conclusion that should not be reached on the basis of delay alone. The conclusion should be arrived at only if there is an evidentiary basis supporting such a decision. A trial judge should not conclude that, by reason of delay alone, no accused can remember sufficient details of the circumstances surrounding an alleged offence to properly defend him or herself against the allegation. [101]

This would appear to leave open the possibility that a defendant charged with speeding, who is served with a summons to appear on the basis of photoradar evidence, may yet raise, as a basis for a stay of proceedings, the delay period between the offence and when she was served with the summons if an intervening event such as departure of a crucial witness, or loss of evidence makes defence of the charge impossible then the stay may be granted. Clearly, however, the onus is on the defendant to put this evidence before the court. [102]

(c) Chain Measurement and Aerial Surveillance

In *R. v. King*, [103] the defendant was charged with speeding after being observed by officers engaged in aircraft surveillance. His speed was determined on the basis of the time it took him to go past markings on the highway that had been measured with a chain. The chain had a marking on it affixed by the manufacturer that stated it was 200 feet in length.

The defendant's appeal from conviction to Divisional Court was successful. Robins J. held that evidence as to measurements made by the use of a chain, it not being an instrument or device whose purpose is to make measurements, is not admissible without further evidence as to the accuracy of its instruments. This is simply because the mark apparently affixed by the manufacturer is hearsay. It would have been different had the distance between the two markings been measured by an instrument used or designed for the purpose of reading measurements or if the chain itself had been measured by the officers with such an instrument. If that had been done there would have been *prima facie* evidence before the court of the distance between the markers. In the circumstances of the charge, the calculations, including distances, must be established with specificity.

---

101 *Ibid.*, at 241.
102 See, for example, *R. v. Uarmadi*, [1998] B.C.J. No. 390.
103 (1977), 35 C.C.C. (2d) 424 (Ont. Div. Ct.).

(d) Pacing

The Ontario Court of Appeal held in *R. v. Bland*[104] that where evidence is given that over a measured level distance the police officer's speedometer recorded steadily at the speed alleged, this is *prima facie* evidence that the defendant was driving at that speed. In the absence of some evidence, elicited either on cross-examination or by defence witnesses, that would suggest that the police speedometer was inaccurate, this is enough to convict. In reaching its decision, the Court made reference to *Nicholas v. Penny*,[105] which stands for the proposition that a conviction for speeding can be made where the police officer gives evidence as to the speed of the defendant based on the officers reliance on his own speedometer. That speedometer need not be tested to make the *prima facie* case.

Another Canadian case that relied on *Nicholas v. Penny* is *R. v. Tait*.[106] There, Dickson Co. Ct. J. held that evidence of a police officer that he clocked the defendant on his speedometer at a speed of 40 m.p.h. for a distance of three-tenths of a mile in a 30 m.p.h. zone is, if believed, sufficient evidence to support a speeding conviction, It is not necessary that the accuracy of the speedometer be proved to justify such a conviction. The law with respect to accepting speedometer evidence is canvassed in *R. v. Purdy*[107] and *R. v. Taggart*.[108]

Of course, there is no reason why the defence cannot put forward evidence of a speedometer reading in order to raise a reasonable doubt. For example, where the prosecution has elicited evidence that a defendant was clocked by radar travelling at an excessive speed, the defendant may testify that he was watching his speedometer and it indicated that he was travelling within the speed limit. Such evidence, if not disbelieved, should be sufficient to have the charge dismissed, notwithstanding that there was no evidence lead as to the accuracy of the defendant's speedometer: *R. v. Morris*.[109]

9. RADAR: BLINDED BY SCIENCE[110]

(a) Establishing a Prima Facie Case

R. v. O'Reilly[111] dealt with what evidence the Crown must present in order to establish a *prima facie* case. At trial, the appellant was convicted of speeding.

---

104 (1974), 20 C.C.C. (2d) 332 (Ont. C.A.).
105 [1950] 2 All E.R. 89 (U.K. K.B.).
106 [1965] 1 C.C.C. 16 (N.B. Co. Ct.).
107 (1963), 6 Cr. L.Q. 510 (N.S. Co. Ct.).
108 (1956), 114 C.C.C. 274 (N.S. C.A.).
109 Rendered September 28 1987, Paris Prov. J. unreported.
110 See also the discussion in Chapter 4, under the heading "Expert Evidence."
111 (1979), 3 M.V.R. 228 (Alta. Dist. Ct.). See also *Keenan, supra*, note 38.

The Crown had called only one witness, a constable, who stated in evidence that he had tested the radar set both before and after the reading in question and was satisfied that it was operating properly. He testified that he was trained in the operation of radar equipment and had considerable experience in the area. He had used a tuning fork and had obtained appropriate readings, which were set out in the certificate of the qualified tester. The certificate was tendered in evidence in accordance with s. 152(2) of the *Highway Traffic Act* (Alberta). The officer was not asked whether the radar device that he reported using was capable of accurately registering speeds or whether the tests conducted by him were approved tests.

McFadyen D.C.J. allowed the appeal and the conviction was set aside. The Court held that in view of the Crown's failure to adduce evidence that the radar set was capable of accurately measuring speeds and that the tests were approved tests, the case had not been made out, although this evidence could have been given by the officer who testified.[112]

In reaching this conclusion His Honour made reference to the Ontario Court of Appeal decision in *R. v. Grainger*.[113] In that case Roach J.A. considered whether there was evidence upon which to base a decision. He wrote:[114]

> The substance of Mr. Ross's argument in this Court was that the record supplied by the radar speedmeter amounted to nothing unless and until it was first established that such a machine, when properly used, was capable of registering the speed of a motor vehicle on a highway, that the machine at the relevant time was in good working condition and was properly used.
>
> In my respectful opinion, it is implicit in the police officer's evidence as summarized in the case stated, that this particular radar speedmeter, when properly used, is capable of registering the speed of a motor vehicle and that, at the time in question, it was being properly used and in good working order. True, the officer admitted that he was not an electronics expert, and, therefore, could not explain all of the scientific mechanism that made up the machine and resulted in it recording accurately the speed of a motor vehicle. He was, however, familiar with the manner in which the machine was intended to be used, and from his familiarity with it over a two weeks' period he stated that the data furnished by it was extremely accurate.
>
> It is possible for any machine to get out of order. On the day in question, however, the officer calibrated this machine by use of a tuning fork and testified that by the use of that device he ascertained that the machine was in good working order.

---

112 See *R. v. Cox* (1996), 180 A.R. 229 (Alta. Q.B.) where comparison of the laser unit to radar equipment, together with the visual estimate of the speed for the motor vehicle satisfied the circumstantial guarantee of trustworthiness. Evidence of tests performed on the laser unit, that the unit was working properly and capable of measuring speed sufficient to establish a *prima facie* case. On the same issue, see also *R. v. Alladina* (1994), 4 M.V.R. (3d) 180 (Alta. Q.B.) and *R. v. Sutherland* (1993), 47 M.V.R. (2d) 254 (Alta. Prov. Ct.), affirmed (1994), 3 M.V.R. (3d) 317 (Alta. Q.B.).

113 (1958), 28 C.R. 84 (Ont. C.A.).

114 *Ibid.*, at 85-86.

Although he could not give a scientific explanation of the operation, he stated that when the vibrations of a given tuning fork set up certain results in the machine, that in the light of his experience the machine was in good working order and capable of recording the speed of a motor vehicle.

A further case referred to in *O'Reilly* was *R. v. Jacobs*.[115] This case is useful because it sets out the essential elements upon which a conviction for speeding may be founded. Judge Patterson concisely summarized his review of the applicable authorities as follows:

Summarizing the foregoing cases, it would appear to me that the following conclusions can be reached:

(1) That the testimony of readings of less sophisticated devices, such as stop watches and speedometers, can be accepted by the Court as prima facie evidence, without proof of the accuracy of such devices. This rule would apply in the absence of legislative intervention with which I will deal shortly.

(2) That readings taken from radar instruments can be accepted as *prima facie* evidence in the following circumstances:

(a) The instrument must be operated by someone trained in its operation. He need not have knowledge of the electronics or mechanism of the device but must be thoroughly familiar with its use.

(b) The operator must give evidence that at the time in question he conducted an approved test of the instrument and that test satisfied him that the instrument was operating properly and was capable of accurately registering speeds. It would be preferable, in my view, for the operator to state that, based on his knowledge of the instrument, such a test satisfied him that the instrument was capable of accurately registering speeds over the entire range of the instrument and what the range was; but the cases do not indicate that this is essential.

(3) The readings from a stop watch, a speedometer or a radar instrument is *prima facie* evidence only. Like any evidence, it is susceptible to rebuttal or raising a reasonable doubt — either by matters elicited on examination or cross-examination or defence evidence.

McFadyen D.C.J. concluded by stating that he was satisfied the law had been accurately stated by Patterson Prov. Ct. J.

In *R. v. Sutherland*,[116] the Court followed *Grainger*, and said:

… the Crown is asking the court to make a quantum leap in accepting the technology of laser readings on the same basis as radar readings. Radar speedmeters have been around for decades. When they were first utilized, empirical evidence of a test car driven through the radar beam at a predetermined speed was adduced together with evidence that the speedometer of the car was checked using a measured mile and a stopwatch. This cumbersome evidentiary process gradually gave

115 Alta. Prov. Ct. D.E. Patterson Prov. J. – unreported.
116 (1993), 47 M.V.R. (2d) 254 (Alta. Prov. Ct.), affirmed (1994), 3 M.V.R. (3d) 317 (Alta. Q.B.).

way to the use of tuning forks as the testing device. These tests thereafter received tacit legislative approval. Section 173 of the *Highway Traffic Act* creates and simplifies admission in evidence of tuning fork test certificates. …

The same cannot be said of the speed determining functions of laser technology. … It seems to me that when new technology which is not generally understood or accepted is placed before a trier of fact, absent expert evidence, there should be some independent empirical evidence to corroborate the litany and scenario created by the manufacturer and related by the operator of the equipment.[117]

(b) Judicial Notice of Radar

In *R. v. Waschuk*,[118] the defendant brought an appeal by way of stated case from a conviction on a charge of speeding. The facts were stated by the trial court as follows:

On the 22nd day of April, A.D. 1970 the accused was operating a motor vehicle in the 2300 block St. George's Avenue, in the City of Saskatoon, Province of Saskatchewan. The accused was identified to my satisfaction as being the operator of the motor vehicle.

A radar reading was taken of his speed and it indicated a reading of 42 m.p.h. It was also proved to my satisfaction that the speed limit in the 2300 block of St. George's Avenue is set at 30 m.p.h. by Saskatoon City Bylaw #4284. The following tests were made of the radar equipment:

> There was a check to see if power was going through the machine. The power read 24 m.p.h. The needle reset at zero when the set was in neutral position. The internal tuner read 60 m.p.h. and the external tuner read 65 m.p.h. Some tickets had been issued prior to the ticket being issued to the accused and the test was made after each ticket with the internal tuner fork and each time it showed 60 m.p.h. No explanation was given as to the meaningfulness of these tests. The beam control was set quite low. The range was set quite low. No patrol car was run through to test the machine. There were no vehicles between the accused's vehicle and the radar machine.

The issue to be decided was essentially whether judicial notice could be taken of the meaningfulness of tests of speed made by a radar machine. MacDonald J. held that judicial notice could not be taken because judicial notice may only be taken of facts which are known to intelligent persons generally. As such persons generally have no idea as to what makes a radar machine work, judicial notice may not be taken of the results of tests of speed, made by a radar machine. Indeed, the facts found by the trial judge would be a complete mystery to most people. Accordingly, the appeal was allowed.

117　*Ibid.*, at p. 258-259. See also *Re Redmond*, [1994] B.C.J. No. 3299. But see *R. v. Joesbury*, [1998] B.C.J. No. 876 where J.P. Makhdoom takes the contra position regarding Laser technology.

118　(1970), 1 C.C.C. (2d) 463 at 464 (Sask. Q.B.).

In *Lawless v. R.*,[119] the appellant contended that the trial judge erred in "not giving weight to the fact that the radar operated by the police officer may have locked on the heater fan which runs continuously in the Appellant's motor vehicle". It had been established in evidence that the police officer involved did not have any scientific knowledge as to how the particular radar gun worked, although he was trained in its operation. The officer also admitted that he had heard instances where radar machines had given speed readings on stationary objects, but he stated that in the present case he had calibrated the instrument after obtaining the reading, and he found it to be working properly.

MacDonald held that the weight of the evidence indicated that the radar machine was in proper working order and would show an accurate reading. It was not sufficient for the appellant to merely cite instances of radar machines taking inaccurate readings without showing that the machine in use was subject to a particular weakness or actually took a wrong reading.

In *R. v. Joudrey*,[120] the radar readings were obtained in atmospheric conditions of fog and drizzle. The defendant argued that the radar readings were wrong, and used a passage from a textbook in cross-examining the police officer regarding the resulting inaccuracies when radar readings are taken in this type of weather. Batiot J. held that the court could take judicial notice of the textbook passages and acquitted the defendant.

(c) Proving the Radar Device

R. v. Wolfe[121] was a case where the conviction was set aside because it could not be supported by the evidence. The officer involved testified that he was trained in the use of the device and that in his opinion the radar machine was working properly, but Arkell Co. Ct. J. held that other evidence cast doubt on the adequacy of his training, which in turn called into question the accuracy of the device and its results. Of particular importance in reaching this decision was the officer's uncertainty with respect to the testing procedure. In this regard, cross-examination of the officer is noteworthy, and a portion of it is set out below:[122]

> Q. Is it a procedure that is prescribed by this machine or do you know that?
> A. No, don't know that.
> Q. You don't know if it's a procedure prescribed for this machine?
> A. No.
> Q. Do you know, if in regard to this machine specifically, if you have had any training that has told you that the tuning fork method is a suitable method for testing this machine?

119 (1981), 11 M.V.R. 296 (P.E.I. S.C.).
120 (1992), 39 M.V.R. (2d) 235 (N.S. Prov. Ct.).
121 (1979), 3 M.V.R. 143 (B.C. Co. Ct.).
122 *Ibid.*, at p. 145.

A. If I had any instructions?
Q. Yes.
A. Only from my colleagues to use it as a check.
Q. That's all?
A. That is all.
Q. Did you have the occasion on this particular — at this particular time, using this particular machine, to test the accuracy of the machine against the actual speed of cars?
A. I'm sorry, how do you mean?
Q. Well, did you run a car through this particular machine, at this time, and determine that it was accurate in that matter?
A. No, I didn't.

In *R. v. Werenka*,[123] an appeal was dismissed where the defence sought to rely on *R. v. O'Reilly*,[124] suggesting that the Crown was obliged to demonstrate that the instrument was capable of accurately registering speeds over the entire range of the instrument, but without calling defence evidence as was the case in *O'Reilly*.

In *Werenka*, the only evidence at trial was given by a police officer on the basis of radar results. He said he had successfully completed a radar course lasting three days given by the police. He had been using the same device for nine months prior to the offence. Tuning fork tests were conducted in accordance with his training and he testified that the device was working and capable of accurately measuring speed. The appellant, he said, had been driving his motor vehicle at 112 k.m.h. in a 90 k.m.h. zone. The officer tendered a certificate in accordance with s. 152(1) of the *Highway Traffic Act* (Alberta), which showed the tuning fork to be accurate at 64 k.m.h. Carusey J. held that the Crown was not obliged to demonstrate that the instrument was capable of accurately registering speeds over the entire range of the instrument where there was no evidence to throw doubt on the officer's evidence.

In *R. v. Lehane*,[125] there was no evidence before the trial judge to indicate that the radar device had been recently tested to determine whether or not the device was operating properly and was capable of accurately measuring speeds. In adopting the reasons of Mcfadyen J. in *O'Reilly*, above, and allowing the appeal, Quigley J. stated, "In my opinion it would be an easy matter for police officers to test the accuracy of radar devices by means of a calibrated tuning fork or by some other means before and after a duty shift during which the device is used."[126]

R. v. Giffin[127] is a case in which the officers involved described the appellant as travelling at 107 k.m.h. in an area with an 80 k.m.h. maximum.

---

123 (1981), 11 M.V.R. 280 (Alta. Q.B.).
124 *Supra*, note 111.
125 (1982), 15 M.V.R. 160 (Alta. Q.B.).
126 *Ibid.*, at p. 161.
127 (1980), 8 M.V.R. 313 (N.S. Co. Ct.).

The purpose or functioning of the radar gun was not testified to, nor was the speed described in terms of kilometres per hour.

The defendant cited *Waschuk*[128] for the proposition that it must be explicitly stated in the evidence that the radar machine was capable of recording the speed of the vehicle being tested. In dealing with this ground of appeal, O'Hearn Co. Ct. J. held that it is apparent "radar" is part of the ordinary language of the Canadian community, and that the use of the device, although not its exact functioning, of course, is within the knowledge of the community.

The appellant's other principal objection dealt with the fact that "80 kilometres" and "107 kilometres" are not expressions of speed but rather of distance. In dealing with this ground, O'Hearn Co. Ct. J. stated as follows:[129]

> A faint suspicion arises from the transcript that the police may be using "kilometres" as expressions of the same nature as "knots", i.e., as expressions of speed rather than of distance. Whether this is so or not, when the questioned expressions are taken in the context of the evidence given in the case, there can be no doubt that they were used as expressions of speed and that everybody present at the trial so understood them, and no one reading the transcript could have any doubt either. While the slack use of language is to be deplored, it is not the function of the Court to correct the language of witnesses or to act as a sort of sergeant major of language, but to administer the law by ascertaining what was communicated by the evidence. In cases where the language fails a Court must, of course, refuse the proof, but where, however slovenly, the language communicates the intended meaning sufficiently clearly, there is no case for rejecting it because it is technically imprecise. In the instant case the communication was sufficient and the appellant fails on this point.

The appeal was thus dismissed.

Giffin, above, may be contrasted with the decision of Zimmerman Prov. Ct. J. in the unreported case of *Meyer v. R.*[130] At trial, Ms. Meyer was convicted of speeding. On appeal to the Provincial Court (Criminal Division), defence counsel advanced the argument that it had not been explicitly stated in evidence by the investigating police officer that, having tested the machine and found it to be working accurately, the machine was capable of measuring the speed of a motor vehicle across the full range of the set. On this ground, the appeal was allowed.

On the issue of testing the radar device, the case of *R. v. Furlong*[131] is informative. At trial, an officer had given evidence as follows: The machine was tested at 5:39 and 5:56 and was working accurately per the manufacturer's specifications. What he did not say was that it was he who had tested the machine, nor is there evidence that he alone was in the police vehicle. A motion

128 *Supra*, note 118.
129 *Supra*, note 127, at 319.
130 Ont. Prov. Ct., August 23, 1984.
131 Ont. Prov. Ct. Palmer Prov. J., unreported. See also *R. v. Cox*, [1996] A.J. No. 57.

for a directed verdict was denied by the learned Justice of the Peace. This argument proved successful on appeal, however, Palmer Prov. Ct. J. simply noted that the Court has to be satisfied on the evidence before it that the machine was tested by a qualified operator and was in working condition.

In *Joliette (Ville) v. Delangis*[132] the Court held that to convict on the offence of speeding the prosecution must prove that the operator of a laser device was qualified, and that the device could measure speed accurately. This latter issue must be proven by indicating comparison at a specified time with conventional radar or a speedometer.

R. v. Woolridge[133] was an appeal by the defendant from his conviction on a charge of speeding, contrary to s. 131(2) of the *Highway Traffic Act* (Newfoundland)).[134] The trial judge had accepted the evidence of the police officer that the defendant had been speeding and that the radar device was operating properly. It was not open to the Court on appeal to reverse the trial judge's finding on fact unless those findings were unreasonable or not supported by the evidence. In the circumstances here, there was no evidence that, if believed by the trial Judge, would justify a finding that the defendant had committed the offence. The appeal was dismissed.

(d) The Problems of Tuning Fork Accuracy

In *R. v. Bourque*,[135] a defendant appealed his conviction for speeding. At trial, he had given evidence that he had been travelling within the speed limit. The officer involved, who had clocked the defendant on radar, testified that he had tested the radar set with a tuning fork and found it to be working properly. No document was tendered by the Crown certifying the tuning fork was accurate, nor was there any evidence that the radar set was capable of properly registering the speed of the defendant's vehicle.

Moshansky J. allowed the appeal, holding that where the Crown seeks to rely on electronic devices for convictions, then it must be prepared to establish beyond a reasonable doubt that such devices are operating properly and capable of performing the functions for which they are intended. If a tuning fork is used to test the performance of the radar set and is not itself proven to be performing accurately, then there has to be a reasonable doubt on the evidence as to the reliability of the readings given by the radar set. The benefit of any such reasonable doubt must be given to a defendant.[136]

---

132 (1997), 35 W.C.B. (2d) 378 (Que. S.C.).
133 (December 17, 1987), G-217/87 (Nfld. T.D.), summarized at 3 W.C.B. (2d) 313.
134 R.S.N. 1970, c. 152.
135 (1985), 38 M.V.R. 110 (Alta. Q.B.), reversed (1986), [1989] A.W.L.D. 356 (Alta. C.A.).
136 See also *Cook, supra* note 25.

10. "REASONABLE AND PRUDENT SPEED" STATUTES

O'Hearn Co. Ct. J., in *R. v. Parsons*[137] had occasion to deal with certain sections of the Nova Scotia Act that created a built-in defence if the defendant could show that his speed did not exceed the permitted speed by more than a prescribed amount and was reasonable and prudent under the existing conditions. This is similar to a defence of due diligence.

At trial, a charge of speeding had been dismissed against the respondent. He explained in his evidence that he had pushed his accelerator in a normal fashion and it stuck. This caused him to believe the engine was idling too high and so he gave the accelerator a quick push but the acceleration did not stop. The respondent then observed the pedal stuck on the floor mat and reached down to free it. The trial Judge found the respondent credible and that the defence of due diligence was available and had been made out.

In allowing the Crown's appeal, O'Hearn Co. Ct. J. held that where the Legislature had prescribed a defence of a nature analogous to due diligence but defined in narrower terms, there was no justification for enlarging the defence so that it extended to the range generally permitted under the canon of strict liability.

This did not conclude the matter, however. There are defences that apply to all crimes, whether they are indictable or summary offences. Incapacity, such as infancy and insanity, as well as necessity, compulsion and duress fall into this category. The absence of volition may still be raised in absolute liability matters. The defendant was entitled to the defence that his driving at the speed in question was involuntary in the sense that it was the result not of his own volition but of an extraneous factor, not subject to his control nor caused by his negligence. In view of the respondent's admission that the floor mat had caused problems in the past, and in view of the fact that the trial judge did not follow the correct premises of law, the appeal was allowed and the matter remitted to a new trial.[138]

In *R. v. Kennedy*,[139] it was not disputed that the posted speed limit was 90 k.m.h. and that the respondent's vehicle was clocked by police aircraft at over 100 k.m.h. The only issue that arose was whether, as held by the trial judge, the respondent was charged under the proper section of the *Motor Vehicle Act* (Nova Scotia).[140] He was charged under s. 94(1) rather than s. 96(2), and it fell to the Appeal Court to determine whether such charging justified an acquittal or, in the alternative, if the charge was not "wrong", the respondant should be permitted to rely on the defence under s. 94(2) that his speed was "reasonable and prudent under the conditions at the time existing".

Sections 94 and 96 provided:

---

137 (1981), 11 M.V.R. 39 (N.S. Co. Ct.).
138 See also *R. v. Racimore* (1975), 25 C.C.C. (2d) 143 (Ont. H.C.).
139 (1972), 7 C.C.C. (2d) 42 (N.S. Co. Ct.).
140 R.S.N.S. 1967, c. 191, now R.S.N.S. 1989, c. 293, ss. 104(1), 104(2), 106(1), 106(2).

94. (1) Notwithstanding the foregoing provisions of this Act the Minister or a traffic authority with the approval of the Provincial Traffic Authority may fix such maximum rates of speed as he may see fit to approve for motor vehicles traversing any part or portion of a highway and may erect and maintain signs containing notification of such rate of speed so fixed and approved by him, and thereafter while such signs remain so erected and displayed the operator or driver of any vehicle exceeding the rate of speed so fixed and approved shall be guilty of an offence under this Act.

(2) It shall be a defence in any prosecution for a violation of this Section if the defendant can show that the speed at which the vehicle was being driven was reasonable and prudent under the conditions at the time existing.

96. (1) Notwithstanding any other provision of this Act, but subject to subsection (2), no person shall drive a motor vehicle at a speed in excess of sixty miles per hour on any highway at any time.

(2) The Minister may fix rates of speed in excess of sixty miles per hour for certain highways and may erect and maintain signs containing notification of such rate of speed, and the driver of a motor vehicle who exceeds that rate of speed so fixed shall be guilty of an offense against this Act.

At trial, the learned County Court Judge apparently considered that where, as here, the posted limit was over 80 k.m.h. and the posting therefore presumably made under s. 96(2), the charge "should" be laid under section 96(2), and that a charge under s. 94(1) should be laid only where the limit posted was 80 k.m.h. or less. The Appeal Court, however, disagreed, noting that nothing in s. 94 limits its application to exceeding posted speed limits of 80 k.m.h. or less. Here the police officer could have charged the respondent either under s. 94(1) or under section 96(2). Since all of the elements of the offence created by s. 94(1) were here proven, the learned judge on appeal should have affirmed the conviction, unless the respondent could have employed the defence created by s. 94(2).

With respect to the second issue, or a charge under s. 94(1), a defence under s. 94(2) cannot succeed under the following conditions: (1) where no limit was posted and the speed was over 80 k.m.h.; (2) where a limit of 80 k.m.h. or less was posted and the actual speed was over 80 k.m.h.; (3) where, as here, a limit of over 80 k.m.h. was posted and that limit was exceeded. Speed that is illegal cannot be "reasonable and prudent".

In *R. v. Peebles*,[141] the defendant was driving a car in excellent condition at 50 m.p.h. in a 35 m.p.h. zone in daylight on a straight country highway with which he was very familiar and on which there was no other traffic. There were very few buildings along the road and weather conditions were perfect. Sisson J. held that the appellant was not driving at a rate of speed that was unreasonable having regard to all of the existing circumstances. The appeal was therefore allowed.

---

141 (1960), 127 C.C.C. 240 (N.W.T. Terr. Ct.).

6

Careless Driving

1. INTRODUCTION

Section 130 of the *Highway Traffic Act*, R.S.O. 1990, c. H.8 provides:

130. Every person is guilty of the offence of driving carelessly who drives a vehicle or streetcar on a highway without due care and attention or without reasonable consideration for other persons using the highway and on conviction is liable to a fine of not less than $200 and not more than $1000 or to imprisonment for a term of not more than six months, or to both, and in addition his or her licence or permit may be suspended for a period of not more than two years.

This short section sets out one of the most serious offences found in the Ontario *Highway Traffic Act* and certainly one of the most litigated. Almost identical provisions are found in other provincial traffic statutes.[1] Defendants convicted of careless driving receive six demerit points. The wording of the section is wide, however, and many defendants, rather than face the vagaries of a trial on such a charge, opt to plead guilty to a less serious offence. In our view, too many charges of careless driving are laid in the absence of sufficient evidence. The vagueness of the wording invites 'over charging' where the investigating officer is unsure of the defendant's wrongful act. Discretion should be exercised in the application of s. 130. Where possible, it is preferable to charge persons with a more specific offence. Of course, as with all criminal and quasi-criminal offences, the burden on the Crown is the same: proof beyond a reasonable doubt.[2]

---

1 R.S.A. 1980, c. H-7, s. 123; R.S.B.C. 1996, c. 318, s. 144; S.M. 1985-86, c. 3, s. 188; R.S.N.B. 1973, c. M-17, s. 7; R.S.N. 1990, c. H-3, s. 110; R.S.N.S. 1989, c. 293, s. 100; R.S.P.E.I. 1988, c. H-5, s. 176; S.S. 1996, c. H-3.2, s. 44; R.S.Y. 1986, c. 118, s. 179; R.S.N.W.T. 1988, c. M-16, s. 154.

2 See *R. v. Gooding* (1977), 33 N.S.R. (2d) 98 (N.S. Co. Ct.).

2. CONFLICT BETWEEN FEDERAL AND PROVINCIAL LAWS

In *R. v. Mann*,[3] the Supreme Court of Canada held that s. 60, the predecessor to s. 130 of the *Highway Traffic Act*, was valid provincial legislation as it was in relation to the regulation of highway traffic. The argument had been advanced that the provincial offence of careless driving had been rendered inoperative by Parliament introducing into the *Criminal Code* the offence of dangerous driving. The Court found, however, that this was not the case. Dangerous driving is concerned with conduct that is something more than mere inadvertence, or mere negligence, or mere error of judgment. Unlike s. 130 [then s. 60] of the *Highway Traffic Act*, the *Criminal Code* offence requires a manner of driving that is dangerous to the public.

In *O'Grady v. Sparling*[4] the Supreme Court of Canada held that the provincial section dealt with "inadvertent negligence" while the relevant provisions of the *Criminal Code* dealt only with "advertent negligence." The two offences, then, not only set out different degrees of negligence, but are different in kind.

The Ontario Court of Appeal in *R. v. Yolles*[5] held that the offence of careless driving is valid provincial legislation in relation to the administration and control of traffic upon highways in the province. It is not legislation in relation to criminal law nor is it in conflict with the *Criminal Code*. Chief Justice Porter held that careless driving is in a sense a residual catch-all provision designed to ensure safety on highways in the province and covering situations that might arise which are not covered by the more specific rules of the road. The test here is whether the federal and provincial enactments are *pari materia*[6] and in conflict with each other so that their provisions could not be in force at the same time. The relevant *Criminal Code* provisions deal with a high degree of negligence, and careless driving involves a different offence created for a different purpose. The fact that circumstances supporting the higher offence might include those supporting the lesser does not oust the provincial enactment because this does not make the two enactments in *pari materia* or bring them into conflict.

3. DOUBLE JEOPARDY

The plea of *autrefois acquit* is not available to a person charged with dangerous driving following his conviction on a charge of careless driving. The two are not identical charges.

---

3 (1966), [1966] S.C.R. 238 (S.C.C.).

4 (1960), [1960] S.C.R. 804 (S.C.C.).

5 (1959), [1959] O.R. 206 (Ont. C.A.).

6 Translates roughly as "of the same matter."

In *R. v. Anthony*[7] the defendant was arraigned on a charge of careless driving which the Crown then withdrew. He was subsequently arraigned on a charge of dangerous driving. The Nova Scotia Appeal Court concluded that dangerous driving and careless driving were not identical offences and not amenable to the special pleas of *autrefois acquit/convict* or the common law defence of *res judicata*.[8]

In *R. v. Stadelbauer*[9] the appellant was convicted on April 19, 1991 of the charge of careless driving. On September 20, 1991 she was convicted of dangerous driving out of the same facts or series of facts. On appeal, the issue was whether the principle barring multiple convictions for similar charges[10] involving the same set of facts applied in the case of dangerous and careless driving. Mr. Justice Salhany said it did not. Firstly, the charge of careless driving is not the same as dangerous driving, since dangerous driving imports an element of danger to members of the public actually present or who might reasonably have been expected to be in the particular vicinity at the time the driving took place.[11] Careless driving, on the other hand, "does not necessarily" involve the public at all. Also, dangerous driving involves advertent negligence whereas careless driving involves only inadvertent negligence. Secondly, Salhany J. held that it is inappropriate to apply the rule barring multiple convictions for the same offence if the two offences were created by different legislative bodies.[12] Thus, if the driving is bad enough, the defendant is exposed to the dual sting of convictions for dangerous driving under the *Criminal Code*, and careless driving under the provincial act.[13]

4. THE MENTAL ELEMENT OF THE OFFENCE

Legislation does not assist as to whether or not *mens rea* must be proved to secure a careless driving conviction. In *R. v. McIver*,[14] the Court held that the Crown need only prove that the defendant committed the prohibited act. Unless he can show that such act was done without negligence or fault on his part[15] he will be convicted.[16] *McIver* thus stands for the proposition that

---

7 (1982), 16 M.V.R. 160 (N.S. S.C.).

8 See also *R. v. Lainey*, unreported, December 3, 1976, Ont. H.C.; *R. v. Landman* (1984), 33 M.V.R. 89 (B.C. Prov. Ct.).

9 (1992), 36 M.V.R. (2d) 181 (Ont. Gen. Div.).

10 *R. v. Kienapple* (*sub nom. Kienapple v. R.*), [1975] 1 S.C.R. 729, 1 N.R. 322 (S.C.C.).

11 *Supra* note 9 at p. 7. *Beaudoin* (1973), 12 C.C.C. (2d) 81 (Ont. C.A.).

12 Quare whether Salhany J.'s reasons do not, in and of themselves, lend support for the opposite conclusion since His Honour is saying ultimately that dangerous driving is simply a more extreme version of careless driving, analogous to the offences of theft and robbery.

13 See also *R. v. Landman* (1984), 33 M.V.R. 89 (B.C. Prov. Ct.).

14 [1965] 4 C.C.C. 182 (Ont. C.A.), affirmed [1966] 2 C.C.C. 289 (S.C.C.). See also *R. v. Kozun* (1997), 34 W.C.B. (2d) 171 (Sask. Q.B.).

15 See also *R. v. Pyszko* (1998), 38 W.C.B. (2d) 25 (Ont. Prov. Ct.).

16 Reference may also be made to *R. v. Johnson* (1983), 45 N.B.R. (2d) 371 (N.B. Q.B.) and *R. v. Therrien* (September 6, 1991), Doc. 5606 (Ont. Gen. Div.). Contra see *R. v. Lucki* (1955),

careless driving is not an offence requiring *mens rea*, but an acquittal should be entered if the defendant can establish that she was duly diligent.

It is sometimes said in traffic court that in the case of a motor vehicle collision, the prosecutor need only make out a *prima facie* case of careless driving to secure a conviction. *McIver*[17] is often used in support of this proposition. In our view, this is erroneous and misleading.[18] If the prosecution is to prove the charge, it must still, even in the absence of defence evidence, make out an act of careless driving beyond a reasonable doubt. Sometimes, obviously, without answering the charge by way of defence, the prosecution will meet this threshold in the course of presenting its case.

In *R. v. Skorput*[19] the court observed that in order to prove the charge of careless driving, the Crown must prove as part of its case that the fact alleged (in this case an accident), is not merely an accident but conduct prohibited by s. 130 of the Act.[20] After this has been done, the onus shifts back to the defendant to show that she was not negligent.[21] Thus, in order to prove the mental element of careless driving, the prosecution must initially show that there is no due diligence or explanation for the driving, within its own case. If such an explanation does exist, via witnesses or expert evidence, or any other evidence, then the defendant is entitled to an acquittal. If such an explanation does not exist within the Crown evidence, then the onus is on the defendant to provide evidence of due diligence. If she cannot do this on a balance of probabilities, and if the conduct is deserving of punishment, then a conviction should be entered.[22]

5. "DESERVING OF PUNISHMENT"

It is this last criterion — that the driving must be considered "deserving of punishment" — which is most problematic and which leads to inconsistent applications of the section. It could be said that it imparts a *mens rea* element to the offence.

---

17 W.W.R. 446 (Sask. Police Court), where the position is taken that careless driving is an offence involving full *mens rea*.

17 *Supra*, note 14.

18 See *R. v. Kotar*, [1994] O.J. No. 763 (Ont. Prov. Ct.) where the Court noted "it is inappropriate for the offence of careless driving to require a shifting burden of proof on a balance of probabilities that what was done without negligence on the defendant's part."

19 (1992), 72 C.C.C. (3d) 294 (Ont. Prov. Div.).

20 *Ibid.*, at p. 301.

21 See also *R. v. Reber*, (September 16, 1992), Stone Prov. J. (Ont. Prov. Div.); *R. v. Skorput*, and *R. v. Kozun* (1997), 34 W.C.B.(2d) 171 (Sask. Q.B.).

22 In *Reber* Stone J. said (at p. 4) that:

> ... it is not inappropriate that an accused should bear the onus of establishing diligence on a balance of probabilities, since his or her actions are peculiarly within his or her knowledge. A by-stander can only guess, or in some cases try to infer what an accused

In *R. v. Grosvenor*[23] the Appellant had driven a motor vehicle in close proximity to a person lying on the ground. At trial he was convicted of careless driving.[24] Veit J. allowed the appeal and ordered a new trial saying,

> There are potential custodial sanctions for a person found guilty of the offence of careless driving ... Therefore, in the prosecution of this offence, although a provincial offence and not a crime, *the Crown must prove not only that the accused committed the careless act, but also*, that he had the requisite guilty mind.[25]

Veit J. then likened the requisite *mens rea* in careless driving to that of homicide. First, there must be a prima facie case of *mens rea*, and secondly, it must be proven that the defendant had the capacity to appreciate the risk flowing from the conduct.[26]

What seems crucial to Veit J. is that a careless driving conviction carries potential custodial punishment. This, it appears, imports the concept of "deserving of punishment" into the *mens rea* analysis. In other words, before a defendant is convicted of careless driving and exposed to a possible six-month term of incarceration, there must be a guilty mind.[27]

This was the approach taken by Cartwright D.C.J. in *R. v. Divizio*.[28] On the issue of *mens rea*, His Honour stated as follows:

> In my view, the trial judge failed to appreciate that the essential element of *mens rea* has to be proven beyond a reasonable doubt before a verdict of guilty may be found. This finding has *perforce* to be made from indirect evidence; no one can read what went on in the defendant's mind at the time of the accident, and the trial judge should therefore have directed himself that he may in law find the presence of that essential ingredient in the mind of the defendant at that time if he was satisfied beyond a reasonable doubt that the presence of *mens rea* was the only reasonable inference to be drawn from the facts that he found proven from the evidence before him: *R. v. Cooper* (1977), 34 C.C.C. (2d) 18 at pp. 31-3, 74 D.L.R. (3d) 731, [1978] 1 S.C.R. 860 (S.C.C.).[29]

Grosvenor and *Divizio* are at odds with *McIver* insofar as the former cases place proof of *mens rea* and proof of capacity to appreciate risk in the list of matters requisite to a conviction. *McIver* stands for the opposite proposition, viz. absence of proof of *mens rea* is not a bar to conviction.

---

actually saw, heard or felt, and how the driver's responses flowed from those sensations.

23 (1993), 50 M.V.R. (2d) 95 (Alta. Q.B.).

24 Under s. 123(a) *Highway Traffic Act*, R.S.A. 1980, c. H-7.

25 *Supra*, note 23 at p. 98 (emphasis added).

26 Citing *R. v. Creighton* (1993), 83 C.C.C. (3d) 346 (S.C.C.) per McLachlin J.

27 The difficulty with such analysis is that Veit J. does not explicitly refer to "deserving of punishment."

28 (1986), 1 M.V.R. (2d) 226 (Ont. Dist. Ct.).

29 His view accords with that taken by Gerein D.C.J. in *Mogenson v. Wright*, note 92, below. In his view, the words "due" and "reasonable" clearly bring *mens rea*, actual or constructive,

In the authors' view, *Grosvenor* and *Divizio* should be approached with caution until such reasoning has been endorsed by appellate courts.[30]

Contrary to *Divizio*, is *Lower*[31] where it was held that momentary inattention at speeds of 20-30 m.p.h., if proved, may be sufficient to constitute a *prima facie* case. It was further held that the Court is not obliged to conclude that the defendant drove in a manner deserving of punishment and *mens rea* is not a necessary element of the offence of careless driving.[32]

In *R. v. Globocki*[33] the Court concluded that the process for determining blameworthiness in careless driving cases is similar to the process involved in cases of criminal negligence. While the impugned conduct in careless driving will necessarily be less serious than cases of criminal negligence, in both situations, it is open to the trier of fact to conclude that the indifference in the sense of a negative mind,[34] is as deserving of punishment as a positive intention to drive carelessly.

Ultimately, the question of blameworthiness is a question to be determined by the trier of fact in light of prevailing community standards. In *R. v. Yorston*[35] the Appellant had hit another car while negotiating a "U-Turn." Hall J. resorted to the concept of the fair-minded person.

In this case the appellant was acting in the course of his duties as a police officer. Part of his duty as such was to enforce the provisions of the *Motor Vehicle Act*.

> He observed what he believed to be a violation of the Act. In the course of attempting to pursue the violator he made an error of perception. After making a number of checks and satisfying himself that the highway was clear he failed to see the other vehicle on the highway. *In my opinion no fair-minded person would say that this was conduct deserving of punishment in the nature of criminal-type sanctions.*[36] (Emphasis added)

The authors' take the view that this is an appropriate manner of determining what is "deserving of punishment."

---

into the section. "It is not an absolute prohibition against ordinary negligence which carries with it only civil liability."

30 Especially since neither the *Grosvenor*, nor *Divizio* judgments consider the leading case of *R. v. McIver*, *supra*, note 14.

31 [1982] B.C.W.L.D. 1421 (B.C. Co. Ct.).

32 See also *R. v. Matheson* (January 9, 1990), Doc. 295/90 (Ont. Gen. Div.) – Huneault J., held that a conviction for careless driving did not require proof of *mens rea*.

33 (1991), 26 M.V.R. (2d) 179 (Ont. Prov. Ct.).

34 Following *R. v. Sharp* (1984), 12 C.C.C. (3d) 428 (Ont. C.A.).

35 (1991), 32 M.V.R. (2d) 285 (N.S. Co. Ct.).

36 *Ibid.*, at p. 291.

6. EXAMPLES OF CONDUCT HELD TO BE SUFFICIENT TO SUPPORT CONVICTION

In *R. v. Namink*[37] Killeen J. held that momentary inattention or a simple error of judgment is insufficient to justify a conviction of careless driving. The offence is "driving carelessly" which, the *Act* provides, may be done in one of two ways: without due care and attention or without reasonable consideration for other persons using the highway as per *R. v. MacKenzie*.[38] Mere inadvertent negligence (whether of the slightest type or of some more significant form) will not necessarily sustain a conviction for careless driving. The Crown must prove beyond a reasonable doubt that the defendant either drove his vehicle on a highway without due care and attention or that he operated it without reasonable consideration for other persons using the highway. One of these ingredients must be proven to support a conviction.[39]

R. v. Jacobsen[40] holds that "inadvertent negligence denotes no more than absence of thought, of due care and attention, the failure to observe which is an offence per se, excluding the considerations that the conduct must constitute a breach of duty to the public and be deserving of punishment in a criminal way."[41]

In *R. v. Beauchamp*[42] the Ontario Court of Appeal held that the standard of care and skill to be applied is not that of perfection. A driver is required to exercise a reasonable amount of skill, and to do what an ordinary prudent person would do in the circumstances. The use of the term "due care", which means the care owing in the circumstances, makes it clear that, while the legal standard of care remains the same in the sense that it is always what the ordinary prudent person would do in the circumstances, the factual standard is always shifting, depending on road, visibility, weather and traffic conditions that exist, or may reasonably be expected, and any other conditions that an ordinary prudent driver would take into consideration. The standard is an objective one, fixed in relation to the safety of other users of the highway, and in no way related to the degree of proficiency or experience attained by the individual driver whose conduct is in question. It is not, however, enough that the defendant's conduct should be shown to fall below this standard. Since the offence is quasi-criminal, it must also appear that the defendant's conduct

---

37 (1979), 27 Chitty's L.J. 289 (Ont. Co. Ct.).
38 (1956), 114 C.C.C. 335 (Ont. H.C.).
39 See *R. v. Wilson* (1971), 1 C.C.C. (2d) 466 (Ont. C.A.). See also *R. v. Turgeon* (1958), 120 C.C.C. 248 (Sask. Dist. Ct.).
40 (1964), 48 W.W.R. 272 (B.C. C.A.).
41 See also *R. v. Haley* (August 9, 1991), Welland 8642/91 (Ont. Gen. Div.), where the driver's attention was "somewhat diverted" by a dog in the back seat of the vehicle.
42 (1953), [1953] O.R. 422 (Ont. C.A.).

has been of such a nature that it can be considered a breach of duty to the public, and so deserving of punishment by the state.[43]

(a) Cumulative Effect of Several 'Careless' Actions

A good example of the type of evidence needed to found a conviction for careless driving is *R. c. Marceau*.[44] There, police officers came across two vehicles that appeared to be speeding. The officers chased the vehicle for a distance of some four miles and speeds reached 85 m.p.h. in a 55 m.p.h. zone. On two separate occasions, the cars passed vehicles after crossing double white lines. Ultimately, one of the police cars intercepted one of the speeders. The other police car continued to pursue the remaining speeder, who was the appellant. The appellant went through a village at 55 m.p.h. when the maximum speed was 25 m.p.h.. He passed two other vehicles while on the wrong side of a double white line. Lastly, he went through a stop sign at 30 m.p.h. The Crown argued that the offence was made out on an accumulation of actions which disclosed the requisite fault. Dugas J. of the Quebec Superior Court agreed. He held that a conviction may be based on evidence of a number of circumstances that disclose carelessness and it wouldn't be appropriate to take a compartmentalised view of the driving in question. Here, speeding for a long distance, passing cars improperly and going through a stop sign all point to a contravention of the applicable section. One is permitted to view the conduct as a whole.[45]

In *R. v. Rousseau*,[46] it was held that improper driving may be manifested by recklessness on the part of the driver, negligence or a speed incompatible with public safety, or any disregard of the public.

In *R. v. McDorman*,[47] the defendant, a professional truck driver, was charged with careless driving and with having faulty brakes. He was transporting cyanide, unfamiliar with the particular route he was taking, and missed

---

43 See also *R. v. Seabrook* (1952), 103 C.C.C. 7 (Ont. H.C.) where it was held that in discussing the offence of careless driving it is fallacious to introduce a discussion of degrees of negligence. It is entirely a matter of applying the language of the Act in its ordinary connotation to the facts of the case, and the essence of the matter is danger to the public, actual or potential to which the concept of civil negligence has no application. See also *McCrone v. Riding*, [1938] 1 All E.R. 157 (K.B.); *R. v. Parsons* (1952), 15 C.R. 409 (Alta. Dist. Ct.) and Segal et al. *Manual of Motor Vehicle Law* (Toronto: Carswell, 1983). Note, contra, that whether or not there was actual or potential danger to the public has also been held to be irrelevant to the offence: *R. v. Smallman* (1946), [1946] 1 C.C.C. 340 (P.E.I. S.C.).

44 (1978), 2 M.V.R. 202 (Que. C.S.).

45 See also *R. v. Rieswyk* (1978), 54 A.P.R. 602, 1 M.V.R. 177 (N.S. Co. Ct.). In *R. v. Rogers* (1981), 34 N.B.R. (2d) 353 (N.B. Q.B.) where it was held that speeding, passing on the left, failing to yield the right of way and an accident were, on the facts, held to be sufficient indices of careless driving.

46 (1938), 70 C.C.C. 252 (Ont. C.A.).

47 (1983), 23 M.V.R. 165 (B.C. Prov. Ct.); affirmed (1984), 27 M.V.R. 37 (B.C. Co. Ct.).

two signs leading to a by-pass around Kamloops. He had been driving for 30 hours when he descended a steep grade in the downtown district of the city. Although within the speed limit as he approached an intersection, his brakes failed totally and he drove into a number of parked vehicles causing a considerable amount of damage. He sounded his horn at the time, but in retrospect admitted he might have pulled the air-brake buttons in the truck. The brake linings were found to be worn beyond acceptable limits and the brake drums required changing. Other inadequacies were found which would have been revealed by a simple test before the journey. The defendant was convicted of careless driving. His conduct as a whole was examined. Weighed together, each of these factors viewed objectively (i.e. failure to use the air brake, failure to follow directions etc.) constitute the offence.

Clearly, there is not one standard for ordinary drivers and another for drivers who are just learning to drive or whose skill is above that of an ordinary driver. In *Skowronnek v. R.*[48] the defendant, a highly-qualified rally driver, was driving a specially-equipped rally car in a remote area of Saskatoon specially chosen for that purpose. The outward and visible signs of the offence of driving without due care and attention were speed, "fishtailing", "kicking up" of gravel by the motor vehicle driven by the appellant, and a police "chase." Walker D.C.J., of the Saskatchewan District Court, held that the offence calls for consideration of an objective standard of care and attention not related to the degree of proficiency or experience of the particular defendant involved. There is not one standard for ordinary drivers and another for others.[49]

(b) "Driving"[50]

To be convicted, the defendant must have been driving and not merely positioned in the driver's seat. In *R. v. Jacobs*,[51] the defendant drove his automobile on the wrong side of a fairly busy road on a dark night and stopped it momentarily opposite some letter boxes in order to extract his mail. He left his headlights on and his engine running, and he did not get out of his car. This was at a place 500 feet east of a brow of a hill. Another driver, proceeding east on his right-hand side of the road, on coming over the brow of the hill saw the defendant's lights ahead of him and drove to pass the defendant on

---

48 (1980), 9 M.V.R. 36 (Sask. Dist. Ct.).
49 See also *R. v. Malleck-Lacroix* (1991), 35 M.V.R. (2d) 46 (Ont. Prov. Div.) where it was held that a school bus driver was held to have a higher degree of care than the common driver. This seems to suggest that all things being equal, such special drivers may have their impugned actions more deserving of punishment than others.
50 *Black's Law Dictionary* defines "driving" in the following manner:
"To urge forward under guidance, compel to go in a particular direction, urge onward, and direct the course of."
51 (1955), 113 C.C.C. 73, 22 C.R. 154 (B.C. C.A.).

the right; realising too late that the defendant was stationary on the wrong side of the road. He collided with the mail boxes and the left rear side of defendant's car.

At trial the defendant was convicted of driving "without due care and attention" within the meaning of s. 57 of the *Motor Vehicle Act*. On Appeal the issue was whether Jacobs was "driving" while in his stationary vehicle so as to constitute an offence of careless driving.

The appeal was dismissed. The British Columbia Court of Appeal held that a person does not cease to drive an automobile merely because he stops temporarily for some purpose, e.g., in order to see if he can turn around in safety. Being stopped under such circumstances is an incident in the operation of the automobile which may fairly be described as driving it.

This is at odds with the decision of Toy J. in *R. v. James*[52] in the British Columbia Supreme Court. There, the defendant was charged with the offence of having the care and control of a motor vehicle while his ability to drive was impaired by alcohol or a drug under s. 234 of the *Criminal Code*, R.S.C. 1970, and had been convicted at trial. The issue arose as to what constituted "care and control" as distinct from "driving." Toy J. held that as a minimum requirement, driving entailed a movement of the vehicle and a governing of the direction of the vehicle by the person in charge. It could not be concluded, however, that one who was driving did not, as well, have care or control. "Care or control" has a wider scope than "driving" in that "care or control" can be exercised when the vehicle is stationary or not under power. It is inconceivable for one to "drive" a motor vehicle that is not in motion.

The British Columbia Court of Appeal attempted in 1992, to resolve the apparent contradiction between *Jacobs* and *James*. In *R. v. Steeden*,[53] the Appellant had left his bus parked behind another bus while he took a break. He left the vehicle without engaging the parking brake. The bus in front pulled away some minutes after Steeden left his vehicle. Steeden's bus then rolled down a hill mounting a curb killing two pedestrians and damaging much property. At issue on appeal was whether Steeden was the driver of the rolling bus for purposes of the careless driving charge under s. 149 of the British Columbia *Motor Vehicle Act*.[54]

Wood J.A. was of the view that the definition of "driver" must be given an ordinary meaning, as opposed to a definition specific to s. 149. In order to be driving, there must be "movement of the vehicle and control of that movement by the person said to be driving."[55] Crucial to this definition is the exercise of control over a vehicle in motion. This follows a line of English

---

52 (*Sub nom. R. v. Jones*) (1974), 17 C.C.C. (2d) 221 (B.C. S.C.).

53 [1995] B.C.J. 1413 (C.A.).

54 R.S.B.C. 1979, c. 288.

55 *Supra*, note 53 at p. 1413.

Authorities from that Court of Appeal.[56] Since Steeden was never in control of the bus while it careened down the hill, he was acquitted.

What distinguishes *Steeden* from *Jacobs* is arguably (i) that Steeden left his vehicle, (ii) Steeden intended to leave his vehicle stationary, and (iii) stopping a vehicle as Jacobs did (ie. while in the driver seat on the wrong side of the road with headlights on) is completely different from (i) and (ii). In fact, Wood J.A. remarked that *Jacobs* has no effect on the ruling in *Steeden* since Jacobs' action was a "manoeuvre."

(c) On a Highway

The question of where one drives so as to fall within the scrutiny of the section has, of course, also been litigated. "Highway" has been defined under s. 1(1) of the *Highway Traffic Act* as follows:

> "highway", includes a common and public highway, street, avenue, parkway, driveway, square, place, bridge, viaduct or trestle, any part of which is intended for or used by the general public for the passage of vehicles and includes the area between the lateral property lines thereof.

In *R. v. Mcmeekin*[57] it was held that the purpose of the British Columbia careless driving legislation was to protect the public by punishing dangerous and careless driving in places to which the public has access. An apartment complex parking lot which is not available for public use is not a "highway" as it is defined in the definitional section of the B.C. *Motor Vehicle Act*. Consequently, a person cannot be convicted under this section for driving a motor vehicle without due care and attention in such a locale. In *R. v. Wall*[58] it was held that a "sidewalk" is not included in the term "highway" which is where the offence must arise.[59]

(d) Wording of Charge

In *R. v. Archer*,[60] the defendant was charged following the wording of the then section which made it an offence to drive "without due care and attention" or "without reasonable consideration for other persons using the highway." This was found to be duplicitous. Owing to the abbreviated wording permitted

---

56 Namely *R. v. Roberts* [1965] 1 Q.B. 85; and also *R. v. MacDonagh*, [1974] Q.B. 448 (U.K. C.A.). See also *Blayney v. Knight* [1974] 60 Cr. App. R. 269 (Div. Ct.).

57 (1982), 16 M.V.R. 27 (B.C. Co. Ct.).

58 (1968), 11 Cr. L.Q. 223.

59 See *R. v. Hughes* (1958) (Alta. Dist. Ct.): conviction valid where driving in National Park; *Glibbery, Re*, [1963] 1 C.C.C. 101 (Ont. C.A.): accused properly convicted where driving on National Defence establishment. In *R. v. Keenan*, [1998] A.J. No. 505 (Alta. Prov. Ct.), a "grassy berm" separating a parking lot from the roadway was held not to fall within the definition of "highway".

60 (1955), 20 C.R. 181, 110 C.C.C. 321 (S.C.C.).

pursuant to the relevant provisions of the *Provincial Offences Act*, a charge would now be sufficient if it simply read "careless driving."

R. v. MacKenzie, supra, holds that since the offence may be committed in one of two ways under the present section, it is sufficient to charge a person with driving "without due care and attention." Obviously, care should be taken when particularising the manner in which the offence took place. In *R. v. Skirzyk*[61] the charge was dismissed where the evidence led at trial revealed that what should have been particularised was the alternative mode of driving not mentioned in the information. Consider too, *R. v. Fry,*[62] which held that a charge is void for duplicity if it charges both careless driving and speeding.

An information which stated that the defendant, the owner of an automobile, "unlawfully did permit [it] to be operated ... without due care and attention", etc. does not disclose any offence, since the Act does not make it an offence to "permit" driving contrary to the statute: *R. v. Greenfield*[63] Section 181(2) of the *Highway Traffic Act* states that the owner of a vehicle, unless he is also the driver, is not liable to a charge of careless driving.

In *R. v. Vandale,*[64] the appellant was convicted of driving "without due care and attention".[65] At trial a conviction was entered because evidence had shown that the defendant vehicle had numerous mechanical problems such as water in the brake system, an air leak, windshield wiper problems, maladjusted brakes, loose tie rod, leaky exhaust etc. The trial judge held that the vehicle should not have been on the road. This was held on appeal to be insufficient to convict on the basis of "without due care and attention." If, on the other hand, the Crown had simply amended the charging document to allege driving "without reasonable consideration for other persons using the highway" under s. 149(1)(b) of the British Columbia *Motor Vehicle Act*, it is submitted that Vandale might have been properly convicted.

(e) Circumstantial Evidence, Accidents and the Proof of Negligence

Mogenson v. Wright[66] involved a defendant who had been driving at night at a normal speed in a normal way and ran into a car which was either parked

---

61 (1981), 29 A.R. 291 (Alta. Prov. Ct.).

62 (1972), 8 C.C.C. (2d) 573 (Ont. H.C.), affirmed (1972), 9 C.C.C. (2d) 242n (Ont. C.A.).

63 (1954), 108 C.C.C. 107 (Ont. H.C.); Segal et al., *Manual of Motor Vehicle Law* (Toronto: Carswell, 1983) at 5.8.

64 (1989), 22 M.V.R. (2d) 288 (B.C. Co. Ct.).

65 *Motor Vehicle Act*, R.S.B.C. 1979, c. 288, as amended by S.B.C. 1987, c. 43, s. 55, s. 149(1) reads:

>   A person shall not drive a motor vehicle on a highway
>   (a) without due care and attention;
>   (b) without reasonable consideration for other persons using the highway; or
>   (c) at a speed that is excessive relative to the road, traffic, visibility or weather conditions.

66 (1962), 39 C.R. 56 (Sask. Dist. Ct.).

or travelling at a very slow speed. On appeal, the conviction was overturned. The court held that an obstacle directly in the path of travel is always conceivable but so rare that to attach quasi-criminal sanctions in such circumstances would be placing an extraordinary duty on a driver. The relevant section of the Saskatchewan legislation did not intend to impose criminal consequences upon a defendant confronted with hidden traps, freak conditions or unusual and sudden emergencies.

In *R. v. Smith*,[67] the defendant was unfamiliar with the area in question. He had been driving along a poorly lighted narrow road on a dark night when he crashed into the retaining wall of a river dyke beside the road. The only evidence against him was the fact of the accident itself. This was held to be insufficient to support the charge. In reaching this conclusion, the Court noted that the civil doctrine of *res ipsa loquitur* does not apply to criminal or quasi-criminal proceedings.[68] Moreover, it is impossible to say that the mere happening of the accident gave rise to a presumption of lack of due care and attention in the circumstances. The accident might well have been caused by the presence of an animal or pedestrian on the road or by some other distressing factor.[69]

In *R. v. Corke*,[70] the defendant appealed her conviction for careless driving. The defendant had driven over the crest of a hill and attempted to avoid a street cleaner which was virtually stopped in front of her, slightly striking the rear of the equipment as she attempted to pull into another lane. No warning signs had indicated the presence of the street cleaner, although there had been evidence that the defendant had been momentarily distracted prior to the accident while looking for a tube of lipstick, but she had testified that the lipstick had been in her hand as she was driving, and such evidence was not rejected by the trial Judge. The trial Judge had concluded that the defendant had simply been unable to handle the situation, rather than indicating that the defendant had been distracted by the lipstick, and it was thus held on appeal that the conviction could not stand. This evidence was coupled with that of another driver who said that he likewise had probably crashed in the same circumstances. The trial Judge had failed to direct his mind to the critical issue of whether there had been a lack of attention to the defendant's driving.

In *R. v. Hall*,[71] the defendant was following a woman who stopped to make a turn onto a side street. When she stopped, the car driven by the

---

67 (1961), 130 C.C.C. 177 (B.C. Co. Ct.).

68 See also *R. v. Koole* (1946), 1 C.R. 297 (Alta. Dist. Ct.).

69 See also *R. v. Simoneau* (1952), 102 C.C.C. 282 (Ont. Dist. Ct.); *R. v. Johnson*, [1967] 3 C.C.C. 26 (B.C. C.A.); *R. v. Buchanan* (1967), 10 Cr. L.Q. 246 (Ont. Mag.) Contra see *R. v. Ayotte* (1962), 132 C.C.C. 55 (Ont. Co. Ct.).

70 Summarized at 3 W.C.B. (2d) 396 (B.C. Co. Ct.). Similar facts arose in *R. v. Devine* (1953), 106 C.C.C. 129 (Ont. Co. Ct.) with the same result in that the accused was given the benefit of the doubt.

71 Unreported, October 12, 1979, Ont. Dst. Ct. - Street J.

defendant came into collision with her because he was unable to stop in time. At the time the weather conditions were adverse. It was snowing and blowing and the streets were slippery. The defendant saw her vehicle when he was a long way back. Her saw her turn signal and then her brake signal and tried to stop, but was unable to do so. On appeal His Honour Judge Street found that he could not be satisfied beyond a reasonable doubt that the defendant was driving without due care and attention as he had seen the car and stated that he saw it a long way back. He may well have been driving without due care and attention but it is equally possible that he had simply been unable to stop because the street was slippery and that through no fault of his own, he slid a long way. In the result, the conviction was set aside.

In *R. v. Ashton*,[72] the evidence disclosed the following. The defendant and three young male companions were together at a party and the defendant had a beer. Blood tests taken after the accident disclosed traces of marihuana. After the party, the four young men went for a ride on two motorcycles along country side roads. At one point, two of the young men got off the motorcycles to urinate at the roadside. The other two drove away after advising that they would return in a couple of minutes. The other driver took the lead, drove southbound at 90-100 k.m.h. leaving the defendant some distance behind. After an undisclosed period of time, the lead driver observed that the defendant was turning around to head back north. He turned to pursue the defendant at 90-100 k.m.h. and succeeded in closing the gap to about 50 feet. He observed the brake light of the respondent's bike and saw it hit the other two young men who were lying down wrestling in the middle of the road. One of them was killed and the other seriously injured.

Keenan D.C.J. reviewed the law and held that the Crown could establish a *prima facie* case of careless driving if:

1. There is evidence from which an inference can be drawn that the defendant drove carelessly; and

2. There is no evidence which supports a rational alternative conclusion.

Assuming a *prima facie* case has been made out, the defendant is left with the practical burden of presenting an explanation in order to avoid a finding of guilt.

Here, there was no evidence which supported an inference of careless driving. The fact that the two friends were lying in the middle of the road could not have been foreseen. There was evidence that the defendant had a temporary licence which did not permit him to drive in the evening, but there was no logical connection between this breach and the offence charged. After the accident the defendant passed a roadside ALERT test and the trace of mari-

---

72 (1985), 36 M.V.R. 100 (Ont. Dist. Ct.).

huana in his blood was not sufficient to support an inference that his ability to drive was impaired. His Honour held that "none of the bits of evidence relied upon by the Crown is evidence of lack of due care and attention, either directly or circumstantially. Taken together, their combined value is no greater than the sum of the parts, which is still zero." Accordingly, he held that as there was no evidence of careless driving, the trial Judge was right in not calling for a defence. "It was his duty to dismiss the charge because there was no evidence of the commission of the offence."

In *R. v. Reber*,[73] the investigating officer found a hydro pole on the northeast corner of an intersection. The pole had fresh scratches and dents, and there was debris from the vehicle. The main part of the severely damaged vehicle was found on the roadway some 10 metres south-west of the pole. The accident occurred in a 50 k.m.h. zone on a wet road, apparently after dark. There was no evidence as to exactly how the accident took place.

At trial the Justice of Peace had speculated as to why the vehicle came to hit the pole, and acquitted Reber. On Appeal Judge Stone held that this was wrong in law, and ordered a new trial. Having found that the car hit the pole, and since the defendant did not testify, it was wrong for the trier of fact to speculate as to what might have innocently caused the accident. Without an explanation from the defendant, the Crown case gave rise to an inference of careless driving, for which an acquittal was unwarranted.[74]

All of the above cases support the proposition that in the case of a motor vehicle accident, an absence of direct evidence (ie. an eyewitness) is no bar to conviction for careless driving. To succeed in this scenario, the prosecutor must show that no rational explanation exists for the accident other than careless driving. For the defendant, an explanation such as brief inattentiveness, or unavoidable obstruction must be raised either within the Crown case, or as part of the defence evidence.

(f) Lesser and Included Offences[75]

Speeding is not a "lesser or included" offence of careless driving. That is, while a defendant might enter a plea to such an offence, he or she could not be convicted of that as an alternative to the offence charged. In *R. v. Carey*,[76] the defendant was charged with careless driving. He entered a

---

73 (September 16, 1992), Stone Prov. J. (Ont. Prov. Div.).

74 It appears that Judge Stone would have simply substituted a finding of guilt in the case except that at a crucial point in the transcript, the comments by the Justice of the Peace were inaudible, and so it was unclear on Appeal precisely what happened at trial. Presumably, but for the inaudible transcript, Reber would have been convicted on appeal.

75 Careless driving is itself a lesser included offence to Impaired Driving and Over 80 under s. 253 of the *Criminal Code*. See *R. v. Fisher*, [1997] O.J. 4424 (Ont. Prov. Ct.).

76 (1973), 10 C.C.C. (2d) 330 (Man. C.A.).

plea of not guilty and the trial proceeded. The trial Judge convicted him of driving at a speed greater than is reasonable and prudent contrary to the relevant provision of the Manitoba *Highway Traffic Act*. An appeal was allowed and the conviction quashed. The Court adopted a working rule with respect to what is and what is not an included offence: "If the whole offence charged can be committed without committing another offence, that other offence is not included." Applying this rule to the offence of careless driving, it is obvious that a person may drive in a careless fashion without speeding.

A later case from the Nova Scotia Supreme Court, Appeal Division, *Smith v. R.*,[77] came to the same conclusion as did the Ontario Court of Appeal in *R. v. Yolles*[78] on somewhat different facts. In *Yolles*, the trial Judge held that as a matter of law if the speed of an automobile attains 80 m.p.h. or more on a highway it constitutes careless driving. The Court of Appeal held this to be an arbitrary rule that cannot govern all cases. What the trial Judge has to decide is not only what the rate of speed was but whether, taking the rate of speed into consideration together with all other circumstances, the defendant was driving "a vehicle on a highway without due care and attention or without reasonable consideration for other persons using the highway."

In *R. v. Rose*,[79] the defendant was originally charged with driving without due care and attention contrary to s. 110(1)(b) of the *Highway Traffic Act*.[80] At trial he was convicted of the offence of improperly completing a passing manoeuvre.[81] On appeal, Easton J. held that improper passing was not an included offence to that of careless driving and so the conviction was improper. While the conduct proven may have supported the charge of improper passing, the information must be properly amended prior to verdict.

7. COMMON FACTUAL SITUATIONS

(a) Driver swerves to avoid obstruction in roadway and causes a collision

In *John Charles Thompson v. The Queen*,[82] the appellant drove into a ditch to avoid hitting four or five large dogs that ran out in front of him from a cornfield on the side of the road. He was convicted at trial by a Justice of the Peace who, after reviewing *R. v. McIver, supra*, took the position that the onus actually shifts to the defendant to show that the accident was not caused by negligence or fault on his part. Street J. ruled that *McIver* had been misapplied and that the correct reading of the decision was that if the evidence indicates carelessness and there is no other rational explanation, a conviction is

77 (1982), 15 M.V.R. 161 (N.S. S.C.).

78 (1958), 122 C.C.C. 209 (Ont. H.C.), reversed in part (1959), 123 C.C.C. 305 (Ont. C.A.).

79 (1996), 26 M.V.R. (3d) 136 (Nfld. T.D.).

80 R.S.N. 1990, c. H-3.

81 *Ibid.*, section 96(1).

82 Unreported, June 12, 1980, Ont. Dist. Ct. - Street J.

justified, but not (in law) required. In this case, however, there is an explanation which is quite reasonable, and accordingly the conviction was quashed.

(b) Driver of vehicle travelling at an excessive speed

In *R. v. Tyndall*,[83] the vehicle was travelling at 160 k.m.h. in a 90 k.m.h. zone at 1:30 a.m. A police chase ensued, which lasted some 20 minutes. In convicting the defendant of careless driving Duval J. said

> The potential dangers of travel at such speed both to passengers in the accused's vehicle, as well as to likely users of the highway, and the inability to cope with an emergency situation by reason of the excessive speed at which the said vehicle was travelling can only lead to the conclusion that the driving occurred without due care and attention and without reasonable consideration for any persons using the highway.[84]

In *Royal Canadian Mounted Police v. Wilson*[85] the defendant had approached a bicyclist travelling in the same direction on a narrow road. The defendant had been riding a motorcycle at lease 22 k.m.h. faster than the speed limit. The bicyclist had veered into the path of the defendant, was struck and died. Judge Lampert convicted Wilson saying,

> For the accused to attempt to pass within a foot or two, or perhaps mere inches, of Miss Brine at a speed exceeding 90 k.m.h. without being assured that she was aware of his approach was, in my opinion, and act that certainly constituted driving a motor vehicle on a highway without reasonable consideration for another person using that same highway. Mr. Wilson's action were, I believe, a clear departure from the standard of care any ordinary prudent motorist would have exercised in the circumstances.[86]

(c) Motor vehicle collision – No evidence that Defendant attempted to avoid the collision, no evidence of fortuitous intervening event

In this case it is suggested that a conviction for careless driving may be appropriate. In *R. v. Therrien*,[87] the defendant was driving on a "nice day", turned to look at a park, and then rear ended another vehicle. There were no skid marks. According to Houston J., it was obvious that the defendant was driving without due care and attention, and the conviction for careless driving was upheld.

---

83 (1988), 15 M.V.R. (2d) 336 (Man. Prov. Ct.).

84 *Ibid.*, at p. 340. Note that the accused in this case was not the driver but the owner of the vehicle who was a passenger in the car. Under the Manitoba *Highway Traffic Act*, S.M. 1985-1986 c. 3, s. 229 the owner of the vehicle can be convicted of careless driving if he cannot satisfy the court that his motor vehicle was in the possession of another without the owner's consent at the relevant time.

85 (1997), 34 M.V.R. (3d) 68 (N.B. Prov. Ct.).

86 *Ibid.*, at p.77-78.

87 (September 6, 1991), Doc. 5606 (Ont. Gen. Div.).

In *R. v. Oakes*,[88] the driver skidded into a parked vehicle on a roadway of loose but well-packed gravel. There being no evidence upon which a Judge could conclude that the accident was a result of an error of judgment, the only possible conclusion was that the driver was not operating the vehicle without the required care and attention.

In *R. v. Martinez*,[89] the appellant had been travelling 50 k.m.h. on a straight, dry road bearing a 70 k.m.h. speed limit. He approached a stop sign at an intersection. Warning of the impending stop was also given in the form of a "Stop ahead" sign. Martinez had gone through the intersection and collided with another vehicle killing the other driver. Evidence disclosed that the appellant made no attempt to stop until he was halfway through the intersection, just before the collision. The appellant was originally charged with dangerous driving but pleaded guilty to the charge of careless driving. He appealed only his sentence. The Court of Appeal described this fact pattern as "a clear...case of careless driving."[90]

(d) Motor vehicle collision where there is evidence of an attempt to avoid the collision or else a fortuitous event prior to impact

In this fact scenario a conviction may be less certain. Courts have taken the view that skid marks etc, may be indicative of an effort by the defendant to take all available steps to avoid the collision. A fortuitous and unpredictable event such as a sudden mechanical failure, animal in the roadway, changing road conditions etc. again shifts the blameworthiness for the accident away from the defendant.

In *R. v. Wallings*,[91] the defendant had been travelling on a straight piece of road. He passed a car and upon returning to his side of the road his left front wheel seized with the result that his car veered to the left and went into a spin. He attempted to straighten the wheel, but was unsuccessful. He further admitted he may have inadvertently hit the accelerator instead of the brake. On appeal, the court quashed the conviction, and reiterated the principle that the mere fact an accident occurred does not constitute driving without due care and attention, and stated:[92]

> The police in their zeal to improve driving standards and to enforce this section, are, in cases where a motorist has suffered an accident, laying this charge and to substantiate it are placing before the Courts the mute evidence of skids, their lengths, intensity and direction together with weather conditions and any other thing pertaining thereto, and virtually forcing the unfortunate motorist to come

88 (1981), 6 W.C.B. 91 (Sask. Dist. Ct.).
89 (1996), 21 M.V.R. (2d) 106 (Ont. C.A.).
90 See also *R. v. Pyszko* (1998), 38 W.C.B. (2d) 25 (Ont. Prov. Ct.).
91 (1961), 130 C.C.C. 128.
92 *Ibid.*, at p. 130.

into Court and prove his innocence. The section was never meant for this. It is not a corollary that after every accident a charge should follow.

With respect to the fact that there was evidence the defendant had accelerated by mistake instead of braking, His Honour referred to the following passage in *R. v. Beauchamp*:[93]

> The law does not require of any driver that he should exhibit "perfect nerve and presence of mind, enabling him to do the best thing possible." It does not expect men to be more than ordinary men. Drivers of vehicles cannot be required to regulate their driving as if in constant fear that other drivers who are under observation, and apparently acting reasonably and properly, may possibly act at a critical moment in disregard of the safety of themselves and other users of the road.

Accordingly, such error of judgement does not constitute careless driving.[94]

In *R. v. David Whalley*,[95] the Defendant hit a bump in the centre of an intersection. This caused his glasses to fall off. He continued for approximately 125 yards before he came into contact with another vehicle and during this period searched for his glasses. The court held that it was not satisfied that because the defendant chose to look for his glasses rather than putting on his brakes right away, that such conduct falls within the meaning of the section so as to constitute careless driving.[96]

In *Mogenson v. Wright*,[97] the Court found as a fact that the defendant's semi-trailer drove at normal highway speeds into the rear of a vehicle which was either stationary or travelling much slower on the roadway, and without tail lights. The defendant had given evidence that there were dark spots on the road due to drifting snow. He did not see the other vehicle until he was 30 or 40 feet away, turned to the right hand ditch to avoid, but hit the car before going down into the ditch. In quashing the conviction, Gerein D.C.J. remarked that,

> I do not think that this section[98] intends to impose criminal consequences for hidden traps, freak conditions, or other unusual and sudden emergencies.[99]

---

93 *Supra*, note 42 at 431. MacKay J.A. is quoting Mazengarb, Dr. *Negligence on the Highway* (2nd ed.) 1952 at p. 176-7.

94 See also *R. v.Turgeon* (1958), 120 C.C.C. 248 (Sask. Dist. Ct.).

95 Unreported, October 9, 1979, Street, D.C.J.

96 See also *R. v. Johnson* (1983), 45 N.B.R. (2d) 371 (N.B. Q.B.) where the accused had dropped a cigarette on the seat and, while attempting to put it out, drove on the wrong side of the road causing a collision. On appeal, the conviction was set aside. See also *Masters*, [1980] Ont. D. Crim. Conv. 5525-07 (Co.Ct.) where the accused emerged from an underpass, where the roadway was wet to an icy road surface. The driver lost control of the vehicle, and collided with a light standard. Accused was acquitted.

97 *Supra* note 66.

98 *Vehicles Act*, S.S. 1957, c. 93, s. 127.

99 *Supra* note 66 at p. 59.

This would suggest that anything unusual which could be said to be the primary cause for the accident will shift the blame in a careless driving charge away from the defendant.[100]

(e) Pedestrian Collisions

In *R. v. Milner*,[101] the defendant was southbound on a slushy, snow covered road. After going through an intersection, his car executed a complete 360 degree circle and spun around on the highway. The defendant chose not to testify at trial but he did give a statement to the police which was admitted. Therein, he indicated that he didn't know why the vehicle went into a spin. The Court held that whatever it was that caused the vehicle to spin was not known, and that it had not been shown beyond a reasonable doubt that the cause could be anything more than a momentary lapse of attention or inadvertent negligence. Accordingly, the charge was dismissed.

Failure to keep a proper lookout has been held to be one of the indices of careless driving. In *R. v. Schoemaker*,[102] the defendant was driving in the central square of the city around midnight. He was a long-time resident of the city and was familiar with the area. As he approached a crosswalk, his vision was obstructed by other vehicles and he hit a pedestrian whom he had spotted a mere five or ten feet in front of him. A moment prior to the accident, he was looking to see who the other drivers were rather than paying attention. The defendant accelerated to a speed of at least 30 m.p.h. to pass the vehicles in front of him despite not having a clear view of the sidewalk. This constituted careless driving, although the result may have been different had the defendant been a stranger in town, unfamiliar with the painted cross-walks.

Similarly, in *R. v. James*,[103] the defendant approached a school crossing with which he was familiar and slowed down, he thought all was clear he kept on going. When he reached a point near the intersection, his car struck a woman. Apparently, he did not see the woman until after the collision and as such failed to keep a proper look-out. The defendant was therefore found guilty of careless driving.[104]

---

100 See, for example, *R. v. Kotar, supra*, note 18, where falling asleep with the resulting jerk of the steering wheel caused the vehicle to enter the wrong lane. This was found to be evidence of an intervening event such as to warrant an acquittal.

101 Unreported, October 9, 1979. Street-D.C.J.

102 (1979), 2 M.V.R. 27 (Ont. Co. Ct.). Other cases where convictions have been registered for failing to keep a proper look-out include *R. v. Fernets* (1963), 42 W.W.R. 309 (Sask. Dist. Ct.) where the accused attempted to pass without first making sure it was safe to do so, and *R. v. B.* (1963), 44 W.W.R. 482 (B.C. S.C.) where again the accused struck a pedestrian on a crosswalk.

103 (1952), 14 C.R. 231 (B.C. Mag. Ct.).

104 See also *R. v. Walker* (1954), 109 C.C.C. 376 (B.C. Co. Ct.) where accused risked passing another vehicle without first taking a proper look and *R. v. Peacock* (1975), 11 N.B.R. (2d)

In *R. v. Globocki*,[105] the Defendant had struck a jay-walking Pedestrian. He was found not guilty of careless driving. In registering the acquittal Macdonnel J. said,

> ... the defendant cannot be required to have regulated her driving behaviour as if in a constant fear that other users of the road might possibly act at a critical moment in disregard of themselves.[106]

Thus it seems that if the pedestrian is acting irrationally a conviction will be more difficult to make out. In *R. v. Keenan*[107] (a picket line striker had sat on the defendant's car as she attempted to leave a picket line. The defendant, terrified for her safety, had continued driving slowly with the pedestrian on the car until the picketer dismounted. She was acquitted of careless driving.

---

579 (N.B. Co. Ct.) where the accused motorcyclist was convicted of careless driving after hitting a child on a crosswalk.

105 *Supra*, note 33.

106 *Ibid.*, at p. 193.

107 [1998] A.J. No. 505 (Alta. Prov. Ct.).

7

Common Defences

1. DUE DILIGENCE, REASONABLE MISTAKE OF FACT

(a) Generally

This is the most common defence to a strict liability offence. By raising the defence of due diligence, the defendant says, in effect, "I did all that I could to avoid breaking the law." In the leading case, *R. v. Sault Ste. Marie*[1] the court said this about the defence:[2]

> Offences in which there is no necessity for the prosecution to prove the existence of *mens rea*; the doing of the prohibited act *prima facie* imports the offence, leaving it open to the accused to avoid liability by proving that he took all reasonable care. This involves consideration of what a reasonable man would have done in the circumstances. The defence will be available if the accused reasonably believed in a mistaken set of facts which, if true, would render the act or omission innocent, or if he took all reasonable steps to avoid the particular event.

The defendant must prove the defence on a balance of probabilities, and the defendant should anticipate calling evidence to positively make out due diligence if such a foundation is not found in the prosecution's case. As Dickson J. said in *Sault Ste. Marie*,

> In a normal case, the accused alone will have knowledge of what he has done to avoid the breach and it is not improper to expect him to come forward with the evidence of due diligence.[3]

---

1 [1978] 2 S.C.R. 1299 at 1326 (S.C.C.).

2 *Ibid.*, at 1325.

3 *Ibid.*, at 1325.

When there is no such evidence, the defence is not made out.[4] More recently, the Supreme Court has soundly endorsed this passage.[5]

The test to be applied is an objective one: what would the reasonable and prudent driver have done in the circumstances? If the defendant has done everything reasonably possible, what purpose is served in punishing the behaviour. Punishing such a person can only bring the administration of justice into disrepute.

Some common examples of the due diligence defence are:

- Failing to yield right of way to a pedestrian within a crosswalk where the accused failed to notice the pedestrian until the last minute because his attention was concentrated on making a left turn.[6]

- Defendant's bicycle collided with a parked car causing serious injury requiring medical attention.[7] Defendant waited at the scene of the accident for five minutes before proceeding to hospital. Defendant then waited at hospital for one hour for police but eventually left. Original five minute wait was held to be a proper exercise of due diligence in relation to charge of Fail to Remain at Scene of accident.[8]

- Offence of overloading a vehicle where the driver supervised the loading of the vehicle to ensure the load fell within the allowable weight.[9]

- Failing to display appropriate placards during transportation of hazardous materials[10] where the corporate defendant had established that it had in place at the time of offence controls and mechanisms specifically implemented to prevent the offence itself from taking place.[11]

---

4 See *R. v. Davis* (1996), 21 M.V.R. (3d) 65 (N.S. C.A.), *R. v. Lowe* (1991), 29 M.V.R. (2d) 265 (N.S. C.A.).

5 See *R. v. Pontes*, (1995), 13 M.V.R. (3d) 145 (S.C.C.).

6 *R. v. Stone* (1996), 21 M.V.R.(3d) 59 (N.S. C.A.).

7 *R. v. Weir* (1992), 36 M.V.R. (2d) 118 (Ont. Prov. Ct.).

8 *Highway Traffic Act*, R.S.O. 1990, c. H.8, S.O. 1997, c. 12, s. 13.

9 *R. v. Boyde* (1988), 15 M.V.R. (2d) 228 (B.C. Co. Ct.), *R. v. Nickel City Transport (Sudbury) Ltd.* (1993), 47 M.V.R. (2d) 20 (Ont. C.A.). On the issue of availability of due diligence in the case of overloaded vehicles see the helpful commentary by M.G. Forbes at 47 M.V.R. (2d) 57 and his case comment on *R. v. Lafarge Can. Inc.* (1989), 19 M.V.R. (2d) 110 at 117.

10 *Dangerous Goods Transportation Act*, R.S.O. 1990, c. D.1; S.S. 1984-85-86, c. D-1.2; R.S.N.S., 1989, c. 119, s. 5; R.S.N. 1990, c. D-1, s. 5; R.S.P.E.I. 1988, c. D-3, s. 3; see also the *Transportation of Dangerous Goods Control Act*, S.A. 1982, c. T-6.5; and also the *Transporation of Dangerous Goods Act*, R.S.C. 1985, c. T-19 (amended 1992, c. 34; 1944, c. 26, ss. 69-73); R.S.B.C. 1996, c. 458; R.S.N.B. 1988, c. T-11.01; R.S.N.W.T. 1988, c. T-6, s. 5. Section 5 of the Ontario Regulations to the *Dangerous Goods Transportation Act* provides that "It is a defence to a charge under this act for the accused to establish that the accused took all reasonable measures to comply with the Act. 1981, c. 69, s. 5." Reading this section it is apparent that a defence of due diligence is 'explicitly' allowed by an accused.

11 *R. v. Motorways* (1989), 16 M.V.R. (2d) 38 (Ont. Prov. Ct.); *R. v. Midland Transport Ltd.* (1992), 37 M.V.R. (2d) 44 (N.S. Prov. Ct.).

(b) Delegation and Due Diligence

A person may delegate responsibility for fulfilling some duty on a driver to another person, provided this is done reasonably. In *R. v. Azzoli*,[12] the defendant had asked his secretary to deal with his outstanding fines. When his licence was suspended for non-payment, his delegation was held to be reasonable and to be a valid excuse:[13]

> I cannot criticize the [defendant] for the conduct that he participated in getting the matter taken care of. He went about it in a way that any reasonable man would have done, gave it to his secretary, asked her to look after it ... [H]e assumed it was done as I think a reasonable person could assume it was done.

Similarly, the cases indicate that if a person acts reasonably to delegate responsibility for insuring a vehicle, a defence to the charge of driving with no insurance will exist.[14]

(c) Absolute Liability Offences

Due diligence only applies to offences of strict liability; it is no defence to a charge of absolute liability.[15] It is thus no defence to the charge of, for example speeding, to say that the defendant was diligently following her speedometer at the legal speed limit.

(d) Mistake of Fact

A defence of mistake of fact has been accepted in the following circumstances:

i) Shooting more game than allowed where the defendant reasonably believed that he had not killed the first deer which he shot;[16]

ii) Employing youth under minimum age while reasonably believing that employee was over age;[17]

iii) Driving under suspension while reasonably believing that licence was not suspended;[18]

---

12 (1983), 24 M.V.R. 205 (Ont. Prov. Ct.).

13 *Ibid.*, at p. 208-209.

14 See Chapter Six and the discussion of the defence under the heading "*Compulsory Automobile Insurance Act.*"

15 *R. v. Morrison* (1979), 31 N.S.R. (2d) 195 (N.S. C.A.); *R. v. Jones*, [1991] 3 S.C.R. 110 (S.C.C.).

16 *R. v. Richardson* (1981), 62 C.C.C. (2d) 417 (Ont. Div. Ct.), affirmed (1982), 39 O.R. (2d) 438n (Ont. C.A.), leave to appeal refused (1983), 48 N.R. 228 (S.C.C.).

17 *R. v. Servico Ltd.* (1977), 2 Alta. L.R. (2d) 388 (Alta. C.A.).

18 *R. v. Briand* (1979), 32 N.S.R. (2d) 615; *R. v. Christman* (1985), 29 M.V.R. 1 (Alta. C.A.); *R. v. Bellomo* (1995), 14 M.V.R. (3d) 63 (Ont. Prov. Ct.); *R. v. Sept* (1995), 14 M.V.R. (2d)

(e) Mistakes as to Matters not Elements of the Offence

There is no requirement the mistake be with regard to one of the elements of the offence. Any mistake of fact which would have rendered the actions of the defendant innocent will satisfy the defence; it need not negate a specific element which the prosecution has to prove.[19]

2. MISTAKE OF LAW AND OFFICIALLY INDUCED ERROR

(a) Introduction

It is well established that, as a general rule, a mistake of law offers no defence. A mistake of law is merely a subspecies of the rule in the case of ignorance of the law[20] and *ignorantia juris neminen excusat* (no one is excused from liability because of ignorance of the law). This common law principle had been given statutory form by s. 19 of the *Criminal Code*[21] and that provision has been repeated verbatim in the Ontario *Provincial Offences Act*, s. 81.[22] The statutory rule reads:

> Ignorance of the law by a person who commits an offence is not an excuse for committing the offence.

While it is not the purpose of this short discussion to reargue the merits or flaws of the rule,[23] it is worthwhile restating the principle policy arguments in its favour. They are:[24]

(1) allowing a defence of ignorance of the law would involve the courts in insuperable evidential problems;

(2) it would encourage ignorance of the law where knowledge of the law is socially desirable;

---

263 (Alta. Prov. Ct.); *R. v. Boivin* (1994), 12 M.V.R.(3d) 21 (Alta. Prov. Ct.); *R. v. Anderson* (1997), 30 W.C.B. (2d) 100 (N.B. C.A.).

19 *R. v. Roche* (1985), 20 C.C.C. (3d) 524 (Ont. C.A.), *R. v. Smithers*, [1978] 1 S.C.R. 506 (S.C.C.).

20 G. Williams, *Criminal Law: The General Part* (2d), 1961, pp.151-2, quoted in N.S. Kastner, "Mistake of Law and the Defence of Officially Induced Error" (1987), 28 Crim. L.Q. 308 at 309.

21 *Criminal Code*. R.S.C. 1985, c. C-46.

22 R.S.O. 1990, c. P.33.

23 The pros and cons of the rule have been thoroughly worked over by the many authors who have considered this topic. The best and most up-to-date examination of this area is the Kastner article (*supra*, note 20). Also helpful in understanding the larger issues are E.R. Keedy "Ignorance and Mistake in Criminal Law" (1980), 22 *Harv. L. Rev.* 75 and D. O'Connor "Mistake and Ignorance in Criminal Cases" (1976) 39 *M.L.R.* 644.

24 D. Stuart, *Canadian Criminal Law*, 1982, pp. 261-8, cited with approval in E.G. Ewaschuk, *Criminal Pleadings and Practice in Canada* (2d) , para. 21:7020; *Canadian Criminal Law: A Treatise*, 3rd ed. (Toronto: Carswell, 1995) at pp. 295-298.

(3) Every person would be a law unto himself, infringing the principle of legality and contradicting the moral principles underlying the law; and

(4) ignorance of the law is blameworthy in itself.

The idea that everyone knows the law and acts to bring his or her behaviour within its confines is really nothing more than a legal fiction.

Some of the most difficult issues arise from those cases where the mistake of the defendant could be classified as either fact or law. These hard cases probably defy any principled resolution though many have tried. In his text *Criminal Pleadings and Practice in Canada,*[25] Mr. Justice Ewaschuk adopts Don Stuart's proposed distinction:

> A mistake of fact exists when the accused is mistaken in his belief that certain facts exist when they do not, or that they do not exist when they do. By contrast, a mistake of law exists when the mistake relates not to the actual facts but rather to their legal effect.

The problem is lessened in regulatory cases by the need for a mistake of fact to have been reasonable and the growing recognition of a defence of officially induced mistake or error of law (discussed below) where non-negligence is shown. In these cases it seems that it is reasonableness and not the characterization of the error as 'factual' or 'legal' which will test a defence.

There are two well accepted exceptions to the rule stated above. The first is impossibility or non-publication. Section 5 of the *Regulations Act*[26] provides:

> **5.**(1) Every regulation shall be published in *The Ontario Gazette* within one month of its filing.
> (2) The Minister may at any time by order extend the time for publication of a regulation and the order shall be published with the regulation.
> (3) A regulation that is not published is not effective against a person who has not had actual notice of it ... [Emphasis added]

The federal *Statutory Instruments Act*[27] contains a provision to the same effect. In other words, a defendant charged with conduct rendered illegal on the face of an unpublished subordinate statute (i.e., a regulation) can plead the defence of no notice. On the other hand, a defendant charged with an offence under a published piece of subordinate legislation is guilty *prima face*, whether or not s/he has notice of the legislation or not.[28] Again, ignorance of the law is no excuse. If the justification for the rule is the fiction that everyone knows

---

25 *Ibid.,* at para. 21:7040.

26 R.S.O. 1990, c. R.21, s. 5; R.S.Y. 1986, c. 151, s. 3; S.S. 1995, c. R-16.2, s. 6; S.N.B. 1991, c. R-7.1; R.S.B.C. 1996, c. 402, s. 5; R.S.A. 1980, c. R-13, s. 3; R.S.N.S. 1989, c. 393, s. 4; *Statutory Instruments Act,* R.S.N.W.T. 1988, c. S-13, ss. 9-10; *Statutes and Subordinate Legislation Act,* R.S.N. 1990, c. S-27, s. 11.

27 R.S.C. 1985, s-22, s. 6; S.C. 1993, c. 34, s. 113(f).

28 *R. v. Williams* (1988), 44 C.C.C. (3d) 58 (Y.T. Terr. Ct.).

the law then this exception makes sense. The most diligent, astute citizens lining up to the highest standard of informing themselves about the law could not possibly be expected to make their behaviour conform with a literally unknowable law.

The other well-established exception is in the colour of right cases. In these matters the statutory definition of the offence requires that the defendant have a specific understanding of the legal status or quality of their actions. Thus, for example, a tow truck driver who removes a car he honestly believes is illegally parked will not be guilty of theft even if the vehicle was legally parked. He does not have the requisite mental appreciation of what he is doing and will be excused from liability even though his error is one of law.

(b) Officially Induced Error

Until recently the courts have been resolute in their protection of the integrity of the error of law rule. The two exceptions set out above were viewed as derogations from a principle which depended on uniform application for justification. Recent years have seen a break with this approach, especially in the area of regulatory offences.

Regulatory schemes usually present the most complex and inaccessible form of laws. They depend upon detailed statutory regimes supported by even more intricate regulation administered by bureaucrats answering to policy manuals and a Minister of the Crown. The system regulating the use of motor vehicles in the province is such a scheme.[29] While these materials may be physically available to the public in that they are published, it is a cruel fiction to pretend that a person knows what the law says.

The most natural reaction of an individual faced with this monolith of state regulation is to either take legal counsel or, more likely, to seek an answer from the governmental official responsible for the scheme. Am I allowed to fish here? Is this machine considered safe? Will my licence be restored as soon as I pay the fine? Each of these questions requires a legal answer and if the answer is wrong and the individual asking acts on the wrong information, then that person is contravening the regulatory scheme under a mistake of law.

---

29 The regulation of motor vehicles and highways depends on a number of statutes and regulations. The standard office consolidation, *Highway Traffic Act and Related Statutes and Regulations*, prepared by the Ministry of Government Services, includes all or part of the following: *Highway Traffic Act*, R.S.O. 1980, c. H.8; *Provincial Offences Act*, R.S.O. 1990, c. P.33; *Compulsory Automobile Insurance Act*, R.S.O. 1990, c. C-25; *Negligence Act*, R.S.O. 1990, c. N.1; *Criminal Code*, R.S.C. 1985, c. C-46; *Motorized Snow Vehicles Act*, R.S.O. 1990, c. M.44; *Public Vehicles Act*, R.S.O. 1990, c. P.52; *Dangerous Goods Transportation Act*, R.S.O. 1980, c. 69; *Off-Road Vehicles Act*, R.S.O. 1990, c. O.4. The consolidation also includes some sixty regulations promulgated under the various Acts. This is not an exhaustive list.

Is it fair to convict a person who has, acting on good faith, taken all reasonable steps to find out the law bearing on his proposed course of action, but who, being misinformed, reasonably mistakes the state of the law? The equities of such situations are compelling.[30] The objectives of the law are not furthered by convicting such an individual. The injustice of the situation, apparent to a lay person, brings the administration of justice into disrepute.

In *R. v. MacLean*,[31] a 'trail blazing and innovative' judgment, a Nova Scotia court accepted a defence based on officially induced error of law or due diligence resulting in a mistake of law. The defendant was charged with driving while under suspension under the old *Criminal Code*[32] provisions. He worked at the Halifax International Airport and, as part of his employment, was required to drive a vehicle around the airport. When his licence was suspended for refusing to provide a breath sample, he telephoned the Office of the Registrar of Motor Vehicle to enquire as to whether he could still drive on airport property. No licence was needed, he was told, to drive on federal government property. This, of course, was wrong as federal regulations require that drivers on federally governed undertakings be licenced.

O'Hearn Co. Ct. J. began his consideration of the defence by examining the regulations themselves, their complexity and inaccessibility. These statutory instruments were so obscure that neither the provincial authorities nor the defendant supervisors at the Department of Transport (the agency responsible for the regulations) were able to see the error until after the defendant had been charged. Reasoning from the rule in cases of non-publication the court adopted the defence as it had been stated in the headnote of an American case arising in the context of a charge of bigamy.[33] A mistake of law will provide a defence where the defendant[34]

> made a bona fide diligent effort to ascertain and abide by law by adopting course and resorting to sources and means as appropriate as any afforded under our legal system and acted in good faith reliance on result of such effort.

The defendant was acquitted on the facts. He had made a reasonable, if faulty, inquiry into his legal position and his mistake of law arose from this inquiry.

After *MacLean* the status of the defence was left in some doubt. While that case was a 'trailblazer,' few seemed inclined to follow. In a 1980 Ontario case, *R. v. Walker*[35] Mr. Justice Martin of the Ontario Court of Appeal refused to apply the defence to the facts. In this case, the defendant misunderstood

---

30 And may provide justification for a light sentence. See Stuart, *supra*, note 24.

31 (1974), 17 C.C.C. (2d) 84 (N.S. Co. Ct.). See also *R. v. MacDougall* (1981), 10 M.V.R. 236 (N.S. C.A.), reversed (1982), 18 M.V.R. 180 (S.C.C.).

32 *Criminal Code*, s. 238(3).

33 *Long v. State (Delaware)* (1949), 65 A.2d 489, quoted by Judge O'Hearn at p. 104.

34 *Ibid.*, at 104.

35 (1980), 51 C.C.C. (2d) 423 (Ont. C.A.).

reporting obligations under customs regulations. The error, however, arose from the defendant's own failure to comprehend the legislation and regulations and not from some "misinformation" by official sources. The trail was apparently closed later that same year when the Supreme Court of Canada in *R. v. Molis*[36] volunteered some *obiter* statements on officially induced error in a case where the defendant was simply ignorant of a newly promulgated and published regulation. Were it not for the judgment of the Supreme court of Canada in *R. v. MacDougall*[37] almost two years later the defence might have been stifled by *Molis* for ever.

MacDougall was another Nova Scotia case dealing with motor vehicles, in this case a charge of driving while suspended. The defendant had had his licence restored pending his appeal of an earlier conviction. He was lead to believe that his licence would remain valid until he received formal notice that the appeal had been refused from the Registrar of Motor Vehicles. The appeal was refused and the defendant continued to drive awaiting the official notice of his suspension. In fact his licence was resuspended from the moment of the appeal decision and no such notice was necessary. While awaiting such notice he was charged with driving while suspended. He successfully argued that his error, while one of law, was induced by the incorrect information provided by the registrar.

The Nova Scotia Court of Appeal[38] had approved of and applied the defence of officially induced error. Mr. Justice MacDonald observed the policy and equities behind making a defence of officially induced error available in the case of regulatory offences. He writes[39]

> The defence of officially induced error has not been sanctioned, to my knowledge, by any appellate Court in this country. The law, however, is ever-changing and ideally adapts to meet the changing mores and needs of society. In this day of intense involvement in a complex society by all levels of Government with a corresponding reliance by people on officials of such Government, there is, in my opinion, a place for the defence of officially induced error, at least so long as a mistake of law, regardless how reasonable, cannot be raised as a defence to a criminal charge.

While the Supreme Court of Canada did not agree that the defence was available on the facts of the case, Mr. Justice Ritchie clearly believed that the defence was not incompatible with the common law rule. He says in his judgment[40]

> It is not difficult to envisage a situation in which an offence could be committed under mistake of law arising because of, and therefore induced by, "officially

---

36 (1980), 55 C.C.C. (2d) 558 (S.C.C.).

37 (1982), 1 C.C.C. (3d) 65 (S.C.C.).

38 (1980), 10 M.V.R. 236 (N.S. C.A.), reversed [1982] 2 S.C.R. 605 (S.C.C.).

39 *Ibid.*, at 160.

40 *Ibid.* at p. 613 [S.C.R.].

induced error" and if there was evidence in the present case to support such a situation existing it might well be an appropriate vehicle for applying the reasoning adopted by MacDonald J.A. In the present case, however, there is no evidence that the accused was misled by an error on the part of the registrar.

In *R. v. Robertson*,[41] the defence was considered in the context of a driving under suspension charge under the *Highway Traffic Act*. The defendant had been lead to believe that her licence was reinstated after being suspended for non-payment of fines. In fact she had inadvertently sent her payment to the wrong address and her licence was never corrected. Provincial Judge Langdon considered the authorities and concluded that at common law there is a defence of officially induced error. The minimal elements of the defence were, in his opinion:[42]

> 1. The actor must advert to his legal position, i.e., he must be (or become) mistaken as to the law after inquiry, not merely ignorant of the law.
>
> 2. The actor must seek advice from an official, who will usually be a member of a government or a government agency.
>
> 3. That official must be one who is involved in the administration of the law in question.
>
> 4. The official must give erroneous advice.
>
> 5. The erroneous advice must be apparently reasonable.
>
> 6. The error of law must arise because of the erroneous advice.
>
> 7. The actor must be innocently misled by the erroneous advice, i.e., he or she must act in good faith and without reason to believe that the advice is indeed erroneous.
>
> 8. The actor's error of law must be apparently reasonable.
>
> 9. The actor, when seeking the advice of the official, must act in good faith and must take reasonable care to give accurate information to the official whose advice he solicits.

The court, however, was unsure whether the defence survived the statutory enactment of the *ignorantia juris* rule in s. 81 of the *Provincial Offences Act*. Nova Scotia, where *MacDougal* originated, had no such statutory rule and so it was unnecessary to consider whether the effect of the legislation was to displace the common law defence. His Honour writes,[43]

> ... [S]uch a defence may be available in appropriate circumstances. ... As I read the other authorities, however, it seems to me to make a great deal of difference whether or not that common rule has been enacted by statute. Where, as in Nova

---

41 (1984), 43 C.R.(3d) 39 (Ont. Prov. Ct.).

42 *Ibid.*, at p. 47.

43 *Ibid.*, at p. 48.

Scotia, the rule applies only by force of the common law, the defence of officially induced error as an exception thereto can emerge to meet the changing needs of modern society. Is the situation the same where Parliament or the legislature has chosen to codify the principle? While s. 7(3) of the *Criminal Code* permits the development of "new" common law defences ..., it does not appear to do so if such defences conflict plainly with valid statutory provisions.

The real breakthrough came in *R. v. Cancoil Thermal Corp.*[44] where the Ontario Court of Appeal embraced the defence and acquitted a defendant charged with operating a manufacturing machine without the safety guard required by the regulations. In concluding that the defendant had been misinformed by an inspector, thus being mistaken as to the legality of their equipment, Mr Justice Lacourciere said[45]

> The defence of "officially induced error" exists where the accused, having adverted to the possibility of illegality, is led to believe, by the erroneous advice of an official, that he is not acting illegally. ... The defence of "officially induced error" is available as a defence to an alleged violation of a regulatory statute where an accused has reasonably relied upon the erroneous legal opinion or advice of an official who is responsible for the administration or enforcement of the particular law. In order for the accused to successfully raise this defence, he must show that he relied on the erroneous legal opinion of the official and that his reliance was reasonable. The reasonableness will depend upon several factors, including the efforts he made to ascertain the proper law, the complexity or obscurity of the law, the position of the official who gave the advice and the clarity, definitiveness and reasonableness of the advice given.

His Lordship adopted the statements of Peter Barton in his article "Officially Induced Error as a Criminal Defence: A Preliminary Look"[46] when he said:

> Where the advice is given by an official who has the job of administering the particular statute, and where the actor relies on this advice and commits what is in fact an offence, even if the agency cannot be estopped does it follow that the actor should not be excused? To do so is not to condone an illegality or say that the agency is estopped into a position of illegality, but to recognize that the advice was illegal but excused the actor because he acted reasonably and does not deserve punishment.

It is clear that in the case of offences of strict liability the defendant will bear the burden of persuasion on this issue. As we have discussed above, defences negating the mental element or aspect of this category of offences are subject to the rule from *Sault Ste. Marie* as to proof.

---

44 (1986), 52 C.R. (3d) 188 (Ont. C.A.).

45 *Ibid.*, at pp. 198-9. See also *R. v. Jorgensen*, [1995] 4 S.C.R. 55 (S.C.C.). In that case, the accused was charged with selling obscene material without lawful justification or excuse. Lamer C.J.C. stated that "Officially induced error of law exists as an exception to the rule that ignorance of the law does not excuse. *This principle is available, not only in the case of charges of regulatory offences, but as here, where the accused is charged with a true criminal offence.*" (at p. 99, emphasis added).

46 (1980), 22 Crim. L. Q. 314, at 331.

It is as yet unclear how far this new defence will go in opening a hole in the *ignorantia juris* rule. There is no logical reason for limiting the defence to "officially" induced errors. The case of a defendant who in good faith takes counsel from a good lawyer, or police officer,[47] is no less compelling, (especially where counsel rely on some judicial pronouncement of authority later overturned in advising) on its equities than that of a defendant who seeks a quick answer from an overworked clerk at a government office. Further, the "official" requirement introduces an element of uncertainty which may promote litigation. Who is an official? Must he or she act in some official capacity when dealing with the defendant, or may a more casual situation invite advice? What if the official acts outside his or her authority? Several authorities[48] have convincingly argued that the true test should be the reasonableness of the defendant's reliance on the advice and not the characterization of the advisor. This conforms with the proper theoretical underpinnings of the defence (advertence of the defendant, rather than estoppel against the government), the equities of the cases and the general principle that someone who exercises due diligence in conforming his or her behaviour to the regulatory scheme should be excused from liability.

In *R. v. Elgar*,[49] the Court gave some guidance as to the limits of this defence. The defendant had been convicted of driving over 80 under the *Criminal Code*. Upon conviction he was prohibited from driving for one year under the mandatory *Criminal Code* driving prohibition imposed in sentencing. A clerk administering the provincial *Highway Traffic Act* gave Elgar advice that he could drive, notwithstanding his driving prohibition. The Court held that, because the official inducing the error was not responsible for *Criminal Code* matters, he could not plead the defence of officially induced error. Unfortunately, the Court also held that because the official was essentially incompetent to give the advice, the mistake was one of law. Presumably then, the defendant pleading officially induced error must also be in a position to show that s/he took proper steps to confirm that s/he was relying on the right official.

In *R. v. Ross*,[50] the Court considered conflicting official inducements. The defendant was stopped by Highway Traffic Board officers who told him he could not drive his truck with the particular class of license he held. However, the defendant relied upon what a government official had told him and continued to drive, subsequently pursued by the officers. The Court held that in

47 See *R. v. Petrie* (1993), 44 M.V.R. (2d) 311 (Alta. Q.B.) where the accused had been told by a police officer that his mufflers were fit was not a defence to the charge of operating a a vehicle without an adequate exhaust muffler under s. 46 (1) of the *Highway Traffic Act* (Alta.). The defence of officially induced error could not be applied to an absolute liability offence as it is to a strict liability offence.

48 Stuart, *supra*, note 24; Kastner, *supra* note 20; Barton, *supra* note 46.

49 (March 2, 1990), Doc. CA 434/88 (Ont. C.A.).

50 (1985), 14 W.C.B. 436.

this scenario the defence of officially induced error was open to the defendant. An important factor was the defendants multiple visits at vehicle inspection stations where his license had been inspected without incident. The defendant was thus reasonable in believing his license was valid.

3. DE MINIMIS NON CURAT LEX

(a) Applicability

It is unclear whether the principle of *de minimis non curat lex* (the law is not concerned with trifling or slight violations) has any place in criminal or quasi-criminal law as a defence. The classic statement of the principle is found in "*The Reward*";[51]

> The Court is not bound to strictness at once harsh and pedantic in the application of statutes. The law permits the qualification implied in the ancient maxim *De minimis non curat lex*. — Where there are irregularities of very slight consequence, it does not intend that the infliction of penalties should be inflexibly severe. If the deviation were a mere trifle, which, if continued in practice, would weigh little or nothing on the public interest, it might properly be overlooked.

Its primary application has been in cases of possession of contraband, either drugs or, in an earlier age, liquor.

In *R. v. Peleshaty*,[52] the Manitoba Court of Appeal applied the doctrine to acquit an individual charged with possession of then illegal alcohol. The defendant was found with two bottles containing about ten drops each. The court observed,[53]

> The Act was not intended to be used to prosecute for having ten drops of liquor, which is not a usable quantity. Convicting him for having ten drops of liquor in each of two bottles is so trifling that the law should take no notice of it.

The cases involving possession of minute quantities of drugs (resin in a pipe used to smoke marijuana or traces of heroin in a spoon used to prepare the drug)[54] have fallen on both sides of the argument over the defence.[55]

In *R. v. Webster*,[56] the defendant was charged with a parking infraction under a municipal by-law. He had parked on a street marked "snow removal route." The winter season was over and the seasonal time frame set out in the prohibiting signs was eight days from closing. There was no snow on the ground and no realistic chance of such snow developing. The delict of the

---

51 (1818), 165 E.R. 1482 at 1484.
52 (1950), 96 C.C.C. 147 (Man. C.A.).
53 *Ibid.*, at p. 156.
54 *Ibid.*, at 156-157.
55 See generally B.A. MacFarlane, *Drug Offences in Canada* (3d ed.) (Toronto: Canada Law Book, 1996).
56 (1981), 10 M.V.R. 310 (Ont. Dist. Ct.).

defendant was minor — a purely technical violation in no way related to the purpose of the prohibition. In accepting the defence and dismissing a Crown appeal Vannini Dist. Ct. J. relied on s. 80 of the *Provincial Offences Act* and held that the maxim was a part of the common law of Ontario and had been preserved as a defence. The real question is whether, under the by-law the municipality could ever have indented so minor a violation to be punishable. His Honour writes:[57]

> Having regard to the special circumstances established in evidence the police would not have exposed themselves to criticism or censor by the public if, in the exercise of their discretion whether to ticket or not, they determined to overlook the infraction. Indeed, to ticket a motorist in such circumstances might bring the police and their enforcement of the law into ridicule and contempt.
>
> A conviction of the accused would serve little purpose. Having regard to the absence of snow and that the prohibition was to expire in eight days, a conviction would not in any way further the intention and purpose of council to facilitate snow removal or act as a general deterrent to other motorists or as an individual deterrent to the respondent against breaching the by-law for the remainder of the seasonal prohibition. Instead it would indeed be "artificial and divorced from reality" and "an absurdity" and bring the administration of justice into ridicule and contempt as well as the police notwithstanding the minimal monetary punishment to which he was liable, although a refusal to pay the fine as a matter might result in his going to jail.
>
> Because:
>
>> (1) the only purpose of the section of the by-law was to facilitate snow removal from the street and there was no snow on the ground at the time;
>>
>> (2) the respondent had parked his car in ignorance of the prohibition for a period of only two-and-a-half hours and would not have parked in prohibition of the by-law had he been aware of it from seeing the signs that were erected and on display;
>>
>> (3) the finding by the Justice that the respondent had committed a technical breech of the law and did not believe that justice would be served by punishing the respondent, and
>>
>> (4) because the application of the maxim is totally discretionary,
>
> I cannot find that the Justice erred in exercising his discretion in the manner that he did and in dismissing the information.

The acquittal of the defendant was upheld.

In a British Columbia case the defendant was charged with driving while impaired even though he had only moved the vehicle a few feet to correct its parking position. (He had called a taxi to take him home.) The court of Appeal rejected the trial judge's conclusion that the defence was properly

---

57 *Ibid.*, at 318-9.

available in a criminal case and added that in this case it was, in any event, not available on the facts.[58]

The position of the defence remains in some doubt in Ontario in light of a 1984 decision of Mr. Justice Montgomery of the High Court. In *R. v. Li*,[59] the defendant relied on *de minimis* to avoid conviction on a minor shoplifting charge. He had taken a drill bit valued at less than a dollar. He said,[60]

> The wealth of authority, in my view, is that the principle of de minimis non curat lex had no application to the criminal law. That certainly has been the disposition in appellate courts in Canada in drug related offences: *R. v. Quigley* (1954), 111 C.C.C. 81 … The matter was also addressed by Lord Scarman in *R. v. Boyesen*, [1982] 2 W.L.R. 882. Lord Scarman cited *Bocking v. Roberts*, [1974] Q.B. 307, where Lord Widgery C.J. said [at p.309]:
>
>> In my judgment it is quite clear that when dealing with a charge of possessing a dangerous drug without authority, the ordinary maxim of de minimis is not to be applied.
>
> If the law were as conceived by the learned provincial court judge rather than inhibiting shoplifting the law would encourage it. It would be possible for an individual to acquire items of small value from a number of stores and do a sizeable shopping with impunity.

This would appear to be contrary to *R. v. Jacobson*[61] where the Ontario Court of Appeal held that the maxim could be applied to acquit a defendant charged with stealing a library book.

The position of the defence in true criminal matters is clearly in flux. In the case of regulatory offences, by their nature involving a civil element, the arguments against allowing the defence in appropriate cases is less compelling. This is especially true when one considers the sometimes harsh administrative consequences which must flow for even the most technical violation (license suspension or demerit points).

4. NECESSITY

(a) Application

Necessity will operate as a defence to an offence of full *mens rea*, strict liability, or absolute liability.[62] To invoke the defence the defendant must have had no legal alternative. In *R. v. Walker*,[63] the court considered the case of a police officer who had failed to stop at a stop sign (an absolute liability offence). While the defence of necessity was not available on the facts of that

---

58 *R. v. Chessa* (1983), summarized at 10 W.C.B. 393.
59 (1984), 16 C.C.C. (3d) 382 (Ont. H.C.).
60 *Ibid.*, at 384.
61 (1972), 9 C.C.C. (2d) 59 (Ont. C.A.).
62 *R. v. Kennedy* (1972), 7 C.C.C. (2d) 42 (N.S. Co. Ct.).
63 (1979), 5 M.V.R. 114 (Ont. Co. Ct).

case, the court observed that the defence would be available in an appropriate fact situation. The classification of the offence as one of absolute liability did not preclude the defendant from invoking the defence:[64]

> Did [the Supreme Court of Canada] really mean that a driver who drove through a stop sign on the orders of his kidnapper who was holding a gun to his head would have no defence at all? What if the driver was a five-year-old child who had somehow managed to set the car in motion? What if the driver was suffering from a condition of non-insane automatism? ... On a reading of the whole judgment, particularly [the] formulation of the three categories, it appears to me that [the Court] was directing [its] mind to the defence of reasonable care ... [and not to defences such as necessity].

In *R. v. Perka*,[65] the Supreme Court confirmed that necessity is a defence without addressing the issue of its application to strict or absolute liability offences. There are four principle limitations on the defence: a) there must be 'clear and imminent peril' calling out for action without deliberation; b) there must be no reasonable legal alternative to the illegal act; c) the harm inflicted by the illegal action must be less than would be present if the 'clear and imminent peril' were manifested; and finally, d) if the harm which forms the basis for the defence was clearly foreseeable and avoidable at an earlier time without any illegality, the defence is unavailable.

In *R. v. Goltz*,[66] Mr. Justice Gonthier suggests that[67] the defence of necessity may be available in the case of driving while under suspension. Gonthier J. gives the example of a grandfather who must drive his grandson because of a medical emergency from a remote fishing hut to a hospital. Notwithstanding that his license is suspended for accumulated demerit points, the grandfather properly could avail himself of the defence of necessity. The act of driving while suspended would be a "morally involuntary" decision to act. The defence would only apply "in circumstances of immediate risk, where the action was taken to avoid a direct and immediate peril."[68]

In *R. v. West*[69] the defendant, arguing the defence of necessity, was acquitted of the charge of impaired driving. The defendant was having a party at his home when the situation became rowdy and violent. He feared for both himself and his wife. He was unable to phone the police from home because the telephone wires had been pulled out of the wall and his cell phone became unusable. Instead of walking a short distance to use a payphone, the defendant

---

64 *Ibid.*, at pp.134-5.
65 [1984] 2 S.C.R. 232, at pp. 238-9 (S.C.C.).
66 8 C.R. (4th) 82 (S.C.C.).
67 *Ibid.*, at p. 109.
68 *Ibid.*, at p. 110.
69 [1994] N.J. No.303 (N.S.S.C.). See also *R. v. Freire* (1993), 47 M.V.R. (2d) 199 (Ont. Prov. Div.) where the accused was disallowed the defence of necessity because he did not avail himself of the reasonable legal alternative of police assistance.

drove because he suffered from angina and was experiencing chest pains. The trial court, and ultimately the Nova Scotia Supreme Court, held that the defendant met the elements of the defence of necessity because:

1. The situation was one of *immediate peril*. The Court held that any reasonable person after having been assaulted and threatened, and with his wife still in the precarious situation, would conclude that there was an immediate peril. This was furthered heightened by the defendant experiencing chest pains.

2. The peril of the situation was not subsiding. The situation, or reasonable expectation of the situation, did not subside once the defendant had called the police.

3. The test of reasonableness is objective. The Court held that any reasonable person would have acted the same as the defendant under the circumstances.

4. There was no other reasonable legal alternative available to the defendant. The Court considered the facts that the defendant had already been assaulted and threatened by an individual still present in the home, the delay in going to a neighbour's home to call the police, the chest pains experienced by the defendant, the distance to the payphone, and the apparent noise that the defendant heard when outside trying to use his cellular phone.

5. The defendant did not create the immediate peril, and was therefore not the author of his own misfortune.

5. PROCEDURAL DEFENCES

(a) Section 3(4) of the *Provincial Offences Act*:

Section 3(4) of the *Provincial Offences Act* states that:[70]

upon the service of an offence notice or summons, the person charged may be requested to sign the certificate of offence, but the failure or refusal to sign as requested does not invalidate the certificate of offence or the service of the offence notice or summons.

The section may properly be divided into two parts. The first part requires a Provincial Offences officer to request from the person charged that he sign the certificate of offence. The second part qualifies this first requirement. A certificate of offence is not invalid if the reason for the lack of the defendant's signature was his refusal to sign the certificate upon request.

The argument that has been advanced in numerous cases both in the Provincial Offences Court and the Provincial Court (Criminal Division) deals with the issue of whether or not the failure of a Provincial Offences officer to request the person charged to sign the certificate of offence invalidates the certificate.

Owing to the saving provision contained within s. 3(4), the fact that the certificate of offence does not bear the signature of the person charged is not a defect apparent on the face of the charging document. Again, this is because

---

70 R.S.O. 1990, c. P.33, s. 3(4).

a person charged may refuse to sign the certificate. Thus, it seems clear that in order to determine whether the certificate of offence was not signed there has to be some evidence led, and therefore a motion to quash cannot be brought prior to plea.

The argument underlying such a motion was carefully canvassed by His Honour Judge W.A. MacDonald of the Provincial Court (Criminal Division), Brantford, Ontario, in reasons given orally on August 13th, 1986 in the case of *R. v. Poos*. His Honour began by making reference to the history of the *Provincial Offences Act*. Prior to the coming into force of the Act, when a defendant ignored or did nothing upon receiving a ticket, it was still the case that for a conviction to register, an officer had to attend court and testify under oath to support the charge. Trials were, of course, held *ex parte*. Under the *Provincial Offences Act* where a defendant does not plead guilty or notify the court of his intention to plead not guilty within the prescribed period of time, the default provisions apply and a conviction will register without there having been a trial, albeit one held *in absentia*.

Judge MacDonald noted that this obviously meant an enormous saving of police time and State money. As His Honour noted at page 2 of his reasons for judgment and following:

> The *Provincial Offences Act*, it appears, is a statutory document and has fundamentally changed the concept and method of laying an offence. No longer does a charge have to be laid before a justice before an accused can be summonsed. Under the *Provincial Offences Act* the accused is summonsed by an officer. The information is later confirmed by a justice. All of these not unreasonable, but nevertheless substantial changes in procedure for the benefit of the State are statutory in nature. The same statute provides certain prerequisites must be complied with before the State must act in this fashion. Section 3 in total sets out a procedure for the commencement of proceedings. In addition to the normal way of swearing an information before a justice, it sets out the requirements that must take place.

His Honour continued,

> If the Legislature wanted the failure of the officer to request a signature not to invalidate the certificate of offence they could have done so in that section by the addition of a couple of words. The fact they did not is strong evidence that the Legislature intended a failure to request a signature to be fatal to a certificate. The language, "the officer shall request a person sign the certificate" is clearly mandatory. The fact is that the Legislature provides no remedy for the lack of request by the officer, but in the same paragraph provides a remedy for the lack of signature by the person charged. It leads to no other interpretation other than what the Legislature intended, the lack of request by the officer shall invalidate the certificate of offence.

In the result, the Appellant's appeal was allowed and the conviction overturned.[71]

---

71 See also *R. v. Ecclestone* unreported, Prov. Ct. (Crim. Div.), Barrie, Ontario June 27, 1986 which is to the same effect as *R. v. Poos*.

This is not to say, however, that the issue is free from controversy. In rebuttal, the argument has been advanced that this does not amount to a procedural error, but is a jurisdictional matter. Thus, once the defendant has attorned to the jurisdiction, the question of whether or not the officer asked the person charged to sign the certificate of offence becomes irrelevant. A further argument in rebuttal is that the irregularity or defect is one that is subject to amendment pursuant to the relevant sections of the *Provincial Offences Act* or is one where the defect is not of such a nature as to invalidate the proceedings.

(b) Proof of By-Laws

The basic rule with respect to municipal by-laws is that judicial notice cannot be taken of them. The common law required judicial notice to be taken of public or general statutes but not of private enactments or subordinate legislation such as regulations or orders-in-council.

Section 29 of the *Evidence Act*, R.S.O. 1990, c. E.23[72] is to the same effect. It reads:

> **29.** Where the original record could be received in evidence, a copy of an official or public document in Ontario, purporting to be certified under the hand of the proper officer, or the person in whose custody such official or public document is placed, or of a document, by-law, rule, regulation or proceeding, or of an entry in a register or other book of a corporation, created by charter or statute in Ontario, purporting to be certified under the seal of the corporation and the hand of the presiding officer or secretary thereof, is receivable in evidence without proof of the seal of the corporation, or of the signature or of the official character of the person or persons appearing to have signed the same, and without further proof thereof.

R. v. Clark[73] stands for the proposition that speed limit signs are *prima facie* proof of compliance with the regulations under the *Highway Traffic Act*. These regulations passed pursuant to the *Highway Traffic Act* require the posting of speed limit signs and limit the authority to post such signs to municipal corporations or authorities. Applying the presumption of regularity, the fact that traffic signs were posted leads to the conclusion that a proper by-law is in place which proscribes what is indicated on the traffic sign. In reaching its decision, the Ontario Court of Appeal considered approvingly the English case of *Gibbins v. Skinner*.[74] There, the relevant provision of the English *Road Traffic Act* required traffic signs to be erected and maintained by local auth-

---

72 See *Evidence Act*, R.S.B.C. 1996, c. 124, s. 28; R.S.A. 1980, c. A-21, s. 34; S.A. 1983, c. L-10.1, s. 57; R.S.N. 1990, c. E-16, s. 21; R.S.N.W.T. 1988, c. E-8, s. 41; R.S.N.S. 1989, c. 154, s. 13; R.S.Y. 1986, c. 57, s. 31.

73 (1973), 14 C.C.C. (2d) 73 (Ont. C.A.), reversed (1974), 18 C.C.C. (2d) 52 (Ont. C.A.).

74 [1951] 1 All E.R. 1049 (Eng. K.B.).

orities for the purpose of securing that adequate guidance be given to the drivers of motor vehicles as to a direction being in force in respect of a length of road deemed to be in a built-up area. The appellant had argued that as it had not been formally proved by the production of the original order in writing that a direction was in force that the road should be deemed to be in a built-up area, an essential element of the prosecution's case was lacking and the mere presence of speed limit signs could not prove that the road was restricted. Lord Goddard C.J. stated that "we must presume that the local authority carry out their duties." He further held:[75]

> In my opinion, in view of the provisions of s. 1(7) of the *Road Traffic Act,* 1934, the prosecution have established a *prima facie* case. It would, indeed, be a serious thing if the police, every time they prosecuted a person for driving over thirty miles an hour on a stretch of road which was deemed to be in a built-up area, had to produce a witness from the local authority to give formal proof of the order containing the direction that the road was to be so deemed ... The fact that it was proved or admitted that appropriate signs had been erected was, in my opinion, *prima facie* proof that the necessary directions and steps had been taken to direct that the road be deemed to be in a builtup area.

Proof that an actual direction had been given was thus held not to be a necessary ingredient of the offence.

In *R. v. McLaren,*[76] the defendant was charged with failing to yield to a pedestrian at a pedestrian crossover. On appeal to the Provincial Court (Criminal Division) it was successfully argued that the by-law had not been proved, and as such the conviction should be quashed. On further appeal to the Ontario Court of Appeal, the Court held that *Clark* should have been applied, and that there had therefore been sufficient proof with respect to the existence of the by-law. Thus, although the Crown must prove the existence of the by-law designating a crossover, this burden may be discharged by putting forward evidence that signs and markings existed of a kind that are commonly used with pedestrian crossovers in the province.

R. v. Blet[77] was a case where the defendant was charged with contravening a municipal by-law relating to building safety. A copy of the by-law was tendered in evidence. It had been certified by the proper officer of the municipal corporation to be a true copy of the by-law and under the seal of the municipal corporation and thus complied with the relevant provisions of the *Municipal Act,* R.S.O. 1960 and the *Evidence Act,* R.S.O. 1960. However, issue was taken with the fact that it had been certified prior to the date of the commission of the alleged offence. In overturning the acquittal, the Ontario Court of Appeal held that unless evidence is led to attack either the existence or the validity

---

75 *Ibid.,* at p. 1052.

76 (1981), 10 M.V.R. 42 (Ont. C.A.). See also, *R. v. Potapchuk* [1963] 1 O.R. 40. But see, *contra, R. v. Hauca* (1966), 56 W.W.R. 683 (Alta. D.C.).

77 [1966] 3 C.C.C. 184 (Ont. C.A.).

of the by-law at the date of the alleged offence, the presumption of regularity will apply and the by-law will be presumed to exist and be valid on the date in question on which the Court is required to act.

Another by-law case of note is *R. v. Snelling.*[78] There, Barlow J. had occasion to deal with a stated case following the conviction of a defendant for failing to stop "before entering or crossing through Carling Avenue, a through highway," contrary to then s. 41(3) of the *Highway Traffic Act*. The *Highway Traffic Act*, as it then was, provided that "through highway" meant "any highway or part of a highway designated as such by the Minister or by by-law of a municipality approved by the Department."

The defendant was convicted at trial although no by-law designating Carling Ave. a through highway was proved in evidence. The trial Judge was of the view that as such a by-law had been proven before him on other occasions he could take judicial notice of its existence.

Barlow J. held that judicial notice could not be taken of the passing of a by-law and overturned the conviction. He emphasized that "[s]uch a by-law, and the terms thereof, must be proved, and it must be shown that there was a compliance therewith as to 'stop' signs and the position thereof." As a result, there was no evidence before the trial Judge upon which to convict.[79]

Snelling, supra, focuses on an important but often overlooked principle; as judicial notice may not be taken of the existence of a by-law *it must actually be placed in evidence.* It is not sufficient for the prosecutor to merely indicate to the presiding justice that he has a copy of the relevant by-law available for his perusal should he deem it appropriate. Rather, the by-law is to be marked as an exhibit and tendered as part of the Crown's case. This is surely a cumbersome procedure but it is the only way in which the Crown may prove its case.

The section dealt with in *Snelling* was legislatively altered so as to obviate the need to prove the by-law. As was pointed out by Mackay J.A. in *R. v. Ross,*[80] at the time Barlow J. rendered his decision in *Snelling*, the section of the *Highway Traffic Act* in issue required proof of the by-law or Regulation authorizing the erection of stop signs. In *Ross*, which post-dated *Snelling*, then s. 64 of the *Highway Traffic Act* required that a driver should bring his vehicle to a full stop "upon approaching a stop sign at an intersection." Prior to this, the section had provided that a driver must stop "before entering or crossing a through highway." As earlier pointed out, "through highway" was defined as meaning designated by the Minister or by by-law. It was therefore obvious

---

78 [1952] O.W.N. 214.

79 *Ibid.,* at p. 215. See also *Peterborough (City) v. Lockyer* (1992), 12 O.R. (3d) 214 (Ont. Prov. Div.) where Collins, J. held that a municipal by-law was an "enactment within the *Interpretation Act*, R.S.O. 1990 and so proof of such by-law/enactment was unnecessary."

80 [1966] 2 O.R. 273 (Ont. C.A.).

"that s. 64 was drafted in such a way as to avoid the necessity of proving the by-law or regulation providing for the erection of the stop sign."

6. OWNER LIABILITY

In all provinces the owner of the motor vehicle is liable for offences committed by another. In many provinces, the owner can be held "vicariously liable"[81] for any traffic infraction committed by the driver.[82] In Ontario, The *Highway Traffic Act* sets out a list in s. 207(2) of offences which *may not* be committed by the owner of a vehicle unless the owner is also the driver at the time of the incident. This list includes: driving without seatbelt; careless driving; driving too slow; as well as most of the rules of the road in Part X of the Act,[83] regulations relating to these provisions; and any by-law prohibiting turns on the highway.

The section also provides that an owner may properly be convicted of any offence for which the driver is liable, unless at the time of the offence the vehicle was in the possession of someone who did not have the owner's consent. Therefore, if the owner is charged with an offence not listed above, s/he may still raise the defense that no consent was given to the driver.[84]

(a) Constitutional Limits

In determining the liability of an owner for traffic offences committed by another, it is crucial to determining at the outset whether the charging offence withstands scrutiny under the Charter. In the seminal decisions *Sault Ste. Marie*[85] and *Reference re s. 94(2) of the Motor Vehicle Act (British Columbia)*[86] the Supreme Court held that legislation which provides for the possibility of imprisonment offences of absolute liability is contrary to s. 7 of the *Charter*. Thus, if the defendant stands to be sentenced to a term of incarceration, the offence must be at least one of strict liability. Clearly, when an owner is exposed to a jail term because another is guilty of a traffic offence, Constitutional limits are engaged.

---

81 See Stuesser "Convicting the Innocent Owner: Vicarious Liability under Highway Traffic Legislation" (1989) 67 C.R. (3d) 316.

82 See *Highway Traffic Act*, R.S.A. 1980, c. H-7, s. 170; Motor Vehicle Act, R.S.B.C. 1996, c. 318, s. 83; *Highway Traffic Act*, S.M. 1985-86, c. H60 (also C.C.S.M., c. H60) [now R.S.M. 1987, c. H60 (also C.C.S.M., c. H60)], s. 229; *Motor Vehicle Act*, R.S.N.B. 1973, c. M-17, s. 270; S.N.B. 1998, c. 30, s. 22; *Highway Traffic Act*, R.S.N. 1990, c. H-3; *Motor Vehicle Act*, R.S.N.S. 1989, c. 293; *Highway Traffic Act*, R.S.P.E.I. 1988, c. H-5; *Highway Traffic Act*, S.S. 1986, c. H-3.1, s. 93; S.Y. 1992, c. 54, s. 7; *Motor Vehicles Act*, R.S.Y. 1986, c. 118, s. 225.

83 Specifically ss. 129-168, 172, 175, 176, 182, and 199.

84 See *Widdis (Litigation Guardian of) v. Hall* (1995), 9 M.V.R. (3d) 252 at 262, (*sub nom. Widdis v. Hall*) (Ont. Gen. Div.).

85 *Supra*, note 1.

86 [1985] 2 S.C.R. 486 (S.C.C.).

In *R. v. Geraghty*,[87] the British Columbia Court of Appeal held that s. 76 of the *Motor Vehicle Act*[88] violates s. 7 of the *Charter* and is therefore unconstitutional because it exposed the vehicle owner to a term of incarceration because of the acts of the driver.

Owner liability under any legislation is thus unconstitutional if a) it exposes the owner to a term of incarceration and b) it is an absolute liability offence.[89]

In *R. v. Wilson*[90] the defendant, the owner of a motor vehicle charged with failing to stop for school bus exhibiting flashing red lights under s. 188(1) of the New Brunswick *Motor Vehicle Act*.[91] Owner liability for s. 188(1) offences is established under s. 133(1.2) of the Act.

> The owner of a motor vehicle shall be guilty of a violation of subsection (1) committed by any person operating the motor vehicle unless the owner establishes that another person
>
>   (i)   was operating a motor vehicle and had possession of it without the owner's consent, express or implied, at the time of the alleged violation,
>   (ii) has been charged with and convicted of the violation, or
>   (iii) admits to being the driver of the vehicle at the time of the alleged violation.

At trial, the charge was dismissed on the basis that s. 188(1.2) violated both sections 11[92] (c)[93] and 11(d)[94] of the *Canadian Charter of Rights and Freedoms*. The Crown appealed the acquittal, ultimately to the New Brunswick Court of Appeal. There the Court noted that s. 188(1) must contemplate an absolute liability offence because s. 188(1.2) does not allow the defence of due diligence. Rather than strike down the whole provision of the *Motor Vehicle Act* as offensive to the *Charter*, the Court opted to "read down" the provision so as to allow the defence of due diligence in s. 188(1.2). Thus, an intermediate ground is possible when owner liability provisions offend the *Charter*. The result in *Wilson* is that an absolute liability offence becomes one of strict liability.

---

87 (1990), 22 M.V.R. (2d) 57 (B.C. C.A.).
88 R.S.B.C. 1979, c. 288.
89 See also *R. v. Pellerin* (1989), 10 M.V.R. (2d) 165 (Ont. C.A.), *R. v. Free* (1990), 25 M.V.R. (2d) 30 (Alta. Q.B.), *R. v. Burt* (1987), 7 M.V.R. (2d) 146 (Sask. C.A.); *R. v. Sutherland* (1990), 22 M.V.R. (2d) 35 (N.S. C.A.), *R. v. Ruff-Dickinson* (1994), 4 M.V.R. (3d) 185 (N.B. Q.B), leave to appeal refused (1994), 4 M.V.R. (3d) 185n (N.B. C.A.).
90 (1997), 31 M.V.R. (3d) 238 (N.B. C.A.).
91 R.S.N.B. 1973, c. M-17.
92 "Any person charged with an offence has the right..."
93 "not to be compelled to be a witness in proceedings against that person in respect of the offence;"
94 "to be presumed innocent until proven guilty according to law in a fair and public hearing by an independent and impartial tribunal."

(b) Defending the Owner

Until 1994 it had been assumed that the term "owner" was restricted in the *Highway Traffic Act* context, to the registered owner. This argument was fuelled by the decision *R. v. Sherman*.[95] In that case the registered owner of a vehicle had argued that she was relieved of her duty to produce documentation under the *Motor Vehicle Accident Claims Act*.[96] Her argument was premised on the fact that, while she was listed as the registered owner of the vehicle, it was in fact her son that was the owner, for all intents and purposes. She had only been registered as owner to enable her son to finance the purchase of the car. McGillivray J.A. dismissed this argument saying that,[97]

> in the opinion of the Court ... "owner" as it appears in the Act must mean registered owner rather than owner at common law if any effect is to be given this legislation.

The Ontario Court of Appeal altered it's position on this issue in the more recent case *R. v. Zwicker*.[98] In that case, a fact pattern opposite to *Sherman* was presented, viz. the "owner" had recently purchased the vehicle, but not yet registered or insured it. Upon being stopped, she was unable to produce any insurance documentation. She was convicted at trial of the charge of operating a motor vehicle without insurance under s. 2(1) (a) of the *Compulsory Automobile Insurance Act*.[99] The Court of Appeal took a different view of ownership this time. According to Robins J.A. under the new legislation, the term owner includes not only the registered owner, but the "common law owner" as well.[100] It is therefore not a defence to a charge under the *Compulsory Automobile Insurance Act*, to claim that the defendant was not the registered owner, but only the "common law owner." The issue of whether the reasoning in *Zwicker* applies to the *Highway Traffic Act* was not addressed in the case. However, litigants who attempt to raise the defence of "common law ownership" to ownership offences under the *Highway Traffic Act* should, in light of *Zwicker*, proceed with caution.

In *Widdis v. Hall*,[101] J had sold his car to R, agreeing to maintain the insurance on the vehicle until the balance of the purchase price was delivered in one week. R had agreed to keep the vehicle at his father's and not to use it until it had been mechanically certified, and registered as sold with the Min-

95 [1972] 1 O.R. 503 (Ont. C.A.).
96 R.S.O. 1970, c. 281.
97 *Supra*, note 95 at p. 506.
98 17 O.R. (3d) 171 (Ont. C.A.).
99 R.S.O. 1990, c. C.25, s. 2.
100 *Zwicker, supra*, note 98 at 172.
101 (1994), 24 C.C.L.I. (2d) 124, (*sub nom. Widdis v. Hall*) 21 O.R. (3d) 238 (Ont. Gen. Div.), additional reasons (1995), 9 M.V.R. (3d) 252 at 262, (*sub nom. Widdis v. Hall*) 22 O.R. (3d) 187 (Ont. Gen. Div.).

istry of Transportation. R, however, did not so register the vehicle, and J. cancelled his insurance. R was involved in a car accident. The issue was whether for purposes of a civil claim for damages, J was considered the "owner" under s. 192 of the *Highway Traffic Act*. On the preliminary issue of determining ownership Judge Misener said,

> I do not see how it is open to me to do other than declare that Joseph Hall was the owner ... at the time of the accident. Admittedly, the ownership permit had been delivered over to Randall Hall with the application for transfer signed in blank and with authority in Randall Hall to enter his name as purchaser and have the Ministry substitute him as the holder of it. Nevertheless, Joseph Hall remained the holder of the permit at the time of the accident. In fact, Joseph Hall retained legal title to the Plymouth ... I would think that that the most significant incident of ownership is the right to ... determine the use of, a chattel. Joseph Hall had had that exclusive right. He had the right to insist the Plymouth remain stationary until it was paid for in full, and indeed he testified it was because of that right that he felt comfortable in instructing Tamara Stofega to cancel the insurance. [102]

This analysis is different[103] than what the Court of Appeal had used in the earlier decision of *Zwicker*.[104] That, of course, was a determination of ownership under the *Compulsory Automobile Insurance Act*, and not the civil liability provisions of the *Highway Traffic Act*. Notwithstanding the obvious differences in policy considerations under the two pieces of legislation, it is also important to point out that in *Hall* the trier of fact would be deciding the ownership issue on the civil burden of proof, namely a balance of probabilities. In *Zwicker* the burden of proof is beyond a reasonable doubt.

(c) The Corporate Owner

Cases are frequently brought before the Courts alleging traffic infractions against Corporations which own fleets of vehicles. In such cases the owner is charged with a moving violation and is then pressed to defend the charge. In such cases, the due diligence defence is often raised. The success of such a defence is, not surprisingly, fact specific. In *R. v. Tilden Car Rental Inc.*[105] a car rental agency was charged, as owner, with speeding under the Alberta photoradar provisions. The defendant attempted to argue that it had been duly diligent in its attempts to dissuade renters from speeding. The defence was rejected, largely because Tilden had made no attempts to obtain the renter's driving history and driving attitude. Such details were found to be an important factor if the owner was truly concerned with the fate of his or her vehicle in the hands of a third party. Absent such information, the owner cannot say he

---

102 *Ibid.*, at p. 131.
103 In fact Misener J. does not even mention *R. v. Zwicker* in the course of his judgment.
104 *Supra*, note 98.
105 (1991), 15 W.C.B. (2d) 126 (Alta. Prov. Ct.).

or she was duly diligent in the circumstances. It also seems to have been a factor in *Tilden Car Rental* that the owner could pass on the cost of the photorador ticket directly to the offending customer/driver.[106]

In *R. v. B.C. Transit*,[107] the owner succeeded in raising the due diligence defence. The defendant transit company had been issued a photoradar speeding ticket for one of its public buses. The court heard that "... the management was doing virtually everything within its power, short of putting inspectors on every bus, to ensure that their drivers did not speed ...".[108] In such circumstances therefore, the due diligence defence succeeds.

---

106 See also *R. v. Black Top Cabs Ltd.*, [1998] B.C.J. No. 322 and *R. v. Best Buy Car & Truck Rentals*, [1997] B.C.J. No. 3051 where the due diligence defence failed on the facts.

107 [1997] B.C.J. No. 3047.

108 *Ibid.*, at para. 15.

8

Common Offences

2. FAIL TO REPORT

(a) The Duty

Part XIV of the Ontario *Highway Traffic Act* imposes special legal obligations on drivers involved in accidents. Its objective is to provide the authorities with a clear picture of all the hazards associated with motor vehicle travel. Section 199 (1)-(3) of the Act provides that;

> (1) Every person in charge of a motor vehicle or street car who is directly or indirectly involved in an accident shall, if the accident results in personal injuries or in damage to property apparently exceeding an amount prescribed by regulation, report the accident forthwith to the nearest provincial or municipal police officer and furnish him or her with the information concerning the accident as may be required by the officer under subsection (3).

> (1.1) If, on reporting the accident to the nearest provincial or municipal police officer under subsection (1), the person is directed by the officer to report the accident at a specified location, the person shall not furnish the officer described in subsection (1) with the information concerning the accident but shall forthwith attend at the specified location and report the accident there to a provincial or municipal police officer and furnish him or her with the information concerning the accident as may be required by the officer under subsection (3).

> (2) Where the person is physically incapable of making a report and there is another occupant of the motor vehicle, the occupant shall make the report.

> (3) A police officer receiving a report of an accident, as required by this section, shall secure from the person making the report, or by other inquiries where necessary, the particulars of the accident, the persons involved, the extent of the personal injuries or property damage, if any, and the other information as may be

necessary to complete a written report concerning the accident and shall forward the report to the Registrar within ten days of the accident.

(b) "On a Highway"

Unlike other motor vehicle offences, there is nothing in this section to limit its application to accidents which occur on the highway. Every accident in which a driver is directly or indirectly involved must be reported if the apparent damage meets the monetary threshold.[1] It would seem, therefore, that the controversy which sometimes surrounds the applicability of certain sections to Aboriginal reserve territory is also avoided by the absence of the phrase "on a highway."

(c) The Mental Element of the Offence

Given the carefully structured regulatory scheme to ensure complete reporting and recording of accidents that Part XIV describes, the offence is presumptively one of strict liability.[2] Thus, unlike the *Criminal Code* offence, the prosecution is not obliged to prove any mental element. The Crown makes out a *prima facie* case upon proof of the accident, the apparent value of the damage and the failure to report "forthwith."

Apart from the question of the use to which statements made under this section are put,[3] it has not been subject to such an attack to date, and such an attack would be difficult to sustain, particularly under s. 1, in light of the objective of the section, the non-penal sanctions and the almost impossible evidentiary burden which would inevitably be placed on the Crown.[4] It is always open to the defendant to raise a defence of due diligence, as well as defences against the *actus reus* constituting the offence.[5] A succesful due diligence defence, however, would require the driver to show that he or she made an honest and reasonable effort to comply, or had an honest and reasonable belief in a set of facts that, if true, would have made the failure to report blameless. In *R. v. Clarke*,[6] the Court rejected the defendant's claim that she did not possess the requisite mental element for the offence because she did not believe there had been an incident causing any damage. The Court held that there was no basis for any such "honest belief" on the part of the defendant, and that any such belief on her part arose from a negligent assumption which

---

1 *R. v. Berg* (1956), 116 C.C.C. 204 (Ont. Co. Ct.); *R. v. Cheadle* (1972), 9 C.C.C. (2d) 111 (Alta. T.D.); *Bell v. Fader* (*sub nom. Bell v. R.*), [1969] 2 C.C.C. 9 (Sask. Q.B.).

2 See the discussion in chapter 1.

3 See chapter 4: *R. v. White* (1998), 32 M.V.R. (3d) 161 (B.C. C.A.), leave to appeal to S.C.C. granted September 17, 1998.

4 See *R. v. Sutherland* (1990), 22 M.V.R. (2d) 35 (N.S. C.A.).

5 See chapter 1.

6 (1984), 27 M.V.R. 65 (B.C. Co. Ct.).

was merely "wishful thinking." In other words, the defendant may have believed there was no accident, but her belief was unreasonable.

(d) "Forthwith"

Under section 199(1) the driver is required to make his or her report "forthwith."[7] In *R. v. Pearson*[8] the defendant had been in a single car accident on a country road at 3 o'clock in the afternoon. He did not contact the police until 9 o'clock that evening. In concluding that this was an acceptable period between event and reporting the court held that "forthwith" meant "within a reasonable time having regard to all the circumstances of the case ..."[9] In determining whether or not the time elapsed is reasonable, the court should have regard to the seriousness of the damage or injury resulting and the availability of communications. A significant delay in notifying police of a minor accident which would be difficult to report may be excused while the failure to report a more serious accident in the same circumstances might not be.

In order to establish a *prima facie* case under this section, the Crown must prove that the defendant failed to make the report "forthwith."

In *Bell v. Fader*,[10] the defendant trucker had been in an accident on an isolated construction site at about noon. His vehicle was the only one involved in the accident and it was operative after the incident. The defendant used his vehicle for the remainder of the work day. He drove into town at the end of the day and made his report at seven o'clock in the evening, moments after arriving in town. The trial court had convicted the defendant saying that he was required to either report the accident "at the first opportunity" or see that someone else did. In acquitting the defendant, the appeal court rejected the "first opportunity" test and referred to the *Pearson* standard. The duty imposed was to report "as promptly as is reasonably possible or practicable under all the circumstances ..."[11]

The suggestion is that to prove the *actus reus* in a case where a belated report was made, the Crown must prove that an earlier report was possible. To the same effect is the statement in *R. v. Marler*[12] that the defendant must make his or her report, "by the quickest means of communications available to him." If the defendant can show that he or she exercised due diligence in making a report, he or she should be acquitted.

In *R. v. Bakker*,[13] the court considered an appeal where the defendant had been involved in a single vehicle accident late in the evening. About 12:30

---

7 Some statutes use the phrase "as soon as possible.".
8 (1960), 32 W.W.R. 457 (Sask. Mag. Ct.).
9 *Ibid.*, at p. 461.
10 *Supra*, note 1.
11 *Ibid.*, at p. 677.
12 (1972), 17 N.B.R. (2d) 663 (N.B. Co. Ct.).
13 (1986), 41 M.V.R. 190 (Ont. Prov. Ct.).

a.m. he had run his car off the road. He left his vehicle without assessing the damage and returned to his hotel. The phones at the hotel had been closed for the evening and so he could not contact police. The next day at nine o'clock in the morning he returned to the site where he found his vehicle to be seriously damaged. He contacted police within a half an hour. The judge concluded that unless the defendant is "physically prevented from reporting, is ill, is injured, unconscious, or taken to hospital"[14] the report must be made. Here the defendant might have been able to make a report when the hotel phones opened in the morning rather than waiting until he had reattended at the scene of the accident.

(e) Assessing the Value of the Damages

It is also clear that the section requires the operator of a vehicle to make an assessment of the damage. The threshold amount of property damage is set by regulation.[15] The defendant in *Bakker* had also tried to argue that his duty to make a report did not arise until the quantity of damage became "apparent". Concluding that, on the facts, this defence was not available, the trial judge held that the driver of a vehicle is under an obligation from the time that the damage would be "apparent on a reasonable examination".[16]

It should be noted that the quantum of damage done is not merely relevant to the penalty (as is the case under some legislation).[17] Unless the prosecution establishes the minimum level of damage no offence is made out.

Similarly in *R. v. Marler*[18] the court held that the use of the word "apparent" required that the driver make some reasonable inspection to assess the damage caused by the accident. The court observed,[19]

> In my opinion that by using the word "apparent", the legislature meant that the value of the property damaged was *clearly and plainly evident, that it would be obvious and readily understood by a reasonable person after a reasonable inspection*. The photographs in evidence confirm very extensive damage to the front, left front and side, one fender was badly torn and twisted. In my opinion it would be apparent to any reasonable person that this was extensive damage well in excess of [the amount fixed by the legislation]. [Emphasis added]

---

14 *Ibid.*, at p. 192.

15 In Ontario, the amount is currently set at $1,000. O. Reg. 537/97.

16 Section 192.

17 See *R. v. Poteri* (1980), 39 N.S.R. (2d) 250 (N.S. Co. Ct.); *Motor Vehicle Act*, R.S.N.S. 1967, c. 191, s. 87.

18 *Supra*, note 12.

19 *Ibid.*, at p. 665.

(f) What Must be Done to Satisfy the Duty?

The defendant is only obliged to provide the investigating officer with such "particulars of the accident, the persons involved, the extent of the personal injuries or property damage, if any, and such other information as may be necessary to complete a written report"[20] in the form approved of by the ministry.[21]

Prior to 1969, statements made to the police in compliance with this section could not be used against the defendant in a trial for a traffic offence except for the purpose of proving compliance with the section. With the repeal of the statutory prohibition of using these statements, the defendant had to turn to the common law rule regarding confessions.[22] This rule holds that inculpatory statements made to police are only admissible in court if the accused gave the statement "voluntarily." In law, voluntariness has a special meaning in these circumstances. To be voluntary a statement must be made "without promise of favour or fear of loss."[23] The question then is whether a statement made in compliance with a statutory duty is voluntary. That is, are such statements admissible under the well-developed rule regarding confessions?

This problem was considered in the context of a federal *Criminal Code* prosecution before the 1969 repeal in which the provincial prohibition against using the statement was held to be inapplicable. In *R. v. Marshall*[24] the Supreme Court of Canada held that in determining the admissibility of a statement made in compliance with a statutory requirement, the appropriate test is voluntariness. The statutory compulsion present in the section is merely one factor to be weighed in assessing whether the statement is admissible. The particular use to which the statement can be put, however, would seem to be limited to fulfilling the regulatory objectives of the statutory scheme, and would not encompass the use for criminal liability.[25]

2. FAIL TO REMAIN

(a) Introduction

Section 200(1) of the *Highway Traffic Act* provides that:

200. (1) Where an accident occurs on a highway, every person in charge of a vehicle or street car that is directly or indirectly involved in the accident shall,

---

20 Section 199(3).
21 Section 199(4).
22 Some provinces have retained an equivalent provision, however. See Segal, Murray D., *Manual of Motor Vehicle Law* (3rd ed.) (Toronto: Carswell, 1982 looseleaf) Chapter 14.
23 *R. v. Rothman* (1981), [1981] 1 S.C.R. 640 (S.C.C.).
24 (1961), 129 C.C.C. 232 (S.C.C.).
25 The Supreme Court of Canada will have an opportunity to consider this issue in the near future: *R. v. White, supra*, note 4.

(a) remain at or immediately return to the scene of the accident;

(b) render all possible assistance; and

(c) upon request, give in writing to anyone sustaining loss or injury, or to any police officer or to any witness, his or her name, address, driver's licence number and jurisdiction of issuance, motor vehicle liability insurance policy insurer and policy number, name and address of the registered owner of the vehicle and the vehicle permit number.

In short, the duty is on a person in charge of a vehicle involved in an accident to remain at or immediately return to the scene of the accident; render all possible assistance; and, upon request give to anyone who has sustained loss or injury, or to a police officer or witness, his or her name, the vehicle owner's name and address, and the permit number for the vehicle.

In *R. v. Gummer*,[26] Martin J.A. articulated the strict policy motivations of the *Criminal Code* offence of fail to remain:

In our view, the court has a duty to bring home to persons having the charge of a motor vehicle which has been involved in an accident that the courts of this country will not countenance the failure to remain at the scene and discharge the duties required by the *Criminal Code*.

The provincial offence of fail to remain can be distinguished from the offence of failing to report on the basis that the charge of fail to remain requires that the accident take place "on a highway,"[27] and it has no threshold damage amount. In other words, the duties imposed by section 200 arise regardless of where the accident occurs[28] or how slight the accident may seem.

(b) The Relationship Between the Provincial and *Criminal Code* Offences

Both Fail to Report and Fail to Remain in the provincial statutes should be distinguished from the *Criminal Code* offence of fail to stop,[29] which makes it an offence for anyone having care or control of a vehicle that is involved in an accident with another person to fail to stop at the scene of the accident in order to avoid civil or criminal liability. Both offences further require that the person who is involved in the accident must give his or her name and address and, if there are injuries, offer assistance.

While the provincial offence provides more detail with respect to the reporting duties of a police officer receiving an accident report, the criminal offence contains an additional mental element to the offence, namely that the *actus reus* of failing to stop must be accompanied by the requisite mental element, namely the "intent to escape civil or criminal liability."

---

26 (1983), 25 M.V.R. 282 (Ont. C.A.).

27 For a consideration of this term, see *R. v. Wong* (1997), 29 M.V.R. (3d) 194 (B.C. S.C.).

28 Subject, of course, to the definition of "Highway" in s. 1(1).

29 R.S.C. 1985, c. C-46, s. 252.

Both offences are *intra vires* their respective legislatures,[30] and the *Code* offence has withstood challenges to its validity under s. 11(*d*) of the *Charter*.[31] The provincial offence of fail to remain has been held to be an included offence in the *Criminal Code*.[32]

It has been held that the specified duties imposed by the *Criminal Code* offence must be discharged at the scene of the accident.[33] Further, the *Criminal Code* offence presumes the requisite intention of avoiding liability unless there is evidence to the contrary, and the consumption of alcohol is capable of constituting such evidence on the basis that it would negate the requisite intention.[34]

(c) The Mental Element of the Offence

Prior to the decision in *Sault Ste. Marie*, the mental element necessary to sustain a conviction under s. 200 was in doubt. In 1974, the Supreme Court of Canada in *R. v. Hill*[35] had rejected the defendant's position that the Crown had to prove that the accused knew there had been an accident in order to sustain a conviction. Dickson J., as he then was, held that "[I]gnorance in this case affords no greater defence than in the case of a driver who unwittingly exceeds the speed limit or inadvertantly goes through a red light … [W]hatever Mrs. Hill believed or did not believe is irrelevant."[36]

In *Hill* the defendant knew of the accident but denied knowledge of the extent of the damage done. In *R. v. Racimore*,[37] Mr. Justice Grange considered the situation where the defendant claimed no knowledge of the accident or damage — the entire event had escaped his notice. Concluding that without knowledge of the accident, the failure to remain, the *actus reus* of the offence, was involuntary, the Court acquitted the defendant. His Lordship wrote:[38]

> His failure to remain was dictated by an ignorance of essential fact [*sic*] and was involuntary, and even though *mens rea* is not a part of the offence he is not guilty.

Thus if the defendant can raise a doubt about his knowledge of an accident, he should be acquitted on the absence of any voluntary *actus reus*.

Since *Sault Ste. Marie*,[39] offences created within the provincial sphere of legislative competence are presumed to be strict liability. That is, while the

---

30 A.G. *Québec v. Gagne*, [1969] R.L. 534 found the corresponding Québec statute to be constitutional.
31 *R. v. Gosselin* (1988), 9 M.V.R. (2d) 290 (Ont. C.A.); *R. v. T. (S.D.)* (1985), 43 C.R. (3d) 307 (N.S. C.A.).
32 *R. v. Vanboeyen* (1992), 40 M.V.R. (2d) 13 (Alta. Prov. Ct.).
33 *R. v. Romanowicz* (1998), 14 C.R. (5th) 100 (Ont. Gen. Div.).
34 *Ibid.*
35 (1973), 14 C.C.C. (2d) 505 (S.C.C.).
36 *Ibid.*, at 511.
37 (1975), 25 C.C.C. (2d) 143 (Ont. H.C.).
38 *Ibid.*, at p. 147.
39 [1978] 2 S.C.R. 1299.

prosecution is not required to prove any positive mental element (save perhaps voluntariness which is properly considered under *actus reus*,) the defendant may escape conviction by demonstrating, on a balance of probability, an innocent mental state. This can be done by showing that the defendant exercised all "due diligence" or that the defendant reasonably believed in a set of facts which, if they had been true, would have made his or her actions innocent. It should be noted that the measure of due diligence and reasonable belief are objective, looking at what the reasonable person would do or believe in the same circumstances.

That this offence is at least strict liability (rather than absolute liability) is made clear by the judgment in *Reference re s. 94(2) of the Motor Vehicle Act (British Columbia)*[40] in which the Supreme Court held that absolute liability could not be assigned to offences which involved the *possibility* of imprisonment.

(d) Possible Defences

The offence of "failing to remain or return to the scene" is a single wrongful act and an information so worded will not be duplicitous. That is, it would not mislead a defendant in preparing his or her defence. See generally *R. v. Budden*.[41] On the other hand, an information or notice which alleged failures under s. 174 (b) or (c) together, or which used improper short forms, should be amended before the defendant pleads. The defendant should know the exact nature of the failure alleged against him or her. A multifarious information or notice should not be allowed. The defendant has a right to a clearly-worded charge stating explicitly the wrongful act alleged.

The duty to provide information to "anyone sustaining loss or injury, or to any constable or other police officer, or *to any witness*" includes anyone having immediate knowledge of the accident, whether they saw it or not. Thus in one case[42] the court concluded that any person who could give evidence in a court in relation to the accident could require the driver to provide the information to them. In that case an "ear witness" who had heard but not seen the accident and had later seen the place where the vehicles came to rest was held to be a witness under the section. The failure of the driver to provide information to that witness was violation of the section.

The provision of information raises questions as to the use to which such information can be put subsequently. In *R. v. Sarkonak*,[43] the accused's state-

---

40 36 M.V.R. 240 (S.C.C.).
41 (1964), [1964] 2 C.C.C. 290 (Ont. Mag. Ct.).
42 *R. v. Rees* (1981), 10 M.V.R. 147 (N.S. Co. Ct.).
43 (1990), 53 C.C.C. (3d) 542 (Man. Q.B.).

ments on reporting an accident were held not to meet the voluntariness requirement since the requirement to report under the Act constituted an inducement to the accused to respond to the police officer's questions. The statements were thus inadmissible in a trial for the *Criminal Code* offence of fail to remain.

While the duty to provide information in Ontario only arises upon the request of a named person this is not the case in all provinces. In Alberta, the statute has no such provision and the defendant must give the information required unless there has been an explicit waiver by the witness or person sustaining loss.[44] This is clearly a higher duty than that which is placed on Ontario drivers.

In *R. v. Hannam*,[45] the Court considered whether any contact between vehicles was necessary to sustain a conviction for leaving the scene under the *Criminal Code*. The accused had been racing and jockeying for position, but there had been no collision or even contact between the vehicles. The defence argued that the accused had not been "involved in an accident." This reasoning was rejected. It was held that involvement in an accident is not dependent on physical contact between the vehicles.

As a strict liability offence, the defence of due diligence is of course open to the defendant. In *R. v. Weir*,[46] the defendant left the scene after a five minute delay. The Court held that this was a proper exercise of due diligence since he required medical assistance. Further, there was no obligation on the defendant to return to the scene of the accident after receiving medical attention.

3. MANDATORY SEATBELT LEGISLATION

(a) Introduction

Every province has legislation requiring drivers and passengers to wear seatbelts. In Ontario, s. 106(3) of the *Highway Traffic Act* states:

> ... [E]very person who drives on a highway a motor vehicle [or is a passenger in a vehicle] in which a seat belt assembly is provided for the driver shall wear the complete seat belt assembly in a properly adjusted and securely fastened manner.

Certain categories of driver are exempt from the requirement to wear a seatbelt. A driver is responsible for ensuring that any passenger under the age of 16

---

44 *R. v. May* (1975), 24 C.C.C. (2d) 505 (Alta. S.C.).

45 (1987), 1 M.V.R. (2d) 361 (Alta. Q.B.).

46 (1992), 36 M.V.R. (2d) 118 (Ont. Prov. Div.).

is wearing a seatbelt.[47] Since the exemptions are statutorily defined, the offence is, to all intents and purposes one of absolute liability.[48]

(b) Constitutional Considerations

Not surprisingly, seatbelt legislation was subject to a great many Charter challenges in the 1980s. Many people found it somehow wrong that the legislature should pass a law requiring one to do something which seemingly does not affect any other person in any way whatsoever, and this was reflected in the rate of compliance and enforcement. However, the constitutional validity of the legislation is now well settled, and the public acceptance of the benefits of seatbelts seemingly higher than ever. In addition, while the enforcement of the provisions is still one which is subject to the exercise of considerable discretion by police officers, the periodic 'zero tolerance' blitz on seatbelts by police forces, and increased public awareness of the costs to society of not wearing a seatbelt suggest that it is probably enforced to a greater extent than it may have been in the past.

Most of the constitutional challenges to seatbelt legislation failed. The cases generally held that the law is aimed at protecting the physical well-being of users of the highways, and whether or not it is a wise or unwise law is a political question and one upon which reasonable persons will differ. Clearly, the courts were loathe to interfere, and the grounds for any constitutional challenge are now essentially exhausted.

The following constitutional principles in the application of seatbelt legislation are entrenched:

- Seatbelt legislation is properly within the ambit of provincial legislative authority.[49]

- Section 7 is not violated just because some injuries may be caused by the use of a seatbelt.

- Just because categories of individuals are exempt from the requirement does not create a distinction sufficient to engage s. 15 of the *Charter*.[50]

---

47 Section 106 has been amended. Ontario has now repealed the exemptions from the legislation, and they will instead appear in the regulations: Bill 55 *Road Safety Act, 1996,* S.O. 1996, c. 20, s. 22(3), (4). Section 22(2) of the same Act amends the section to make it clear that passengers 16 and over responsible for wearing seatbelts, while those under 16 are the responsibility of the driver. The amendments also allow a police officer to request identification from a "passenger in a motor vehicle who appears to be at least 16 years old" for the purposes of enforcing the legislation (s.106(8), (8.1))The Bill received Royal Assent on June 27 1997, but these particular sections had not yet been proclaimed in force at the time of writing.

48 Although technically it is, as discussed below, one of strict liability.

49 *Paquin v. Montréal (City)* (1981), 12 M.V.R. 123 (Que. S.C.).

50 *R. v. Powless* (1996), 27 M.V.R. (3d) 15, (N.W.T. S.C.); *R. v. MacIntyre* (1989), 22 M.V.R. (2d) 331 (P.E.I. Prov. Div.); *Léger c. Montréal (Ville)* (1985), 39 M.V.R. 60 (Que. S.C.),

- There is no s. 7 violation in requiring the use of seatbelts: "[t]he risk of injury or death is decreased when a seatbelt is worn; moreover, failure to wear a seatbelt puts other persons, both in the vehicle and outside it, at increased risk."[51]
- Where an individual may hold personal beliefs as to the exercise of his or her free will, mandatory seatbelt legislation does not infringe freedom of religion under s. 2(a) of the *Charter.*[52]

(c) The Application of the Statute

The offence is one of strict liability. Thus, where a police officer testified that he was not wearing his seatbelt as he was arriving at an emergency situation which may require him to draw his weapon to preserve life, the defence of necessity was made out.

The requirement that the seatbelt be "properly adjusted" requires only that it be securely fastened to a sufficient degree of snugness. Thus where the accused was wearing the torso part of the seatbelt under his arm as opposed to over his shoulder, but the seatbelt was otherwise securely fastened, he was in compliance with the section.[53]

In Ontario the statutory exemptions (aside from age) apply in the following circumstances:[54]

(1)   the driver is going in reverse;

(2)   the person holds a valid medical certificate stating that the person is unable to wear a seatbelt for reasons of illness or physical characteristic;

(3)   the person is actually engaged in work which requires entering and exiting the vehicle frequently, and where the speed does not exceed 40 km/h;

With respect to the interpretation of these exemptions, the following principles have been applied:

---

affirmed (*sub nom. Montréal (Ville) v. Léger*) (1986), 41 M.V.R. 85 (Que. C.A.); *R. v. Kennedy* (1987), 3 M.V.R. (2d) 88 (B.C. C.A.), leave to appeal refused (1988), 22 B.C.L.R. (2d) xxx, 4 M.V.R. (2d) xxxviii, 87 N.R. 236 (note) (S.C.C.).

51 *R. v. Maier* (1989), 21 M.V.R. (2d) 134 (Alta. C.A.), leave to appeal refused (1990), 44 C.R.R. 199n (S.C.C.). The Court of Appeal restored the original conviction on the basis that the appellate court below had improperly interfered with the findings of fact made by the trial judge.

52 *R. v. Thompson* (1986), 41 M.V.R. 158 (B.C. C.A.), affirmed (1986), 45 M.V.R. 136 (B.C. C.A.).

53 *R. v. Merchant* (1990), 25 M.V.R. (2d) 234 (Sask. Q.B.); *R. v. Bessic* (1993), 146 A.R. 86 (Alta. Prov. Ct.).

54 The regulations also contain exemptions for certain specified drivers and passengers, primarily for emergency personnel in certain situations: R.R.O. 1990, Reg. 613.

- The section requires the accused to have the letter or certificate from a physician in his or her possession at the time of driving.[55] However, depending on the particular statutory language in each province, evidence of medical disability may in some circumstances be demonstrated at trial, thus allowing for an acquittal even where a medical certificate was not in the driver's possession at the time of driving. In one case, the accused was able to bring himself within the exemption by calling evidence at his trial demonstrating that he suffered from claustrophobia.[56]

- The exemption for those engaged in employment which required them to frequently leave a vehicle, the exemption only applies to one who is "actually engaged in" work of that kind.[57]

A seatbelt charge is difficult to defend succesfully. The defence will often have little choice but to test the officer's evidence as to his observation of the accused and the seatbelt. Thus defence counsel should cross-examine carefully on the exact time, place and conditions under which he or she purported to observe the accused.

4. FOLLOW TOO CLOSELY

(a) Introduction

Prohibition on following another vehicle too closely is covered by s. 158 of the *Highway Traffic Act*, under the rather awkward heading, "Headway of Motor Vehicles." The section states:

> **158.** (1) The driver of a motor vehicle or street car shall not follow another vehicle or street car more closely than is reasonable and prudent having due regard for the speed of the vehicle and the traffic on and the conditions of the highway.
>
> (2) The driver of a commercial motor vehicle when driving on a highway at a speed exceeding 60 kilometres per hour shall not follow within 60 metres of another motor vehicle, but this shall not be construed to prevent a commercial motor vehicle overtaking and passing another motor vehicle.[58]

In the context of a dangerous driving case, the British Columbia Court of Appeal had this to say about the offence of following too closely:

> Driving without sufficient space behind the vehicle in front creates a number of hazards. The view ahead is obstructed. That is particularly so in a case like this where the vehicle being followed is a large truck.

---

55 *R. v. Bixby* (1987) 3 W.C.B. (2d) 225 (Nfld. S.C.).

56 *R. v. Brannen* (1994), 7 M.V.R. (3d) 295 (N.S. S.C.).

57 *R. v. Matthews* (1987), 3 W.C.B. (2d) 445 (Nfld. S.C.).

58 Section 159(2) makes it an offence to follow a fire department vehicle responding to an alarm at a distance of less than 150 metres.

Another obvious hazard is that there is insufficient stopping distance if something unexpected happened. ...[59]

A breach of the statutory duty establishes a *prima facie* case of civil negligence.[60]

(b) Proving the Case

An early British Columbia case held that it is insufficient to charge a driver merely with allowing his or her vehicle to "follow another too closely," since the statutory elements of the offence include the requirement that the driving not be "reasonable and prudent" in the circumstances.[61] In Ontario, however, it is acceptable for the charging document to contain the wording "follow too closely." Both the regulations [Item 463 in Schedule 43 of R.R.O. 1990, Reg. 950] and s. 13 of the *Provincial Offences Act* allow for such wording in the charging document.[62]

The offence is undoubtedly one of the hardest for the prosecution to prove. This is in a large measure due to the holding in the leading case of *R. v. Ouseley*[63] which makes it clear that the mere fact of a rear end collision will not suffice to make out a *prima facie* case of following too closely. In *Ouseley*, the Crown led evidence showing that the accused's car struck the vehicle which it was following. The driver of the lead vehicle had occasion to slow down gradually and stop just before the impact. Apart from the collision itself, there was no evidence as to how closely behind the lead vehicle the accused's car was being driven at any time. The Crown introduced a statement by the accused wherein he stated: "I saw her brake ahead of me. I braked and started to skid and hit her." Moreover, it was shown that the surface of the street was icy and not in good condition.

The Court of Appeal held that more needed to be proven than the fact of the collision. This is because the impact itself would sustain logical inferences other than that the respondent was following too closely. For example, the collision may have been caused by inattention on the part of the accused, or by his excessive speed. As stated by Gale C.J.O. for the Court, "[h]e was not charged with careless driving, however, and we can see no reason why he should have been convicted of this offence, where there was no evidence whatever as to the distance which separated the two cars until the actual impact." Since other explanations for a rear end collision are invariably available, the Crown should be particularly scrupulous in determining whether there is a reasonable prospect of conviction. In addition, eyewitness evidence, which is effectively a prerequisite to a conviction, is often lacking.

---

59 *R. v. Sara* (1992), 40 M.V.R. (2d) 45 (B.C. C.A.).
60 *Murray v. Brum* (1990), 27 M.V.R. (2d) 64 (Ont. Gen. Div.).
61 *Oskey, Re* (1959), 29 W.W.R. 415 (B.C. S.C.).
62 See Chapter 2 concerning the validity of the charging document.
63 [1973] 10 C.C.C. (2d) 148 (Ont. C.A.).

R. v. Walsh[64] goes somewhat further than *Ouseley* in holding that there can be no conviction in the absence of any, or any reliable, evidence as to the distance between the two cars. A conviction may not be founded on the fact that an accused was not keeping a proper lookout.[65]

"Reasonable and prudent" is another nebulous term similar to the term "due care" used in the context of careless driving. Each case is really decided on its own facts. Both concepts impart a similar legal standard of care, namely, what the average reasonable person would have done in like circumstances. In the context of careless driving, *R. v. Beauchamp*[66] is authority for the proposition that the factual standard is a constantly shifting one depending on road, visibility, weather conditions, traffic conditions that exist or reasonably may be expected and any other conditions that ordinarily prudent drivers would take into consideration. With respect to a charge under s. 158, the provision itself specifies that a vehicle shall not follow another vehicle more closely than is "reasonable and prudent having due regard for the speed of such vehicle and the traffic on and the conditions of the highway." These factors are essential elements of the offence and must be proven beyond a reasonable doubt for a conviction to be sustained. Similar legislation in British Columbia has been held to be an offence of strict liability.[67]

In *R. v. Robbins*,[68] the accused was convicted of following another vehicle too closely, contrary to then s. 164(1) of the *Motor Vehicle Act*, R.S.B.C. 1979, c. 288 [Now R.S.B.C. 1996, c. 318, s. 162 (i) (follow too closely)]. He was operating his motor vehicle in the vicinity of construction work. The vehicle ahead of him went through an underpass and, upon exiting, stopped abruptly in response to a flagman's signal which the driver thought read "stop" and not "slow" as was the case. The accused attempted to stop in time but was unable to do so. His vehicle collided with the vehicle in front of him as he swerved to the left in an attempt to avoid a collision. His vehicle ended up in a ditch on the opposite side of the road.

In allowing the accused's appeal, it was held that:[69]

I think that the words "follow another vehicle more closely than is reasonable and prudent," import the concept of distance between two moving vehicles. It

64 (1960), 130 C.C.C. 201, 33 W.W.R. 91 (Sask. Mag. Ct.).

65 Although see *R. v. Sara, supra* note 59: the accused had been looking down at his gauges for an appreciable time when the view ahead was blocked by a truck, the traffic was heavy, and the accused was so close behind the truck that he could not cope with an unexpected event. The Court of Appeal held that these were sufficient circumstances for the accused to be convicted of the *Criminal Code* offence of dangerous driving, leading to the somewhat anomalous possibility that the traffic offence of following too closely demands more onerous proof than the *Criminal Code* offence.

66 [1953] O.R. 422, 106 C.C.C. 6 (Ont. C.A.).

67 *R. v. Ishkanian* (1985), [1986] B.C.W.L.D. 634 (B.C. Co. Ct.).

68 (1990), 22 M.V.R. (2d) 201 (B.C. Co. Ct.).

69 *Ibid.*, at p. 207-208.

seems to me that, if the vehicle ahead suddenly stops, that creates an emergency situation which is not contemplated by the enactment.

The essence of the offence is following too closely. The section instructs the trier of fact to determine whether the driver behind was following more closely than is reasonable and prudent, having due regard for the speed of the vehicles and the amount and nature of the traffic, and on the condition of the highway. The phrase "speed of the vehicles" indicates to me that the section contemplates that both vehicles are moving.

The appellant may well have been civilly negligent in driving faster than was reasonable and prudent. But as Bence P.M. (Sask. Magistrate's Court) pointed out in *R. v. Walsh* (1960), 33 W.W.R. 91 at 92, 130 C.C.C. 201 at 202, "[r]ear-end collisions occur for various reasons, often failure to keep a proper lookout, or too high speed, or faulty brakes, and any one of which could create civil liability." But this is a quasi-criminal charge, and the Court must find that the defendant was following more closely than was reasonable and prudent.

5. RADAR WARNING DEVICES

(a) Introduction

Radar warning devices, colloquially known as 'fuzz-busters' became popular in the mid-to-late 1970's when technology made it possible to produce small, affordable units to detect radar speed monitoring equipment. The devices were outlawed in 1977 as they were seen to be contrary to public safety by inviting individuals to break the law and by helping them to escape detection. Particularly in the post-*Charter* era, the offence is conceptually interesting in that the device in and of itself is not harmful. The device is the conceptual equivalent of an accomplice to a crime (the 'lookout' in a robbery for example). However, it is hard to imagine any productive use for the device in the hands of a motorist other than that of concealing the commission of the offence of speeding.

Section 79(1) of the *Highway Traffic Act* defines a 'radar warning device' as:

> … any device or equipment designed or intended for use in a motor vehicle to warn the driver of the presence of radar speed measuring equipment in the vicinity and includes any device or equipment designed or intended for use in a motor vehicle to interfere with the effective operation of radar speed measuring equipment.[70]

The balance of s. 79 sets in place the legislative framework for the control of such devices. The Act provides,

> (2) No person shall drive on a highway a motor vehicle that is equipped with or that carries or contains a radar warning device.

---

70 Proposed amendments remove the word radar from the section in order to accomodate newer technologies (e.g. laser).

(3) A police officer may at any time, without a warrant, stop, enter and search a motor vehicle that he or she has reasonable grounds to believe is equipped with or carries or contains a radar warning device contrary to subsection (2) and may seize and take away any radar warning device found in or upon the motor vehicle.

(4) Where a person is convicted of an offence under this section, any device seized under subsection (3) by means of which the offence was committed is forfeited to the Crown.

(5) Every person who contravenes subsection (2) is guilty of an offence and on conviction is liable to a fine of not less than $100 and not more than $1000.

(6) Subsection (2) does not apply to a person who is transporting radar warning devices in sealed packages in a motor vehicle from a manufacturer to a consignee.

(7) No person shall sell, offer or advertise for sale a radar warning device by retail.

(8) Every person who contravenes subsection (7) is guilty of an offence and on conviction is liable,

(a) for a first offence, to a fine of not more than $1000; and

(b) for each subsequent offence, to a fine of not more than $5,000.

(b) Constitutional Considerations (1): Division of Powers

The legislation was first challenged with respect to the division of powers, and the provincial authority to legislate in an area concerning radio and tele-communications (a federal head of power). In *R. v. Boivin*,[71] the constitution-ality of that provision (then section 52(a)) was held to be within the power of the provincial legislature. Holland J. held that "in pith and substance" the Legislature purported to legislate concerning highway traffic in the province rather than the use of radio waves. While the legislation incidentally dealt with radio communications this did not make it unconstitutional.[72]

Boivin also raised the issue of whether the section was, in pith and sub-stance, in relation to criminal law rather than highway traffic. Arguably that a charge could be laid under s. 139 of the *Criminal Code* which renders it an offence to obstruct a police officer in the execution of his or her duty. Holland J. rejected this suggestion: while it might be possible to lay a charge under the federal legislation, that did not necessarily mean that the provision was outside its jurisdiction. Nor does it mean that the section necessarily con-flicts with existing federal legislation.[73] This has not, however, prevented the offence of obstructing justice from playing a significant role in the charging and prosecution of this offence.

---

71 (1978), 1 M.V.R. 44 (Ont. H.C.).

72 To the same effect see *R. v. Van Dermark* (1994), 5 M.V.R. (3d) 274 (Nfld. T.D.); *R. v. Crosstown Motors Ltd.* (1975), 22 C.C.C. (2d) 404 (Alta. Prov. Ct.); *R. v. Olin* (1978), 41 C.C.C. (2d) 241 (Alta. T.D.).

73 On this point see *O'Grady v. Sparling* (1960), [1960] S.C.R. 804 at p. 810 (S.C.C.).

(c) Elements of the Offence

The Crown must prove beyond a reasonable doubt (a) that the device is a radar warning device; (b) that the accused was on a highway, and (c) that the device was in the vehicle. In *R. v. Shuler*,[74] the Alberta Court of Appeal had occasion to deal with the issue of whether the driver of a vehicle equipped with a radar detector from which the fuse is missing, is guilty of an offence under section 61(1) of the Alberta *Highway Traffic Act*.[75] Laycraft J.A., in delivering the judgment of the Court held that it would have frustrated the legislation's clear intention to hold that a radar detector with a fuse missing is not a device capable of detecting radar emissions when that fuse can be easily "popped in or out" as the evidence indicated in this case. It would be absurd to conclude otherwise.

(d) Proving the Offence: the Role of Expert Evidence

In *R. v. Henuset*,[76] a police constable operating a running, moving radar in an unmarked car, noticed the accused's vehicle suddenly dropping in speed immediately after coming within range of the radar beam. The constable seized from the accused's vehicle a device which he considered to be a radar detector. He then hooked the unit up to his vehicle's lighter. The device emitted a warning buzzer and light when tested by the officer by turning on his own radar unit. The prosecution adduced no expert evidence at trial. The accused was convicted of unlawfully having a radar device contrary to s. 185(3) of the *Highway Traffic Act* of Manitoba, fined $75 and the device was confiscated.

Counsel for the accused had argued that the Constable's evidence alone, and his description of his testing of the device, could not be evidence that the device seized is in fact one "for detecting radar speed determination equipment." In support of this argument, counsel referred to the constable's evidence under cross-examination. This dealt with the effect of the Constable having to cut the wires to remove the device, and having to re-connect them in what he hoped was the same order. He wasn't able to say, however, that he put them back in the same order. Further, under cross-examination the constable had indicated as follows:[77]

> Q. Well, can you testify that that, in fact, is the case, then that this instrument was in the same operating condition, as it were, when you tested it as it was when it was in the vehicle?
> A. No, for the main reason because I had to cut the wires and putting the wires back together colour for colour … that I just followed what would be naturally colour for colour or …

---

74 (1983), 21 M.V.R. 189 (Alta. C.A.).

75 R.S.A. 1980, c. H-7.

76 (1983), [1983] 4 W.W.R. 267 (Man. Co. Ct.).

77 *Ibid.*, at p. 271.

Further, the constable testified he did not test the device in the same vehicle in which his radar was installed but in another police vehicle; that he was not an electronics expert, although he had dabbled for some years with amateur radio; and that the constable in no way examined the insides of either of the two small boxes to determine how they functioned or to determine what the device was really designed to do. The constable's following candid admission was the most telling evidence:

> Q. Do you have any electronic credentials at all, I mean, I fix my toaster but that doesn't make me an expert.
> A. No, I never indicated I was an expert, just some knowledge of radios but I'm not — I wouldn't even consider myself as an expert.
> Q. Well, if that's the case then, Constable, perhaps you can tell me whether or not it's true that the device that you hold in your hand could be, unless you saw the inside of it, could be almost anything, couldn't it?
> A. That is correct, yes.
> Q. All right, and all that you know is that after you hooked it up with a piece of police equipment and plugged it into the cigarette lighter in your police car, that it reacted to your radar set?
> A. Exactly, yes, that's all I can say.
> Q. And that's all you know?
> A. Yes, and just the sudden drop in speed led me to believe that it might be an instrument capable of detecting radar in a vehicle.
> Q. That it might be?
> A. Because I was driving an unmarked police car and I was a fair distance away before it.
> Q. I see. Did you take it near a radar or a radio tower of any kind to see if it would react?
> A. This equipment?
> Q. Yes.
> A. No, I did not.

The County Court Judge held as follows:

> While the court in this case is highly suspicious and suggests the accused is probably guilty of the offence charged because of the circumstances, in the absence of a definition, description or explanation or other absolute proof as to what this "device" actually is, those suspicions alone are not enough to warrant a conviction in the circumstances here, and the learned Provincial Judge erred in finding guilt, mainly it would seem on the basis of a "sudden speed drop" and a subsequent testing in a really non-scientific way.

> In this day and in our push-button society, when electronic sciences are such that even the experts find difficulty in keeping abreast, legislatures who pass laws authorizing the use of, and the prohibition of possession of certain types of electronic gadgets, must be prepared to provide the necessary resources to insure proper enforcement of such laws. This applies particularly to the increasing appearance in Manitoba of devices employed by those intent on circumventing the speed laws, namely the type of device similar to what was seized here and purporting to be a "device for detecting radar speed determination equipment",

often commonly referred to as "Fuzz Busters", "Fox Hunters", "Bear Killers" and "Speed Smellers". There are states and provinces, of course, where such devices are not illegal, but Manitoba as yet is not one of those, and when a charge is laid the Crown must be prepared to prove its case beyond doubt.

It follows then that the appeal is allowed, the fine, if paid, refunded and the confiscated device returned to counsel for the accused to dispose of as he may determine!

The case of *R. v. Wasylyshen*,[78] however, rejected the reasoning found in *Henuset*. In *Wasylyshen*, the Crown was successful on appeal from the accused's acquittal on a charge of unlawful possession of a radar detecting device. Smith J. held that expert evidence is not necessary in every case to prove that such a device is in fact a radar detector. In any event, in that case, there was clear evidence of that fact from a police officer who identified the object as being a radar detector and who had experience with those devices.

Spademan v. R.[79] considered the question of determining whether or not expert evidence is required to show that the device seized is in fact a radar warning device. The evidence of the officer was that he seized the device from the accused's vehicle but did not take the power cord. The officer then took the device to his own vehicle, and using his own power cord, plugged it into the cigarette lighter. He then flipped a switch and it went "beep". The court concluded that this test was not sufficient. As no proper test was performed, there was no proof before the court that the unit in question was designed to be a radar warning device. Accordingly, the appeal was allowed.

(e) Constitutional Considerations (2): Search & Seizure

Subsection 79(3) empowers a police officer to stop, enter and search a vehicle that he or she has reasonable grounds to believe is equipped with a radar warning device, and may seize the device. A conviction under the section can result in the device being forfeited to the Crown according to s. 79(4) of the Act. This has been held not to violate s. 8 of the *Charter*.[80]

In *R. v. Fehr*[81] a police officer stopped the vehicle for a routine check and "on a hunch" resulting from an odd movement of the defendant's vehicle. He conducted a search of the glove compartment and seized what he believed was a radar detector device. Ferg J. held the search of the glove compartment to have been unreasonable and illegal as it was based on no probable or reasonable grounds. However, he found that the evidence should not have been excluded pursuant to s. 24(2) of the *Charter*:[82]

---

78 (1987),7 M.V.R. (2d) 273 (Man. Q.B.).
79 (October 25, 1985), Stiles Prov. J. (Ont. Prov. Div.).
80 *R. v. Munn* (1990), 23 M.V.R. (2d) 118 (Nfld. T.D.).
81 (1984), 29 M.V.R. 63 (Man. Q.B.).
82 *Ibid.*, at p. 65-6.

> Here, the illegality of possessing a radar detector is a minimal thing certainly not heinous, given that several provinces and many of the United States do not prohibit the possession of, indeed the actual use of such machines; the constable's conduct to simply open the glove compartment did not invade to any great degree the accused's personal privacy and was done with no objection or opposition whatever; and the constable's thinking (albeit wrongly) that his investigation was not infringing the accused's rights was simply done in the course of his duties to root out and discover criminal activity as he is sworn to do. His conduct cannot be condoned but is not such so as to warrant alleged illegal conduct on the part of the accused to be overlooked and forgotten about.

The decision was not appealed. It is submitted that where the legislation includes a general power to stop, then the impugned action in *Fehr* will be allowed.

What about the situation in which the driver has concealed the radar warning device on his or her person before being stopped by the police officer? In *R. v. Arseneau*,[83] the accused was pulled over when the police officer suspected that he had a radar warning device in his vehicle. The officer searched the vehicle as he was permitted to do under then s. 61(3) of the Act. The officer found a wire leading from a plug into the cigarette lighter of the motor vehicle and this wire led to an area on the dash where he found a clip typically used to hold a radar warning device. The officer then noticed an object in the accused's pocket that looked like a radar warning device. The accused denied having the device, and the officer proceeded to arrest the accused for obstructing justice. The officer then searched the accused and retrieved the device. The trial judge held that:

> there was nothing in law to compel the defendant to turn over the radar warning device to the officer from his possession. With no such compulsion the officer, albeit frustrated, had no reasonable and probable grounds to arrest the defendant for obstruction.

Thus the search incident to arrest was unlawful and the evidence of the warning device was excluded.[84]

A similar issue arose in *R. v. Dunne*[85] under virtually identical circumstances. The appeal court judge found that the seizure of the warning device as an incident of arrest for the offence of obstructing justice constituted a violation of the accused's s. 8 rights, and the evidence was excluded. Section 79 of the *Highway Traffic Act* provides no power to search a person, nor does it provide a power of arrest. Further, the section is not included among offences for which arrest without warrant may be made under s. 217. Thus:

> [T]he refusal on the part of the defendant to deliver, from his person, what the officer believed was such a device, cannot constitute in law the offence of

---

83 [1988] O.J. No. 2525 (Prov. Div.).

84 See also *Lavin c. Québec (Procureur général)* (1992), 16 C.R. (4th) 112 (Que. C.A.).

85 [1992] O.J. No. 1884 (Prov. Div.).

obstructing the officer in the lawful execution of his duty. The defendant here had a common law right to remain silent and had no obligation to assist the officer in establishing the commission of an offence.

These decisions should not be taken as holding that an accused can never be convicted of the offence unless the actual device is produced. It is open to the Crown to lead other evidence of the presence of a warning device sufficient to warrant conviction.

(f) Radar Warning Device Detectors

The difficulties in proving the presence of a radar warning device have been somewhat alleviated by the use of warning device detectors. Police officers now routinely carry units capable of detecting the presence of radar warning devices. These devices act as both investigative and evidentiary tools, since they can not only detect motorists who might be carrying warning devices, and assist in proving that they were indeed in the vehicle. This latter use is particularly important in light of the limitations placed on the right to search the driver's person outlined above.

In *R. v. Didunyk*,[86] it was held that the use of these electronic radar detectors by the police did not constitute surreptitious electronic surveillance and thus violate the right to be free from unreasonable search under s. 8 of the *Charter of Rights and Freedoms*. In that same case, the Crown called as an expert witness the provincial radar coordinator with the Ontario Provincial Police. The appeal court judge summarized the witness' explanation of the operation of the VG2 interceptor as follows:

> the radar warning devices are designed to operate in a specific frequency in the microwave portion of the spectrum of radio waves, namely 11.55 gigahertz. As they are being operated, they emit or 'leak' certain transmissions of this frequency. The interceptor VG2 on the other hand is designed to detect these leakages in that wave length. It is an electronic radio receiver, comprised of an antenna and an oscillator tuned to that specific frequency. It can detect such emissions not only from radar warning devices but from other sources of microwave trans-mission including alarm systems and automatic door openers. As it receives such signals it warns the operator by means of a series of lights and an audio tone. As the source of the emissions gets progressively closer, the lights increase in number up to ten, and the alarm increases in speed until it becomes a steady tone. All the displays stop the moment that the source, in this case the radar warning device, passes by. The instrument is even tested by injecting a 11.55 gigahertz frequency signal into the apparatus. If it needs to be said, it makes no permanent record, and is not capable of picking up conversations.

This obviously provides some potential avenues for cross-examination of the officer in these relatively new cases.

---

86 (1992) 15 W.C.B. (2d) 164 (Ont. Prov. Div.).

There has always been an issue as to the extent of disclosure to which the accused is entitled in cases involving radar equipment. With respect to the police use of radar warning device detectors, the Ontario Court of Appeal has held that the Crown will only be obliged to disclose the operation manual of the VG2 radar interceptor device used by the police where such disclosure is relevant to the case. While that principle only follows the general disclosure guidelines laid down by the Supreme Court of Canada in *R. v. Stinchcombe*,[87] the issue was considered in relation to the specific offence: absent the Crown relying on the use of the device to prove that the accused's device was indeed a radar detector, or an application to exclude the evidence of the detector for a *Charter* violation, disclosure will not be ordered.[88] In other words, the device has a testimonial capacity which, if used by the Crown to prove its case, would require disclosure in order that the accused can challenge what amounts to the testimonial factors of the device — its capacity, functioning and accuracy.

Where there is a defence motion to exclude the evidence on the basis that the seizure of the device found in the accused's car, and the consequential arrest were made without reasonable and probable grounds, then the functioning of the detector could also be relevant and disclosure may be appropriate depending on the circumstances of the case. Otherwise the technical specifications of the device are irrelevant to the trial. It would seem that where a police officer used the device simply as evidence of his or her grounds for stopping the vehicle, then absent a *Charter* challenge, disclosure of the manual is not necessary.

6. COMPULSORY AUTOMOBILE INSURANCE

(a) Introduction

Every province has legislation requiring vehicles to be insured. In Ontario, the *Compulsory Automobile Insurance Act*[89] was first passed in 1979. The legislature wanted to be certain that every person suffering loss or injury would have access to insurance money as a result of a motor vehicle accident. The Act recognized that some drivers, because of poor records, could not get any insurance from a normal automobile underwriter.

To ensure that no driver should face an absolute bar to driving because of the unavailability of coverage in compliance with the Act, the Facility Association was established. This is a mechanism which pools insurance risks so that high risk drivers can obtain motor vehicle insurance in circumstances where insurance might not otherwise be available. This is not a guarantee of affordable insurance; it merely provides expensive insurance to drivers who

---

87 (1991), [1991] 3 S.C.R. 326 (S.C.C.).

88 *R. v. Shannon* (1992), 42 M.V.R. (2d) 128 (Ont. C.A.).

89 R.S.O. 1990, c. C.25.

would otherwise be completely uninsurable. Under s. 10 of the Act, the superintendent (now the commissioner) has the power to approve or disallow the rates prepared by the Facility Assocation.

(b) Operating an Uninsured Vehicle

It is an offence for the owner of a vehicle to operate or allow someone else to operate a vehicle on a highway unless that vehicle is insured. Section 2 (1)-(3) of the Ontario Act provides:

2. (1) Subject to the regulations, no owner or lessee of a motor vehicle shall,

  (a) operate the motor vehicle; or

  (b) cause or permit the motor vehicle to be operated,

on a highway unless the motor vehicle is insured under a contract of automobile insurance.

(2) For the purposes of subsection (1), where a permit for a motor vehicle has been issued under subsection 7(7) of the *Highway Traffic Act*, "contract of automobile insurance" with respect to that motor vehicle means a contract of automobile insurance made with an insurer.

(3) Every owner or lessee of a motor vehicle who,

  (a) contravenes subsection (1) of this section or subsection 13(2); or

  (b) surrenders an insurance card for inspection to a police officer, when requested to do so, purporting to show that the motor vehicle is insured under a contract of automobile insurance when the motor vehicle is not so unsured,

is guilty of an offence and is liable on a first conviction to a fine of not less than $5,000 and not more than $25,000 and on a subsequent conviction to a fine of not less than $10,000 and not more than $50,000 and, in addition, his or her driver's licence may be suspended for a period of not more than one year.

As can be seen, the monetary penalties are severe, the amounts having been recently raised.[90]

Subsection 2(2) has the effect of requiring that owners of vehicles registered in Ontario insure with an underwriter licensed by the Ontario Superintendent of Insurance. The reference to the regulations in subsection 2(1) relates to a special exemption granted to members of the conservative Mennonite community.[91] Vehicles owned or operated on behalf of the federal government are also exempted.

---

90 And, although for a lesser amount, have and should survive consitutional scrutiny: *R. v. Raymond* (1996), 27 M.V.R. (3d) 257 (Alta. Prov. Ct.).

91 Conservative Mennonites are opposed to insurance on moral and religious principles. An individual's exemption from the operation of s. 2 is dependent on the Mennonite community

(c) What is a "Contract of Insurance"?

The contract of "automobile insurance" that the owner must carry is defined in the Act as:

insurance against liability arising out of bodily injury to or the death of a person or loss of or damage to property caused by a motor vehicle or the use or operation thereof, and which,

(a) insures at least to the limit required by section 251 of the *Insurance Act*,

(b) provides the statutory accident benefits set out in the *Statutory Accident Benefits Schedule* under the *Insurance Act*, and

(c) provides the benefits prescribed under section 265 of the *Insurance Act*.[92]

In essence, these provisions require that every vehicle carry insurance for third parties and certain "no fault" benefits. It is not possible to buy insurance from an Ontario licensed insurer that will provide less than the minimum coverage, and as vehicles registered in Ontario must deal with Ontario insurers, it follows that only vehicles registered outside the province could carry policies that failed to meet the minimum standards set out in the definition.

(d) Fail to Produce Proof of Insurance

The driver of a vehicle is required to have an insurance card with the vehicle at all times, to prove that here is a valid policy subsisting on the vehicle. Section 3 provides:

3. (1) An operator of a motor vehicle on a highway shall have in the motor vehicle at all times,

(a) an insurance card for the motor vehicle; or

(b) an insurance card evidencing that the operator is insured under a contract of automobile insurance,

and the operator shall surrender the insurance card for reasonable inspection upon the demand of a police officer.

(2) Despite subsection (1), an operator of a motor vehicle who is named as an excluded driver under the contract of automobile insurance under which the vehicle is insured shall have in the vehicle at all times an insurance card evidencing that the operator is a named insured under another contract of automobile insurance, and the operator shall surrender the insurance card for reasonable inspection upon the demand of a police offficer.

---

organizing and maintaining a financial responsibility plan called the Conservative Mennonite Automobile Brotherhood Assistance Plan. The individual exempted must be a member in good standing of the Conservative Mennonite Church and must be accepted under the plan.

92 Section 1(1).

(3) A person who contravenes this section is guilty of an offence and on a conviction is liable to a fine of not more than $400.

The power to demand production of documentation granted a police officer does not violate a motorist's rights under the *Charter*.[93] Many officers and prosecutors will elect not to prosecute this offence if the driver, through an honest oversight, has simply forgotten to have the proper proof of insurance card with them. Showing a card that was valid on the date of the charge may sometimes be enough to have the charge withdrawn.[94]

(e) The Mental Element: Due Diligence as a Defence

It is well established that the offences of driving without insurance and failing to produce an insurance card are strict liability offences. Once the prosecutor has established that the vehicle was driven without insurance or that the driver did not produce an insurance card for inspection, the offence is made out. If, however, the accused can show that he acted with all due diligence or that he was acting on a mistaken set of facts in which he or she reasonably believed, he or she may be excused.

In *R. v. McGilvery*,[95] the accused was charged with being the owner of a vehicle that had been driven on a highway while it was not insured. He was, however, only the paper title-holder. The vehicle had been purchased by his wife, but was registered in his name, because at the time his wife was not licensed. The vehicle was eventually given to the couple's daughter, and the accused left instruction that the vehicle's ownership was to be transferred and the insurance to be put in good standing. The wife and daughter failed to do so. The Court concluded on these facts that the father should be acquitted because "the accused reasonably believed in a mistaken set of facts which, if true, would the act or ommission innocent."[96]

In a similar case, *R. v. Tjelta*,[97] the wife of the accused was responsible for dealing with the family's insurance matters. The policies normally came due in April, but in the case of the vehicle in issue it came due in January. The Court concluded that the accused's reliance on his wife's report that his vehicle was covered was reasonable and hence constituted a valid defence.

This was also the case in *R. v. Gallagher*,[98] where the accused inadvertently failed to renew her policy after her broker informed her of the pending

---

93 *R. v. Hufsky* (1988), [1988] 1 S.C.R. 621 (S.C.C.); *R. v. Rubb* (1997), 36 W.C.B. (2d) 4 (Ont. Prov. Div.).

94 This is no guarantee. A driver who, though insured, has failed to produce the card, is in violation of the *Compulsory Automobile Insurance Act* even if the vehicle is fully insured.

95 (1979), 19 A.R. 447 (Alta. Dist. Ct.).

96 *Ibid.*, at 449, per Belzil J.

97 (1983), 25 M.V.R. 274 (B.C. S.C.).

98 (1985), 35 M.V.R. 228 (Nfld. Dist. Ct.).

renewal date. An accident two days after the policy had lapsed revealed that the accused was driving without insurance. Her belief was reasonable and her actions were therefore innocent and she was acquitted.

Simply delegating responsibility of insuring a vehicle will not always be a "reasonable" excuse. The person driving must actually turn his or her mind to whether the vehicle is insured before going out on the highway. In *R. v. Carter*,[99] the appellant was charged with operating a vehicle without insurance. She left all insurance dealings to her husband and was unaware of renewal periods or coverage. She was, therefore, genuinely surprised when she learned that she was not covered by a policy of insurance. In discussing the defence of reasonable mistake of fact in compulsory automobile insurance cases, the Court hearing the appeal observed:[100]

> I am satisfied, as was the trial Judge, that the appellant here honestly believed that her husband had covered his motor vehicle with an insurance policy as required by [the provincial legislation]. *The question is whether her ignorance of the fact that he had neglected to keep it in good standing so exonerates her from liability under [the compulsory automobile insurance provisions]* ... While in such a case it is not necessary to prove *mens rea* on the part of the appellant, once the prohibited act has been established, the onus was on the appellant to exonerate herself by showing that she committed the act reasonably believing in a mistaken set of facts which, if true, would render the act innocent, providing, however, there was no negligence upon her part. If she had been correct in her belief, there would have been no offence. She had taken it for granted that her husband had obtained an insurance policy and was surprised when looking through a billfold in the car that she could not find evidence of this insurance. It was his responsibility to provide the insurance and to leave an insurance card or evidence of the policy in the car to indicate that the appropriate insurance was in effect. He neglected to do this.

> While I have great sympathy for the appellant in this instance because there was no responsibllity upon her to cover the car with insurance, and she quite naturally assumed her husband had attended to it, the *Highway Traffic Act* provides that a driver of a motor vehicle must be able to produce evidence that a motor vehicle insurance policy is in effect upon it. This means that it is an offence to drive a motor vehicle without such evidence. *The appellant did not check to see if there was evidence of insurance in the car before driving it or, in fact, whether any insurance was in effect. Since the [provincial legislation] clearly places the burden upon her to so determine, it is not a defence to say that she believed that there was proof of insurance in the vehicle at that time.* In my view, the legislation clearly envisaged the situation at hand as constituting an offence under s. 78(6)(b). It declared that a person shall not operate a motor vehicle unless it has been covered by appropriate insurance. The section obviously purports to prohibit all persons, including non-owners, from driving motor vehicles without such coverage. This means that a non-owner driver of a motor vehicle must ensure that the vehicle is covered with insurance before driving it. Had the appellant checked

---

99 (1985), 34 M.V.R. 294 (Nfld. Dist. Ct.).

100 *Ibid.*, at p. 299-300.

upon this, she would have discovered that there was no insurance upon the vehicle. *The offence on her part flows from her failure to check if there was insurance in effect upon her husband's automobile. She made an honest mistake in believing that there was coverage, but her mistake arose out of lack of diligence on her part. Where there is such neglect the defence of honest error must fail.*

The whole purpose of the legislation is to ensure that persons injured in motor vehicle accidents through the fault of one of the operators would be able to recover damages through appropriate insurance coverage in effect upon the vehicle at fault. It was designed to protect persons in situations such as occurred in this case. Accordingly, I must reject this ground of appeal. [Emphasis added].

While the appellant's belief was honest, it was not reasonable. That is, she was negligent in failing to take any real steps to even inquire into the existence of a valid subsisting policy.

It is difficult to reconcile a case such as *Carter* with the decision in another case, *R. v. Blackburn.*[101] There the British Columbia Court of Appeal concluded that driving an uninsured vehicle was a strict liability offence and held that, on the facts of the case, the defence of reasonable mistake of fact was available. The accused was the purchaser of a used vehicle. She had recently sold her own car and taken the plates and insurance from that vehicle and physically transferred them to her recently acquired car. There was never a formal transfer of the plates, nor a new policy for the second car. In quashing the conviction, the Court observed:

> ... [t]he appellant honestly believed on reasonable grounds that at the relevant time she was insured and was using a licence plate in a manner permissible in the circumstances.[102]

This case may be explained on the basis that the appeal judge felt that he was bound by what the trial judge had concluded as to the reasonableness of the error.

An error, if it is to provide a defence under a compulsory insurance charge, must be reasonable.

(f) Who is the "Owner"?

In *R. v. Sherman,*[103] the Court considered who the "owner" of a vehicle is in the context of mandatory insurance provisions. The mandatory insurance requirement arose under the old *Motor Vehicle Accident Claims Act.*[104] In evaluating the meaning to be given to the word "owner", the Court said:

---

101 (1980), 57 C.C.C. (2d) 7 (B.C. C.A.).

102 *Ibid.*, at p. 9.

103 (1972), 5 C.C.C. (2d) 247 (Ont. C.A.).

104 R.S.O. 1970, c. 281, s. 3.

[A] word or phrase is to be interpreted in light of the mischief which the provision is obviously intended to prevent ... The purpose of the Motor Vehicle Accident Claims Act is made apparent by its various provisions ... That purpose is to protect the public from loss due to the negligence of an uninsured motorist by setting up a motor vehicle accident claims fund with a contributory fee. [The section] accordingly, requires the owner to pay this fee or to have the vehicle insured and a penalty is provided for failing to do so. To lend any force to these provisions the police authorities must be able to determine the identity of the owner. The only way this can be assured is through the registration procedure. It follows in the opinion of the Court that "owner" as it appears in the Act must mean registered owner rather than owner at common law if any effect is to be given to this legislation.

In *R. v. Zwicker*,[105] however, the Ontario Court of Appeal rejected an argument based on *Sherman* in interpreting the *Compulsory Automobile Insurance Act*. The Court considered whether the word "owner" in section 2 of the Act applied only to the registered owner of the vehicle, and held that:

That argument cannot succeed. In our opinion, the interpretation of "owner" in *R. v. Sherman* is not applicable to s. 2(1) of the *Compulsory Automobile Insurance Act*. The word "owner" as used in this provision is not restricted to the "registered owner" of a motor vehicle but includes the "common law owner" as well.[106]

The *Compulsory Automobile Insurance Act* differed significantly from the previous legislation which was considered in *Sherman*. Given the provisions of the provincial highway traffic legislation requiring the removal of licence plates at the time of the conveyance of a vehicle, registration is no longer the sole means of identifying the owner of a given vehicle. Thus the reasoning in *Sherman* is inapplicable to the current statutory scheme.

7. DRIVE WHILE SUSPENDED

(a) Introduction

A driver's licence may be suspended as a part of the penalty imposed upon conviction for certain *Highway Traffic Act* offences;[107] it may be suspended automatically as a result of certain *Criminal Code* convictions;[108] a suspension may result from an accumulation of demerit points;[109] or it may be suspended as a consequence of an unsatisfied civil judgment or unpaid fines.[110] The strict enforcement of suspensions is at the heart of highway traffic

---

105 (1994), 1 M.V.R. (3d) 1 (Ont. C.A.).
106 For indicia of common law ownership, see *Honan v. Gerhold* (1975), [1975] 2 S.C.R. 866 (S.C.C.); *Keizer v. Hanna* (1975), 10 O.R. (2d) 597 (Ont. C.A.), affirmed (1978), [1978] 2 S.C.R. 342 (S.C.C.); *R. v. Fisher* (1988), 4 W.C.B. (2d) 253 (Ont. Prov. Ct.).
107 For example, Fail to Remain, s. 200(a).
108 Ontario *Highway Traffic Act*, s. 41.
109 See below, chapter 9.
110 Section 198.

legislation, since it is the primary means of attempting to keep irresponsible drivers off the road, and encouraging compliance with motor vehicle laws.[111]

Section 53 of the *Highway Traffic Act* provides:

> **53.** (1) Every person who drives a motor vehicle or street car on a highway while his or her driver's licence is suspended under an Act of the Legislature or a regulation made thereunder is guilty of an offence and on conviction is liable,
>
>> (a) for the first offence, to a fine of not less than $500 and not more than $5,000; and
>>
>> (b) for each subsequent offence, to a fine of not less than $1000 and not more than $5,000,
>
> or to imprisonment for a term of not more than six months, or to both.
>
> (2) Where a person who has previously been convicted of an offence under subsection (1) is convicted of the same offence within five years after the date of the previous conviction, the offence for which he or she is last convicted shall be deemed to be a subsequent offence for the purpose of clause (1)(b).
>
> (3) The driver's licence of a person who is convicted of an offence under subsection (1) is thereupon suspended for a period of six months in addition to any other period for which the licence is suspended, and consecutively thereto.

Also of potential significance to prosecutions for "driving while suspended" is s. 52(1) of the *Highway Traffic Act*, concerning service of a notice of suspension:

> **52.** (1) Notice to a person of the suspension of his or her driver's licence is sufficiently given if delivered personally or sent by registered mail addressed to the person to whom the licence was issued at the latest current address of the person appearing on the records of the Ministry and where notice is given by registered mail it shall be deemed to have been given on the fifth day after the mailing unless the person to whom notice is given establishes that he or she did not, acting in good faith, through absence, accident, illness or other cause beyond his or her control, receive the notice.

In *Goltz*, the Supreme Court of Canada reflected on the nature of this type of offence:[112]

> In partial summary, it must be said that commission of the offence specified by s. 86(1)(a)(ii) and s. 88(1) of the *Motor Vehicle Act* is grave. It may involve a risk to the lives and limbs of innocent users of the province's roads, by persons designated bad drivers by a fair and cautious identification system, who knowingly step outside the law.

---

111 In *R. v. Goltz* (1991), [1991] 3 S.C.R. 485 (S.C.C.), evidence was introduced at the accused's trial on the equivalent charge in British Columbia which showed that a small number of bad drivers are involved with a disproportionate number of traffic-related accidents overall. One estimate adduced by counsel for the Crown claimed that five percent of the drivers in British Columbia are involved in 44 percent of the reported accidents.

112 *Ibid.*, at p. 160.

(b) The Elements of the Offence

To constitute an offence the defendant must a) drive, b) a motor vehicle, c) on a highway, d) while his or her licence is suspended. This last requirement must be read in light of s. 54 which provides that, for the purposes of the Act, a person who does not hold a licence, but has been the subject of a suspension, is deemed to have had a licence suspended,[113] and shall have no permit or licence issued to him or her until the suspension has been served and the appropriate reinstatement fee paid.[114]

The certificate should ideally state that the accused is disqualified from "driving", although where the certificate on a complete reading fulfills the requirements it will not be fatal.[115]

The accused should be provided with adequate particulars of his or her suspension on the certificate. Thus it has been held that an accused must be informed of both the reason for and the statutory provision authorizing the suspension.[116]

Under s. 52, which requires reasonable notice be given to the accused in writing of the intention to use certificate evidence of disqualification, the notice served on the accused should refer to the particular proceeding in which the certificate is to be used against the accused.[117] It is important that all the details of the accused's name are correct.

The elements of the offence which have received some judicial attention are considered below.

(i) *"On a Highway"*

The prosecution must prove that the accused was driving "on a highway." Usually, of course, this element of the offence presents no difficulty for the prosecution. The issue has arisen in the context of private property and Indian reserves.

The meaning of "highway" in context of an Indian reserve will depend on the facts of how the road in question is used, regulated and understood. Thus in *R. v. Thunderchild*,[118] the road was held not to be one intended for or used by the general public, since there was no evidence that the persons described as users of the road were not treaty Indians. A road that was restricted to band members, their employees and peace officers stationed on the reserve

---

113 *R. v. Marini* (1997), 28 M.V.R. (3d) 46 (Ont. Prov. Div.).

114 Section 54 was recently amended to include a subsection concerning reinstatement of the suspended driver's licence: Bill 55 *Road Safety Act, 1996*, S.O. 1996, c. 20, s. 11, not yet proclaimed in force.

115 *R. v. Olney* (1988) 6 W.C.B. (2d) 216 (Sask. Q.B.).

116 *R. v. Thomas* (1988) 6 W.C.B. (2d) 315 (Sask Q.B.).

117 *R. v. Hayward* (1988) 5 W.C.B. (2d) 438 (Sask. Q.B.).

118 (1995), 29 W.C.B. (2d) 121 (Sask. Q.B.).

for the protection of band members, was not "open to the public." In *R. v. Bellegarde*,[119] however, it was.

(ii) *"Under Suspension"*

Section 53 requires that the defendant be "under suspension" when the driving in issue occurs. In *R. v. Zembal*,[120] the defendant had paid his fines on the day before he was alleged to have driven. His licence had not been reinstated, however, through the normal administrative delay between payment and the lifting of the suspension.

The court observed that on the day in question the defendant could have applied to a court for an order compelling the Registrar to reinstate the licence:[121]

> It is not completely accurate to say the accused's licence was under suspension. It had been under suspension. It is more accurate to say that the accused was legally entitled to reinstatement of his licence at the time of the offence. His position can more accurately be described as "pending reinstatement" than "under suspension". As a matter of law I am not convinced that the accused's driver's licence was under suspension when he was driving. *A fortiori* when one considers the very serious minimum fine and mandatory suspension that are consequent upon conviction of this offence.

Alternatively, the court was prepared to hold that the "particularly technical offence" in issue did not deserve the punishment imposed (the defendant would lose his driver's licence and consequently his job if convicted).

In some provinces[122] this offence only arises where the driver is "disqualified," a technical term which only arises where the loss of driving privileges arises from some violation related to the drivers capacity to drive.

(iii) *Distinguishing the Offence*

This offence should be distinguished from the *Criminal Code* offence under s. 259(4). The *Code* provision requires that the suspension or disability arise as a direct or indirect result of a *Code* conviction.[123] A disqualification from driving arising out of a conviction under the *Highway Traffic Act* does not constitute a disqualification punishable under s. 259(4) of the *Criminal Code*.[124]

---

119 (1989) 8 W.C.B. (2d) 705 (Sask. Q.B.).

120 (1987), 1 M.V.R. (2d) 335 (Ont. Prov. Ct.).

121 *Ibid.*, at p. 337.

122 See for example *R. v. Bear* (1985), 39 M.V.R. 50 (Sask. Prov. Ct) and *Carton v. R.* (1985), 32 M.V.R. 244 (Sask. Q.B.).

123 See the closing words of s. 259(5). Note also s. 42 of the *Highway Traffic Act*.

124 *R. v. Dunn* (1992), 15 W.C.B. (2d) 525 (Ont. Prov. Div.).

(iv) *Proving the Suspension*

The Registrar is not required to personally sign each notice of suspension. A facsimile of the signature is significant.[125] There is no obligation on the Registrar to hold a formal hearing before imposing the term of suspension mandated by the Act. The Registrar has a broad discretion and only has a common law duty not to act capriciously or unfairly.[126]

The Court has no authority on its own motion to order a hearing into whether an accused's license should be suspended.[127]

(v) *The Mental Element*

Driving while suspended is a strict liability offence.[128] The Crown need not prove that the accused knew of his or her licence suspension, but, as s. 52(1) states, it is open to a defendant to raise a defence of due diligence or reasonable mistake of fact, showing on a balance of probabilities that through no fault of his or her own, exercising all reasonable care, did not know of the suspension.[129] As discussed below, a recent decision has held that the burden implicit in the legislation violates the *Charter*: although it does not state it specifically, the section implies that the accused must "establish" the non receipt of the notice. It would seem, then, that an accused need only raise a reasonable doubt as to the knowledge of suspension.[130] In *R. v. MacDougall*,[131] the Supreme Court of Canada held that the parallel Nova Scotia provision created an offence, "concerning the public welfare [and that] it was properly characterized as 'an offence of strict liability' within the meaning of the classification stipulated by Mr. Justice Dickson [as he then was, in *R. v. Sault Ste. Marie*]".

It has been held that an accused who is unaware of suspension because of the failure to notify the Registrar of his change of address cannot be held to have exercised due diligence.[132] It is open to debate as to whether this failure is sufficiently proximate to the fault involved in driving while suspended.

---

125 *R. v. Mayer* Sept 15 1983 unreported Man. C.A.; *R. v. Malik* (1992), 17 W.C.B. (2d) 119 (Man. Prov. Ct.).

126 *R. v. O'Reilly* (1993), 19 W.C.B. (2d) 489 (Nfld C.A.); *Raichura v. Manitoba (Registrar of Motor Vehicles)*; *Green v. Manitoba (Registrar of Motor Vehicles)* (1992), 16 W.C.B. (2d) 286 (Man. C.A.).

127 *R. v. Power* (1989), 7 W.C.B. (2d) 216 (Nfld. S.C. T.D.).

128 For a recent and comprehensive analysis of this aspect of the offence, see *R. v. Bellomo* (1995), 14 M.V.R. (3d) 63 (Ont. Prov. Div.).

129 *R. v. Anderson* (1997), 27 M.V.R. (3d) 97 (N.B. Q.B.); *R. v. Christman* (1985), 29 M.V.R. 1 (Alta. C.A.).

130 *R. v. Bellomo, supra*, note 128.

131 (1982), 1 C.C.C. (3d) 65, 18 M.V.R. 180, at 184 (S.C.C.). See also *R. v. MacLellan* (1983), 23 M.V.R. 236 (N.S. A.D.).

132 *R. v. Lowe* (1991), 29 M.V.R. (2d) 265 (N.S. C.A.); *R. v. L'Hirondelle* (1993), 45 M.V.R. (2d) 264 (Alta. Q.B.). See O. Reg. 340/90, s. 33.

In *Bellomo*, Fairgrieve P.C.J. considered in detail the constitutional legitimacy of the requirement that the accused demonstrate due diligence. He held
that, in line with the well-established principles laid down in *R. v. Sault Ste.
Marie*, and *Reference Re. The B.C. Motor Vehicles Act* the requirement violates
sections 11(d) and 7 of the *Charter*. His Honour held that the violation could
not be justified under s. 1 of the *Charter* since the effects of the measure
limiting the accused's *Charter* rights were disproportionate to the objective
sought to be achieved by the legislation. The measures failed to limit the
accused's *Charter* rights as little as possible:[133]

> I see no reason why the obvious alternative measure, convicting only those who
> have not raised a reasonable doubt as to their knowledge of the suspension, would
> not be regarded as achieving the objectives of enforcing compliance with the rules
> of the road and compelling the payment of fines just as effectively. If the focus
> is only on the collection of fines, then one might question the current system
> that allows for the renewal of driver's licences every three years, rather than an
> annual renewal where the payment of any outstanding fines could be regarded
> as a pre-condition to receiving a new licence. Why that clerical process would
> be regarded as less effective than suspending licences, prosecuting people in the
> Provincial Offences Court, and in some cases imprisoning people, is not com-
> pletely clear. Moreover, even if the Legislature preferred the suspension and prose-
> cution route, it could still have chosen one of the alternative, less intrusive means
> referred to by Lamer C.J.C. in *Wholesale Travel*, i.e., either mandatory pre-
> sumption of knowledge rebuttable by raising a reasonable doubt as to the driver's
> awareness of the suspension, or, if the persuasive burden on the accused was main-
> tained, removing imprisonment as a potential penalty.[134]

In *R. v. Jack*,[135] the defendant had driven while his licence was automatically
suspended after an impaired driving conviction. The trial judge held that, unless
the prosecutor proved that the defendant knew of the suspension, a conviction
could not be entered. This was an error. While the defendant might escape
conviction by demonstrating that he did *not*, after reasonable diligence, know
of the suspension, there was no duty on the crown to prove that he had such
knowledge.

In *R. v. Pontes*,[136] the accused was charged with driving a motor vehicle
at a time when he was prohibited from driving under s. 92 of the British
Columbia *Motor Vehicle Act*, contrary to s. 94(1) of that Act. Section 92 provided that a person convicted of an offence under certain sections of the Act,
including s. 94(1), is "automatically and without notice" prohibited from
driving a motor vehicle for 12 months. Section 94(1) provided that a person
who drives a motor vehicle on a highway while he is prohibited from driving
under certain sections of the Act, including s. 92, commits an offence and is

---

133 *R. v. Oakes* (1986), [1986] 1 S.C.R. 103 (S.C.C.).
134 *Bellomo, supra*, note 128 at p. 88.
135 (1983), 21 M.V.R. 198 (B.C. S.C.).
136 [1995] 3 S.C.R. 44 (S.C.C).

liable to a fine and to imprisonment. The accused was acquitted at trial. The trial judge found that s. 94(1), in combination with s. 92, created an absolute liability offence for which imprisonment was a penalty, thereby contravening s. 7 of the *Charter.* The Supreme Court held that because the prohibition on driving in s. 92 is automatic and without notice, s. 94(1) effectively prevents an accused who is unaware of the prohibition from raising that defence. In those circumstances, the offence ought to be characterized as one of absolute liability.

Nevertheless the absolute liability offence created by s. 94(1) and s. 92 did not contravene the *Charter.* This conclusion flows from the application of s. 4.1 and of s. 72(1) of the British Columbia *Offence Act.* These sections respectively indicate that, notwithstanding the provisions of any other Act, no person is liable to imprisonment for an absolute liability offence, and that the non-payment of a fine will not result in imprisonment. Thus, an accused convicted under ss. 94(1) and 92 faces no risk of imprisonment and there is, accordingly, no violation of the right to life, liberty and security of the person under s. 7 of the *Charter.*

A person may delegate the task of putting a licence in good standing to another person. In *R. v. Azzoli*,[137] the defendant had asked his secretary to pay his outstanding fines while he was out of the country, on the understanding that if this was done he could avoid suspension. When he returned and was charged with driving while suspended he was genuinely surprised. The court, commenting on the defendant's actions observed[138]

> I cannot criticize the respondent for the conduct that he participated in getting the matter taken care of. He went about it in a way that any reasonable man would have done, gave it to his secretary, asked her to look after it. ... [H]e assumed it was done as I think a reasonable person could assume it was done.

The defendant had been duly diligent even if his unfortunate secretary had not!

(vi) *The Defence of Officially Induced Error*

Because the offence of driving while suspended depends on an official act (the existence of a suspension) and the varied reasons such an action could come to be, it invites a defence of honest and reasonable mistake of law induced by officials. A number of cases since *MacDougall* have applied the defence to this charge.

In *R. v. Christman*,[139] the Alberta Court of Appeal observed:

---

137 (1983), 24 M.V.R. 205 (Ont. Prov. Ct.).
138 *Ibid.*, at pp. 208-9.
139 *Supra*, note 129.

The defence of "due diligence" is for the accused to establish from his own or other evidence in the case. It would "be available if the accused reasonably believed in a mistaken set of facts which, if true, would render the act ... innocent": per Dickson J. in *R. v. Sault Ste. Marie*. In this context the accused would establish that though he was disqualified from driving, he reasonably believed he was not. In my opinion the decisions in both *Sault Ste. Marie* and *MacDougall* make it clear that, once the Crown proved the prohibited act, no further evidence was required to negative due diligence.

The defendant can escape conviction if he can establish an innocent mental state, whether through due diligence or officially induced error.

(vii) *Facts Where the Defence has been Accepted*

The defence of officially induced error has been successful in a number of cases. In *R. v. Coleman*,[140] the defendant was disqualified from driving. The certificate from the Registrar was sent to his last known address, but had been returned "unknown". The defendant had never received notice of the suspension. The court, in acquitting, observed:[141]

> We are dealing here with a charge of driving while disqualified, and that implies a degree of awareness on the part of the respondent. Inasmuch as the respondent did not receive notice of his suspension, is it a reasonable inference that he did not reasonably believe in a set of facts (i.e., in his right to drive in Manitoba) which, if true, would be a defence to this charge? This is not a case where the accused is relying on an explanation of "due diligence". Had that been the case, then obviously, as was pointed out by Dickson J. in *Sault Ste. Marie*, ... the onus would have been on the accused to come forward "with evidence of due diligence". What the respondent claims in this case is that since he was not notified that his licence to drive was suspended, he believed (as would a reasonable man) that he had the right to drive in Manitoba. ...
>
> ... The issue I must address is, was the respondent operating the vehicle reasonably believing in a mistaken set of facts which, if true, would have rendered the act innocent?

The facts allowed a reasonable inference that the defendant was acting under an exculpatory mistake. As the court notes, it was because the accused was charged with an offence dependant on bureaucratic action (suspension) of which he had no knowledge, that he was acquitted. The defendant reasonably believed that the legal status of his licence was constant until such time as he received knowledge to the contrary.

This case would appear to be similar to *Robichaud c. R.*[142] There the defendant was mailed a notice of suspension resulting from accumulated

---

140 (1985), 31 M.V.R. 258 (Man. Q.B.).

141 *Ibid.*, at p. 261.

142 (1984), 29 M.V.R. 190 (N.B. Q.B.).

demerit points. The statute[143] provided that notice would be deemed to have occurred four days after posting and that the suspension was effective from that date. Robichaud, however, only received his notice some days after his alleged transgression, though more than four days after it had been posted. The court held that the legislature clearly attached importance to the receipt of the notice. The law provided for notice where other provinces allowed for automatic suspension. The legislative provision which deemed notice to have occurred four days after posting could be displaced by evidence that the defendant had in fact remained ignorant of the suspension through no fault of his own.

An excellent review of the law on officially induced error and mistake of law is to be found in *R. v. Robertson*,[144] though that judgment must be read in light of the conclusion of the Ontario Court of Appeal in *R. v. Cancoil Thermal Corp.*[145]

In *R. v. McFerran*,[146] the defendant claimed that he misunderstood the letter from the Superintendent informing him of the suspension. He said that he believed that the notice was simply a letter asking him to show cause why his licence should not be suspended. The defendant has received such letters in the past; he responded with a letter as he had in previous occasions. The trial judge rejected this evidence. He said that, in his opinion, the defendant and his witnesses were not credible and that the letter to the Superintendent was a subterfuge. Having rejected this evidence, it was proper for the trial judge to have convicted.

(viii) *Double Jeopardy and the Criminal Code*

It would appear that a conviction for driving while suspended does not preclude a conviction for driving without a valid licence. In the British Columbia case of *R. v. Moody*[147] the defendant was stopped and given the equivalent of an offence notice charging him with driving without a valid licence (a much less serious offence than driving while under suspension). He pleaded guilty and paid the set fine. The plea was accepted and a conviction entered. Shortly thereafter, the officer realized that, in fact, the defendant was under suspension at the time and proceeded to lay an information charging the more serious offence. On appeal the court held that, as the gravamen of the two offences was different (one directed at those who had no licence, while the other was directed at those who ignored suspensions), the defendant could be convicted of both.

---

143 *Motor Vehicle Act*, R.S.N.B. 1973, c. M-17, s. 300(3).
144 (1984), 30 M.V.R. 248 (Ont. Prov. Ct.).
145 (1986), 52 C.R. (3d) 188 (Ont. C.A.).
146 (1983), 24 M.V.R. 303 (B.C. Co. Ct.).
147 (1985), 33 M.V.R. 198 (B.C. Co. Ct.).

This decision ignores the reasoning of Smith, Prov. J. in *R. v. Preeper*[148] applying the principle against multiple convictions for the same wrongful act, sometimes called the "Kienapple" principle.[149] He had held that a defendant who had pleaded guilty and effectively been 'sentenced' by paying his fine could not subsequently be convicted on a second occasion for the more serious offence.

It is submitted that the reasoning of *Preeper* is to be preferred to that in *Moody*. This is especially true in an age of instantaneous computer access to driving records. If an officer is considering a charge of driving while suspended there is little administrative hardship in requiring that a check be done before filing the certificate.

(ix) *Sentencing Issues*

Some provinces include a mandatory term of imprisonment on conviction for this charge where the suspension was a result of a poor driving record. In *R. v. Goltz*,[150] the Supreme Court of Canada commented on the rationale behind the relatively severe penalties for this offence:

> The administrative scheme for the prohibition of bad drivers and imposition of mandatory minimum sentences was enacted as a consequence of the extensive study by the [B.C.] Motor Vehicle Task Force. It had found that the more penalty points a driver had as a result of driving infractions, the more likely it was that the individual would not be a responsible, safe driver....
>
> ... because the offence is difficult to detect — since a police officer will not know a driver has been prohibited until that driver is stopped and questioned — there is a great temptation on the part of many prohibited drivers to commit the offence. Consequently, a legislature may rationally conclude that for the purpose of deterrence, a serious penalty must attach to it. ...
>
> ... [T]he offence is not trivial or arbitrary. On the contrary, the mandatory minimum sentence contained in s. 88(1)(c) and applicable to s. 86(1)(a)(ii) is based squarely on a legislative concern to isolate bad drivers for the better protection of the public. Most importantly, it demonstrates that a person who has been given this panoply of safeguards against wrongful or inappropriate prohibition, yet knowingly violates the notice in contempt of the public interest and the sanction which seeks to protect it, commits a graver offence than a person who violated the prohibition unwittingly and who had not been given this range of intermediate opportunities to mend his ways, to inquire into the reasons for the prohibition, and to appeal the Superintendent's decision.

Goltz had accumulated numerous penalty points for a variety of driving infractions, causing the Superintendent to deem the Respondent's driving record

---

148 (1984), 28 M.V.R. 193 (B.C. Prov. Ct).

149 After the leading case, *R. v. Kienapple* (*sub nom. Kienapple v. R.*), [1975] 1 S.C.R. 729 (S.C.C.).

150 *Supra*, note 111 at p. 157.

unsatisfactory and to declare that the public interest required that he be prohibited from driving. The B.C. legislation, *Motor Vehicle Act*, R.S.B.C. 1979, c. 288, provided that:

> **86.** (1) Notwithstanding that a person is or may be subject to another prohibition from driving, where the superintendent considers it to be in the public interest, he may, with or without a hearing, prohibit the person from driving a motor vehicle
>
> (a) where the person ...
>
> (ii) has a driving record that in the opinion of the superintendent is unsatisfactory.[151]

The Court held that it does not infringe s. 12 of the *Charter* when the prohibition from driving is made pursuant to s. 86(1)(a)(ii) of the Act. That section provided for imprisonment where the accused was suspended as a result of s. 86(1)(a)(ii) because it is especially those drivers who are dangerous to innocent citizens using the roads in a responsible manner. The gravity of the offence must be assessed in light of the legislative purpose and the underlying driving offences giving rise to the prohibition. An order of prohibition made under s. 86(1)(a)(ii) is aimed in large measure at safeguarding the health and lives of citizens using the highways of a province, as reflected in the requirements that the prohibited individual must have built up an "unsatisfactory driving record" and that the prohibition be in "the public interest".

"Subsequent conviction" for the purposes of s. 52 includes the second conviction where an accused is convicted of more than one offence even where that conviction is on the same day before the same Court. The only consideration in determining whether a conviction is a subsequent conviction is the sequence of convictions and not whether any offence occurred before or after any conviction.[152]

The former *Criminal Code* provision dealing with driving while disqualified (old s. 238(3)) was found unconstitutional in *R. v. Boggs*.[153] The issue in *R. v. Courchene*[154] was whether old convictions under the now unconstitutional (and since repealed) section could be proved as an aggravating factor upon a provincial charge of driving while suspended. The court concluded that such convictions could be placed before the court as facts in aggravation of the sentence. While they were convictions without constitutional authority, they were nonetheless part of the record of the defendant and in the absence of an order quashing them (an order apparently precluded by s. 776 of the *Code*) they are relevant in sentencing.

---

151 The equivalent Ontario provision is s. 47(1)(d).
152 *Ficko v. Ontario (Registrar of Motor Vehicles)* (1989) 7 W.C.B. (2d) 76 (Ont. C.A.); *Sentes v. Saskatchewan (Highway Traffic Board)* (1988) 4 W.C.B. (2d) 194 (Sask. C.A.).
153 (1981), [1981] 1 S.C.R. 49 (S.C.C.).
154 (1984), 25 M.V.R. 204 (Man. Prov. Ct.).

It is inappropriate for a judge passing sentence for a conviction under the *Criminal Code* to resort to the authority of the provincial *Highway Traffic Act* in order to impose a greater term of licence suspension than that authorized by the *Criminal Code.*[155]

8. FAILING TO STOP WHEN SIGNALED BY POLICE OFFICER

(a) Introduction

Section 216 of the *Highway Traffic Act* was introduced as section 189a of the Act in late 1981.[156] It gives a police officer a general power to stop a vehicle when the officer is lawfully acting in the execution of his or her duties. The provisions were the Legislature's response to the Ontario Court of Appeal decision of *R. v. Dedman*[157] which had held that there was no provision in the *Highway Traffic Act* authorizing a stop by a police officer in the execution of his or her duty or placing a corresponding duty on the part of the motorist to comply. This section is reproduced in its entirety:

216. (1) A police officer, in the lawful execution of his or her duties and responsibilities, may require the driver of a motor vehicle to stop and the driver of a motor vehicle, when signalled or requested to stop by a police officer who is readily identifiable as such, shall immediately come to a safe stop.

(2) Every person who contravenes subsection (1) is guilty of an offence and on conviction is liable to a fine of not less than $500 and not more than $5,000 or to imprisonment for a term of not more than six months, or to both.

(3) Where a person is convicted of an offence under subsection (2) and the court is satisfied on the evidence that the person wilfully continued to avoid police while a police officer gave pursuit, the court shall make an order suspending the driver's licence of that person for a period of three years, and the suspension shall be in addition to any other period for which the licence is suspended and consecutively thereto.

(4) In a proceeding for a contravention of subsection (1) in which the circumstances set out in subsection (3) are alleged and before the court accepts the plea of the defendant, the clerk or registrar of the court shall orally give notice to such person to the following effect:

"The Highway Traffic Act provides that upon conviction of the offence with which you are charged, in the circumstances indicated therein, your driver's licence shall be suspended for three years."

(5) The suspension of a driver's licence under this section shall not be held to be invalid by reason of failure to give the notice provided for in subsection (4).

---

155 *R. v. Brady* (1992), 18 W.C.B. (2d) 50 (B.C. C.A.).

156 S.O. 1981, c. 72, s. 2. All references to the original section in cases discussed in this chaper have been replaced with the current section.

157 (1985), [1985] 2 S.C.R. 2 (S.C.C.), affirming (1981), 10 M.V.R. 59 (Ont. C.A.).

(6) An appeal may be taken from an order of suspension under subsection (3) or a decision to not make the order in the same manner as from a conviction or an acquittal under subsection (2).

(7) Where an appeal is taken from an order for suspension under subsection (6), the court being appealed to may direct that the order being appealed from shall be stayed pending the final disposition of the appeal or until otherwise ordered by that court.

There is very little consistency across the country with respect to the specific language used in provincial highway traffic legislation to justify stopping of motorists by peace officers for various purposes.[158] The jurisprudence has generally held, however, that such legislation, though varying in specific wording, generally authorizes random stopping of motorists by police at least for purposes connected with highway regulation and safety. Nevertheless, it is clear that the statutory language must specifically authorize the type of stop made.[159] The power to stop will not generally be inferred from the mere existence of a statutory duty on motorists simply to carry and produce documents or to maintain vehicles properly.[160]

(b) Constitutional Considerations (1): Division of Powers

In *R. v. Hisey*,[161] the Ontario Court of Appeal considered whether s. 216 was *ultra vires* the province or rendered inoperative because it was in conflict with the obstruct police provision of the *Criminal Code* (then s. 118a). Morden J.A. (as he then was), writing for the Court, ultimately concluded that s. 216 was validly enacted by the province.

In *Hisey*, the appellant conceded that his conviction and the sentence imposed (which included the mandatory three-year suspension of his licence under s. 216(3)) were proper apart from the issue of the constitutional validity of the section. His Lordship observed that a conflict between federal and provincial legislation does not result in and of itself in the invalidity of the provincial legislation, but only in its inoperability. No question of paramountcy, which can result in the provincial legislation being held to be inoperative, can arise unless the two pieces of legislation submitted to be in conflict are each constitutionally valid.

---

158 British Columbia: s. 100 of the *Motor Vehicle Act*, R.S.B.C. 1996, c. 318; Alberta: s. 119 of the *Highway Traffic Act*, R.S.A. 1980, c. H-7; Saskatchewan: s. 40(8), (9) of the *Highway Traffic Act, 1996*, S.S. 1996, c. H-3.1; New Brunswick: s. 15(1)(d) of the *Motor Vehicle Act*, R.S.N.B. 1973, c. M-17; Nova Scotia: ss. 18, 78(2) and 83(1) of the *Motor Vehicle Act*, R.S.N.S. 1989, c. 293.

159 *R. v. Angell* (1996), 31 W.C.B. (2d) 123 (N.B. Prov. Ct.).

160 *Dedman, supra*, note 157; *R. v. Heiber* (1995), 29 W.C.B. (2d) 323 (Ont. Gen. Div.).

161 (1985), 40 M.V.R. 152 (Ont. C.A.), leave to appeal to the S.C.C. refused (1986), 40 M.V.R. 152n (S.C.C.).

With respect to the issue of paramountcy, it was held that this would require conflict or contradiction between the two sections. To the extent that the two provisions are the same, in the sense that they "duplicate" each other, such qualities have been observed to be the "ultimate in harmony" in other cases, and Mr. Justice Morden followed suit. While his Lordship did not suggest that there was duplication, he held that the absence of any conflict between the two provisions (in the sense that one could obey both laws at the same time) meant that the paramountcy test was not met.

Is s. 216 valid provincial legislation? In what really is the crux of his decision, Morden J.A. held as follows:[162]

> It is clear that the real purpose of [s.216] is to confer on police officers the power, in the lawful execution of their duties and responsibilities, to require drivers of motor vehicles to stop. This is the gravamen of the section. Its offence-creation feature, which includes the aggravated example provided for in [s.216(3)], is subsidiary and ancillary to the conferral of the power to stop. Its particular purpose is to provide a sanction to make the exercise of the power more effective. With the foregoing in mind I do not think that it can reasonably be said that the main purpose of [s.216] is to prohibit certain kinds of driving with penal consequences, not that this in itself would necessarily result in the legislation being considered to be in relation to criminal law and outside the sphere of provincial competence. All of these considerations emphasize the primarily regulatory feature of the law which make it more concerned with property and civil rights or a matter of merely a local or private nature than with criminal law.

Accordingly, the appeal was dismissed.

(c) The Operation of the Section

The offence is clearly one of the most serious in the Act. The section contemplates two types of offenders — those who fail to stop, and those who, having done so, wilfully continue to evade a pursuing police officer. Following a conviction under s. 216(1), a finding of escape by flight may be made. If such a finding is made, the conviction will result in a mandatory three-year licence suspension. A finding of flight under subsection (3) cannot be made unless and until a conviction has been entered under subsection (1). It would seem that the Crown is required to plead the particulars of subsection (3) in the information, but the evidence adduced with respect to the offence under subsection (1) would be identical to that led in support of a finding of flight or escape. In other words, no new evidence is permitted to be led.

The information must aver to the elements of subsection (1) in order for a finding under subsection (3) to follow, however, since the latter is only a subsequent finding which is dependent upon the establishment of the offence

---

162 *Ibid.*, at p. 158.

in subsection (1). Thus in *Day v. R.* [163] Hurley Dist. Ct. J. held the information to be insufficient because it did not create an offence known to law. The charge alleged that the accused,

> On or about July 26th, 1984 at the City of Kingston [...] did commit the offence of being the driver of a motor vehicle did fail to immediately come to a safe stop when signalled or requested to stop by a police officer readily identifiable as such and did wilfully continue to avoid police while a police officer gave pursuit and did thereby commit an offence contrary to the *Highway Traffic Act*, s. [216(3)]

The principle underlying the pleading requirement is that it ensures a person charged with contravening s. 216(1) is reasonably informed prior to trial of the further allegation made against him or her. Moreover, Hurley J. also observed that an essential ingredient of an offence under the latter section was that the officer had been in the lawful execution of his duties. Note too, that when the Crown intends to pursue a finding under s. 216(3), the defendant must be notified in court prior to plea of that fact. [164]

The Ontario Court of Appeal first considered the section in *R. v. Dilorenzo*. [165] The central issues facing the court were:

- The standard of proof required by s. 216(3);
- Whether, in the facts of the case, the police officer was readily identifiable as such;
- Whether the trial judge had a discretion to impose less than a three-year suspension;
- The significance of an absence of an allegation of the circumstances set out in s. 216(3).

With respect to ss. 216(1) and (2), the Court held that these created strict liability offences in which there was no necessity for the prosecution to prove the existence of *mens rea*. Once the *actus reus* of the offence is proved, it is for the accused to show he or she took all reasonable steps to bring his or her actions within the law. [166]

These provisions, however, are to be distinguished from the wilful escape by flight provision, s. 216(3), which requires proof of *mens rea*. The conduct envisioned under this sub-section is of an aggravated variety in that the accused must be shown to have "*wilfully* continued to avoid police while a police officer gave pursuit". In other words, he or she must have intended to avoid the police.

---

163 (1985), 36 M.V.R. 221 (Ont. Dist. Ct.).
164 Pursuant to s. 216(4), although subsection (5) states that the suspension of a driver's licence under this section shall not be held to be invalid by reason of failure to give the notice provided for in subsection (4).
165 (1984), 26 M.V.R. 259 (Ont. C.A.). This remains the leading case on the proper interpretation of the section.
166 See also *R. v. Bunting* (1983), 26 M.V.R. 23 (B.C. Co. Ct.).

As was seen in *Day*, s. 216(3) does not create a specific offence but rather relates to penalty in that it imposes a mandatory three-year licence suspension. *Mens rea*, the special intention to avoid police, must be proved beyond a reasonable doubt. It had been argued on appeal that the use of the word "satisfied" had the effect of providing for a test on the balance of probabilities but the Court rejected this assertion.[167]

An essential ingredient of the offence constituted by s. 216(1) is that the police officer who requests a person to stop is "readily identifiable" as a police officer, such as wearing a blue O.P.P. shirt with identifying shoulder patches that were plainly visible.[168]

It would also seem that a police officer only has the authority to stop where that order is made "on a highway" and the prosecution must prove that this was the case.[169]

The Court further held that s. 216(3) made it mandatory that a person's licence was to be suspended for three years, no more, no less, and this is a fixed penalty. The Legislature has not given the courts any discretion to impose a less onerous licence suspension.

Section 216(6) gives the defendant a right of appeal from the s. 216(3) finding, and s. 216(7) permits the defendant to obtain a stay pending appeal.

(d) Application of Principles

In *R. v. Traves*,[170] the investigating officer gave evidence that he had followed the accused to his home and that, upon arriving home, the accused turned his motorcycle into the driveway and around the rear of his residence. The officer's cruiser lights and siren remained on as he followed the accused. The accused made continued efforts toward opening the door with his key despite the officer informing him that he was under arrest for the *Criminal Code* offence of dangerous driving. Morrisey Dist. Ct. J. concluded that this evidence was not so weak that a verdict of guilty could be said to be unreasonable. In so ruling, he found that the Crown had proven beyond a reasonable doubt that the accused had the requisite *mens rea* of wilfully avoiding police pursuit.

It is sufficient indication of a demand to stop that a police officer activate emergency lights and siren. There is no further obligation to announce or manually signal the demand to stop.[171] The fact that the accused did not succeed in evading the police officer does not imply that an attempt was not

---

167 See *contra*, *R. v. Worth* (1983), 21 M.V.R. 89 (Ont. Co. Ct.).
168 See also *R. v. Friesecke* (1996), 31 W.C.B. (2d) 300 (Ont. Prov. Div.).
169 *R. v. Douglas* (1997), 29 M.V.R. (3d) 161 (Ont. Prov. Div.); *R. v. Mansour*, [1979] 2 S.C.R. 916.
170 (1986), 43 M.V.R. 188 (Ont. Dist. Ct.).
171 *R. v. Smood* [1985] B.C.W.L.D. 1295 (Co. Ct.).

intended to be made.[172] It would seem, however, that the phrase "readily identifiable" in s. 216(1) relates to the police officer and not the unmarked vehicle which the officer might be operating.[173]

(e) Multiple Convictions and The *Kienapple* Principle

In *R. v. Kennedy*,[174] the two accused had been convicted of charges under s. 216 of the *Highway Traffic Act*. The defendant Brisson had further been charged with careless driving but had been acquitted on the basis of the application of the principle in *Kienapple v. R.*[175] disallowing multiple convictions for matters arising out of the same delict or wrongful act. The accused Kennedy had also been charged with dangerous driving but had been convicted. Both contended that it was appropriate in the circumstances to apply the principle against multiple convictions as laid down in *Kienapple*.

Mr. Justice Brooke held that *Kienapple* was not applicable to either Kennedy's situation or Brisson's. In doing so, he pointed out that whereas ss. 216(1) and (2) of the *Highway Traffic Act* make it an offence for a driver to fail to stop in response to the command of a police officer, s. 216(3) does not create an offence but goes to the question of what penalty to impose on a driver who is guilty of the offence created by s. 216(1) and (2). *Kienapple* does not deal with penalties. Moreover, the duty to stop in response to an order of a police officer and to avoid police chases is quite different from the duty to drive with care which can, depending on the circumstances, give rise to a conviction of careless driving or perhaps dangerous driving under the *Criminal Code*.[176]

Houlden J.A., with Howland C.J.O. concurring, agreed with Mr. Justice Brooke's assessment but shed further light on why *Kienapple* was inapplicable. The *Kienapple* principle applies when the act that underlies the offence is sought to be used again to constitute the factual basis of a conviction for another offence. Here, however, in order to obtain a conviction for careless driving or dangerous driving, the Crown had to establish that the accused had done something beyond what was required to be established under s. 189a. Accordingly, *Kienapple* was of no relevance to these cases.[177]

---

172 *R. v. Parker* (1992), 41 M.V.R. (2d) 257 (Ont. Gen. Div.).

173 *R. v. Lauzon* (1996), 31 W.C.B. (2d) 178 (Ont. Gen. Div.). Although it is not clear that this would really be fair in all circumstances.

174 (*sub nom. R. v. Brisson*) (1986), 37 M.V.R. 313 (Ont. C.A.), affirming (1984), 29 M.V.R. 145 (Ont. Co. Ct.).

175 *Supra*, note 149.

176 For example, a person could drive with care around a corner and hide in a driveway and that would be enough to bring down the additional penalty under s. 216(3).

177 See also *R. v. Ueffing* (1980), 7 M.V.R. 155 (N.S. C.A.) where it was found that the *Kienapple* principle was not offended where the provincial violation preceded the dangerous driving and was a separate matter.

(f) Constitutional Considerations (2): The *Charter*

The section raises readily apparent concerns with respect to ss. 8 and 9 of the *Charter*. In *R. v. Hufsky*,[178] the appellant was stopped at random in a spot check by police; there had been nothing unusual about his driving. The spot check was for the purposes of checking licences, insurance, mechanical fitness of cars and sobriety of the drivers with the only guideline being that at least one marked police car be engaged in spot check duty. There were no criteria, standards, guidelines or procedures to determine which vehicles should be stopped; it was in the discretion of the police officer. Eventually, the appellant was charged with refusing to provide a breath sample contrary to then s. 234.1 of the *Criminal Code*.

Ultimately, an appeal was brought in the Supreme Court of Canada. One of the issues raised was whether s. 216(1) of the *Highway Traffic Act* contravened the right not to be arbitrarily detained pursuant to s. 9 of the *Charter*. The Court held that s. 216(1) prescribed a limit on the right not to be arbitrarily detained. However, in view of the importance of highway safety and the role to be played in relation to it by a random stop authority for the purpose of increasing both the detection and the perceived risk of detection of motor vehicle offences, many of which cannot be detected by the mere observation of driving, the limit imposed by s. 216(1) is reasonable and is demonstrably justified in a free and democratic society, within the meaning of s. 1 of the *Charter*.[179]

In *R. v. Ladouceur*,[180] the Supreme Court of Canada was faced with *Charter* considerations involving random stops conducted by police under the authority of s. 216(1), as opposed to the organized system of spot checks dealt with in *Hufsky*. The court held that the section authorized conduct that was in violation of the accused's right to be free from arbitrary detention under s. 9 of the *Charter*, since it gave an officer absolute discretion in determining whether to make the request to stop.[181] However, the infringement was justifiable under s. 1 of the *Charter*. Further, the random stop was not in violation of s. 8 of the *Charter*, there being no distinction in law between random stops and organized 'R.I.D.E.' type stops. As long as the stop is made in accordance with the statutory scheme, there is no infringement.

There is a limit on police action following a stop, however. The ambit of s. 216 stops was considered by the Ontario Court of Appeal in

---

178 (1988), [1988] 1 S.C.R. 621 (S.C.C.).

179 See also *R. v. Parton* (1983), 25 M.V.R. 177 (Alta. Q.B.) where s. 119 of the Alberta *Highway Traffic Act*, which parallels s. 189a was held not to contravene ss. 7, 8 or 9 of the *Charter*. To the same effect is *R. v. Moretto* (1984), 28 M.V.R. 290 (Man. Q.B.) dealing with s. 71(2) of the Manitoba Act.

180 (1990), 21 M.V.R. (2d) 165 (S.C.C.). See also *R. v. Wilson* (1990), 56 C.C.C. (3d) 142 (S.C.C.) For a similar holding in relation to the Alberta *Highway Traffic Act*.

181 See also *R. v. MacLennan* (1995), 97 C.C.C. (3d) 69 (N.S. C.A.).

R. v. Simpson.[182] Doherty J.A. held that the section only authorized stops made for the purpose of enforcing traffic laws and ensuring the safe operation of motor vehicles. The use of power for the purposes of investigating a possible narcotics offence was not authorized and would constitute a breach of s. 8 of the *Charter*.[183] That does not mean that the discovery of a *Criminal Code* offence in the course of executing a s. 216 stop will be illegitimate. In *R. v. Belnavis & Lawrence*[184] the Supreme Court of Canada considered the legality of a search conducted subsequent to a s. 216 stop. In dismissing the accused's appeal, the majority included the statement in its reasons that the officer was entitled to ask questions, look for documents in the vehicle, and check it for safety in the course of a s. 216 stop.[185]

As mentioned, the legislation must specifically authorize a stopping power. The significance of specific legislation empowering police officers to stop a vehicle was recently considered by the Newfoundland Court of Appeal in *R. v. Griffin.*[186] In allowing the accused's appeal the Court noted that, "[t]he Newfoundland legislation does not contain the broad general powers to stop that exist in some other provincial statutes nor does it contain amendments such as have occurred in Ontario by the enactment of s. 216 and 48."[187] Thus the random stopping of a vehicle without articulable cause could not constitute a justifiable use of police powers associated with duties to enforce highway traffic law. Although s. 162 of the Newfoundland Act contains the reference, "to stop … to ensure that this Act and regulations are being complied with", this does not give an additional express power to stop, and may only refer

---

182 (1993), 79 C.C.C. (3d) 482 (Ont. C.A.).

183 See also *R. v. Poirier* (1996), 31 W.C.B. (2d) 425 (Ont. Gen. Div.).

184 [1997] S.C.J. No. 81.

185 The particular facts of each case will determine whether the search subsequent to the stop was reasonable. For a consideration of the scope of police power after the suspect has fled from the police after being requested to stop, see *R. v. Tricker* (1995), 96 C.C.C. (3d) 198 (Ont. C.A.), leave to appeal to S.C.C. refused (1996), 16 M.V.R. (3d) 235 (note) (S.C.C.).

186 (1996), 28 M.V.R. (3d) 1 (Nfld. C.A.), leave to appeal refused (1997), 215 N.R. 399 (note) (S.C.C.).

187 The Newfoundland *Highway Traffic Act*, R.S.N. 1990, c. H-3 contains the following potentially relevant provisions:

29. A driver, owner or person having the care and control of a vehicle shall produce the vehicle licence issued for the vehicle for inspection when a peace officer or inspector so requests.

162. Where a traffic officer reasonably considers it necessary

(a) to ensure orderly movement of traffic;

(b) to prevent injury or damage to persons or property;

(c) to permit proper action in an emergency; or

(d) to stop a motor vehicle on a highway to ensure that this Act and the regulations are being complied with,

the officer may direct traffic according to his or her discretion, notwithstanding anything in this Part, and every person shall obey the officer's directions.

to situations where another vehicle has been stopped under the Act and it is necessary to direct the movement of the target vehicle to ensure efficient traffic management; it is limited to stops for the purpose of enforcing the *Highway Traffic Act* and regulations.

9. TURNS, RIGHTS OF WAY AND INTERSECTIONS

(a) Introduction

Part X of the *Highway Traffc Act* sets out the "Rules of the Road", that is, the rules which govern the orderly movement of vehicles using highways. Its principal concern is the regulation of vehicles approaching or passing through intersections and of vehicles passing or overtaking other highway users.[188] The various offences contained in the part comprise a significant percentage of traffic offences charged and tried.

Section 134 provides an overarching authority to a police officer under certain emergency-type situations to direct traffic or close any portion of a highway according to his or her discretion, and a concomitant obligation on drivers to obey that direction.[189] Section 182(1) provides the general authorization for the placing of signs on any highway. Aside from the provisions of individual offences, there is a general statutory obligation on drivers to "obey the instructions or directions indicated on any sign so erected."

(b) Turns

Every turn that a driver may conceivably make on a highway is governed by the *Highway Traffc Act*. To be legal a turn must be i) allowable, ii) properly signaled, and iii) properly executed. By allowable we mean that there is no prohibition against such a turn being made. Such a prohibition would usually appear in the form of a regulation or by-law indicated by a duly erected sign. Section 144 (9) of the *Highway Traffc Act* specifies the offence of failing to obey any sign erected at an intersection (for example, a 'no left turn' sign).

(i) *Signalling the Turn*

If a turn is allowable it must be properly executed. A driver turning left or right, manoeuvering between lanes must first ensure that the manoeuvre can be made safely and "if the operation of any other vehicle may be affected by such movement", the driver must signal the intended turn in a manner which

---

188 A number of the provisions dealing with the 'rules of the road' have been the subject of civil litigation arising from automobile accidents occurring at intersections. These are collected in Chapter 10 of Segal, Murray *Manual of Motor Vehicle Offences, supra*, note 21.

189 For instances of the broad discretion granted to officers, see *R. v. Bothwell* (1986), 45 M.V.R. 1 (Ont. C.A.); *R. v. Williams* (1986), (sub nom. *Williams v. R.*) 39 M.V.R. 153 (N.S. C.A.).

is "plainly visible" to the other driver.[190] The Act creates two distinct offences: failure to see that the particular movement can be made in safety, and the failure to give a signal plainly visible to the operator of any other vehicle that might be affected.[191]

It should be noted that the duty to signal only arises where the operation of another *vehicle* is affected. The prosecution must therefore prove this fact beyond reasonable doubt to obtain a conviction. A turn may be signalled by indicator lights or by hand signals.[192] A turn to the left may be manually signalled by extending the hand and arm horizontally and beyond the left side of the vehicle;[193] a turn to the right may be signalled by extending the hand and arm upward and beyond the left side of the vehicle.[194] A stop is indicated by extending the hand and arm downward and beyond the left side of the vehicle.[195] Turns are, of course, more commonly indicated by the vehicle's flashing light indicator, the quality of which is governed by the Act.[196] It must only be used to indicate the turns or movements permitted by the Act.[197]

(c) Executing the Turn

When executing the turn, the driver must use the appropriate lane or, where lanes are not marked on the highway, the appropriate portion of the roadway. Thus, when turning to the left one must use the lane or portion of road immediately to the right of the centre line;[198] when turning to the right one must use the lane or portion of road immediately to the left of the curb.[199] The exception to this rule is multilane roads which have more than one designated turning lane. When turning a vehicle the driver must enter the "target road" in the lane which corresponds to that from which the turn was made.[200] This is most important where there are multiple turn lanes, but applies to all turns. Long vehicles or vehicles with trailers often cannot turn sharply enough to comply fully with these requirements (i.e., it is impossible to make a clear ninety degree turn without, at least momentarily, entering a lane other than the one required by the legislation). In such cases the driver is excused from

---

190 Section 142(1). Section 142(2) requires the same caution of drivers setting a vehicle in motion
      from a parked or stopped position, and s. 142(8) governs stopping and sudden braking.
191 *R. v. Lebedorf* (1962), [1963] 2 C.C.C. 95 (Ont. H.C.).
192 Section 142(3).
193 Section 142(4)(a).
194 Section 142(4)(b).
195 Subsections 142(8)(a).
196 Section 142(6).
197 Section 142(7).
198 Section 141(6).
199 Section 141(2).
200 Section 141(3), (7).

using the appropriate lane if he or she complies with the various provisions as closely as practicable.[201]

In *R. v. Harding*,[202] the court considered the requirement that a driver keep as close as possible to the centre line. The court held that the words "as close as practicable" within the forerunner of the section[203] meant "what is reasonable under the circumstances".

One of the more common traffic incidents is the left turn or "T-Bone" collision. Section 141(5) places the onus on a driver turning left at an intersection across the path of another vehicle to afford "a reasonable opportunity to the driver or operator of the approaching vehicle to avoid a collision."

(d) Right of Way

A variety of obligations arise under the general concept of right of way. A right of way is the legal right of one user of the highway to require and expect that another user will modify his or her behaviour to allow safe passage of the first user. Thus, for example, a pedestrian who enters onto a crosswalk with a green light can expect that an approaching driver will stop to allow him or her to pass unharmed.

The following rights of way, and concomitant duties of care are provided for in the Act:

- Drivers entering the highway from a private road or driveway, have the duty not to create a hazard. While the duty of care is a high one,[204] it ceases and the more general duty of care applies once the entry has been made.[205] The Ontario Court of Appeal recently considered this offence and held that there is no onus upon an individual charged with this offence to explain his or her action. In other words, the prosecution must demonstrate that the entry was made without due care for approaching traffic.[206]

- A driver must yield right of way to pedestrians or wheelchair users within a pedestrian crosswalk. While the section distinguishes between pedestrians according to which side of the crosswalk they are on, to all intents and purposes, vehicles shold stop whenever a pedestrian is in a crosswalk.[207]

- Pedestrians have an equal duty not to enter a crosswalk when a vehicle is "so close that it is impracticable for the driver of the vehicle or streetcar

---

201 Section 141(9).

202 (1971), 2 C.C.C. (2d) 341 (Ont. Co. Ct.).

203 *Highway Traffic Act*, R.S.O. 1960, c. 172, s. 68(3).

204 *Boutilier v. Atton* (1964), 50 M.P.R. 131 (N.S. C.A.).

205 Section 139. *R. v. Perry* (1941), 77 C.C.C. 103 (N.B. Co. Ct.); *R. v. Hornstein* (1973), 11 C.C.C. (2d) 197 (Ont. Prov. Ct.); *R. v. Langille* (1980), 31 N.B.R. (2d) 355 (N.B. C.A.).

206 *R. v. Shapero* (February 6, 1991), Doc. CA184/90 (Ont. C.A.).

207 Section 140(1). It is also an offence to overtake within 30 meters of a crosswalk: s. 140(3).

to yield the right of way."[208] The legislation should be interpreted as giving pedestrians greater protection than vehicles, however.[209] The Nova Scotia Court of Appeal has held the offence to be one of strict liability.[210]

• It is proposed to amend the Ontario legislation to require drivers to yield right of way to buses that have indicated an intention to leave a bus bay and re-enter traffic.[211]

(e) Passing Vehicles

The Act contains several specific sections which govern the conduct of vehicles passing each other, either by overtaking, or passing in opposite directions.[212] Section 148 governs procedures and general safety of meeting and overtaking other vehicles. "Fail to turn out to the right"[213] is a section commonly pleaded to in rear-end accident situations. Vehicles being overtaken have a duty to move to the right to allow the overtaking vehicle to pass.[214]

Section 149 requires drivers to stay in their half of the roadway under certain common sense road conditions, namely on approach to the crest of a hill, within 30 metres of a bridge or tunnel where visibility is obstructed,[215] or within 30 metres of a level crossing.[216] The prohibitions do not apply where a highway is divided into marked lanes with more lanes in one direction than the other (i.e. where the lanes in one direction occupy more than half of the roadway). The line markings must be clear.[217]

A driver may overtake to the right of a proceeding vehicle where it can be done safely, and where the driver being passed is about to make, or has signalled his or her intention to make a left turn. The highway must have suffficient room for two vehicles to pass in each direction, or there must be a paved shoulder on which the passing vehicle can travel. In essence, the offence of "pass off roadway" is committed when a vehicle overtakes on the right on an unpaved roadway.[218] The section creates two separate offences — fail to pass in safety and pass off roadway.[219]

---

208 Section 140(4).

209 *R. v. Knutson* (1989), 13 M.V.R. (2d) 158 (Sask. Q.B.).

210 *R. v. Davis* (1996), 21 M.V.R. (3d) 65, 429 A.P.R. 68 (N.S. C.A.).

211 S.O. 1994, c. 27, s. 138(12) [enacted as s. 142.1 of the *Highway Traffic Act*].

212 *R. v. Mailman* (1990), 24 M.V.R. 112 (N.S. C.A.).

213 Section 148(1).

214 Section 148(2).

215 Section 149(1)(a).

216 Section 149(1)(b).

217 Section 149(2)(a); *Plourade c. R.* (1981), 14 M.V.R. 27 (N.B. Q.B.).

218 Section 150.

219 *R. v. Worden* (1962), 132 C.C.C. 197 (Ont. C.A.). Section 154 creates a different offence of "change lane not in safety".

(f) Intersections without Signal Lights or Signs

Where an intersection has no stop or yield sign or signal lights to control traffic, the right of way belongs to the first vehicle entering the intersection.[220] If two or more vehicles arrive at the intersection at the same time, or almost the same time, the right of way belongs to the vehicle on the right.[221] It should be noted that for the purpose of determining rights of way, a streetcar is counted as a vehicle.[222]

(g) Failure to Obey A Signal Light or Sign

One of the most common charges arising from intersection violations is failure to obey a sign or signal light. There a variety of duties imposed on the driver depending on the colour of the light.[223]

The Ontario Court of Appeal has held in the context of an emergency vehicle that the offence of failing to stop at a red light is one of absolute liability, in large measure because, unlike other provisions in the statutory scheme, there was no provision in the section for a due diligence defence.[224] The overall purpose of the legislation, the ease of compliance, and the relatively minor non-penal penalty provided further grounds for categorizing the offence as one of absolute liability.

In *R. v. Higgins*,[225] however, the Nova Scotia Court of Appeal, applying the test from *Sault Ste. Marie*,[226] concluded that the offence was one of strict liability and that a defence of due diligence was available. The trial judge was satisfied that the defendant had done everything a reasonable person could be expected to do to observe and obey the sign in question. A driver who can demonstrate that he or she took reasonable steps to obey the sign, or that through no fault of the driver, the sign was not visible, should be acquitted.

This is not an invitation for quibbling about the quality of signs, however. The erection of a sign need not be perfect to regulate traffic. In *R. v. Priest*,[227] the court was faced with a stop sign which had been erected six inches closer to the road and six inches higher off the ground than the regulations required. The defendant challenged his conviction on the premise that the sign was illegal because it was not in exact accord with the regulations. The Ontario Court of Appeal held that[228]

---

220 Section 135(2).
221 Section 135(3).
222 Section 138(1).
223 Section 144.
224 *R. v. Kurtzman* (1991), 31 M.V.R. (2d) 1 (Ont. C.A.).
225 (1981), 10 M.V.R. 157 (N.S. C.A.).
226 (1978), 40 C.C.C. (2d) 353, 85 D.L.R. (3d) 161, [1978] 2 S.C.R. 1299 (S.C.C.).
227 (1961), 35 C.R. 32 (Ont. C.A.).
228 *Ibid.*, at p. 37.

> ... [A] stop sign that complies, though not strictly, but so substantially, with the regulation as to reasonably indicate that it is authoritatitve and erected by the competent authority in intended compliance with its power under the Act, in my opinion, is equally binding on the driver, provided that he could have seen it if he was keeping a proper lookout.

The test then is a functional one, relying on the ability of the sign to convincingly communicate the valid regulation authorizing its erection.[229] If a sign has been posted but has since been removed or otherwise tampered with or affected by nature, no offence has been committed. The provisions are directed at drivers who are 'approaching a stop sign'; if the sign is gone or somehow transmuted, no offence is committed.[230]

(h) Yield Signs[231]

A yield sign requires a driver to slow down, "to a speed reasonable for the existing conditions", or to stop if necessary. The driver shall then "yield the right of way to traffic in the intersection or approaching so closely that it would constitute an immediate hazard" to vehicles.

It is no defence, however, to a charge of failing to yield that the other driver is in violation of the law. In one case,[232] the defendant claimed that the rule only required the driver approaching a yield sign to give up the right of way to a lawful user of the highway. This defence was rejected: every vehicle entering or approaching the intersection, whether legally driven or not, is entitled to the right of way.

In another case, *R. v. Hornstein*,[233] the Court held that the duty to yield requires the driver to give up the right of way until it is possible to negotiate the entire vehicle safely into the stream of traffic.

(i) Stop Signs

Section 136 (1) prescribes that when approaching a stop sign the driver:

> (a) shall stop his or her vehicle ... at a marked stop line or, if then immediately before entering the nearest crosswalk or, if none, then immediately before entering the intersection; and

> (b) shall yield the right of way to traffic in the intersection or approaching the intersection on another highway so closely that to proceed would constitute an immediate hazard and, having so yielded the right of way, may proceed.

---

229 With respect to signal lights see, *R. v. Potapchuk* (1963), [1963] 1 O.R. 40 (Ont. H.C.).

230 *Sorrie v. Cluting* (1955), [1955] O.W.N. 946 (Ont. C.A.); see also, *Webb v. Moore's Taxi Co.* (1942), [1942] 3 W.W.R. 294 (Man. C.A.); *Kraft v. Prefontaine* (1963), 41 W.W.R. 510 (Sask. C.A.).

231 Section 138.

232 *R. v. Horban* (1959), 31 W.W.R. 139 (Alta. Dist. Ct.).

233 (1973), 11 C.C.C. (2d) 197 (Ont. Prov. Ct.).

It is not enough for a driver to bring his vehicle to a stop at the stop sign: the driver must come to a full stop at the appropriate position, depending on the configuration of the intersection. In *R. v. Manship*,[234] the stop sign was located several feet from the intersection it controlled. The driver stopped at the sign and then proceeded towards the intersection. He did not stop a second time when he arrived at the point where he had a view of approaching traffic (the appropriate point in this case). Rather, he moved slowly and took care not to interfere with cross-traffic. The court held that the legislation required the driver to stop not at the sign but at the point where he had a view. His actions, while prudent, were none the less a violation of the section.

There are several other stoppping requirements in most acts. In Ontario, there are provisions governing stopping at railway crossings,[235] for streetcars,[236] and for school buses.[237]

(j) Signal Lights

Where an intersection is controled by signal lights, the actions of drivers approaching the intersection are controlled by s. 144. The rules set out in s. 144 are subject to special limitations found in the regulations or in by-laws as indicated by special signs.[238] Lane lights may be used to give specific directions to each lane of traffic.[239] The meaning of each signal light or combination of lights is set out in s. 144.

(k) "Anti-Gridlock" Provisions

Municipal councils may pass a by-law making it an offence under the *Highway Traffic Act* to enter an intersection where it appears that it will be impossible to clear the intersection. Unless the "trafffic in front of [the driver] is moving in a manner that would reasonably lead him or her to believe he or she can clear the intersection", before the light turns red, he or she should not enter the intersection.[240]

---

234 (1983), 22 M.V.R. 257 (N.B. Q.B.). The New Brunswick legislation is similar to that in s. 116. See also *R. v. Bannister* (1964), [1964] 2 C.C.C. 299 (N.B. Co. Ct.).

235 Sections 163, 164.

236 Section 166.

237 Section 175.

238 For example, "no right turn on red" signs.

239 Section 144(10).

240 Section 145.

10. COMMERCIAL VEHICLES

(a) **Introduction**

Commercial vehicles, particularly trucks and tractor-trailers, are heavily regulated, not only under the regulations of the *Highway Traffic Act*, but under other provincial statutes also.[241]

"Commercial Motor Vehicle" is defined in s. 1 of the *Highway Traffic Act* as:

> a motor vehicle having permanently attached thereto a truck or delivery body and includes ambulances, hearses, casket wagons, fire apparatus, buses and tractors used for hauling purposes on the highways.

Note that the class of vehicles known as commercial is simply one subclass of "motor vehicles" which is also defined in s. 1. Thus operators of commercial vehicles are subject to the same rules of the road as drivers of motor cars.[242] They are also subject to the general permit and licence requirements as other drivers.[243] The main differences between private motor cars and commercial vehicles lies in some differing registration and licencing requirements, and the safety-oriented, largely regulatory regime for standards, inspections and maintenance.

The *Highway Traffic Act* regulates not only that broad class of vehicles which fall under the designation "commercial", but imposes licencing and other conditions for the operation of various commercial activities associated with motor vehicles. Thus, s. 39 governs vehicle rental agencies, requiring them to ascertain that the lessor is validly licenced to drive. The Act also provides for the making of regulations governing driving instructors,[244] as well as car dealers (new and used),[245] wreckers,[246] and garages doing repairs.[247]

---

241 See R.R.O. 1990, Reg. 575 — Commercial Motor Vehicle Inspections; O. Reg. 424/97 — Commercial Vehicle Operator's Registration Certificates; O. Reg. 4/93 — Hours of Work, as well as the *Truck Transportation Act*, R.S.O. 1990, c. T.22, and the *Public Vehicles Act*, R.S.O. 1990, c. P.54.

242 Some offences contain specific applications to commercial vehicles, for example the offence of "following too closely" in s. 158 stipulates that, except when overtaking, commercial vehicles, when driving over 60 k.m.h. must stay at least 60 metres behind any other motor vehicle.

243 For example, the general requirements respecting issuing, holding and cancellation of permits found in s. 7; the V.I.N. requirement in s. 10(2); drive without licence, s. 32(17); the general suspension powers of the Registrar, s. 47.

244 Section 58 and R.R.O. 1990, Reg. 586 (although as the section suggests, this profession is governed by Municipal by-laws).

245 Sections 59, 60 (in addition to the provisions of the *Motor Vehicle Dealers Act*, R.S.O. 1990, c. M.42).

246 Sections 59(1), 60.

247 Sections 59(8), 60. Section 60 imposes broad record-keeping and reporting requirements upon operators of such premises, designed to assist police in investigating offences involving vehicles.

(b) Administrative Requirements

Drivers and operators of commercial motor vehicles are required to be in possession of a valid "Commercial Vehicle Operator's Registration Certificate" (C.V.O.R.),[248] and are required to carry it and other documentation in the vehicle at all times. A police officer is entitled to demand inspection of those documents at any time,[249] and is authorized on reasonable belief that the vehicle is being driven without the proper permit[250] to detain the vehicle and seize its permit and number plates.[251] The issuing of a C.V.O.R. is an administrative act which must be carried out where all the requirements are met.[252]

In addition to the minimum requirements under the *Compulsory Automobile Insurance Act*, operators of commercial vehicles are required to carry additional insurance in an amount specified by regulation, proof of which must be carried and is subject to examination on demand by a police officer.[253]

Operators issued permits under a reciprocity agreement with another jurisdiction are subject to particular requirements and conditions.[254] Unless exempt by regulation, commercial vehicles are required to have the name of its owner attached to or painted on both sides of the vehicle.

Section 190 of the Act requires operators of commercial vehicles to maintain and carry with them at all times a daily log, and they are required to surrender it to a police officer upon demand. Regulations made under this section prescribe the type of logs, as well as hours of work, periods of rest and other requirements concerning the safe operation of commercial vehicles. In *R. v. Kleysen Transport Ltd.*,[255] an interprovincial carrier was charged with violating the regulations governing the maximum number of hours allowed before requiring off-duty time. Notwithstanding that a regulation under the federal *Motor Vehicle Transportation Act, 1987*[256] created the same offence, the provincial regulation was valid since it only duplicated but did not conflict with the federal regime.

(c) Technical Requirements

There are a multitude of technical requirements and equipment standards imposed on all vehicles, and commercial vehicles generally have their own

---

248 Section 16(2).
249 Section 16(4).
250 Under s. 16(2) or s. 47(8).
251 Section 20(2).
252 Section 17(1).
253 Section 23(3).
254 Sections 24, 25.
255 (1990), 31 M.V.R. (2d) 121 (Ont. Prov. Div.).
256 R.S.C. 1985, c. 29 (3rd Supp.).

governing provisions which address the specific characteristics of those vehicles. Part VI of the *Highway Traffic Act* sets out equipment requirements of all vehicles, including lights,[257] brakes,[258] mudguards and windshield wipers,[259] reflectors,[260] and tires.[261]

Recent legislative changes have brought in specific penalties for commercial vehicles which are in violation of the equipment requirements. Section 64, for example, as well as providing broad authority for a police officer to inspect to ensure that the a vehicle's brakes are "maintained in good working order" and in conformance with the regulations, provides for a fine of up to $20,000 where a commercial vehicle or trailer is in violation of the section's requirements.[262]

The purpose of these sections is, of course, one of public safety on the highways, and the general penalty provision applies to commercial vehicles, again with increased fines:

> **84.** (1) No person shall drive or operate or permit the driving or operation upon a highway of a vehicle, a street car or vehicles that in combination are in such a dangerous or unsafe condition as to endanger any person.
>
> (2) Every person who contravenes this section is guilty of an offence and, if the offence was committed by means of a commercial motor vehicle within the meaning of subsection 16(1), on conviction is liable to a fine of not less than $400 and not more that $20,000.[263]

Section 107 of the Act requires operators of commercial vehicles to inspect, repair and maintain their vehicles and trailers, the duty being imposed upon operators to ensure safety and to ensure that drivers of commercial vehicles conduct such safety inspections, and drivers are not to operate the vehicle unless the proper inspection has taken place.

Part VII of the *Highway Traffic Act* specifies the limits on loads and dimensions. In *R. v. Lafarge Canada Inc.*,[264] the Ontario Provincial court dealt with the question of the mental element required for this offence. The corporate accused had been convicted at trial on the basis that the offence of operating an overweight vehicle was one of absolute liability. On appeal, it was held

---

257 Sections 62, 103(3).

258 Section 64.

259 Section 66.

260 Section 103(2).

261 Sections 69, 70.

262 Section 64(9) (S.O. 1996, c. 20, s. 14). Similar provisions exist for violation of other equipment requirements.

263 Subsection (2) was proclaimed in force on October 28, 1996 S.O. 1996, c. 20, s. 19. A new addition to the section, 84(1.1) deems any commercial motor vehicle having one or more critical defects to be "in such dangerous or unsafe condition as to endanger any person," S.O. 1997, c. 12, s. 11, in force Feburary 2, 1998.

264 (1989), 19 M.V.R. (2d) 110 (Ont. Prov. Ct.).

that the offence was one of strict liability designed to ensure safety on the roads within an overall regulatory framework which provided for exemptions to the weight and dimension requirements. The Court also held that the complexity of the regulations made it difficult for transport drivers to understand them. It would be unreasonable to construe the offence as one of absolute liability.[265] The related s. 111 respecting the proper securing and overhanging of loads requires the court to consider various factors, including the nature and positioning of the load, and the nature of the journey undertaken. Thus, the load must be secured in order to negotiate any obstacles that might disturb it.[266]

Similar provisions regarding weight limits are found in Part VIII of the Act. There are detailed requirements concerning various aspects of weight restrictions, including the power for a police officer to require the vehicle to be weighed on reasonable and probable grounds that the weight restrictions are being breached.[267]

Section 122 imposes load limits during certain "reduced load periods", but subsection 122(4) exempts from the application of that section vehicles "operated by or on behalf of a municipality transporting waste."[268] In *R. v. Tricil Ltd.*,[269] the distinction created by the legislation was held to be violative of s. 15 of the *Charter*, since it conferred a benefit on one group of operators simply by virtue of the fact that they were transporting on behalf of the municipality. The charges were stayed in that case. It is not clear that the now well-developed principles guiding the application of the equality provision of the *Charter* (namely that the distinction must apply to a category of actors analogous to or listed in s. 15(1)) could withstand analysis today. Nevertheless, the distinction does seem arbitrary and unfair.[270] The issue has not been litigated further, likely because charges which would bring the distinction to light have not since been laid.

On a charge of being the owner of an overweight vehicle, it is open to the Court to acquit the accused where it is satisfied that the excess weight over the tolerance specified in the regulations was not wholly attributable to the accused. It has been held to be reversible error if the trial judge fails to address that issue, particularly when it is raised by counsel for the accused.[271]

---

265 The appeal was nevertheless dismissed on the basis that the accused had not demonstrated the required due diligence.

266 *Walker-Trowbridge v. D.P.P.*, [1992] R.T.R. 1822 (Div. Ct.).

267 In *R. v. Breau* (1989), 19 M.V.R. (2d) 29 (P.E.I. C.A.), the search provision was held to violate the accused's rights under s. 8 of the *Charter*.

268 Presumably the analysis that follows would also apply to subsection 114(3) — subject probably to some modification of the analysis of constitutional justification.

269 (1989), 16 M.V.R. (2d) 62 (Ont. Prov. Ct.).

270 *R. v. George Smith Transport* (1989), 6 W.C.B. (2d) 259 (Man Q.B.).

271 It is submitted that the judge in *Tricil* should logically have struck down or severed the offending legislation.

The proper characterization of the mental element of weight restriction offences has been the subject of some disagreement. The leading case on the mental element of the weight restrictions in the Act is *R. v. Nickel City Transport (Sudbury) Ltd.*[272] There, the accused was charged with carrying a load on its triple axle in excess of the permissible weight. The Court held that the offence was one of strict liability. Arbour J.A. held that the offence, as written and intended, was one of absolute liability, but that the possibility of imprisonment in default without exceptions for inability to pay made the offence one of strict liability. Tarnopolsky and Grange J.A. held that the offence was simply strict liability.

---

272 (1993), 47 M.V.R. (2d) 20 (Ont. C.A.). See also the annotation by Murray G. Forbes, 47 M.V.R. (2d) 57.

9

Sentencing in Traffic Cases

1. INTRODUCTION

In many cases the most significant stage in the proceedings occurs when the presiding justice or judge sentences the defendant. As the Supreme Court of Canada has observed in the criminal context, "From the offender's point of view, sentencing is the most critical part of the whole process, it is the 'gist of the proceeding.'"[1] In addition, in traffic offence cases, the administrative sanctions attached to a conviction are often equally important to the accused. In this chapter we look at some of the legal issues which arise in relation to the consequences of a conviction for a traffic offence.

A number of sentencing options are available to a justice or judge dealing with a traffic offence charge. These may range from a discharge or suspended sentence to substantial fines and, in extreme cases, imprisonment. While this broad discretion exists, the vast majority of cases will result in relatively modest fines.[2] More substantial fines are reserved for truly serious circumstances or particularly bad offenders; imprisonment is rare.

It is important to distinguish the sentence imposed for a traffic offence from the administrative or regulatory sanctions associated with a finding of guilt. All provincial regimes designed control the use of vehicles and highways include provisions to attach such sanctions to traffic offence convictions.

---

1 *R. v. Gardiner*, [1982] 2 S.C.R. 368 at 406.

2 In Ontario, for example, the *Provincial Offences Act* R.S.O. 1990, c.P.33, s.12, creates a maximum fine for cases where the prosecution proceeds by under Part I (by ticket, the overwhelming majority of cases) of $500. The availability of some dispositions, such as discharges, will depend on the particular statute: *R. v. Sztuke* (1993), 16 O.R. (3d) 559 (Ont. C.A.). The form and quantum of sentences are always a product of statute.

Indeed, the central purpose of such legislation is to keep bad drivers off the roads.[3] These administrative consequences exist apart from the immediate sentence imposed for a particular traffic offence. They serve to control who drives, and under what limitations. Licence revocations and suspensions serve to withdraw the privilege of driving from road users who have demonstrated — through their traffic offence convictions and otherwise — their inability to do so with an appropriate degree of skill or care.

2. RANGE OF SENTENCE AVAILABLE

The range of sentences available to the trial court is fixed by statute. The range may be fixed by the statute creating the offence, or by a general procedural statute. The available penalties are usually limited by the manner in which the prosecution has been initiated. The *Provincial Offences Act* and the *Highway Traffic Act* in Ontario have general provisions that determine the standard penalty ranges that apply if no specific range of penalties is stated in the section creating the offence. If no specific range is set out in the offence creating statute, the Ontario *Highway Traffic Act* provides that the violation is subject to a fine of not less than $60 and not more than $500.[4] If a person is convicted for an offence committed as a pedestrian, or while in a wheelchair, there is no minimum fine, and the maximum penalty is $50, unless the offence creating provision includes some larger amount.[5]

Where the prosecution has been initiated by certificate under Part I of the Ontario *Provincial Offences Act*, the maximum penalty is set at $500, notwithstanding any other penalty provision related to the offence charged.[6] Similarly, under the Ontario statute, where a set fine is in place and the defendant pleads guilty "with an explanation" on a certificate prosecution, the eventual fine imposed cannot exceed that set out as the set fine on the ticket.[7]

In British Columbia it appears that the fine set out in a ticket represents the maximum fine for that prosecution. This is a function of the wording in the ticket itself and the regulations supporting the process of bringing offenders before the courts using this process. In *R. v. Miner*,[8] the British Columbia Court

---

3 *R. v. Pontes*, 13 M.V.R. (3d) 145 (S.C.C.).
4 Ontario *Highway Traffic Act* s. 214(1).
5 Ontario *Highway Traffic Act* s. 214(2).
6 Ontario *Provincial Offences Act*, s. 12.
7 Ontario *Provincial Offences Act* s. 7, which authorizes the court to "enter a conviction and impose the set fine or such lesser fine as is permitted by law." [Emphasis added].
8 (1997), 32 M.V.R. (3d) 108 (B.C. C.A.); affirming [1996] B.C.J. No. 559 (B.C. S.C.).

of Appeal rejected the Crown's argument that once an accused elected to contest a traffic offence ticket, the penalties available became those in the statute, and not those in the ticket. Mr. Justice Hollinrake observed:[9]

> The position of the Crown in this appeal is that the *Offence Act* regulation which sets out the prescribed fines, is restricted to an offender who is not disputing the violation ticket. The Crown says the Supreme Court judge erred in concluding that s. 8 and s. 78 of the *Offence Act* do not apply to the imposition of fines in a case such as is now before us, that is, where the charge is initiated by a violation ticket.
>
> I agree with the conclusion of the Supreme Court judge that:
>
>> Creating a risk of a much higher fine by establishing the right to dispute a ticket is not an interpretation that is supported by the language, legislative intent or the purpose of the law.
>
>> In the absence of language which would clearly support the position of the Crown, I would be loathe to accede to its submission where the effect of that submission is that the offender is lulled into thinking, by the words of the violation ticket, that insofar as any fine goes, it will be "as prescribed", being $100. In my opinion, the only rationale for not advising the offender that, if disputed, the fine could be higher than the "prescribed fine", is that it was not intended that the fine on unsuccessfully disputing the violation ticket could be other than the prescribed fine shown on the ticket itself.

This does not, however, affect the trial court's powers in respect of a licence suspension.[10]

3. PROCEDURE ON SENTENCING

(a) Introduction

What sentence will be appropriate in a given case will depend on the particular facts giving rise to the charge and the individual circumstances of the offender. Sometimes, however, the evidence on these points will be in conflict. For example, the defendant may plead guilty to careless driving but disagrees with the prosecutor as to what precise form this driving took, or the volume of surrounding pedestrian or vehicle traffic. If the prosecution claims, for example, that there were many school-age children in the area and that the road traffic was busy (facts that would make the offence more serious), these facts must be proved by evidence before the court can consider them in sentencing. In all such cases, the prosecution is obliged to prove beyond a reasonable doubt the facts that it alleges (and which the defence denies) in

---

9 *Ibid.*, at p. 112.
10 *R. v. Mordo* (1997), 30 M.V.R. (3d) 320 (B.C. C.A.); *R. v. McKinnon* (1997), 30 M.V.R. (3d) 280 (B.C. S.C.).

aggravation.[11] In such a case, the prosecution may rely on evidence that might not otherwise be admissible because it is hearsay or otherwise not normally accepted because it violates some evidentiary rule. The procedure on sentencing hearings is less formal than that at trial. There are, however, some minimal rules.

(b) Submissions by the Parties

Before imposing sentence on any defendant, the trial court must invite both the prosecutor and the defendant to make submission as to the appropriate sentence. Where the defendant is not represented, the trial court must ask the defendant if he has anything to say before sentence is passed.[12] While the failure to invite a defendant or the prosecutor to make submissions is not a fatal error (in that it does not ordinarily effect the validity of the proceedings)[13] a *refusal to hear* submissions from either side should be considered a jurisdictional error. That is, a failure to allow either side to make its case on sentencing is a serious error that a superior court will consider when reviewing the sentence.[14]

(c) Enquiries by the Court

No one is ordinarily required to give information to the court if that information would harm his or her position. That is, the defendant does not have to provide the prosecution with the factual basis for its case on sentencing. However, procedural statutes in traffic offences sometimes specifically provide that the trial court may ask the defendant whatever questions it considers appropriate, including what the defendant's financial circumstances are. The court may even ask that such statements be given under oath. The defendant cannot, however, be forced to answer such questions[15] nor should the court be permitted to draw an adverse inference from an accused's refusal to answer any such question.

If the court wishes to impose a fine that is to be payable 'forthwith' or immediately, it must first be satisfied that the defendant will be able to pay a fine on such terms. Ordering a fine to be payable immediately without an appropriate inquiry or proof of ability to pay is an error in principle that is subject to review and correction on appeal.[16]

---

11 *R. v. Gardiner*, [1982] 2 S.C.R. 368 (S.C.C.); *R. v. Brown* (1991), 30 M.V.R. (2d) 1 (S.C.C.). In the criminal context many of these procedural rules are now codified in Part XXIII of the *Criminal Code*.

12 This is the common law principle of allocutus, codified in various procedural statutes: see s. 57(1) of the Ontario *Provincial Offences Act*, R.S.O. 1990 c. P.33.

13 See, for example, s. 57(2) of the Ontario statute.

14 *R. v. Taillefer* (1978), 3 C.R.(3d) 357 (Ont. C.A.).

15 *Provincial Offences Act*, R.S.O. 1990, c. P.30 s. 57(3).

16 *R. v. Andrews* (1973), 15 C.C.C.(2d) 43 (B.C. S.C.).

(d) Pre-sentence Reports

When making submissions in a difficult case, a defendant or prosecutor may wish to suggest to the justice or judge hearing the case that a pre-sentence report would be helpful. In serious cases the trial court may seek such assistance in the form of a report prepared by a provincial probation officer or other official.[17]

Generally such reports will outline the educational, employment, family and financial background of the offender. They will usually reveal, for example, if the offender will suffer some special hardship if a substantial fine is imposed, or if a discretionary licence suspension would have a particular impact on the offender. If something negative appears in the pre-sentence report with which the offender disagrees, the offender should put this disagreement on the record before the court. Once this is done the onus is on the prosecutor to prove the fact with evidence if it intends to rely on it as an aggravating factor in its submissions to the court.[18]

A pre-sentence report should not attempt to set out the facts of the offence, as these may be in dispute,[19] nor should the report recommend a specific sentence (though this is a common error).[20] Rather the report should put before the judge the facts related to the offender and any circumstances that might be of interest to the sentencing court.

(e) Sentencing Procedure and Ontario's *Provincial Offences Act*

In Ontario, the province's *Provincial Offences Act*[21] provides a statutory regime to govern the process by which a fit sentence is determined. Sections 56 to 70 deal with the imposition and enforcement of sentence, setting out:

1. The circumstances under which a pre-sentence report might be ordered by the court (s. 56);

2. The right of the parties, prosecution and defence, to make submissions as to penalty (s. 57(1));

3. The potential for fines less than prescribed "minimum" fines (s. 59);

---

17 In Ontario if the proceding was initiated by information (Part III) the trial court upon convicting the defendant, may direct a probation officer to prepared and file such a report with the court (*Provincial Offences Act*, R.S.O. 1990, c. P.33, s. 56(1)). The prosecutor and the defendant (or his or her representative) will automatically receive copies of such reports (s. 56(2)).

18 *R. v. Gardiner*, [1982] 2 S.C.R. 368 (S.C.C.); *R. v. Pindar*, [1923] 2 W.W.R. 997 (Alta. C.A.).

19 *R. v. Martell* (1984), 48 Nfld. & P.E.I.R. 79 (P.E.I. C.A.).

20 *R. v. Bernier* (1978), 5 C.R. (3d) 385 (Que. C.A.).

21 *Provincial Offences Act*, R.S.O. 1990, c. P.33 (as amended by: 1992, c. 20, s. 1; 1993, c. 27, Sched.; 1993, c. 31, s. 1; 1994, c. 10, s. 23; 1994, c. 17, ss. 130, 131; 1994, c. 27, s. 52; 1995, c. 6, s. 7.).

4. The authority of the Court to make inquiries as to the defendant's ability to pay a fine (s. 57(2));

5. The place of pre-trial custody in the calculation of a sentence (s. 58);

6. The ordering of costs against a convicted defendant (s. 60);

7. The calculation, imposition, and disposition of "victim fine surcharges" intended to assist victims of crime (s. 60.1);

8. The calculation of sentences and the service thereof (ss. 63, 64);

9. The enforcement of fines (ss. 63 to 70).

4. DETERMINING THE FIT SENTENCE

(a) Generally

The vast majority of traffic offence convictions will result in fines being imposed (with driving licence suspensions being imposed in some cases). When assessing the amount or "quantum" of the fine to be imposed in a particular case, the court will be primarily concerned with the gravity of the offence and the character of the offender.

A fine should be within the offender's financial means.[22] The offender should not be ordered to pay a fine in an amount that would cause undue financial hardship to him or her.[23] Nor should the court order payment of the fine within so short a time as would be unfair or cause hardship.[24] As the Ontario Court of Appeal observed in *Ward*, where a fine is an appropriate penalty, a fine of such magnitude should not be imposed, that having regard to the means of the offender, it cannot be paid within a reasonable time.[25]

The fine imposed should not, however, punish an offender for being wealthy.[26] The correct approach is to fix the appropriate amount of the fine based on the seriousness of the offence and the offender's record. Once this is done, the court is to consider the "economic circumstances" of the offender and, if appropriate adjust the fine downward.[27] Thus, it is not normally open to the prosecution to prove that the offender has some special capacity to pay an unusually high fine, though the prosecutor may attempt to disprove any claim made by the defendant to financial hardship by proving the offenders financial circumstances.

---

22 Section 57(1) of the Ontario *Provincial Offences Act* which mandates inquiries into an offender's 'economic circumstances'.

23 Consider *R. v. Snider* (1977), 37 C.C.C.(2d) 189 (Ont. C.A.) and *R. v. Rasper* (1978), 1 C.R. (3d) S-45 (Ont. C.A.).

24 *R. v. Andrews* (1973), 15 C.C.C. (2d) 43 (B.C. S.C.).

25 *R. v. Ward* (1980), 56 C.C.C. (2d) 15 (Ont. C.A.) at 18.

26 *R. v. Wells* (1977), 7 C.R. (3d) S-17 (Alta. Dist. Ct.).

27 *R. v. Johnson* (1971), 17 C.R.N.S. 329, (1972), 5 C.C.C. (2d) 541 (N.S. C.A.) and *R. v. Fairbairn* [1981] Crim.L.Rev. 190.

One possible exception to this rule is where the commission of the offence has permitted the offender to earn some profit. If, for example, a trucking company achieved some competitive advantage by the commission of a traffic offence or offences, the court might consider that amount to ensure that the fine did not become a simple 'licence fee' which would encourage the offender and others to commit the same offence for economic benefit.

(b) Factors Relevant to Sentence

A number of factors are relevant to the determination of a fit sentence. In the context of traffic offences, where most offences involve monetary penalties, a number of factors will be relevant to the imposition of a sentence.

(i) *Ability to Pay*

Perhaps the most obvious consideration in the imposition of any monetary sentence is the ability of the offender to pay the fine.

(ii) *Sentence Imposed in Similar Cases (the "Tariff")*

In the context of traffic offences, this consideration is often difficult to determine. While no formal "tariff" normally exists to which reference might easily be made, local practice will often determine a standard or typical fine for common offences. Often this figure will reflect the set fine or fine fixed for settlement of a ticketed offence.

(iii) *Driving and Related Criminal Record*

The principal purpose of a regime of highway traffic control is to prevent or at least minimize poor driving practices by road users. This makes specific and general deterrence important sentencing principles. The need for specific deterence — the deterrence of the particular offender from future offences — will be determined by reference to his or her driving record, and any related criminal record.

(iv) *Personal Circumstances of the Offender*

It is fundamentally important that every sentence imposed be responsive to the circumstances of the particular offender. The offender's circumstances — age, marital status, health, background, future prospects — must be considered by the court in passing sentence. In most traffic offence cases, the imposition of a monetary sentence will not be particularly influenced by these factors — the ability of the offender to pay is the only 'personal circumstance' that will usually be relevant to the fine ultimately imposed.

If, however, a custodial sentence is being considered, then the personal circumstances of the offender become critical. Before imposing a custodial sentence the court must consider these circumstances and balance them against the factors tending to suggest a custodial disposition.

(v) *Aggravating and Mitigating Circumstances Arising from the Offence*

Just as a sentence must be tailored to the circumstances of the offender, so too it must reflect the offence committed by that offender. Courts will routinely consider the seriousness of a driver's misconduct or neglect by reference to a number of factors including:

- the degree of actual harm caused as a result of the offence;
- the potential for harm which the commission of the offence created;
- the presence or degree of subjective intention by the offender;
- the presence or absence of other forms of bad driving conduct (e.g., drinking and driving short of the offence of impaired driving);
- the length of time of the commission of the offence (was the poor driving momentary or did it extend over a substantial period of time?).

(c) **Imposing Less than the Minimum Fine**

While numerous provisions creating traffic offences provide for minimum fines[28] (and in some cases even minimum terms of imprisonment) procedural statutes sometimes permit exceptions from such minimums. These sections, where they exist, authorize a court to depart from the statutory minimums in cases where the court is convinced that the statutory minimum would work an injustice in the particular case.

In Ontario, s. 59 of the *Provincial Offences Act*[29] provides that:

Relief against minimum fine

(2) Although the provision that creates the penalty for an offence prescribes a minimum fine, where in the opinion of the court exceptional circumstances exist

---

28 See s. 59 of the Ontario *Provincial Offences Act* referenced below. The British Columbia *Offences Act* R.S.B.C. 1996 c. 338, s. 88 (1), provides that

Despite any other section of this Act or any other Act, in determining the fine to be imposed on conviction, the justice must consider the means and ability of the defendant to pay the fine, and, if the justice is of the opinion that the defendant is unable to pay the amount of the fine that the justice would otherwise impose, the justice may impose a fine in a lesser amount that the justice considers appropriate,

but goes on in s. 88(2) to provide that, "If a minimum fine is established under the *Motor Vehicle Act* for contravention of a provision of that Act, a justice must not impose under subsection (1) a fine of less than the minimum established.

29 *Provincial Offences Act*, R.S.O. 1990, c. P.33.

so that to impose the minimum fine would be unduly oppressive or otherwise not in the interests of justice, the court may impose a fine that is less than the minimum or suspend the sentence.

Idem, re imprisonment

(3) Where a minimum penalty is prescribed for an offence and the minimum penalty includes imprisonment, the court may, despite the prescribed penalty, impose a fine of not more than $5,000 in lieu of imprisonment.

It is worth noting that s. 59 offers no relief for an offender facing a minimum licence suspension. The court has no power to reduce a licence suspension below the minimum set out in the relevant penalty section. In order to consider something less than the minimum fine, the trial judge must be satisfied, on evidence, that exceptional circumstances exist. The onus is on the offender to demonstrate (on a balance of probabilities) that circumstances exist to warrant a departure from the policy established in the statute, and the imposition of something less than the minimum fine or a fine in lieu of a term of imprisonment.[30] Even if the minimum fine is a substantial one, the court must impose it in the absence of showing circumstances which warrant a departure. Thus, in the case of a trial *in absentia*, even where the fine is a substantial one, the court was obliged to impose the minimum fine (in this case $5,000).[31] The imposition of substantial minimium fines, is not cruel or unusual punishment where this sort of relief is available.[32]

---

30 See *R. v. Jansen* (1983), 10 W.C.B. 24 (Ont. Co. Ct.).

31 *R. v. Shears*, [1997] O.J. No. 3081 (Ont. Gen. Div.) dealing with the substantial minimum fines imposed for breaches of the Ontario *Compulsory Automobile Insurance Act*, R.S.O. 1990, c. C.10, as amended by, among others, S.O. 1997, c. 19 (increasing the minimum fines). (The substantial mimimum fines for the offences related to automobile insurance seem to be intended to keep the fine penalty competative with the cost of insuring a vehicle. As the cost of insurance continues to rise, the possibility of fines less than $5,000 may seem minor when compared to the cost of insurance.).

32 *Ibid.*

Appendix A

Table of Key Highway Traffic Provisions

Table of Key Highway Traffic and Procedural Statutory Provisions

Nature of Statute: Jurisdiction	Highway Traffic Statutes	Provincial Offence Procedure Statute	Speeding Offences	Mandatory Insurance	Careless Driving
British Columbia	*Motor Vehicle Act Highways Act* R.S.B.C. 1996 c. 318	*Offence Act* R.S.B.C. 1996. c. 338	*Motor Vehicle Act* ss. 145-147	*Insurance (Motor Vehicle) Act* R.S.B.C. 1996. c. 231	*Motor Vehicle Act* s. 144
Alberta	*Highway Traffic Act* R.S.A. 1980. c. H-7	*Provincial Offences Procedure Act* S.A. 1988. c. P-21.5	*Highway Traffic Act* ss. 69-75	*Motor Vehicle Administration Act* s. 71(1)(a)	*Highway Traffic Act* s. 123
Saskatchewan	*Highway Traffic Act* S.S. 1986. c. H-3.1	*Summary Offences Procedure Act* R.S.S. c. S-63.1 See also *Traffic Safety Court of Saskatchewan Act* 1988. c. T-19.1	*Highway Traffic Act* ss. 36-41	*Automobile Accident Insurance Act* R.S.S. 1978. c. A-35	*Highway Traffic Act* s. 44(1)
Manitoba	*Highway Traffic Act* C.C.S.M. c. H-60	*Summary Convictions Act* S.M. 1985-6, c. 4 – Chap. S230	*Highway Traffic Act* ss. 95-105	*Highway Traffic Act* s. 226(2)	*Highway Traffic Act* s. 188
Quebec	*Highway Traffic Act* L.R.Q.. c. C-24.1	*Code of Penal Procedure* L.R.Q.. c. C-25.1		*Quebec Highway Safety Code* s. 35	
New Brunswick	*Motor Vehicle Act* R.S.N.B. 1973. c. M-17 *Highway Act* R.S.N.B. 1973. c. H-5	*Provincial Offences Procedure Act* R.S.N.B. 1987. c. P.22 *Summary Convictions Act* R.S.N.B. 1973. c. S-15	*Motor Vehicle Act* ss. 140-146	*Insurance Act* R.S.N.B. 1973. Cl-12. Part VII	*Motor Vehicle Act* s. 346

Table of Key Highway Traffic
and Procedural Statutory Provisions — Cont'd

Nature of Statute: Jurisdiction	Highway Traffic Statutes	Provincial Offence Procedure Statute	Speeding Offences	Mandatory Insurance	Careless Driving
Ontario	*Highway Traffic Act* R.S.O. c. H.8	*Provincial Offences Act* R.S.O. 1990. c. P.33	*Highway Traffic Act* ss. 128-130, 132	*Compulsory Automobile Insurance Act* R.S.O. 1990. c. C.25	*Highway Traffic Act* s. 130
Nova Scotia	*Motor Vehicle Act* R.S.N.S. 1989. c. 293	*Summary Proceedings Act* R.S.N.S. 1989. c. 450	*Motor Vehicle Act* ss. 100-106	*Motor Vehicle Act* s. 13 and *Insurance Act* R.S.N.C. 1989. s. 105	*Motor Vehicle Act* s. 100
Prince Edward Island	*Highway Traffic Act* R.S.P.E.I. 1988. c. H-5	*Summary Proceedings Act* R.S.P.E.I. 1988. c. S-9	*Highway Traffic Act* ss. 176-177	*Highway Traffic Act* Part XI	*Highway Traffic Act* s. 176
Newfoundland	*Highway Traffic Act* R.S.N. 1990. c. H-3	*Summary Proceedings Act* R.S.N. 1990. c. S-30	*Highway Traffic Act* ss. 110-111	*Highway Traffic Act* Part IV	*Highway Traffic Act* s. 110
Yukon Territory	*Motor Vehicles Act* R.S.Y. 1986. c. 118	*Summary Convictions Act* R.S.Y. 1986. c. 164	*Motor Vehicle Act* ss. 117, 131-133	*Motor Vehicle Act* s. 68	*Motor Vehicle Act* s. 179
Northwest Territories	*Motor Vehicle Act* R.S.N.W.T. 1988. c. M-16	*Summary Convictions Procedure Act* R.S.N.W.T. 1988. c. S-15	*Motor Vehicle Act* ss. 169-180	*Insurance Act* R.S.N.W.T. 1988. c. 1-4 Part V "Statutory Conditions"	*Motor Vehicle Act* s. 154(1)

Appendix B

Proceedings Commenced by Certificate of Offence

R.R.O. 1990, REG. 950 [am. O. Reg. 620/91; O. Reg. 8/92; O. Reg. 177/92; O. Reg. 238/92; O. Reg. 284/92; O. Reg. 336/92; O. Reg. 682/92; O. Reg. 9/93; O. Reg. 314/93; O. Reg. 364/93; O. Reg. 365/93; O. Reg. 500/93; O. Reg. 610/93; O. Reg. 687/93; O. Reg. 688/93; O. Reg. 689/93; O. Reg. 36/94; O. Reg. 106/94; O. Reg. 276/94; O. Reg. 307/94; O. Reg. 321/94; O. Reg. 410/94; O. Reg. 411/94; O. Reg. 445/94; O. Reg. 465/94; O. Reg. 495/94; O. Reg. 496/94; O. Reg. 507/94; O. Reg. 511/94; O. Reg. 534/94; O. Reg. 614/94; O. Reg. 786/94; O. Reg. 30/95; O. Reg. 91/95; O. Reg. 430/95; O. Reg. 509/95; O. Reg. 485/96; O. Reg. 511/96; O. Reg. 109/97; O. Reg. 180/97; O. Reg. 234/97; O. Reg. 344/97; O. Reg. 536/97; O. Reg. 148/98; O. Reg. 240/98; O. Reg. 241/98.]

Certificate of Offence

ICON
LOCATION
CODE

OFFENCE
NUMBER
N°
D'INFRACTION

FORM 1 PROVINCIAL OFFENCES ACT   ONTARIO COURT (PROVINCIAL DIVISION)
FORMULE 1 LOI SUR LES INFRACTIONS PROVINCIALES   COUR DE L'ONTARIO (DIVISION PROVINCIALE)

CERTIFICATE OF OFFENCE/*PROCÈS-VERBAL D'INFRACTION*

I _____ BELIEVE AND CERTIFY THAT
JE SOUSSIGNÉ(E)   (PRINT NAME/NOM EN LETTRES MOULÉES)   CROIS ET ATTESTE QUE

ON THE _____ DAY OF _____ 19 ___ TIME _____ | M |
LE   JOUR DE   À (HEURE)

NAME _____
NOM   FAMILY/NOM DE FAMILLE   GIVEN/PRÉNOM   INITIALS/INITIALES

ADDRESS _____
ADRESSE   NUMBER AND STREET/N° ET RUE

MUNICIPALITY/MUNICIPALITÉ   P.O./C.P.   PROVINCE   POSTAL CODE/CODE POSTAL

AT/À _____

DID COMMIT THE OFFENCE OF: MUNICIPALITY / MUNICIPALITÉ
A COMMIS L'INFRACTION SUIVANTE : _____

_____

_____

_____

_____

CONTRARY TO:
CONTRAIREMENT À _____

_____ SECT./ART. _____

DRIVER'S LICENCE NO./NUMÉRO DE PERMIS DE CONDUIRE | CVOR/CVU | □

SEX   BIRTHDATE/DATE DE NAISSANCE   MOTOR VEHICLE INVOLVED   PLATE NUMBER   PROVINCE
SEXE D/J   M/M   Y/A   VÉHICULE IMPLIQUÉ   N° DE PLAQUE D'IMMATRICULATION
                        □ YES □ NO
                        OUI   NON

AND I FURTHER CERTIFY THAT I SERVED AN   JE CERTIFIE EN OUTRE QUE J'AI SIGNIFIÉ UN
OFFENCE NOTICE   **AVIS D'INFRACTION**
PERSONALLY UPON THE PERSON CHARGED ON THE OFFENCE DATE /EN MAINS PROPRES À L'ACCUSÉ(E) LE JOUR DE L'INFRACTION

SIGNATURE OF ISSUING PROVINCIAL OFFENCES OFFICER   OFFICER NO.   PLATOON   UNIT
SIGNATURE DE L'AGENT DES INFRACTIONS PROVINCIALES   AGENT N°   PELOTON   UNITÉ

SIGNATURE OF PERSON CHARGED (OPTIONAL)/SIGNATURE DE L'ACCUSÉ(E) (FACULTATIF)

SET FINE (INCLUDING COSTS)   TOTAL PAYABLE/SOMME TOTALE À PAYER
AMENDE FIXÉE (Y COMPRIS LES FRAIS) $ $

SUMMONS ISSUED FOR/ASSIGNATION DÉLIVRÉE POUR   CT.ROOM CODE
                                                SALLE
                                                D'AUDIENCE
                                                   | M |
THE _____ DAY OF _____ 19 ___ AT _____
LE   JOUR DE   À (HEURE)

ONTARIO COURT (PROVINCIAL DIVISION) AT/*COUR DE L'ONTARIO (DIVISION PROVINCIALE) À*

CONVICTION ENTERED/DÉCLARATION DE CULPABILITÉ INSCRITE DATE   D/J   M/M   Y/A
SET FINE IMPOSED
AMENDE FIXÉE IMPOSÉE

                          C.V.O.R. NUMBER (COMMERCIAL VEHICLES ONLY)
                          N° DE L'ICVU (VÉHICULES UTILITAIRES SEULEMENT)

JUSTICE/JUGE

Photo-Radar Certificate of Offence

ONTARIO COURT (PROVINCIAL DIVISION), PROVINCE OF ONTARIO
COUR DE L'ONTARIO (DIVISION PROVINCIALE), PROVINCE DE L'ONTARIO

OFFENCE NO./N° DE L'INFRACTION

FILING DATE/DATE DE DÉPÔT

PHOTO-RADAR CERTIFICATE OF OFFENCE
PROCÈS-VERBAL D'INFRACTION CONSTATÉE
PAR RADAR PHOTOGRAPHIQUE

FORM / FORMULE 2, O. REG./RÉGL. O. 950
PROVINCIAL OFFENCES ACT / LOI SUR LES INFRACTIONS PROVINCIALES

I, ..., believe and certify that
I have viewed the photographic equivalent of a photograph recorded on
roll . . . . frame . . . ., that was obtained through
the use of a prescribed photo-radar system, and I have determined that the motor
vehicle shown therein bears the number plate . . . . and that
it indicates the rate of speed at which the motor vehicle was being driven was
. . . . kilometres per hour when photographed on the . . . . day
of . . . . 19 . . . . at . . . . a.m./p.m.,
and that (Name) . . . .
(Address) . . . .
was the owner of the motor vehicle bearing number plate . . . .
on the date of offence, as recorded with the Ministry of Transportation and shown
in the appended certificate, and on that date the owner did commit the offence of
speeding at or near
(Location) . . . .
(Municipality) . . . .
(Speed Limit) . . . . (Rate of Speed of Vehicle) . . . .
I hereby committing an offence contrary to section 128 and pursuant to section 207
of the *Highway Traffic Act.*
Date of Issue: . . . .
Signature of Issuing Officer: . . . . Officer No.: . . . .
Enforcement Agency: . . . .
Set Fine (including costs) $ . . . .
TOTAL PAYABLE

CERTIFICATE OF QUALIFIED OPERATOR

I, ..., a qualified operator
of the prescribed photo-radar system described herein, certify that I was
operating a . . . . (make and model of machine) on
the . . . . day of . . . . . 19 . . . between . . . . a.m./p.m. and . . . . a.m./p.m.
at or near (location) . . . . in the
municipality/township of . . . .
and that the above system was tested by me in accordance with manufacturer's
specifications prior to and at the conclusion of my operation of the system at
the above noted time, date and location, and found to be in proper working
order, and that this system recorded the speed of, and photographed vehicles
at the date and place set out herein, commencing with roll number . . . . .
frame . . . . and ending with frame . . . .
and that the speed limit at that location on that date was . . . .
kilometres per hour.
Signature of System Operator: . . . .
Date: . . . .
Operator No.: . . . .
Enforcement Agency: . . . .

I certify that I have mailed Offence Notice No. . . . .
to the defendant on . . . .
at the address of the defendant as recorded with the Ministry of Transportation.
Signature of Issuing Officer: . . . .
Officer No.: . . . . Agency: . . . .

CERTIFICATE OF OWNERSHIP

To be inserted or appended.

Je, soussigné(e) . . . ., crois et atteste avoir
vu l'équivalent photographique d'une photographie enregistrée sur le rouleau
. . . . et la photogramme . . . . qui a été obtenu au moyen d'un système
de radar photographique prescrit, et j'ai déterminé que le véhicule automobile qui
y apparaît porte la plaque d'immatriculation . . . .
et qu'il indique que la vitesse à laquelle le véhicule automobile roulait était
de . . . .
kilomètres/heure lorsqu'il a été photographié le . . . . 19. . .
à . . . . (heure), et que (nom) . . . .
(adresse) . . . . était le propriétaire
du véhicule automobile portant la plaque d'immatriculation . . . .
le jour de l'infraction, comme il a été enregistré auprès du ministère des Transports
et comme il ressort du certificat ci-joint, et à cette date, le propriétaire a effectivement
commis une infraction d'excès de vitesse à
(lieu) . . . .
(municipalité) . . . .
(limite de vitesse) . . . . (vitesse du véhicule) . . . .
ou près de cet endroit commettant ainsi une infraction, contrairement à l'art. 128
et conformément à l'art. 207 du Code de la route.
Date d'émission : . . . .
Signature de l'agent de police émetteur : . . . .
N° de l'agent de police . . . .
Organisme chargé de l'exécution . . . .
Amende fixée (y compris les frais) . . . . $
MONTANT TOTAL EXIGIBLE

CERTIFICAT DE L'OPÉRATEUR QUALIFIÉ

Je, soussigné(e) . . . ., opérateur qualifié
du système de radar photographique prescrit, atteste que je faisais
fonctionner . . . . (marque et modèle de machine)
le . . . . . jour de . . . . . 19 . . . . entre . . . . . heure(s) et . . . . . heure(s)
dans la municipalité/canton de . . . .
que j'ai vérifié le système ci-dessus, conformément aux normes du fabricant,
avant et après l'utilisation du système à l'heure, à la date et au lieu indiqués
ci-dessus et qu'il a été jugé en bon état de fonctionnement. En outre, j'atteste
que ce système a enregistré la vitesse et a photographié des véhicules
automobiles, à la date et au lieu indiqués ci-dessus sur le rouleau numéro
. . . . photogramme . . . . jusqu'au
photogramme . . . . et que la limite de vitesse en ce lieu et
à cette date était de . . . . kilomètres/heure.
Signature de l'opérateur du système : . . . .
Date : . . . .
N° de l'opérateur : . . . .
Organisme chargé de l'exécution : . . . .

J'atteste que j'ai expédié par courrier l'avis d'infraction n° . . . .
au défendeur, le . . . . à l'adresse
du défendeur qui est enregistrée auprès du ministère des Transports.
Signature de l'agent de police émetteur : . . . .
N° de l'agent de police . . . . Organisme . . . .

CERTIFICAT DE PROPRIÉTÉ

Le certificat peut-être inséré ici ou annexé.

CONVICTION ENTERED / SET FINE IMPOSED

. . . .
Justice/Judge   Date   D M Y
CD 0817 (06/94)

DÉCLARATION DE CULPABILITÉ INSCRITE / AMENDE IMPOSÉE

. . . .
Juge   Date   J M A

Offence Notice

```
ICON                    OFFENCE
LOCATION                NUMBER
CODE                    N°
                        D'INFRACTION
```

FORM 3 PROVINCIAL OFFENCES ACT ONTARIO COURT (PROVINCIAL DIVISION)
FORMULE 3 LOI SUR LES INFRACTIONS PROVINCIALES COUR DE L'ONTARIO (DIVISION PROVINCIALE)

OFFENCE NOTICE / *AVIS D'INFRACTION*

BELIEVES AND CERTIFIES THAT
CROIT ET ATTESTE QUE

```
ON THE          DAY OF
LE              JOUR DE                              19      TIME            [  ] M
                                                            À (HEURE)
NAME
NOM             FAMILY/NOM DE FAMILLE       GIVEN/PRÉNOM        INITIALS/INITIALES
ADDRESS
ADRESSE
                                        NUMBER AND STREET/N° ET RUE

        MUNICIPALITY/MUNICIPALITÉ      P.O./C.P      PROVINCE        POSTAL CODE/CODE POSTAL
AT/À
```

DID COMMIT THE OFFENCE OF: MUNICIPALITY / *MUNICIPALITÉ*
A COMMIS L'INFRACTION SUIVANTE :

CONTRARY TO:
CONTRAIREMENT À :

```
                                                    SECT./ART
DRIVER'S LICENCE NO./NUMERO DE PERMIS DE CONDUIRE
                                                                        CVOR/CVU
                                                                        [  ]

SEX   BIRTHDATE/DATE DE NAISSANCE  MOTOR VEHICLE INVOLVED    PLATE NUMBER
SEXE  D/J   M/M   Y/A              VÉHICULE IMPLIQUÉ      N° DE PLAQUE D'IMMATRICULATION   PROVINCE
                                   [ ] YES  [ ] NO
                                       OUI      NON
```

I BELIEVE AND CERTIFY THAT THE ABOVE OFFENCE HAS BEEN COMMITTED.
JE CROIS ET ATTESTE QUE L'INFRACTION CI-DESSUS A ÉTÉ COMMISE.

```
SIGNATURE OF ISSUING PROVINCIAL OFFENCES OFFICER
SIGNATURE DE L'AGENT DES INFRACTIONS PROVINCIALES    OFFICER NO   PLATOON   UNIT
                                                     AGENT N°     PELOTON   UNITÉ


        SIGNATURE OF PERSON CHARGED (OPTIONAL)/SIGNATURE DE L'ACCUSÉ(E) (FACULTATIF)

        SET FINE  (INCLUDING COSTS)      TOTAL PAYABLE/SOMME TOTALE À PAYER
        AMENDE FIXÉE (Y COMPRIS LES FRAIS)   $                      $
```

SUMMONS ISSUED FOR/ASSIGNATION DÉLIVRÉE POUR

```
                                                        CT ROOM/CODE
                                                        SALLE
THE       DAY OF                                    M   D'AUDIENCE
LE        JOUR DE              19          AT
                                           À (HEURE)
ONTARIO COURT (PROVINCIAL DIVISION) AT/COUR DE L'ONTARIO (DIVISION PROVINCIALE) À
```

Certificate of Offence (cont'd)

IMPORTANT - PLEASE READ CAREFULLY - WITHIN 15 DAYS OF RECEIVING THIS NOTICE, CHOOSE ONE OF THE FOLLOWING OPTIONS. COMPLETE THE SELECTED OPTION (SIGN WHERE NECESSARY) AND DELIVER IT (AND PAYMENT WHERE APPLICABLE) TO THE ADDRESS SHOWN ON THE NOTICE. IF YOU FAIL TO EXERCISE YOUR CHOICE WITHIN THE 15 DAY PERIOD, OR IF YOU DO NOT APPEAR FOR TRIAL, YOU WILL BE DEEMED NOT TO WISH TO DISPUTE THE CHARGE, AND A JUSTICE MAY ENTER A CONVICTION IN YOUR ABSENCE. UPON CONVICTION YOU WILL BE REQUIRED TO PAY THE SET FINE PLUS COURT COSTS, AN ADMINISTRATIVE FEE IS PAYABLE IF THE FINE GOES INTO DEFAULT, AND THE INFORMATION MAY BE PROVIDED TO A CREDIT BUREAU.

IMPORTANT – VEUILLEZ LIRE ATTENTIVEMENT – DANS LES QUINZE JOURS QUI SUIVENT LA DATE À LAQUELLE VOUS RECEVEZ LE PRÉSENT AVIS, CHOISISSEZ L'UNE DES OPTIONS SUIVANTES. REMPLISSEZ L'OPTION CHOISIE (SIGNEZ LÀ OÙ C'EST NÉCESSAIRE) ET REMETTEZ L'AVIS (AVEC VOTRE PAIEMENT, LE CAS ÉCHÉANT) À L'ADRESSE INDIQUÉE SUR L'AVIS. SI VOUS N'EXERCEZ PAS VOTRE CHOIX DANS LES QUINZE JOURS OU SI VOUS NE COMPARAISSEZ PAS, VOUS SEREZ RÉPUTÉ(E) NE PAS VOULOIR CONTESTER L'ACCUSATION ET UN JUGE POURRA INSCRIRE UNE DÉCLARATION DE CULPABILITÉ EN VOTRE ABSENCE. AUQUEL CAS VOUS SEREZ TENU(E) DE PAYER L'AMENDE FIXÉE AINSI QUE LES FRAIS JUDICIAIRES. DES FRAIS ADMINISTRATIFS S'APPLIQUENT EN CAS DE DÉFAUT DE PAIEMENT DE L'AMENDE ET LES RENSEIGNEMENTS PEUVENT ÊTRE COMMUNIQUÉS À UN SERVICE D'INFORMATIONS FINANCIÈRES.

❶ OPTION 1

PLEA OF GUILTY - PAYMENT OUT OF COURT: I PLEAD GUILTY AND PAYMENT OF THE "TOTAL PAYABLE" IS ENCLOSED (FOLLOW THE INSTRUCTIONS ON THE "PAYMENT NOTICE")

PLAIDOYER DE CULPABILITÉ - PAIEMENT À L'AMIABLE : JE PLAIDE COUPABLE ET J'INCLUS LE PAIEMENT DE LA SOMME TOTALE À PAYER (SUIVEZ LES INSTRUCTIONS SUR L'AVIS DE PAIEMENT)

SIGNATURE

CHANGE OF NAME OR ADDRESS IF APPLICABLE/*CHANGEMENT DE NOM DU D'ADRESSE LE CAS ÉCHÉANT*

NAME/*NOM* _____ (PLEASE PRINT/*EN LETTRES MOULÉES*)

ADDRESS/*ADRESSE* _____

LANGUAGE AT TRIAL/*LANGUE AU PROCÈS :*
I REQUEST MY TRIAL TO BE HELD IN THE / *JE DEMANDE QUE MON PROCÈS SOIT TENU :*
☐ ENGLISH LANGUAGE/*EN ANGLAIS*   OR/*OU*   ☐ FRENCH LANGUAGE/*EN FRANÇAIS*

❷ OPTION 2

PLEAD GUILTY WITH AN EXPLANATION: ATTEND THE COURT OFFICE SHOWN BELOW (OPTION 2) WITHIN THE TIMES AND DAYS SHOWN. YOU MUST BRING THIS NOTICE WITH YOU.

PLAIDOYER DE CULPABILITÉ ACCOMPAGNÉ D'UNE EXPLICATION: PRÉSENTEZ-VOUS AU GREFFE INDIQUÉ CI-DESSOUS, DURANT LES HEURES ET LES JOURS INDIQUÉS. VOUS DEVEZ APPORTER LE PRÉSENT AVIS AVEC VOUS.

DEMANDE DE PROCÈS

ONTARIO COURT (PROVINCIAL DIVISION) | COUR DE L'ONTARIO (DIVISION PROVINCIALE)

❸ OPTION 3: TRIAL OPTION

NOTICE OF INTENTION TO APPEAR IN COURT:
1. I INTEND TO APPEAR IN COURT TO ENTER A PLEA AT THE TIME AND DATE SET FOR TRIAL.
2. I INTEND TO CHALLENGE THE EVIDENCE OF THE PROVINCIAL OFFENCES OFFICER.
☐ NO   ☐ YES

NOTE: IF YOU INDICATE "NO" ABOVE, THE OFFICER MAY NOT ATTEND AND THE PROSECUTOR MAY RELY ON CERTIFIED STATEMENTS AS EVIDENCE AGAINST YOU.

AVIS D'INTENTION DE COMPARAÎTRE :
1. *J'AI L'INTENTION DE COMPARAÎTRE POUR INSCRIRE UN PLAIDOYER AUX DATE ET HEURE FIXÉES POUR LE PROCÈS.*
2. *J'AI L'INTENTION DE CONTESTER LA PREUVE DE L'AGENT DES INFRACTIONS PROVINCIALES.*
☐ NON   ☐ OUI

NOTE : SI VOUS COCHEZ LA CASE «NON» CI-DESSUS, IL SE PEUT QUE L'AGENT NE SOIT PAS PRÉSENT ET QUE LE POURSUIVANT S'APPLIQUE SUR LES DÉCLARATIONS CERTIFIÉES POUR PROUVER VOTRE CULPABILITÉ.

SIGNATURE

Offence Notice

ICON
LOCATION
CODE

OFFENCE
NUMBER
N°
D'INFRACTION

FORM 4 PROVINCIAL OFFENCES ACT   ONTARIO COURT (PROVINCIAL DIVISION)
FORMULE 4 LOI SUR LES INFRACTIONS PROVINCIALES   COUR DE L'ONTARIO (DIVISION PROVINCIALE)

OFFENCE NOTICE/*AVIS D'INFRACTION*

BELIEVES AND CERTIFIES THAT
CROIT ET ATTESTE QUE

| ON THE *LE* | DAY OF *JOUR DE* | 19 | TIME *À (HEURE)* | | M |

NAME
NOM   FAMILY/*NOM DE FAMILLE*   GIVEN/*PRÉNOM*   INITIALS/*INITIALES*

ADDRESS
ADRESSE   NUMBER AND STREET/*N° ET RUE*

MUNICIPALITY/*MUNICIPALITÉ*   P.D./C.P.   PROVINCE   POSTAL CODE/*CODE POSTAL*

AT/*À*

DID COMMIT THE OFFENCE OF: MUNICIPALITY / *MUNICIPALITÉ*
A COMMIS L'INFRACTION SUIVANTE :

CONTRARY TO:
CONTRAIREMENT À :

SECT./*ART.*

DRIVER'S LICENCE NO./*NUMÉRO DE PERMIS DE CONDUIRE*   C/*N./C/N.*

| SEX *SEXE* | BIRTHDATE/*DATE DE NAISSANCE* D/J   M/M   Y/A | MOTOR VEHICLE INVOLVED *VÉHICULE IMPLIQUÉ* ☐ YES *OUI* ☐ NO *NON* | PLATE NUMBER *N° DE PLAQUE D'IMMATRICULATION* | PROVINCE |

I BELIEVE AND CERTIFY THAT THE ABOVE OFFENCE HAS BEEN COMMITTED.
JE CROIS ET ATTESTE QUE L'INFRACTION CI-DESSUS A ÉTÉ COMMISE.

| SIGNATURE OF ISSUING PROVINCIAL OFFENCES OFFICER *SIGNATURE DE L'AGENT DES INFRACTIONS PROVINCIALES* | OFFICER NO. *AGENT N°* | PLATOON *PELOTON* | UNIT *UNITÉ* |

SIGNATURE OF PERSON CHARGED (OPTIONAL)/*SIGNATURE DE L'ACCUSÉ(E) (FACULTATIF)*

| SET FINE (INCLUDING COSTS) *AMENDE FIXÉE (Y COMPRIS LES FRAIS)* $ | TOTAL PAYABLE/*SOMME TOTALE À PAYER* $ |

SUMMONS ISSUED FOR/*ASSIGNATION DÉLIVRÉE POUR*   CT.ROOM *SALLE D'AUDIENCE* CODE

M

| THE *LE* | DAY OF *JOUR DE* | 19 | AT *À (HEURE)* |

ONTARIO COURT (PROVINCIAL DIVISION) AT/*COUR DE L'ONTARIO (DIVISION PROVINCIALE) À*

Offence Notice (cont'd)

IMPORTANT - PLEASE READ CAREFULLY - WITHIN 15 DAYS OF RECEIVING THIS NOTICE, CHOOSE ONE OF THE FOLLOWING OPTIONS. COMPLETE THE SELECTED OPTION (SIGN WHERE NECESSARY) AND DELIVER IT (AND PAYMENT WHERE APPLICABLE) TO THE ADDRESS SHOWN ON THE NOTICE. **IF YOU FAIL TO EXERCISE YOUR CHOICE WITHIN THE 15 DAY PERIOD, OR IF YOU DO NOT APPEAR FOR TRIAL, YOU WILL BE DEEMED NOT TO WISH TO DISPUTE THE CHARGE, AND A JUSTICE MAY ENTER A CONVICTION IN YOUR ABSENCE.** UPON CONVICTION YOU WILL BE REQUIRED TO PAY THE SET FINE PLUS COURT COSTS. AN ADMINISTRATIVE FEE IS PAYABLE IF THE FINE GOES INTO DEFAULT, AND THE INFORMATION MAY BE PROVIDED TO A CREDIT BUREAU.

❶ OPTION 1 - PLEA OF GUILTY - PAYMENT OUT OF COURT: PLEA GUILTY AND PAYMENT OF THE "TOTAL PAYABLE" IS ENCLOSED (FOLLOW THE INSTRUCTIONS ON THE "PAYMENT NOTICE").

SIGNATURE _____

❷ OPTION 2 - TO PLEAD GUILTY WITH AN EXPLANATION: ATTEND THE COURT OFFICE WITHIN THE TIMES AND DAYS SHOWN. YOU MUST BRING THIS NOTICE WITH YOU.

❸ OPTION 3 - TRIAL OPTION - DO NOT MAIL
1. YOU OR YOUR AGENT **MUST** ATTEND THE COURT OFFICE IN PERSON WITHIN THE TIMES AND DAYS SHOWN TO FILE A NOTICE OF INTENTION TO APPEAR IN COURT.
2. YOU OR YOUR AGENT MUST BRING THIS NOTICE WITH YOU.
3. **YOU CANNOT SET A TRIAL DATE BY MAIL.**
4. FOR YOUR CONVENIENCE, AND TO SAVE TIME, YOU MAY CALL THE COURT OFFICE IN ADVANCE FOR AN APPOINTMENT.

IMPORTANT - VEUILLEZ LIRE ATTENTIVEMENT - DANS LES QUINZE JOURS QUI SUIVENT LA DATE À LAQUELLE VOUS RECEVEZ LE PRÉSENT AVIS, CHOISISSEZ L'UNE DES OPTIONS SUIVANTES. REMPLISSEZ L'OPTION CHOISIE (SIGNEZ À LA OÙ C'EST NÉCESSAIRE) ET REMETTEZ L'AVIS AVEC VOTRE PAIEMENT, LE CAS ÉCHÉANT) À L'ADRESSE INDIQUÉE SUR L'AVIS. SI VOUS N'EXERCEZ PAS VOTRE CHOIX DANS LES QUINZE JOURS, OU SI VOUS NE COMPARAISSEZ PAS, VOUS SEREZ RÉPUTÉ(E) NE PAS VOULOIR CONTESTER L'ACCUSATION ET UN JUGE POURRA INSCRIRE UNE DÉCLARATION DE CULPABILITÉ EN VOTRE ABSENCE. AUQUEL CAS VOUS SEREZ TENU(E) DE PAYER L'AMENDE FIXÉE AINSI QUE LES FRAIS JUDICIAIRES. DES FRAIS ADMINISTRATIFS S'APPLIQUENT EN CAS DE DÉFAUT DE PAIEMENT DE L'AMENDE ET LES RENSEIGNEMENTS PEUVENT ÊTRE COMMUNIQUÉS À UN SERVICE D'INFORMATIONS FINANCIÈRES.

OPTION 1 - PLAIDOYER DE CULPABILITÉ — PAIEMENT À L'AMIABLE : JE PLAIDE COUPABLE ET J'INCLUS LE PAIEMENT DE LA SOMME TOTALE À PAYER. (SUIVEZ LES INSTRUCTIONS SUR L'AVIS DE PAIEMENT).

SIGNATURE _____

OPTION 2 - PLAIDOYER DE CULPABILITÉ ACCOMPAGNÉ D'UNE EXPLICATION: PRÉSENTEZ-VOUS AU GREFFE, DURANT LES HEURES ET LES JOURS INDIQUÉS. VEUILLEZ APPORTER LE PRÉSENT AVIS AVEC VOUS.

OPTION 3 - DEMANDE DE PROCÈS - NE PAS ENVOYER PAR LA POSTE
1. *VOUS DEVEZ VOUS PRÉSENTER AU GREFFE, EN PERSONNE OU PAR L'INTERMÉDIAIRE D'UN REPRÉSENTANT, DURANT LES HEURES ET LES JOURS INDIQUÉS, POUR DÉPOSER UN AVIS D'INTENTION DE COMPARAÎTRE.*
2. *VOUS OU VOTRE REPRÉSENTANT DEVEZ APPORTER LE PRÉSENT AVIS.*
3. *ON NE PEUT PAS FIXER LA DATE D'UN PROCÈS PAR COURRIER.*
4. *POUR GAGNER DU TEMPS, VOUS POUVEZ APPELER LE GREFFE POUR PRENDRE UN RENDEZ-VOUS.*

Photo-Radar Offence Notice

PHOTO-RADAR OFFENCE NOTICE / AVIS D'INFRACTION CONSTATÉE PAR RADAR PHOTOGRAPHIQUE

FORM/FORMULE 5, O. REG.   RÉGL. O. 950 – PROVINCIAL OFFENCES ACT / LOI SUR LES INFRACTIONS PROVINCIALES

ONTARIO COURT (PROVINCIAL DIVISION)
COUR DE L'ONTARIO (DIVISION PROVINCIALE)

OFFENCE NO./Nº D'AVIS D'INFRACTION

You/Vous

Photograph or equivalent/photographie ou l'équivalent

(Name/Nom): ....

(Address/Adresse): ....

being the owner of a motor vehicle displaying

en tant que propriétaire d'un véhicule automobile qui porte le nº de

Vehicle Number Plate: .... Province: ....

plaque d'immatriculation suivant: .... Province: ....

are charged with the offence of speeding

êtes accusé de l'infraction d'excès de vitesse

on the ... day   of ....,19 ... at .... (a.m./p.m.)

le .... 19 .... à .... (heure)

at or near

à ou près de (lieu): ....

(Location): ....

....

In the Municipality/Township of: ....

Dans la municipalité ou le canton de: ....

Speed limit: ....

Limite de vitesse: ....

Rate of Speed of Motor Vehicle: ....

Vitesse du véhicule automobile: ....

as shown in the photographic equivalent (or photograph) appended, contrary to s. 128 and pursuant to s. 207 of the Highway Traffic Act.

comme le montre l'équivalent photographique (ou la photographie) qui est joint(e), contrairement à l'art. 128 et conformément à l'art. 207 du Code de la route.

Opérateur du système
de radar photographique: .... Nº de l'opérateur: ....

Photo-Radar System Operator: .... Operator No.: ......

I BELIEVE AND CERTIFY THAT THE ABOVE OFFENCE HAS BEEN COMMITTED.

JE CROIS ET J'ATTESTE QUE L'INFRACTION CI-DESSUS A ÉTÉ COMMISE.

Signature of Officer
Issuing this Notice: .... Issuing Officer No.: ......

Signature de l'agent de
police qui émet cet avis: .... Agent émetteur de l'avis: ....

Enforcement Agency: ....

Organisme chargé de l'exécution: ....

DATE OF DEEMED SERVICE: ....

DATE DE SIGNIFICATION RÉPUTÉE: ....

Please Note that Section 207 of the Highway Traffic Act provides that you as owner are liable for this offence even if you were not the driver at the time, subject to limited exceptions. Neither demerit points nor a driver's licence suspension will result from a conviction for this offence.

Please note further: The operator of the photo radar system used in the detection of this offence has certified that he/she is a qualified operator of the prescribed system used on the above noted offence date at the date and location indicated above, and that the system was tested before and after operation at that date and location and found to be in proper working order; and that photographs obtained at that date and location, (which includes the photograph obtained regarding this offence) were recorded by that system, and that the speed limit at that location on that date was as set out above.

Set Fine (including costs)
Amende fixe (y compris les frais)
Total Payable:/Total à payer:

$ .... $

Veuillez noter que l'art. 207 du Code de la route prévoit que vous-même, en tant que propriétaire, êtes responsable de cette infraction, même si vous n'étiez pas le conducteur au moment où celle-ci a été commise, sous réserve de certaines exceptions. Une déclaration de culpabilité pour la présente infraction n'entraînera aucun point d'inaptitude ni la suspension du permis de conduire.

Veuillez aussi noter que l'opérateur du système de radar photographique, utilisé dans la détection de la présente infraction, a attesté qu'il/elle est un(e) opérateur(trice) qualifié(e) du système utilisé à la date de l'infraction et au lieu indiqués ci-dessus, que le système a été vérifié avant et après son utilisation à cette date et en ce lieu et qu'il a été jugé en bon état de fonctionnement. En outre, il/elle a attesté que les photographies obtenues à cette date et en ce lieu (y compris celle qui concerne la présente infraction) ont été enregistrées par ce système, et que la limite de vitesse en ce lieu, à cette date, était la même que celle indiquée ci-dessus.

NOTICE – within 15 days of the date of deemed service shown above, choose one of the options on this Notice. To pay the set fine, please complete Option 3 - Plea of Guilty – on the bottom of this notice and remit payment with the bottom portion of this form to Court address shown. If you do not pay the set fine shown above, or if you do not deliver a Notice of Intention to Appear in court, or if you do not appear for trial, you will be deemed not to wish to dispute the charge and a Conviction may be entered against you. Upon conviction you will be required to pay the Set Fine plus Court Costs. An administrative fee is payable if the fine goes into default and the information may be provided to a credit bureau. Failure to pay the fine imposed upon conviction will result in refusal to issue validation of your vehicle permit or refusal to issue a vehicle permit until the fine and court costs and fees have been paid.

OPTION 1 – TRIAL OPTION: You or your agent must attend the court office within the times and days shown to file a Notice of Intention to Appear in court. You or your agent must bring this notice with you. YOU CAN NOT SET A TRIAL DATE BY MAIL. For your convenience and to save time YOU MAY CALL THE COURT OFFICE IN ADVANCE FOR AN APPOINTMENT. At the time set for your appointment, a prosecutor or an officer will be available to discuss the charge with you or your agent.

(SHOW COURT ADDRESS AND HOURS)

OPTION 2 – TO PLEAD GUILTY WITH AN EXPLANATION: Attend at the court office shown within the times and days shown. You MUST bring this Notice with you.

AVIS – Dans les 15 jours de la signification réputée à la date mentionnée ci-dessus, choisissez l'une des options du présent avis. Pour payer l'amende fixée, remplissez l'option 3 - plaidoyer de culpabilité – au bas du présent avis et remettez le paiement avec la partie inférieure de la présente formule à l'adresse du tribunal indiquée. Si vous ne payez pas l'amende fixée susmentionnée ou si vous ne remettez pas un avis d'intention de comparaître au tribunal ou si vous ne comparaissez pas pour un procès, vous serez réputé(e) ne pas vouloir contester l'accusation et une déclaration de culpabilité pourra être inscrite contre vous. En cas de déclaration de culpabilité, vous serez tenu(e) de payer l'amende fixée plus les frais de justice. Des droits administratifs seront payables s'il y a défaut de paiement de l'amende et cette information pourra être transmise à un service d'informations financières. À défaut de payer l'amende qui vous est imposée en cas de déclaration de culpabilité, il en résultera un refus de délivrer la validation de votre certificat d'immatriculation de véhicule ou un refus de délivrer un certificat d'immatriculation de véhicule tant que l'amende, les frais de justice et les droits judiciaires n'auront pas été payés.

OPTION 1 – CHOIX DE PROCÈS : Vous ou votre représentant devez vous présenter au greffe dans les délais indiqués pour déposer un avis d'intention de comparaître au tribunal. Vous ou votre représentant devez apporter cet avis avec vous. VOUS NE POUVEZ PAS FIXER UNE DATE POUR LE PROCÈS PAR COURRIER. Dans votre intérêt et pour gagner du temps, VOUS POUVEZ TÉLÉPHONER AU GREFFE À L'AVANCE POUR OBTENIR UN RENDEZ-VOUS. Au moment fixé pour votre rendez-vous, un poursuivant ou un agent pourra s'entretenir avec vous ou avec votre représentant, sur l'accusation. (INDIQUEZ L'ADRESSE ET LES HEURES D'OUVERTURE DU TRIBUNAL)

OPTION 2 – PLAIDOYER DE CULPABILITÉ AVEC UNE EXPLICATION : Présentez-vous au greffe du tribunal indiqué dans les délais et aux heures indiqués. Vous DEVEZ apporter cet avis avec vous.

Photo-Radar Offence Notice (cont'd)

COMPLETE AND DETACH THIS PORTION AND SEND WITH PAYMENT
REMPLISSEZ ET DÉCOUPEZ CETTE PORTION ET ENVOYEZ-LA AVEC VOTRE PAIEMENT

OPTION 3 – PLEA OF GUILTY – PAYMENT OUT OF COURT:
I plead guilty and payment of the set fine is enclosed:

Offence Notice No. . . . .

Sign here: . . . .

TO PAY: Write the number of the Offence Notice on the front of your cheque or money order and make it payable to **ONTARIO COURT (PROVINCIAL DIVISION).** Dishonoured cheques will be subject to an administrative charge. Do not send cash, correspondence or post dated cheques in the self-addressed envelope provided. Please allow sufficient time for your payment to be delivered.

**TOTAL PAYABLE
MONTANT TOTAL EXIGIBLE:**

$ . . . . $

OPTION 3 – *PLAIDOYER DE CULPABILITÉ – PAIEMENT HORS COUR :*
Je plaide coupable et le paiement de l'amende fixée est ci-joint.

N° d'avis d'infraction . . . .

Signer ici: . . . .

POUR PAYER : Écrire le numéro d'avis d'infraction au recto de votre chèque ou de votre mandat et libellez-le à l'ordre de la COUR DE L'ONTARIO (DIVISION PROVINCIALE). Les chèques refusés feront l'objet de frais administratifs. N'envoyez pas d'argent comptant ou de chèques par correspondance ni de chèques postdatés dans l'enveloppe-réponse qui est fournie. Veuillez prévoir un délai suffisant pour la livraison de votre paiement.

Name: . . . .
Nom:

Address: . . . .
Adresse:

. . . .

Cheque/Money Order enclosed: ☐   Visa ☐   Mastercard ☐
Chèque ou mandat joint:

Card No.: . . . . Expiry Date: M . . . . Y . . . .
N° de carte :   *Date d'expiration: M*   *A*

Signature of Cardholder: . . . .
Signature du titulaire de la carte.

CD 0818 (06/94)

Summons

ICON
LOCATION
CODE

FORM 8 PROVINCIAL OFFENCES ACT ONTARIO COURT (PROVINCIAL DIVISION)
FORMULE 5 LOI SUR LES INFRACTIONS PROVINCIALES COUR DE L'ONTARIO (DIVISION PROVINCIALE)

SUMMONS/*ASSIGNATION*

BELIEVES AND CERTIFIES THAT
CROIT ET ATTESTE QUE

ON THE / LE   DAY OF / JOUR DE   19   TIME / À (HEURE)   M

NAME / NOM   FAMILY/NOM DE FAMILLE   GIVEN/PRÉNOM   INITIALS/INITIALES

ADDRESS / ADRESSE   NUMBER AND STREET/N° ET RUE

MUNICIPALITY/MUNICIPALITÉ   P O /C P   PROVINCE   POSTAL CODE/CODE POSTAL

AT/A

DID COMMIT THE OFFENCE OF:
A COMMIS L'INFRACTION SUIVANTE: MUNICIPALITY / MUNICIPALITÉ

CONTRARY TO:
CONTRAIREMENT À:

SECT./ART.

DRIVER'S LICENCE NO /NUMERO DE PERMIS DE CONDUIRE   CVOR/CVU

SEX/SEXE   BIRTHDATE/DATE DE NAISSANCE D/J M/M Y/A   MOTOR VEHICLE INVOLVED/VÉHICULE IMPLIQUÉ YES/OUI NO/NON   PLATE NUMBER N° DE PLAQUE D'IMMATRICULATION   PROVINCE

OFFICER NO. AGENT N°   PLATOON PELOTON   UNIT UNITE

THIS IS THEREFORE TO COMMAND YOU IN HER MAJESTY'S NAME TO APPEAR BEFORE THE ONTARIO COURT (PROVINCIAL DIVISION)
POUR CES MOTIFS, ORDRE VOUS EST DONNE, AU NOM DE SA MAJESTÉ, DE COMPARAÎTRE DEVANT LA COUR DE L'ONTARIO (DIVISION PROVINCIALE)

CT.ROOM SALLE D'AUDIENCE   CODE   M

ON THE / LE   DAY OF / JOUR DE   19   AT / À (HEURE)
ONTARIO COURT (PROVINCIAL DIVISION) AT/*COUR DE L'ONTARIO (DIVISION PROVINCIALE) À*

AND TO ATTEND THEREAFTER AS REQUIRED BY THE COURT IN ORDER TO BE DEALT WITH ACCORDING TO LAW. THIS SUMMONS IS SERVED UNDER PART I OF THE PROVINCIAL OFFENCES ACT.
ET D'Y ÊTRE PRÉSENT(E) PAR LA SUITE LORSQUE LE TRIBUNAL L'EXIGERA, DE FAÇON À ÊTRE TRAITÉ(E) SELON LA LOI. CETTE ASSIGNATION VOUS EST SIGNIFIÉE AUX TERMES DE LA PARTIE I DE LA LOI SUR LES INFRACTIONS PROVINCIALES.

SIGNATURE OF PROVINCIAL OFFENCES OFFICER/*SIGNATURE DE L'AGENT DES INFRACTIONS PROVINCIALES*

Notice of Intention to Appear

NOTICE OF INTENTION TO APPEAR
AVIS D'INTENTION DE COMPARAÎTRE

Form/Formule 7
O. Reg./Règl. O. 950

TAKE NOTICE THAT I , _____
SACHEZ QUE JE, SOUSSIGNÉ(E) _____
(defendant's name, current address / nom du défendeur, adresse actuelle)

wish to give notice of my intention to appear in court for the purpose of entering a plea and having a trial respecting the
désire donner un avis d'intention de comparaître au tribunal pour inscrire un plaidoyer et faire instruire la question, en ce qui
charge set out in Offence Notice or Parking Infraction Notice _____
concerne l'accusation décrite dans l'avis d'infraction ou dans l'avis
d'infraction de stationnement   Number/Numéro

FOR ANY OFFENCE OTHER THAN PHOTO RADAR SPEEDING COMPLETE THIS SECTION *POUR TOUTE INFRACTION AUTRE QUE CELLE D'EXCÈS DE VITESSE CONSTATÉE PAR RADAR PHOTOGRAPHIQUE, REMPLISSEZ CETTE PARTIE*	At the trial I intend to challenge the evidence of the provincial offences officer who completed the Certificate of Offence or Certificate of Parking Infraction. *Au procès, j'ai l'intention de contester la preuve de l'agent des infractions provinciales qui a dressé le procès-verbal d'infraction ou le certificat d'infraction de stationnement.*	☐ No /Non ☐ Yes /Oui
FOR A PHOTO-RADAR SPEEDING OFFENCE COMPLETE THIS SECTION. *POUR UNE INFRACTION D'EXCÈS DE VITESSE CONSTATÉE PAR RADAR PHOTOGRAPHIQUE, REMPLISSEZ CETTE PARTIE*	At the trial I intend to challenge the evidence of the photo-radar system operator. *Au procès, j'ai l'intention de contester la preuve de l'opérateur du système de radar photographique.*	☐ No /Non ☐ Yes /Oui

If you indicated above that you do not intend to challenge the evidence of the provincial offences officer or photo-radar system operator, the officer or operator may not attend your trial and the prosecutor may rely on certified statements as evidence against you.

Si vous avez coché la case «non», indiquant que vous n'avez pas l'intention de contester la preuve de l'agent des infractions provinciales ou de l'opérateur du système de radar photographique, l'agent ou l'opérateur peut ne pas se présenter à votre procès, et le poursuivant peut s'appuyer sur des déclarations certifiées à titre de preuve contre vous.

I request my trial to be held in the
Je demande que mon procès soit tenu en
  ☐ English language/*anglais*
  ☐ French language/*français*

I request a _____ language interpreter for the trial.
(leave blank if inapplicable)

Je demande les services d'un interprète de langue _____ *pour le procès.*
(à remplir, le cas échéant)

NOTE: IF YOU FAIL TO APPEAR AT THE TIME AND PLACE SET FOR YOUR TRIAL, YOU WILL BE DEEMED NOT TO DISPUTE THE CHARGE, AND A CONVICTION MAY BE ENTERED AGAINST YOU IN YOUR ABSENCE, WITHOUT FURTHER NOTICE.

REMARQUE : SI VOUS NE COMPARAISSEZ PAS À L'HEURE, À LA DATE ET AU LIEU FIXÉS POUR VOTRE PROCÈS, VOUS SEREZ RÉPUTÉ NE PAS CONTESTER L'ACCUSATION, ET UNE DÉCLARATION DE CULPABILITÉ POURRA ÊTRE ENREGISTRÉE CONTRE VOUS EN VOTRE ABSENCE, SANS AUTRE AVIS.

_____
(signature of defendant or agent / signature du défendeur ou du représentant)

_____
date

CD 0813 (05-94)

Notice of Trial

Notice of Trial/*Avis de procès*

Form/*Formule* 8
O. Reg./*Règl.* O. 950

Offence No. ....
Nº de l'infraction

To:
À

┌   ┐

└   ┘

You are charged with the following offence:/*Vous êtes accusé(e) de l'infraction suivante :*

On the/*Le* .... day of/*jour de* ...., 19 .... at/*à* ...... am/pm/*(heure)* at/*à* ....

.... you did commit the offence of/*vous avez commis l'infraction de*

....

contrary to the/*en contravention à la* ....
statute/*loi*   section/*article*

(Set fine including costs) Total Payable/*(Amende fixée, plus frais de justice) Total à payer* $ _____ $

TAKE NOTICE that on the .... day   AVIS VOUS EST DONNÉ que le .... jour de

of ...., 19 ... , ... ,19 ... ,

at ...... a.m./p.m., your trial will be held at: à .... heure, votre procès sera tenu à

Court Address/*Adresse du tribunal*

This will confirm that you have (chosen to/have chosen not to)   *Ceci confirme que vous avez choisi (de contester/de ne pas contester)*
(delete inapplicable)   *(biffez la mention inutile)*
challenge the evidence of the (Provincial Offences Officer/Photo-   *la preuve de l'agent des infractions provinciales/à l'opérateur du système*
radar system operator).   *de radar photographique.*

Your trial will be held on the date and time noted above at the Ontario   *Votre procès se tiendra à la date et à l'heure indiquées ci-dessus à la Cour de*
Court (Provincial Division) shown. You and your witnesses should   *l'Ontario (Division provinciale) susmentionnée. Vos témoins et vous-même devrez*
be ready for your trial at that time. If you do not appear, you will be   *être prêts pour votre procès à cette date. Si vous ne comparaissez pas, vous serez*
deemed not to dispute the charge and the court may convict you in   *réputé(e) ne pas contester l'accusation, et le tribunal pourra vous déclarer*
your absence without further notice.   *coupable en votre absence, sans autre avis.*

Issued at .... this .... day of .... 19 ....
Décerné à ...... *le* .... *jour de*

OFFICE USE ONLY/*RÉSERVÉ AU GREFFE*

I certify that a copy of this Notice was:	I certify that a copy of this Notice was:	I certify that I have given notice to the (Provincial Offences
J'atteste qu'une copie de cet avis a été	*J'atteste qu'une copie de cet avis a été*	Officer/Photo-radar system operator) of the defendant's
		(delete inapplicable)
☐ sent by mail to defendant	☐ sent by mail to prosecutor	intention to challenge the officer's evidence at trial.
envoyée par courrier au défendeur	*envoyée par courrier au poursuivant*	*J'atteste que j'ai donné un avis à l'agent des infractions*
☐ given personally to defendant	☐ given to prosecutor or agent	*provinciales/à l'opérateur du système de radar*
remise en mains propres au	*donnée au poursuivant ou au représentant*	*photographique), de l'intention du défendeur de contester*
défendeur		*(biffez la mention inutile)*
		la preuve de l'agent au procès.

Clerk / Justice /or Designated Person	Clerk / Justice / or Designated Person	Clerk / Designated Person
Greffier / juge de paix / ou personne désignée	*Greffier / juge de paix / ou personne désignée*	*Greffier / Personne désignée*

Date	Date	Date

Notice of Fine and Due Date

ONTARIO COURT (PROVINCIAL DIVISION)
COUR DE L'ONTARIO (DIVISION PROVINCIALE)

NOTICE OF FINE AND DUE DATE
AVIS D'AMENDE ET DATE D'ÉCHÉANCE

Form/*Formule* 9
O. Reg./*Règl.* O. 950

From/*De* :

To/*À* : (Defendant/*Défendeur*)

You have been convicted of the following Offence:
Vous avez été reconnu coupable de l'infraction suivante:

Offence Number . . . .
Numéro de l'infraction
Offence . . . .
Infraction
Offence Date . . . .
Date de l'infraction
Conviction Date . . . .
Date de la condamnation
Amount Due . . . .
Montant dû
Date Due . . . .
Date d'échéance

The above fine has not been paid. You are required to pay the above amount by the due date. Please note, an administrative fee is payable if the fine goes into default, and the information may be provided to a credit bureau. Costs incurred for any civil enforcement may also be added. Failure to pay the fine imposed upon conviction may also result in refusal to issue validation of your vehicle permit or refusal to issue a vehicle permit or driver's licence suspension until the fine and court costs and fees have been paid. (Driver's licence suspension does not apply to photo-radar speeding offences.)

NOTE: Section 66 of the *Provincial Offences Act* provides that you may apply to the court for an extention of time to pay the fine.

[Insert payment instructions]

L'amende susmentionnée n'a pas été payée. Il vous est enjoint de payer l'amende susmentionnée avant la date d'échéance. Veuillez noter que vous devez payer des droits administratifs, en cas de non-paiement de l'amende, et l'information peut être transmise à un service d'informations financières. Des frais de mesures d'exécution pourront aussi être ajoutés. Le défaut de paiement de l'amende imposée peut également, sur déclaration de culpabilité, entraîner le refus de validation ou d'émission de votre certificat d'immatriculation ou la suspension du permis de conduire, tant que l'amende, les frais de justice et les droits judiciaires n'auront pas été payés. (La suspension du permis de conduire ne s'applique pas aux infractions constatées par radar photographique.)

REMARQUE : L'article 66 de la Loi sur les infractions provinciales prévoit la possibilité de présenter une requête en vue d'obtenir une prorogation du délai de paiement de l'amende.

[Insérez les instructions de paiement]

3. This Regulation comes into force on the day the *Provincial Offences Statute Law Amendment Act, 1993* **comes into force.**

32/94

3. Le présent règlement entre en vigueur le jour de l'entrée en vigueur de la *Loi de 1993 modifiant des lois en ce qui concerne les infractions provinciales.*

Ont. Reg. 786/94, s. 1.

Appendix C

Abbreviated Wording to be Used in the Charging Document

Schedule 43

Highway Traffic Act

PART	ITEM	COLUMN 1	COLUMN 2
II	1.	Drive motor vehicle, no permit	clause 7(1)(a)
Permits	2.	Drive motor vehicle, no currently	
		validated permit	clause 7(1)(a)
	3.	Drive motor vehicle, no plates	clause 7(1)(b)
	4.	Drive motor vehicle, fail to	
		display two plates	clause 7(1)(b)
	5.	Drive motor vehicle, plate	
		improperly displayed	clause 7(1)(b)
	6.	Drive motor vehicle, no vali-	
		dation on plate	clause 7(1)(c)
	7.	Drive motor vehicle, validation	
		improperly affixed	clause 7(1)(c)
	8.	Draw trailer, no permit	clause 7(4)(a)
	9.	Draw trailer, no plate	clause 7(4)(b)
	10.	Draw trailer, plate improperly	
		displayed	clause 7(4)(b)
	11.	Fail to surrender permit for motor	
		vehicle	clause 7(5)(a)
	12.	Fail to surrender permit for trailer	clause 7(5)(b)
	13.	Have more than one permit	subsection 7(15)
	14.	Drive motor vehicle, not in accor-	
		dance with permit limitations	section 8
	15.	Permit driving of motor vehicle,	
		not in accordance with permit	
		limitations	section 8
	16.	Make a false statement	subsection 9(1)
	17.	Fail to notify change of address	subsection 9(2)
	18.	Fail to notify change of name	subsection 9(2)
	19.	Fail to notify change of address-	
		lessee	subsection 9(3)
	20.	Fail to notify change of name-	
		lessee	subsection 9(3)
	21.	Drive motor vehicle, no vehicle	
		identification number	subsection 10(1)
	22.	Permit driving of motor vehicle,	
		no vehicle identification number	subsection 10(1)
	23.	Draw trailer, no identification	
		number	clause 10(2)(a)
	24.	Permit drawing of trailer, no	
		identification number	clause 10(2)(a)

Part	Item	Column 1	Column 2
	25.	Draw conversion unit, no identification number	clause 10(2)(b)
	26.	Permit drawing of conversion unit, no identification number	clause 10(2)(b)
	27.	Draw converter dolly, no identification number	clause 10(2)(c)
	28.	Permit drawing of converter dolly, no identification number	clause 10(2)(c)
	29.	Fail to remove plates on ceasing to be owner	clause 11(1)(a)
	30.	Fail to remove plates on ceasing to be lessee	clause 11(1)(a)
	31.	Fail to retain plate portion of permit	clause 11(1)(b)
	32.	Fail to give vehicle portion of permit to new owner	subclause 11(1)(c)(i)
	33.	Fail to give vehicle portion of permit to lessor	subclause 11(1)(c)(ii)
	34.	Fail to apply for permit on becoming owner	subsection 11(2)
	34.1	Fail to provide valid information package for inspection	subsection 11.1(1)
	34.2	Fail to deliver valid information package at time of vehicle transfer	subsection 11.1(1)
	35.	Deface plate	clause 12(1)(a)
	36.	Deface validation	clause 12(1)(a)
	37.	Alter plate	clause 12(1)(a)
	38.	Alter validation	clause 12(1)(a)
	39.	Deface permit	clause 12(1)(a)
	40.	Alter permit	clause 12(1)(a)
	41.	Use defaced plate	clause 12(1)(b)
	42.	Use defaced validation	clause 12(1)(b)
	43.	Use altered plate	clause 12(1)(b)
	44.	Use altered validation	clause 12(1)(b)
	45.	Permit use of defaced plate	clause 12(1)(b)
	46.	Permit use of defaced validation	clause 12(1)(b)
	47.	Permit use of altered plate	clause 12(1)(b)
	48.	Permit use of altered validation	clause 12(1)(b)
	49.	Use defaced permit	clause 12(1)(b)
	50.	Permit use of defaced permit	clause 12(1)(b)
	51.	Remove plate without authority	clause 12(1)(c)

Part	Item	Column 1	Column 2
	52.	Use plate not authorized for vehicle	clause 12(1)(d)
	53.	Permit use of plate not authorized for vehicle	clause 12(1)(d)
	54.	Use validation not furnished by Ministry	clause 12(1)(e)
	55.	Use validation not furnished for vehicle	clause 12(1)(e)
	56.	Permit use of validation not furnished by Ministry	clause 12(1)(e)
	57.	Permit use of validation not furnished for vehicle	clause 12(1)(e)
	58.	Use plate not in accordance with Act	clause 12(1)(f)
	59.	use plate not in accordance with regulations	clause 12(1)(f)
	60.	Use validation not in accordance with Act	clause 12(1)(f)
	61.	Use validation not in accordance with regulations	clause 12(1)(f)
	62.	Permit use of plate not in accordance with Act	clause 12(1)(f)
	63.	Permit use of plate not in accordance with regulations	clause 12(1)(f)
	64.	Permit use of validation not in accordance with Act	clause 12(1)(f)
	65.	Permit use of validation not in accordance with regulations	clause 12(1)(f)
	66.	Confuse identity of plate	subsection 13(1)
	67.	Obstruct plate	subsection 13(2)
	68.	Dirty plate	subsection 13(2)
	69.	Entire plate not plainly visible	subsection 13(2)
	69.1	Obstruct plate, prevent accurate photograph	subsection 13(3)
	69.2	Obstruct plate preventing identification by stoll system	subsection 13(3.1)
	70.	Operate commercial motor vehicle — no valid CVOR certificate	subsection 16(2)
	71.	Drive commercial motor vehicle — no valid CVOR certificate	subsection 16(2)
	72.	Fail to carry fleet limitation certificate	subsection 16(3)

Part	Item	Column 1	Column 2
	73.	Fail to carry CVOR certificate	clause 16(3)(a)
	74.	Fail to carry vehicle lease	clause 16(3)(b)
	75.	Fail to carry vehicle contract	clause 16(3)(c)
	76.	Fail to surrender CVOR certificate	subsection 16(4)
	77.	Fail to surrender vehicle lease	subsection 16(4)
	78.	Fail to surrender vehicle contract	subsection 16(4)
	79.	Fail to surrender fleet limitation certificate	subsection 16(4)
	80.	Fail to notify change of officer's name	section 18
	81.	Fail to notify change of officer's address	section 18
	82.	Fail to notify change of officers	section 18
	83.	Fail to retain copy of lease or contract	section 20
	83.1	Operate commercial motor vehicle — improper insurance	subsection 23(1)
	83.2	Driver of commercial motor vehicle — fail to carry proof of insurance	subsection 23(3)
	83.3	Driver of commercial motor vehicle — fail to surrender proof of insurance	subsection 23(3)
IV Licences, Driver, Driving Instructor	84.	Drive motor vehicle — no licence	subsection 32(1)
	84.1	Drive commercial motor vehicle — no licence	subsection 32(1)
	85.	Drive motor vehicle — improper licence	subsection 32(1)
	85.1	Drive commercial motor vehicle — improper licence	subsection 32(1)
	86.	Drive streetcar — no licence	subsection 32(2)
	87.	Drive vehicle with air brakes — no endorsement	subsection 32(3)
	87.1	Drive commercial motor vehicle with air brake — no endorsement	subsection 32(3)
	88.	Drive motor vehicle in contravention of conditions	subsection 32(9)
	88.1	Drive commercial motor vehicle in contravention of conditions	subsection 32(9)
	89.	Permit unlicensed person to drive motor vehicle	subsection 32(10)
	89.1	Permit unlicensed person to drive commercial motor vehicle	subsection 32(10)

PART	ITEM	COLUMN 1	COLUMN 2
	90.	Permit person with improper licence to drive motor vehicle	subsection 32(10)
	90.1	Permit person with improper licence to drive commercial motor vehicle	subsection 32(10)
	91.	Permit unlicensed person to drive	subsection 32(10)
	91.1	Permit operation of vehicle with air brakes — no endorsement on licence	subsection 32(11)
	91.2	Permit novice driver to drive in contravention of condition or restriction	subsection 32(11.1)
	92.	Driver fail to surrender licence	subsection 33(1)
	92.1	Accompanying driver fail to surrender licence	subsection 33(2)
	93.	Driver fail to give identification	subsection 33(3)
	93.1	Accompanying driver fail to give identification	subsection 33(3)
	94.	Possess illegal licence	clause 35(1)(a)
	95.	Use illegal licence	clause 35(1)(a)
	96.	Possess non-Photo Card portion of cancelled, revoked or suspended licence	clause 35(1)(b)
	97.	Use non-Photo Card portion of cancelled, revoked or suspended licence	clause 35(1)(b)
	98.	Permit another person to use all or part of licence	clause 35(1)(c)
	98.1	Use other person's licence	clause 35(1)(d)
	98.2	Apply for more than one licence	clause 35(1)(e)
	98.3	Secure more than one licence	clause 35(1)(e)
	98.4	Possess more than one licence	clause 35(1)(e)
	98.5	Fail to surrender suspended, revoked or cancelled licence	clause 35(1)(f)
	99.	Driving under licence of other jurisdiction while suspended in Ontario	section 36
	100.	Employ person under 16 to drive	subsection 37(2)
	101.	Permit person under 16 to drive	subsection 37(2)
	102.	Let unlicensed driver hire vehicle	subsection 39(1)
	103.	Fail to produce licence when hiring vehicle	subsection 39(3)
	104.	Apply for permit while prohibited	subsection 47(5)

PART	ITEM	COLUMN 1	COLUMN 2
	105.	Procure permit while prohibited	subsection 47(5)
	106.	Possess permit while prohibited	subsection 47(5)
	107.	Apply for licence while prohibited	subsection 47(6)
	108.	Procure licence while prohibited	subsection 47(6)
	109.	Possess licence while prohibited	subsection 47(6)
	110.	Procure CVOR certificate while suspended	subsection 47(7)
	111.	Apply for CVOR certificate while suspended	subsection 47(7)
	112.	Operate commercial motor vehicle — fleet limitation certificate not carried	clause 47(8)(a)
	113.	Operate commercial motor vehicle — CVOR certificate suspended	clause 47(8)(b)
	113.1	Novice driver fail to provide breath sample	subsection 48.1(3)
	113.2	Novice driver refuse to provide breath sample	subsection 48.1(3)
	113.3	Novice driver fail to provide breath sample	subsection 48.1(4)
	113.4	Novice driver refuse to provide breath sample	subsection 48.1(4)
	113.5	Novice driver fail to surrender licence	subsection 48.1(5)
	113.6	Accompanying driver fail to provide breath sample	subsection 48.2(2)
	113.7	Accompanying driver refuse to provide breath sample	subsection 48.2(2)
	114.	Operate vehicle for which permit suspended	section 51
	115.	Operate vehicle for which permit cancelled	section 51
	116.	Driving while under suspension	section 53
V Garage and Storage Licences	117.	No licence to operate vehicle business	subsection 59(1)
	118.	Interfere with officer inspecting vehicle business	subsection 59(6)
	119.	Fail to keep records	subsection 60(1)
	120.	Deal with vehicle with vehicle identification number altered	subsection 60(2)
	121.	Deface vehicle identification number	subsection 60(3)

Part	Item	Column 1	Column 2
	122.	Remove vehicle identification number	subsection 60(3)
	123.	Fail to notify re vehicle stored more than 2 weeks	subsection 60(4)
	124.	Fail to report damaged vehicle	subsection 60(5)
	124.1	Give false report	subsection 60(6)
VI Equipment	125.	Drive without proper headlights — motor vehicle	subsection 62(1)
	125.1	Drive without proper headlights — commercial motor vehicle	subsection 62(1)
	126.	Drive without proper rear light — motor vehicle	subsection 62(1)
	126.1	Drive without proper rear light — commercial motor vehicle	subsection 62(1)
	127.	Drive without proper headlight — motorcycle	subsection 62(2)
	128.	Drive without proper rear light — motorcycle	subsection 62(2)
	129.	Drive without proper headlights — motorcycle with sidecar	subsection 62(3)
	130.	Drive without proper rear light — motorcycle with sidecar	subsection 62(3)
	131.	Drive with improper headlights	subsection 62(2)
	131.1	Drive with improper headlights — commercial motor vehicle	subsection 62(6)
	132.	Drive with headlamp coated	subsection 62(7)
	132.1	Drive with headlight coated — commercial motor vehicle	subsection 62(7)
	133.	Drive with headlamp covered	subsection 62(7)
	133.1	Drive with headlamp covered — commercial motor vehicle	subsection 62(7)
	134.	Drive with headlamp modified	subsection 62(7)
	134.1	Drive with headlamp modified — commercial motor vehicle	subsection 62(7)
	135.	More than 4 lighted headlights	subsection 62(9)
	135.1	More than four lighted headlights — commercial motor vehicle	subsection 62(9)
	136.	Improper clearance lights	subsection 62(10)
	136.1	Improper clearance lights — commercial motor vehicle	subsection 62(10)
	137.	Fail to have proper identification lamps	subsection 62(11)

Part	Item	Column 1	Column 2
	137.1	Fail to have proper identification lamps — commercial motor vehicle	subsection 62(11)
	138.	Fail to have proper side marker lamps	subsection 62(13)
	138.1	Fail to have proper side marker lamps — commercial motor vehicle	subsection 62(13)
	139.	Use lamp producing intermittent flashes of red light	subsection 62(14)
	139.1	Use lamp producing intermittent flashes of red light — commercial motor vehicle	subsection 62(14)
	140.	Red light at front	subsection 62(15)
	140.1	Red light at front — commercial motor vehicle	subsection 62(15)
	141.	Use V.F.F. lamp improperly	subsection 62(16)
	141.1	Use V.F.F. lamp improperly — commercial motor vehicle	subsection 62(16.1)
	142.	Improper bicycle lighting	subsection 62(17)
	143.	Improper lighting on motor assisted bicycle	subsection 62(17)
	144.	Improper number plate light	subsection 62(19)
	145.	Use parking light while vehicle in motion	subsection 62(20)
	146.	Have more than one spotlamp	subsection 62(22)
	146.1	Have more than one spotlamp — commercial motor vehicle	subsection 62(22)
	147.	Improper use of spotlamp	subsection 62(22)
	147.1	Improper use of spotlamp — commercial motor vehicle	subsection 62(22)
	148.	Improper lights on traction engine	subsection 62(23)
	149.	No red light on rear of trailer	subsection 62(24)
	149.1	No red light on rear of trailer — commercial motor vehicle	subsection 62(24)
	150.	No red light on rear of object	subsection 62(24)
	150.1	No red light on rear of object — commercial motor vehicle	subsection 62(24)
	151.	No proper red lights — object over 2.6 m	subsection 62(25)
	151.1	No proper red light — object over 2.6m — commercial motor vehicle	subsection 62(25)
	152.	No lamp on left side	subsection 62(26)

PART	ITEM	COLUMN 1	COLUMN 2
	152.1	No lamp on left side — commercial motor vehicle	subsection 62(26)
	153.	Improper lights on farm vehicle	subsection 62(27)
	154.	No directional signals	subsection 62(29)
	154.1	No directional signals — commercial motor vehicle	subsection 62(29)
	155.	No brake lights	subsection 62(29)
	155.1	No brake lights — commercial motor vehicle	subsection 62(29)
	156.	No blue flashing light on snow removal vehicle	subsection 62(31)
	157.	Improper use of blue flashing light	subsection 62(32)
	158.	No sign — "right hand drive vehicle"	section 63
	159.	Improper braking system	subsection 64(1)
	159.1	Improper braking system — commercial motor vehicle	subsection 64(1)
	160.	Improper brakes on motorcycle	subsection 64(2)
	161.	Improper brakes on motor assisted bicycle	subsection 64(2)
	161.1	Improper brakes on bicycle	subsection 64(3)
	162.	Improper brakes on trailer	subsection 64(5)
	162.1	Improper brakes on trailer — commercial motor vehicle	subsection 64(5)
	163.	Defective brakes	subsection 64(7)
	163.1	Defective brakes — commercial motor vehicle	subsection 64(7)
	164.	Defective braking system	subsection 64(7)
	164.1	Defective braking system — commercial motor vehicle	subsection 64(7)
	165.	Sell improper brake fluid	clause 65(1)(a)
	166.	Offer to sell improper brake fluid	clause 65(1)(a)
	167.	Install improper brake fluid	clause 65(1)(a)
	168.	Sell improper hydraulic oil	clause 65(1)(b)
	169.	Offer to sell improper hydraulic oil	clause 65(1)(b)
	170.	Install improper hydraulic oil	clause 65(1)(b)
	171.	Improper windshield wiper	clause 66(1)(a)
	171.1	Improper windshield wiper — commercial motor vehicle	clause 66(1)(a)
	172.	No windshield wiper	clause 66(1)(a)
	172.1	No windshield wiper — commercial motor vehicle	clause 66(1)(a)
	173.	Improper mirror	clause 66(1)(b)

PART	ITEM	COLUMN 1	COLUMN 2
	173.1	Improper mirror — commercial motor vehicle	clause 66(1)(b)
	174.	No mirror	clause 66(1)(b)
	174.1	No mirror — commercial motor vehicle	clause 66(1)(b)
	175.	Improper mudguards	subsection 66(3)
	175.1	Improper mudguards — commercial motor vehicle	subsection 66(3)
	176.	No mudguards	subsection 66(3)
	176.1	No mudguards — commercial motor vehicle	subsection 66(3)
	177.	No odometer	subsection 66(5)
	177.1	No odometer — commercial motor vehicle	subsection 66(5)
	178.	Defective odometer	subsection 66(5)
	178.1	Defective odometer — commercial motor vehicle	subsection 66(5)
	179.	Operate motor vehicle — mirrors more than 305 mm	section 67
	180.	No speedometer on bus	section 68
	181.	Defective speedometer on bus	section 68
	182.	Improper tire — damage to highway	subsection 69(1)
	183.	Device on wheels — injure highway	subsection 69(2)
	184.	No lock shoe — animal drawn vehicle	subsection 69(3)
	185.	Improper tires	clause 70(3)(a)
	185.1	Improper tires — commercial motor vehicle	clause 70(3)(a)
	186.	Improper tires — drawn vehicle	clause 70(3)(a)
	186.1	Improper tires — drawn vehicle — commercial motor vehicle	clause 70(3)(a)
	187.	Improperly installed tires	clause 70(3)(b)
	187.1	Improperly installed tires — commercial motor vehicle	clause 70(3)(b)
	188.	Improperly installed tires — drawn vehicle	clause 70(3)(b)
	188.1	Improperly installed tires — drawn vehicle — commercial motor vehicle	clause 70(3)(b)
	189.	Fail to mark rebuilt tire	subsection 71(2)
	190.	Sell unmarked rebuilt tire	subsection 71(3)
	191.	Offer to sell unmarked rebuilt tire	subsection 71(3)

PART	ITEM	COLUMN 1	COLUMN 2
	192.	Sell new vehicle — no safety glass	subsection 72(2)
	193.	Register new vehicle — no safety glass	subsection 72(2)
	194.	Install non-safety glass	subsection 72(3)
	195.	Window obstructed	clause 73(1)(a)
	196.	Windshield obstructed	clause 73(1)(a)
	197.	Have object obstructing view	clause 73(1)(b)
	198.	Drive with window coated — view obstructed	subsection 73(2)
	199.	Drive with windshield coated — view obstructed	subsection 73(2)
	200.	Colour coating obscuring interior	subsection 73(3)
	201.	No clear view to front	clause 74(1)(a)
	202.	No clear view to sides	clause 74(1)(a)
	203.	No clear view to rear	clause 74(1)(b)
	204.	No muffler — motor vehicle	subsection 75(1)
	205.	No muffler — motor assisted bicycle	subsection 75(1)
	206.	Improper muffler — motor vehicle	subsection 75(1)
	207.	Improper muffler — motor assisted bicycle	subsection 75(1)
	208.	Excessive fumes	subsection 75(3)
	209.	Unreasonable noise — signalling device	subsection 75(4)
	210.	Unreasonable smoke	subsection 75(4)
	211.	Unnecessary noise	subsection 75(40
	212.	No horn — motor vehicle	subsection 75(5)
	213.	No horn — motor assisted bicycle	subsection 75(5)
	214.	No horn — bicycle	subsection 75(5)
	215.	Defective horn — motor vehicle	subsection 75(5)
	216.	Defective horn — motor assisted bicycle	subsection 75(5)
	217.	Defective horn — bicycle	subsection 75(5)
	218.	Have a siren	subsection 75(6)
	219.	No slow moving vehicle sign	subsection 76(1)
	219.1	Slow moving vehicle sign not attached to rear of vehicle or trailer	subsection 76(1)
	219.2	Slow moving vehicle sign not attached in accordance with regulations	subsection 76(1)

PART	ITEM	COLUMN 1	COLUMN 2
	219.3	Slowing moving vehicle sign placed on fixed object	subsection 76(4)
	219.4	Prohibited use of slow moving vehicle sign	subsection 76(6)
	220.	No sleigh bells	subsection 77(1)
	221.	Television in front seat	clause 78(1)(a)
	222.	Television visible to driver	clause 78(1)(b)
	223.	Television operating in front seat	subsection 78(2)
	224.	Television operating — visible to driver	subsection 78(2)
	225.	Drive motor vehicle with radar warning device	section 79
	226.	Improper means of attachment	section 80
	226.1	Improper means of attachment — commercial motor vehicle	section 80
	227.	Fail to submit vehicle for tests	subsection 82(3)
	228.	Operate unsafe vehicle	section 84
	228.1	Operate unsafe vehicle — commercial motor vehicle	section 84
	229.	Operate unsafe streetcar	section 84
	230.	Operate unsafe combination of vehicles	section 84
	230.1	Operate unsafe combination of vehicles — commercial motor vehicle	section 84
	231.	Permit operation of unsafe vehicle	section 84
	231.1	Permit operation of unsafe vehicle — commercial motor vehicle	section 84
	232.	Permit operation of unsafe streetcar	section 84
	233.	Permit operation of unsafe combination of vehicles	section 84
	233.1	Permit operation of unsafe combination of vehicles — commercial motor vehicle	section 84
	234.	Operate vehicle — fail to display device	subsection 85(1)
	235.	Permit operation of vehicle — fail to display device	subsection 85(1)
	236.	Issue SSC not provided by Ministry	section 86
	237.	Affix vehicle inspection sticker not provided by Ministry	section 86

Part	Item	Column 1	Column 2
	238.	Unauthorized person issue SSC	subsection 90(1)
	239.	Unauthorized person affix vehicle inspection sticker	subsection 90(2)
	240.	Issue SSC without proper inspection	clause 90(3)(a)
	241.	Affix vehicle inspection sticker without proper inspection	clause 90(3)(a)
	242.	Issue SSC — vehicle not complying	clause 90(3)(a)
	243.	Affix vehicle inspection sticker — vehicle not complying	clause 90(3)(a)
	244.	SSC not made by inspection mechanic	subclause 90(3)(b)(i)
	245.	Vehicle inspection record not made by inspection mechanic	subclause 90(3)(b)(i)
	246.	SSC not countersigned	subclause 90(3)(b)(ii)
	247.	Unlicensed inspection station	subsection 91(1)
	248.	Corporation fail to notify change of officer or director	subsection 91(7)
	249.	Unregistered mechanic certify SSC	subsection 92(1)
	250.	Unregistered mechanic sign vehicle inspection record	subsection 92(1)
	251.	Obstruct inspector	subsection 98(6)
	252.	False statement in SSC	subsection 99(2)
	253.	Sell new vehicle not complying with standards	subsection 102(3)
	254.	Offer for sale new vehicle not complying with standards	subsection 102(3)
	255.	Expose for sale new vehicle not complying with standards	subsection 102(3)
	256.	Sell new vehicle not marked or identified	subsection 102(3)
	257.	Offer for sale new vehicle not marked or identified	subsection 102(3)
	258.	Expose for sale new vehicle not marked or identified	subsection 102(3)
	259.	No name on commercial vehicle	subsection 103(1)
	260.	Less than two reflectors — commercial vehicle	subsection 103(2)
	261.	Less than two reflectors — trailer	subsection 103(2)
	262.	Sell new commercial vehicle without two red rear lights	clause 103(3)(a)

PART	ITEM	COLUMN 1	COLUMN 2
	263.	Offer to sell new commercial vehicle without two rear red lights	clause 103(3)(a)
	264.	Sell trailer without two red rear lights	clause 103(3)(a)
	265.	Offer to sell trailer without two red rear lights	clause 103(3)(a)
	266.	Sell new commercial vehicle without two rear red reflectors	clause 103(3)(b)
	267.	Offer to sell new commercial vehicle without two rear red reflectors	clause 103(3)(b)
	268.	Sell trailer without two rear red reflectors	clause 103(3)(b)
	269.	Offer to sell trailer without two rear red reflectors	clause 103(3)(b)
	270.	No name and address on road-building machine	subsection 103(4)
	271.	Fail to wear proper helmet on motorcycle	subsection 104(1)
	272.	Fail to wear proper helmet on motor assisted bicycle	subsection 104(1)
	273.	Carry passenger under 16 not wearing proper helmet	subsection 104(2)
	273.1	Fail to wear proper helmet on bicycle	subsection 104(2.1)
	273.2	Permit person under 16 not wearing proper helmet on bicycle	subsection 104(2.2)
	274.	Dealing with vehicle not conforming to standard	subsection 105(1)
	275.	Dealing with motor assisted bicycle — no document of compliance	subsection 105(2)
	276.	Drive with seat belt assembly removed	subsection 106(2)
	277.	Drive with seat belt assembly inoperative	subsection 106(2)
	278.	Drive with seat belt assembly modified	subsection 106(2)
	279.	Driver — fail to wear complete seat belt assembly	subsection 106(3)
	280.	Driver — fail to properly adjust complete seat belt assembly	subsection 106(3)
	281.	Driver — fail to securely fasten complete seat belt assembly	subsection 106(3)

Part	Item	Column 1	Column 2
	282.	Passenger — fail to wear complete seat belt assembly	subsection 106(4)
	283.	Passenger — fail to properly adjust complete seat belt assembly	subsection 106(4)
	284.	Passenger — fail to securely fasten complete set belt assembly	subsection 106(4)
	285.	Driver — fail to ensure passenger wears complete seat belt assembly	subsection 106(6)
	286.	Driver — fail to ensure passenger properly adjusts complete seat belt assembly	subsection 106(6)
	287.	Driver — fail to ensure passenger securely fasten complete seat belt assembly	subsection 106(6)
	287.1	Driver — fail to ensure child passenger occupies seat belt assembly equipped position	subsection 106(7)
	288.	Fail to establish system to periodically inspect, repair and maintain commercial motor vehicles	subsection 107(2)
	289.	Fail to inspect commercial motor vehicle or cause inspection	subsection 107(3)
	290.	Fail to repair commercial motor vehicle or cause repair	subsection 107(3)
	291.	Fail to maintain commercial motor vehicle or cause it to be maintained	subsection 107(3)
	292.	Fail to instruct driver to inspect commercial motor vehicle or cause inspection of it	subsection 107(4)
	293.	Drive commercial motor vehicle without prescribed inspection	subsection 107(5)
	294.	Tow trailer without prescribed inspection	subsection 107(5)
	295.	Fail to report vehicle defect	subsection 107(6)
	296.	Fail to report trailer defect	subsection 107(6)
	297.	Drive defective vehicle	subsection 107(7)
	298.	Tow defective trailer	subsection 107(7)
	299.	Permit operation of defective vehicle	subsection 107(8)
	300.	Permit towing of defective trailer	subsection 107(8)
	301.	Fail to maintain documents or cause them to be maintained	subsection 107(9)

Part	Item	Column 1	Column 2
	302.	Fail to carry inspection report	subsection 107(10)
	303.	Fail to surrender inspection report	subsection 107(10)
VII Load and Dimensions	304.	Overwidth vehicle	subsection 109(1)
	305.	Overwidth load	subsection 109(2)
	306.	Overlength vehicle	subsection 109(6)
	307.	Overlength combination of vehicles	subsection 109(7)
	307.1	Operate overlength combination of vehicles	subsection 109(8)
	308.	Overlength semi-trailer	subsection 109(10)
	309.	Overlength bus	subsection 109(11)
	310.	Overheight vehicle	subsection 109(14)
	311.	Fail to carry permit in vehicle	subsection 110(6)
	312.	Fail to produce permit	subsection 110(6)
	313.	Oversize vehicle — violate permit	subsection 110(7)
	314.	Overweight vehicle — violate permit	subsection 110(7)
	314.1	Fail to comply with condition of permit	subsection 110(7)
	315.	Fail to mark overhanging load	subsection 111(1)
	315.1	Fail to mark overhanging load — commercial motor vehicle	subsection 111(1)
	316.	Insecure load	subsection 111(2)
	316.1	Insecure load — commercial motor vehicle	subsection 111(2)
	317.	Overweight on tires ...kg.	clause 115(1)(a)
	318.	Overweight on tires ...kg.	clause 115(1)(b)
	319.	Overweight single axle (single tires) ...kg. Class A Highway	clause 116(1)(a)
	320.	Overweight single axle (dual tires) ...kg. Class A Highway	clause 116(1)(b)
	321.	Overwieght dual axle ...kg. Class A Highway	clause 116(1)(c)
	322.	Overweight triple axle ...kg. Class A Highway	clause 116(1)(d)
	323.	Overweight dual axle (single tires) ...kg. Class A Highway	subsection 116(2)
	324.	Overweight triple axle (single tires) ...kg. Class A Highway	subsection 116(3)
	325.	Overweight single front axle ...kg. No verification. Class A Highway	subsection 116(4)

Part	Item	Column 1	Column 2
	326.	Overweight single front axle ...kg. Exceed rating. Class A Highway	subsection 116(4)
	327.	Overweight two axle group ...kg. Class A Highway	clause 117(a)
	328.	Overweight three axle group ...kg. Class A Highway	clause 117(b)
	329.	Overweight four axle group ...kg. Class A Highway	clause 117(c)
	330.	Overweight vehicle ...kg. Class A Highway	section 118
	331.	Overweight during freeze-up ...kg.	subsection 119(4)
	332.	Overweight on axle ...kg. Class B Highway	section 120
	333.	Overweight vehicle-vilate permit ...kg.	subsection 121(1)
	334.	Fail to have receipt in vehicle	subsection 121(3)
	335.	Fail to produce receipt	subsection 121(3)
	336.	Fail to proceed to scale	subsection 124(6)
	337.	Fail to have load removed	clause 124(7)(a)
	338.	Obstruct weighting, measuring or examination	clause 124(7)(b)
	339.	Cause vehicle to be overloaded	section 126
IX Rate of Speed	340.	Speeding	section 128
	340.1	Owner-speeding pursuant to s. 207	section 128
	341.	Careless driving	section 130
	342.	Unnecessary slow driving	section 132
X Rules of the Road	343.	Disobey officer directing traffic	subsection 134(1)
	344.	Drive on closed highway	subsection 134(3)
	345.	Fail to yield — uncontrolled intersection	subsection 135(2)
	346.	Fail to yield to vehicle on right	subsection 135(3)
	347.	Disobey stop sign — stop wrong place	clause 136(1)(a)
	348.	Disobey stop sign — fail to stop	clause 136(1)(a)
	349.	Fail to yield to traffic on through highway	clause 136(1)(b)
	350.	Traffic on through highway — fail to yield	subsection 136(2)
	351.	Fail to yield — yield sign	subsection 138(1)
	352.	Fail to yield from private road	subsection 139(1)
	353.	Fail to yield from driveway	subsection 139(1)

PART	ITEM	COLUMN 1	COLUMN 2
	354.	Fail to yield to pedestrian	clause 140(1)(a)
	355.	Fail to yield to pedestrian approaching	clause 140(1)(b)
	356.	Fail to yield to person in wheelchair	clause 140(1)(a)
	357.	Fail to yield to person in wheelchair approaching	clause 140(1)(b)
	358.	Pass stopped vehicle at crossover	subsection 140(2)
	359.	Pass stopped streetcar at crossover	subsection 140(2)
	360.	Stopped vehicle at crossover — fail to yield to pedestrian	clause 140(2)(a)
	361.	Stopped street car at crossover — fail to yield to pedestrian	clause 140(2)(a)
	362.	Stopped vehicle at crossover — fail to yield to person in wheelchair	clause 140(2)(a)
	363.	Stopped street car at crossover — fail to yield to person in wheelchair	clause 140(2)(a)
	364.	Stopped vehicle at crossover — fail to yield to pedestrian approaching	clause 140(2)(b)
	365.	Stopped street car at crossover — fail to yield to pedestrian approaching	clause 140(2)(b)
	366.	Stopped vehicle at crossover — fail to yield to person in wheelchair approaching	clause 140(2)(b)
	367.	Stopped street car at crossover — fail to yield to person in wheelchair approaching	clause 140(2)(b)
	368.	Pass front of vehicle within 30 m of crossover	subsection 140(3)
	369.	Pass front of street car within 30 m of crossover	subsection 140(3)
	370.	Pedestrian fail to yield at crossover	subsection 140(4)
	371.	Person in wheelchair — fail to yield at crossover	subsection 140(4)
	371.1	Cyclist — ride in crossover	subsection 140(6)
	372.	Improper right turn	subsection 141(2)
	373.	Improper right turn — multi-lane highway	subsection 141(3)

Part	Item	Column 1	Column 2
	374.	Left turn — fail to afford reasonable opportunity to avoid collision	subsection 141(5)
	375.	Improper left turn	subsection 141(6)
	376.	Improper left turn — multi-lane highway	subsection 141(7)
	377.	Turn — not in safety	subsection 142(1)
	378.	Change lane — not in safety	subsection 142(1)
	379.	Fail to signal for turn	subsection 142(1)
	380.	Fail to signal — lane change	subsection 142(1)
	381.	Start from parked position — not in safety	subsection 142(2)
	382.	Start from stopped position — not in safety	subsection 142(2)
	383.	Start from parked position — fail to signal	subsection 142(2)
	384.	Start from stopped position — fail to signal	subsection 142(2)
	385.	Improper arm signal	subsection 142(4)
	386.	Improper signal device	subsection 142(6)
	387.	Use turn signals improperly	subsection 142(7)
	388.	Fail to signal stop	subsection 142(8)
	389.	Fail to signal decrease in speed	subsection 142(8)
	390.	Improper signal to stop	subsection 142(8)
	391.	Improper signal to decrease in speed	subsection 142(8)
	392.	Brake lights — improper colour	clause 142(8)(b)
	393.	U-turn on a curve — no clear view	clause 143(a)
	394.	U-turn — railway crossing	clause 143(b)
	395.	U-turn near crest or grade — no clear view	clause 143(c)
	396.	U-turn — bridge — no clear view	clause 143(d)
	397.	U-turn — viaduct — no clear view	clause 143(d)
	398.	U-turn — tunnel — no clear view	clause 143(d)
	399.	Improper stop — traffic signal at intersection	subsection 144(5)
	400.	Improper stop — traffic signal not at intersection	subsection 144(6)
	401.	Fail to yield to pedestrian	subsection 144(7)
	402.	Fail to yield to traffic	subsection 144(8)
	403.	Proceed contrary to sign at intersection	subsection 144(9)

PART	ITEM	COLUMN 1	COLUMN 2
	404.	Disobey lane light	subsection 144(10)
	405.	Green light — fail to proceed as directed	subsection 144(12)
	406.	Flashing green light — fail to proceed as directed	subsection 144(13)
	407.	Green arrow — fail to proceed as directed	subsection 144(14)
	408.	Amber light — fail to stop	subsection 144(15)
	409.	Amber arrow — fail to stop	subsection 144(16)
	410.	Amber arrow — fail to proceed as directed	subsection 144(16)
	411.	Flashing amber light — fail to proceed with caution	subsection 144(17)
	412.	Red light — fail to stop	subsection 144(18)
	413.	Red light — proceed before green	subsection 144(18)
	414.	Turn on red light — fail to yield	subsection 144(19)
	415.	Emergency vehicle — proceed when unsafe	subsection 144(20)
	416.	Flashing red light — fail to stop	subsection 144(21)
	417.	Flashing red light — fail to yield	subsection 144(21)
	418.	Pedestrian fail to use crosswalk	subsection 144(22)
	419.	Pedestrian disobey flashing green light	subsection 144(24)
	420.	Pedestrian disobey red light	subsection 144(25)
	421.	Pedestrian disobey amber light	subsection 144(25)
	422.	Pedestrian disobey "don't walk" signal	subsection 144(27)
	422.1	Cyclist — ride in or along crosswalk	subsection 144(29)
	423.	Disobey portable amber light — fail to stop	subsection 146(3)
	424.	Disobey portable red light — fail to stop	subsection 146(4)
	425.	Disobey portable red light — proceed before green	subsection 146(4)
	426.	Disobey portable red light — stop wrong place	subsection 146(5)
	427.	Disobey portable amber light — stop wrong place	subsection 146(5)
	428.	Remove portable lane control signal system	subsection 146(6)
	429.	Deface portable lane control signal system	subsection 146(6)
	430.	Interfere with portable lane control signal system	subsection 146(6)

Part	Item	Column 1	Column 2
	431.	Fail to keep right when driving at less than normal speed	section 147(1)
	432.	Fail to share half roadway — meeting vehicle	subsection 148(1)
	433.	Fail to turn out to right when overtaken	subsection 148(2)
	434.	Fail to share roadway — meeting bicycle	subsection 148(4)
	435.	Fail to turn out to left to avoid collision	subsection 148(5)
	436.	Bicycle — fail to turn out to right when overtaken	subsection 148(6)
	437.	Fail to turn out to left to avoid collision with bicycle	subsection 148(6)
	438.	Motor assisted bicycle — fail to turn out to right when overtaken	subsection 148(6)
	439.	Fail to turn out to left to avoid collision with motor assisted bicycle	subsection 148(6)
	440.	Fail to stop to facilitate passing	subsection 148(7)
	441.	Fail to assist in passing	subsection 148(7)
	442.	Pass — roadway not clear — approaching traffic	clause 148(8)(a)
	443.	Attempt to pass — roadway not clear — approaching traffic	clause 148(8)(a)
	444.	Pass — roadway not clear — overtaking traffic	clause 148(8)(b)
	445.	Attempt to pass — roadway not clear — overtaking traffic	clause 148(8)(b)
	446.	Drive left of centre — approaching crest of grade	clause 149(1)(a)
	447.	Drive left of centre — on a curve	clause 149(1)(a)
	448.	Drive left on centre within 30 m of bridge — no clear view	clause 149(1)(a)
	449.	Drive left of centre within 30 m of viaduct — no clear view	clause 149(1)(a)
	450.	Drive left of centre within 30 m of tunnel — no clear view	clause 149(1)(a)
	451.	Drive left of centre within 30 m of level railway crossing	clause 149(1)(b)
	452.	Drive left of centre — railway crossing	clause 149(1)(b)
	453.	Pass on right — not in safety	subsection 150(1)
	454.	Pass — off roadway	subsection 150(2)
	455.	Disobey official sign	subsection 151(1)

PART	ITEM	COLUMN 1	COLUMN 2
	456.	Drive wrong way — one way traffic	section 153
	457.	Fail to drive in marked lane	clause 154(1)(a)
	458.	Unsafe lane change	clause 154(1)(a)
	459.	Use centre lane improperly	clause 154(1)(b)
	460.	Fail to obey lane sign	clause 154(1)(c)
	461.	Drive wrong way — divided highway	clause 156(1)(a)
	462.	Cross divided highway — no proper crossing provided	clause 156(1)(b)
	462.1	Backing on roadway — divided highway	subsection 157(1)
	462.2	Backing on shoulder — divided highway	subsection 157(1)
	463.	Follow too closely	subsection 158(1)
	464.	Commercial vehicle — follow too closely	subsection 158(2)
	465.	Fail to stop on right for emergency vehicle	clause 159(1)(a)
	466.	Fail to stop — nearest curb — for emergency vehicle	clause 159(1)(b)
	467.	Fail to stop — nearest edge of roadway — for emergency vehicle	clause 159(1)(b)
	468.	Follow fire department vehicle too closely	subsection 159(2)
	469.	Permit attachment to vehicle	section 160
	470.	Permit attachment to streetcar	section 160
	471.	Draw more than one vehicle	section 161
	472.	Drive while crowded	section 162
	473.	Disobey railway crossing signal — stop wrong place	section 163
	474.	Disobey railway crossing signal — fail to stop	section 163
	475.	Disobey railway crossing signal — proceed unsafely	section 163
	476.	Disobey crossing fate	section 164
	477.	Open vehicle door improperly	clause 165(a)
	478.	Leave vehicle door open	clause 165(b)
	479.	Pass streetcar improperly	subsection 166(1)
	480.	Approach open streetcar door too closely	subsection 166(1)
	481.	Pass streetcar on the left side	subsection 166(2)
	482.	Frighten animal	section 167

Part	Item	Column 1	Column 2
	483.	Fail to ensure safety of person in charge of animal	section 167
	484.	Fail to use lower beam — oncoming	clause 168(a)
	485.	Fail to use lower beam — following	clause 168(b)
	485.1	Prohibited use of alternating highbeam headlights	subsection 169(2)
	486.	Fail to take precaution against vehicle being set in motion	subsection 170(9)
	487.	Fail to have warning lights	clause 170(10)(a)
	488.	Fail to use warning lights	subsection 170(11)
	489.	Interfere with traffic	subsection 170(12)
	490.	Interfere with snow removal	subsection 170(12)
	490.1	Offer tow truck services on King's Highway within 200 m of accident or apparent accident	clause 171(1)(a)
	490.2	Offer tow truck services on King's Highway within 200 m of vehicle involved in accident	clause 171(1)(b)
	490.3	Park tow truck on King's Highway within 200 m of accident or apparent accident — sufficient tow trucks available	clause 171(2)(a)
	490.4	Stop tow truck on King's Highway within 200 m of accident or apparent accident — sufficient tow trucks available	clause 171(2)(a)
	490.5	Park tow truck on King's Highway within 200 m of vehicle involved in accident — sufficient tow trucks available	clause 171(2)(b)
	490.6	Stop tow truck on King's Highway within 200 m of vehicle involved in accident — sufficient tow trucks available	clause 171(2)(b)
	491.	Race a motor vehicle	subsection 172(1)
	492.	Race an animal	section 173
	493.	Fail to stop at railway crossing — public vehicle	subsection 174(1)
	494.	Stop wrong place at railway crossing — public vehicle	clause 174(1)(a)
	495.	Fail to look both ways at railway crossing — public vehicle	clause 174(1)(b)

PART	ITEM	COLUMN 1	COLUMN 2
	496.	Fail to open door at railway crossing — public vehicle	clause 174(1)(c)
	497.	Cross tracks using gear requiring change — public vehicle	clause 174(1)(d)
	497.1	Change gears while crossing railway track — public vehicle	clause 174(1)(e)
	497.2	Fail to stop at railway crossing — school bus	subsection 174(2)
	497.3	Stop wrong place at railway crossing — school bus	clause 174(2)(a)
	497.4	Fail to look both ways at railway crossing — school bus	clause 174(2)(b)
	497.5	Fail to open door at railway crossing — school bus	clause 174(2)(c)
	497.6	Cross tracks using gear requiring change — school bus	clause 174(2)(d)
	497.7	Change gears while crossing railway track — school bus	clause 174(2)(e)
	498.	Bus not used to transport adults with developmental handicaps or children, painted chrome yellow	subsection 175(3)
	499.	Prohibited markings	subsection 175(4)
	499.1	Prohibited equipment — school bus stop arm	subsection 175(4)
	500.	Drive chrome yellow vehicle, not used to transport adults with developmental handicaps or children	subsection 175(5)
	501.	Drive vehicle with prohibited school bus markings	subsection 175(5)
	502.	Drive vehicle with prohibited school bus stop arm	subsection 175(5)
	503.	Fail to actuate school bus signals	subsection 175(6)
	504.	Improperly actuate school bus signals	subsection 175(8)
	505.	Improperly actuate school bus signals at intersection controlled by operating traffic control system	clause 175(9)(a)

Part	Item	Column 1	Column 2
	506.	Improperly actuate school bus signals at location, other than an intersection, controlled by operating traffic control system — at sign or roadway marking indicating where stop to be made	subclause 175(9)(b)(i)
	507.	Improperly actuate school bus signals at location, other than an intersection, controlled by operating traffic control system — in area immediately before entering crosswalk	subclause 175(9)(b)(ii)
	507.1	Improperly actuate school bus signals at location, other than an intersection, controlled by operating traffic control system — within 5 metres of traffic control system	subclause 175(9)(b)(iii)
	507.2	Improperly actuate school bus signals within 60 metres of location controlled by operating traffic control system	clause 175(9)(c)
	507.3	Stop school bus opposite loading zone	clause 175(10)(a)
	507.4	Stop school bus improperly at loading zone	clause 175(10)(b)
	507.5	Fail to stop for school bus — meeting	subsection 175(11)
	507.6	Fail to stop for school bus — overtaking	subsection 175(12)
	508.	Guard fail to properly display school crossing stop sign	subsection 176(2)
	509.	Fail to obey school crossing stop sign	subsection 176(3)
	510.	Improper use of school crossing stop sign	subsection 176(4)
	511.	Unauthorized person display school crossing stop sign	subsection 176(5)
	512.	Solicit a ride	clause 177(a)
	513.	Solicit business	clause 177(b)
	514.	Attach to vehicle	subsection 178(1)
	515.	Attach to streetcar	subsection 178(1)
	516.	Ride 2 on a bicycle	subsection 178(2)
	517.	Ride another person on a motor assisted bicycle	subsection 178(3)

Part	Item	Column 1	Column 2
	518.	Person — attach to vehicle	subsection 178(4)
	519.	Person — attach to streetcar	subsection 178(4)
	520.	Pedestrian fail to walk on left side of highway	section 179
	521.	Pedestrian on roadway fail to keep to left edge	section 179
	522.	Litter highway	section 180
	523.	Deposit snow or ice on roadway	section 181
	524.	Disobey sign	subsection 182(2)
	525.	Disobey sign at tunnel	subsection 183(2)
	526.	Deface notice	section 184
	527.	Remove notice	section 184
	528.	Interfere with notice	section 184
	529.	Deface obstruction	section 184
	530.	Remove obstruction	section 184
	531.	Interfere with obstruction	section 184
	532.	Fail to remove aircraft	subsection 187(1)
	533.	Move aircraft improperly	subsection 187(2)
	534.	Aircraft unlawfully take off	subsection 187(3)
	535.	Draw occupied trailer	section 188
	536.	Operate air cushioned vehicle	section 189
	537.	Fail to maintain daily log	subsection 190(3)
	538.	Fail to carry daily log	subsection 190(3)
	539.	Fail to surrender daily log	subsection 190(4)
	540.	Driver in possession of more than one daily log	subsection 190(5)
	540.1	Permit person to drive commercial motor vehicle not in accordance with the regulations	subsection 190(6)
	540.2	Fail to produce proof of exemption	subsection 191(7)
	540.3	Drive motor vehicle — toll device improperly affixed	subsection 191.2(1)
	540.4	Drive motor vehicle — no toll device	subsection 191.2(1)
	540.5	Drive motor vehicle — invalid toll device	subsection 191.2(1)
	540.6	Engage in activity to evade toll system	subsection 191.3(1)
	540.7	Engage in activity to obstruct toll system	subsection 191.3(1)

Part	Item	Column 1	Column 2
	540.8	Engage in activity to interfere with toll system	subsection 191.3(1)
	540.9	Use device to evade toll system	subsection 191.3(1)
	540.10	Use device to obstruct toll system	subsection 191.3(1)
	540.11	Use device to interfere with toll system	subsection 191.3(1)
	540.12	Sell device designed to interfere with toll system	subsection 191.3(4)
	540.13	Offer to sell device designed to interfere with toll system	subsection 191.3(4)
	540.13	Advertise for sale device designed to interfere with toll system	subsection 191.3(4)
	540.15	Sell device intended to interfere with toll system	subsection 191.3(4)
	540.16	Offer to sell device intended to interfere with toll system	subsection 191.3(4)
	540.17	Advertise for sale device intended to interfere with toll system	subsection 191.3(4)
XIV Records and Reporting of Accidents and Convictions	541.	Fail to report accident	subsection 199(1)
	542.	Fail to furnish required information	subsection 199(1)
	542.1	Fail to report accident — specified location	subsection 199(1.1)
	542.2	Fail to furnish required information	subsection 199(1.1)
	543.	Occupant fail to report accident	subsection 199(2)
	544.	Police officer fail to report accident	subsection 199(3)
	545.	Fail to remain	clause 200(1)(a)
	546.	Fail to render assistance	clause 200(1)(b)
	547.	Fail to give required information	clause 200(1)(c)
	548.	Fail to report damage to property on highway	section 201
	549.	Fail to report damage to fence bordering highway	section 201
	550.	Medical practitioner — fail to report	subsection 203(1)
	551.	Optometrist — fail to report	subsection 203(1)
	552.	Failing to forward suspended licence to Registrar	subsection 211(2)
	553.	Fail to surrender suspended driver's licence	subsection 212(2)

Part	Item	Column 1	Column 2
	554.	Refuse to surrender suspended driver's licence	subsection 212(2)
	554.1	Cyclist — fail to stop	subsection 218(2)
	554.2	Cyclist — fail to identify self	subsection 218(2)
	555.	Obstruct officer	subsection 225(5)
	556.	Withhold record	subsection 225(5)
	557.	Conceal record	subsection 225(5)
	558.	Destroy record	subsection 225(5)

References in column 2 relating to items 498 to 507 reflect changes made to the *Highway Traffic Act* which were proclaimed on the 1st day of July, 1991.

O. Reg. 364/93; O. Reg. 365/93; O. Reg. 465/94; O. Reg. 496/94;
O. Reg. 430/95, s. 1; O. Reg. 485/96, s. 1(2); O. Reg. 511/96;
O. Reg. 180/97; O. Reg. 344/97; O. Reg. 536/97.

Schedule 44

Regulation 575 of Revised Regulations of Ontario, 1990 Under the Highway Traffic Act

Item	Column 1	Column 2
1.	Improper inspection report	section 4
2.	Fail to record defect	subsection 5(1)
3.	Fail to forward inspection report to operator	subsection 5(2)
4.	Repair defect — fail to complete inspection report	section 6
5.	Fail to ensure vehicle conforms to standards	section 9
6.	Fail to keep proper documents for vehicle	clause 11(a)
7.	Fail to keep inspection report	clause 11(b)

Schedule 45

Regulation 577 of revised Regulations of Ontario, 1990 Under the Highway Traffic Act

Item	Column 1	Column 2
1.	Load not properly confined	subsection 2(1)
1.1	Load not properly confined — commercial motor vehicle	subsection 2(1)
2.	No covering on load	subsection 2(1)
3.	No covering on load — commercial motor vehicle	subsection 2(1)

O. Reg. 485/96, s. 2.

Schedule 46

Ontario Regulation 340/94 under the Highway Traffic Act

ITEM	COLUMN 1	COLUMN 2
1.	Class L licence holder — unaccompanied by properly licensed driver	subsection 3(1)
2.	Class R licence holder — drive at unlawful hour	subsection 4(1), paragraph 1
3.	Class R licence holder — carry passenger	subsection 4(1, paragraph 2
4.	Class R licence holder — drive on prohibited highway	subsection 4(1), paragraph 3
5.	Glass G1 licence holder — unaccompanied by qualified driver	subsection 5(1)
6.	Class G1 licence holder — drive when blood alcohol concentration above zero	subsection 5(1), paragraph 1
7.	Class G1 licence holder — accompanying driver blood alcohol concentration .05 or above	subsection 5(1), paragraph 2
8.	Class G1 licence holder — carry front seat passenger	subsection 5(1), paragraph 3
9.	Class G1 licence holder — carry excess passengers	subsection 5(1), paragraph 4
10.	Class G1 licence holder — drive on prohibited highway	subsection 5(1), paragraph 5
11.	Class G1 licence holder — drive at unlawful hour	subsection 5(1), paragraph 6
12.	Class G2 licence holder — drive when blood alcohol concentration above zero	subsection 6(1), paragraph 1
13.	Class G2 licence holder — carry excess passengers	subsection 6(1), paragraph 2
14.	Class M1 licence holder — drive when blood alcohol concentration above zero	section 7, paragraph 1
15.	Class M1 licence holder — drive at unlawful hour	section 7, paragraph 2
16.	Class M1 licence holder — carry passenger	section 7, paragraph 3
17.	Class M1 licence holder — drive on prohibited highway	section 7, paragraph 4
18.	Class M2 licence holder — drive when blood alcohol concentration above zero	section 8
19.	Drive without authorized accompanying driver	subsection 23(1)
20.	Class M or M2 licence holder — drive G1 vehicle unaccompanied by qualified driver	subsection 23(2)
21.	Class M or M2 licence holder — drive unauthorized vehicle	subsection 23(2)
22.	Drive bus with unauthorized passengers	subsection 23(3)

ITEM	COLUMN 1	COLUMN 2
23.	Temporary driver's licence holder — operate improper class of vehicle	subsection 24(1)
24.	Contravene licence condition — driving ability	section 25
25.	Fail to notify change of address — licence	subsection 33(1)
26.	Fail to notify change of name — licence	subsection 33(2)
27.	Licence holder — fail to sign driver's licence in ink	section 34

O. Reg. 465/94, s. 2.

Schedule 47

Regulation 586 of Revised Regulations of Ontario, 1990 Under the Highway Traffic Act

ITEM	COLUMN 1	COLUMN 2
1.	Instruct driving without licence	section 2
2.	Fail to display licence	section 11

Schedule 48

Regulation 587 of Revised Regulations of Ontario, 1990 Under the Highway Traffic Act

ITEM	COLUMN 1	COLUMN 2
1.	Use unapproved instrument to test brakes	subsection 1(1)
2.	Test brakes with clutch engaged	subsection 2(1)
3.	Test brakes with motive power applied	subsection 2(2)
4.	Brakes inadequate to stop vehicle	section 3
4.1	Brakes inadequate to stop vehicle — commercial motor vehicle	section 3
5.	Brakes inadequate to stop combination of vehicles	section 3
5.1	Brakes inadequate to stop combination of vehicles — commercial motor vehicle	section 3
6.	Brakes inadequate to stop mobile home	section 4
7.	Push rod stroke exceeds prescribed limit	subsection 5(1)
7.1	Push rod stroke exceeds prescribed limit — commercial motor vehicle	subsection 5(1)
8.	Push rod stroke exceeds manufacturer's maximum	subsection 5(2)
8.1	Push rod stroke exceeds manufacturer's maximum — commercial motor vehicle	subsection 5(2)
9.	Combined brake shoe lining movement exceeds one-eighth of an inch	subsection 5(3)
9.1	Combined brake shoe lining movement exceeds one-eight of an inch — commercial motor vehicle	subsection 5(3)

Item	Column 1	Column 2
10.	Wheel brake not automatically adjustable	subsection 5(5)
10.1	Wheel brake not automatically adjustable — commercial motor vehicle	subsection 5(5)
11.	Wheel brake not equipped with indicator	subsection 5(6)
11.1	Wheel brake not equipped with indicator — commercial motor vehicle	subsection 5(6)
12.	Wheel brake removed	subsection 5(8)
12.1	Wheel brake removed — commercial motor vehicle	subsection 5(8)
13.	Wheel brake rendered inoperable	subsection 5(8)
13.1	Wheel brake rendered inoperable — commercial motor vehicle	subsection 5(8)
14.	Wheel brake operating improperly	subsection 5(8)
14.1	Wheel brake operating improperly — commercial motor vehicle	subsection 5(8)
15.	Unequal braking power	subsection 5(9)
15.1	Unequal braking power — commercial motor vehicle	subsection 5(9)
16.	Fail to display required conspicuity markings	subsection 7(1)

O. Reg. 430/95, s. 2; O. Reg. 485/96, s. 3.

Schedule 49

Regulation 595 of Revised Regulations of Ontario, 1990 Under the Highway Traffic Act

Item	Column 1	Column 2
1.	Vendor fail to return licence to Ministry	subsection 1(4)
2.	Purchaser fail to apply for new licence	subsection 1(4)
3.	Fail to keep record book	section 2
4.	Failure to return permit and number plates	clause 3(d)
5.	Fail to record exchange of engine	section 4

Schedule 50

Regulation 596 of Revised Regulations of Ontario, 1990 Under the Highway Traffic Act

Item	Column 1	Column 2
1.	Improper lights	subsection 2(1)
1.1	Improper lights — commercial motor vehicle	subsection 2(1)
2.	Manufacturer sell substandard seat belt	subsection 9(2)
3.	Manufacturer sell unmarked seat belt	subsection 9(2)

ITEM	COLUMN 1	COLUMN 2
4.	Manufacturer mark substandard seat belt	subsection 9(3)
5.	Sell unmarked seat belt	subsection 9(4)
6.	Improperly mark seat belt	subsection 9(6)
7.	Motorcycle handlebars more than 380 mm high	subsection 10(1)
8.	Motor assisted bicycle handlebars more than 380 mm high	subsection 10(1)
9.	Carry passenger improperly on motorcycle	subsection 10(2)
10.	No footrests for passenger on motorcycle	subsection 10(2)
11.	Passenger improperly seated on motorcycle	subsection 10(3)

O. Reg. 485/96, s. 4.

Schedule 51

Ontario Regulation 4/93 under the Highway Traffic Act

ITEM	COLUMN 1	COLUMN 2
1.	Drive after 60 hours on duty in 7 days	subsection 3(2)
2.	Drive after 70 hours on duty in 8 days	subsection 3(3)
3.	Drive after 120 hours on duty in 14 days	clause 3(4)(a)
4.	Drive without taking 24 hours off duty time	clause 3(4)(b)
5.	Exceed 75 hours on duty time in 14 days	subsection 3(4)
6.	Exceed 13 hours driving time	subsection 4(1)
7.	Drive after 15 hours on duty time	subsection 4(3)
8.	Fail to make daily log	subsection 8(1)
9.	Fail to make proper daily log	subsection 9(1)
10.	Fail to complete graph grid	subsection 9(2)
11.	Fail to sign and certify copy of daily log	subsection 10(2)
12.	Fail to make handwritten daily log upon request	subsection 10(3)
13.	Fail to possess blank log forms	subsection 10(3)
14.	Fail to carry daily logs for previous 7 days	subsection 11(1)
15.	Fail to carry daily logs for previous 13 days	subsection 11(1)
16.	Fail to carry required receipts	subsection 11(1)
17.	Fail to surrender required documents	subsection 11(2)
18.	Fail to make daily log	section 13
19.	Fail to forward daily log	section 14
20.	Fail to forward required documents	section 14
21.	Fail to keep logs	subsection 15(1)
22.	Fail to keep required documents	subsection 15(1)
23.	Fail to surrender logs	subsection 15(3)
24.	Fail to surrender required documents	subsection 15(3)

O. Reg. 364/93, s. 2.

Schedule 52

Regulation 601 of Revised Regulations of Ontario, 1990 under the Highway Traffic Act

ITEM	COLUMN 1	COLUMN 2
1.	Insufficient inspection area	clause 4(1)(a)
2.	Insufficient inspection tools	clause 4(1)(b)
3.	Unsuitable hoist or jack	clause 4(1)(b)
4.	Improper inspection devices	clause 4(1)(c)
5.	Unclean conditions	clause 4(1)(d)
6.	Unsafe conditions	clause 4(1)(d)
7.	Poor condition of equipment	subsection 4(2)
8.	Fail to report termination of mechanic	section 9
9.	Fail to keep copy of certificate on premises	clause 10(a)
10.	Fail to keep record of vehicles inspected	clause 10(b)
11.	Fail to keep record of agents	clause 10(c)
12.	Improper inspection records	clause 10(d)
13.	Fail to display identifying sign	subsection 11(1)
14.	Fail to return identifying sign	subsection 11(2)
15.	Unauthorized display of sign	subsection 11(3)
16.	Fail to return unused vehicle inspection forms and stickers	subsection 12(2)
17.	Fail to return unused SCCs	subsection 12(2)
18.	Fail to return vehicle inspection records	subsection 12(2)
19.	Fail to report missing SSCs, forms or stickers	subsection 13(1)
20.	Incomplete report on missing forms or stickers	subsection 13(2)
21.	Fail to return recovered forms or stickers	subsection 13(3)

O. Reg. 307/94, s. 1.

Schedule 53

Regulation 608 op Revised Regulations of Ontario, 1990 Under the Highway Traffic Act

ITEM	COLUMN 1	COLUMN 2
1.	Prohibited use of left lane on King's Highway	subsection 1(1)

Schedule 54

Regulation 611 of Revised Regulations of Ontario, 1990 Under the Highway Traffic Act

ITEM	COLUMN 1	COLUMN 2
1.	Licensee — fail to remove dump vehicle inspection sticker	clause 5(4)(b)
2.	Authorized person — fail to remove dump vehicle inspection sticker	clause 5(4)(b)
3.	Inspecting mechanic — fail to remove dump vehicle inspection sticker	clause 5(4)(b)
4.	Licensee — fail to properly affix current dump vehicle inspection sticker	clause 5(4)(b)
5.	Authorized person — fail to properly affix current dump vehicle inspection sticker	clause 5(4)(b)
6.	Inspecting mechanic — fail to properly affix current dump vehicle inspection sticker	clause 5(4)(b)
7.	Licensee — fail to remove school purposes vehicle safety inspection sticker	clause 8(3)(d)
8.	Authorized person — fail to remove school purposes vehicle safety inspection sticker	clause 8(3)(d)
9.	Inspecting mechanic — fail to remove school purposes vehicle safety inspection sticker	clause 8(3)(d)
10.	Licensee — fail to remove brake inspection sticker (school purposes vehicle)	clause 8(3)(d)
11.	Authorized person — fail to remove brake inspection sticker (school purposes vehicle)	clause 8(3)(d)
12.	Inspecting mechanic — fail to remove brake inspection sticker (school purposes vehicle)	clause 8(3)(d)
13.	Licensee — fail to remove bus safety inspection sticker	clause 9(6)(d)
14.	Authorized person — fail to remove bus safety inspection sticker	clause 9(6)(d)
15.	Inspecting mechanic — fail to remove bus safety inspection sticker	clause 9(6)(d)
16.	Licensee — fail to remove brake inspection sticker	clause 9(6)(d)
17.	Authorized person — fail to remove brake inspection sticker	clause 9(6)(d)
18.	Inspecting mechanic — fail to remove brake inspection sticker	clause 9(6)(d)

Schedule 55

Regulation 612 of Revised Regulations of Ontario, 1990 Under the Highway Traffic Act

ITEM	COLUMN 1	COLUMN 2
1.	Fail to display "school bus" sign	clause 1(1)(a)
2.	Improper "school bus" sign	clause 1(1)(a)
3.	Fail to display "do not pass when signals flashing" sign	clause 1(1)(b)
4.	Improper "do not pass when signals flashing" sign	clause 1(1)(b)
5.	Fail to have signal lights	clause 1(1)(c)
6.	Improper signal lights	clause 1(1)(c)
7.	Control device not accessible to driver	clause 1(1)(c) para. 3
8.	Control device not equipped to signal driver	clause 1(1)(c) para. 3
9.	No first aid kit	clause 1(1)(D)
10.	Improper first aid kit	subclause 1(1)(d)(i)
11.	Improper first aid kit	subclause 1(1)(d)(ii)
12.	Fail to conceal "school bus" sign	subsection 1(2)
13.	Sell new school bus not conforming to CSA standards	section 2
14.	Offer to sell new school bus not conforming to CSA standards	section 2
15.	Improper mirror	clause 3(1)(a)
16.	No tire chains or snow tires	clause 3(1)(b)
17.	Improper speedometer	clause 3(1)(c)
18.	Inadequate body floor	clause 3(1)(d)
19.	Fail to have two constant-speed windshield wipers	clause 3(1)(e)
20.	Fail to have effective defrosting device	clause 3(1)(e)
21.	Fail to have adequate interior lighting	clause 3(1)(f)
22.	Fail to have interior lighted	clause 3(1)(f)
23.	Fail to have axe or clawbar	clause 3(1)(g)
24.	Axe or clawbar not securely mounted and accessible	clause 3(1)(g)
25.	Fail to have adequate fire extinguisher	clause 3(1)(g)
26.	Fire extinguisher not securely mounted and accessible	clause 3(1)(g)
27.	Fail to have dependable tires	clause 3(1)(h)
28.	Front tires rebuilt	clause 3(1)(h)
29.	Fail to have emergency door or exit	subclause 3(1)(i)(i)
30.	Improper emergency door	subclause 3(1)(i)(i)
31.	Fail to Fail to have required pushout windows	subclause 3(1)(i)(ii)
32.	Fail to have pushout window in rear	subsection 3(2)

Schedule 55.1

Regulation 614 of the Revised Regulations of Ontario, 1990 Under the Highway Traffic Act

Item	Column 1	Column 2
1.	Fail to contain load as prescribed	clause 2(1)(a)
1.1	Fail to contain load as prescribed — commercial motor vehicle	clause 2(1)(a)
2.	Fail to have required number of tiedown assemblies	clause 2(1)(b)
2.1	Fail to have required number of tiedown assemblies — commercial motor vehicle	clause 2(1)(b)
3.	Fail to prevent load from shifting forward	subsection 2(3)
3.1	Fail to prevent load from shifting forward — commercial motor vehicle	clause 2(3)
4.	Fail to properly block or brace load	clause 2(3)(a)
4.1	Fail to properly block or brace load — commercial motor vehicle	clause 2(3)(a)
5.	Use tiedown assembly failing to meet required aggregate working load limit	subsection 3(1)
5.1	Use tiedown assembly failing to meet required aggregate working load limit — commercial motor vehicle	subsection 3(1)
6.	Use defective or damaged tiedown assembly	subsection 3(6)
6.1	Use defective or damaged tiedown assembly — commercial motor vehicle	subsection 3(6)
7.	Fail to secure over-the-centre tiedown tensioner with adequate secondary means	subsection 3(7)
7.1	Fail to secure over-the-centre tiedown tensioner with adequate secondary means — commercial motor vehicle	subsection 3(7)
8.	Fail to contain load as prescribed	section 4
9.	Fail to contain load as prescribed — commercial motor vehicle	section 4

O. Reg. 430/95, s. 3; O. Reg. 485/96, s. 5.

Schedule 56

Regulation 620 of Revised Regulations of Ontario, 1990 Under the Highway Traffic Act

Item	Column 1	Column 2
1.	Speeding — provincial park — more than 70 km/h on highway set out in Schedule	clause 1(a)
2.	Speeding — provincial park — more than 40 km/h	clause 1(b)

Schedule 57

Regulation 625 of Revised Regulations of Ontario, 1990 Under the Highway Traffic Act

ITEM	COLUMN 1	COLUMN 2
1.	Drive with studded tire	section 9

O. Reg. 485/86, s. 6.

Schedule 58

Regulation 627 of Revised Regulations of Ontario, 1990 Under the Highway Traffic Act

ITEM	COLUMN 1	COLUMN 2
1.	Pedestrian using controlled-access highway	subsection 1(1)

Schedule 59

Regulation 628 of Revised Regulations of Ontario, 1990 Under the Highway Traffic Act

ITEM	COLUMN 1	COLUMN 2
1.	Vehicle modified — fail to apply for new permit	section 3

Schedule 60

Regulation 630 of Revised Regulations of Ontario, 1990 Under the Highway Traffic Act

ITEM	COLUMN 1	COLUMN 2
1.	Bicycle on controlled-access highway	clause 1(a)
2.	Motorcycle 50 cc or less on controlled-access highway	clause 1(b)
3.	Motorcycle driven by electricity on controlled-access highway	clause 1(c)
4.	Motor assisted bicycle on controlled-access highway	clause 1(d)

Schedule 1

North Grey Region Conservation Authority—Regulation 126 of Revised Regulations of Ontario, 1990 under the Conservation Authorities Act

ITEM	COLUMN 1	COLUMN 2
1.	Park vehicle in Conservation Area other than where permitted	clause 15(2)(c)

Schedule 2

Sauble Valley Conservation Authority—Regulation 132 of Revised Regulations of Ontario, 1990 under the Conservation Authorities Act

ITEM	COLUMN 1	COLUMN 2
1.	Park vehicle in Conservation Area other than where permitted	clause 15(2)(c)

Schedule 3

Regulation 333 of Revised Regulations of Ontario, 1990 under the Energy Act

ITEM	COLUMN 1	COLUMN 2
1.	Park propane fuelled vehicle with leaks in propane system inside a garage	subsection 2(1) para. 114 clause 16.16.1
2.	Park propane fuelled vehicle with tank filled beyond capacity inside a garage	subsection 2(1) para. 114 clause 16.16.1
3.	Park propane fuelled vehicle near source of heat	subsection 2(1) para. 114 clause 16.16.3
4.	Park propane fuelled vehicle near an open flame	subsection 2(1) para. 114 clause 16.16.3
5.	Park propane fuelled vehicle near source of ignition	subsection 2(1) para. 114 clause 16.16.3
6.	Park propane fuelled vehicle near an open pit	subsection 2(1) para. 114 clause 16.16.3
7.	Park propane fuelled vehicle near a drain	subsection 2(1) para. 114 clause 16.16.3

Schedule 4
Regulation 496 of Revised Regulations of Ontario, 1990 under the Game and Fish Act

ITEM	COLUMN 1	COLUMN 2
1.	Fail to park in designated area	clause 3(a)
2.	Fail to park in designated area	section 4

Schedule 5
Regulation 502 of Revised Regulations of Ontario, 1990 under the Game and Fish Act

ITEM	COLUMN 1	COLUMN 2
1.	Fail to park in designated area	clause 16(a)
2.	Fail to park in designated area	clause 16(a)
3.	Fail to park in designated area	clause 19(h)

Schedule 6
Highway Traffic Act

ITEM	COLUMN 1	COLUMN 2
0.1	Possess illegal disabled person parking permit	clause 27(a)
0.2	Illegally display disabled person parking permit	clause 27(b)
0.3	Fail to surrender disabled person parking permit	clause 27(c)
0.4	Illegally use disabled person parking permit on Crown land	clause 27(d)
1.	Fail to park—off roadway	clause 170(1)(a)
2.	Fail to stop—off roadway	clause 170(1)(a)
3.	Fail to stand—off roadway	clause 170(1)(a)
4.	Park on roadway—no clear view	clause 170(1)(b)
5.	Stop on roadway—no clear view	clause 170(1)(b)
6.	Stand on roadway—no clear view	clause 170(1)(b)
7.	Park on highway—interfere with traffic	subsection 170(12)
8.	Park on highway—interfere with snow clearing	subsection 170(12)
9.	Stand on highway—interfere with traffic	subsection 170(12)
10.	Stand on highway—interfere with snow clearing	subsection 170(12)

O. Reg. 126/91, s. 1.

Schedule 7

Regulation 604 of Revised Regulations of Ontario, 1990 under the Highway Traffic Act

Item	Column 1	Column 2
1.	Parking—improper parallel	section 2
2.	Parking—improper angle	subsection 3(1)
3.	Parking—obstruct sidewalk	subclause 4(1)(a)(i)
4.	Parking—obstruct crosswalk	subclause 4(1)(a)(ii)
5.	Parking—obstruct private entrance	subclause 4(1)(a)(iii)
6.	Parking—obstruct entrance-way	subclause 4(1)(a)(iv)
7.	Parking—obstruct fire hydrant	clause 4(1)(b)
8.	Parking—bridge	clause 4(1)(c)
9.	Parking—hotel entrance	subclause 4(1)(d)(i)
10.	Parking—theatre entrance	subclause 4(1)(d)(ii)
11.	Parking—public hall	subclause 4(1)(d)(iii)
12.	Parking—intersection	clause 4(1)(e)
13.	Parking—signal light	clause 4(1)(f)
14.	Parking—railway crossing	clause 4(1)(g)
15.	Parking—obstruct other vehicle	clause 4(1)(h)
16.	Parking—over time limit	clause 4(1)(i)
17.	Parking—disobey "no parking here to corner" sign	clause 4(2)(a)
18.	Parking—disobey sign at fire hall	clause 4(2)(b)
19.	Parking—disobey sign at school	clause 4(2)(c)
20.	Parking—Schedule .... highway	subsection 5(1)
21.	Parking—exceed time limit	subsection 5(2)

Schedule 8

Regulation 622 of Revised Regulations of Ontario, 1990 under the Highway Traffic Act

Item	Column 1	Column 2
1.	Stop vehicle on part of highway where prohibited	section 1

Schedule 9

Regulation 804 of Revised Regulations of Ontario, 1990 under the Motorized Snow Vehicles Act

ITEM	COLUMN 1	COLUMN 2
1.	Fail to park off roadway	clause 15(1)(a)
2.	Fail to stop off roadway	clause 15(1)(a)
3.	Fail to stand off roadway	clause 15(1)(a)
4.	Park on roadway—no clear view	clause 15(1)(b)
5.	Stop on roadway—no clear view	clause 15(1)(b)
6.	Stand on roadway—no clear view	clause 15(1)(b)
7.	Park on highway—interfere with traffic	subsection 15(4)
8.	Stand on highway—interfere with traffic	subsection 15(4)
9.	Park on highway—interfere with snow clearing	subsection 15(4)
10.	Stand on highway—interfere with snow clearing	subsection 15(4)

Schedule 10

Regulation 829 of Revised Regulations of Ontario, 1990 under the Niagara Parks Act

ITEM	COLUMN 1	COLUMN 2
1.	Park vehicle—area not designated	clause 2(9)(h)
1.1	Park vehicle—area designated for disabled	clause 2(9)(h.1)
2.	Park vehicle—after hours designated	clause 2(9)(i)
3.	Park vehicle—between midnight and 6 a.m. where unauthorized	Clause 2(9)(j)
4.	Park vehicle—within 15 metres of bridge	clause 13(1)(a)
5.	Park vehicle—interferes with movement of vehicles	clause 13(1)(a)
6.	Park vehicle—prohibited area	clause 13(1)(a)
7.	Park vehicle—over one hour limit	subclause 13(1)(b)(i)
8.	Park vehicle—over two hour limit	subclause 13(1)(b)(ii)
9.	Park sight-seeing vehicle—area not designated	clause 13(1)(c)
10.	Park heavy vehicle	subsection 13(9)

O. Reg. 47/92, s. 1.

Schedule 11
Regulation 867 of Revised Regulations of Ontario, 1990 under the Ontario Agricultural Museum Act

Item	Column 1	Column 2
1.	Park vehicle in place not set aside for parking	clause 13(1)(l)

Schedule 12
Regulation 872 of Revised Regulations of Ontario, 1990 under the Ontario Food Terminal Act

Item	Column 1	Column 2
1.	Park vehicle within Terminal—interferes with movement of vehicles	clause 5(a)
2.	Stand vehicle within Terminal—interferes with movement of vehicles	clause 5(a)
3.	Park vehicle within Terminal—in prohibited area	clause 5(b)
4.	Stand vehicle within Terminal—in prohibited area	clause 5(b)
5.	Park vehicle within Terminal—off roadway	section 7
6.	Stand vehicle within Terminal—off roadway	section 7
7.	Park vehicle within Terminal—place not designated for parking	section 7
8.	Stand vehicle within Terminal—place not designated for parking	section 7
9.	Park vehicle other than automobile in area designated for automobiles	clause 13(3)(a)
10.	Park automobile in designated area for over 24 hours	clause 13(3)(b)
11.	Park vehicle other than truck in area designated for trucks	clause 13(4)(a)
12.	Park truck in designated area for over 24 hours	clause 13(4)(b)
13.	Park vehicle in reserved area—decal not properly affixed	subsection 13(6)
14.	Park automobile at rear dock of wholesaler	subsection 14(1)
15.	Stand automobile at rear dock of wholesaler	subsection 14(1)
16.	Park truck at rear dock of wholesaler	subsection 14(1)
17.	Stand truck at rear dock of wholesaler	subsection 14(1)
18.	Park automobile at dock of cold storage section	subsection 14(1)
19.	Stand automobile at dock of cold storage section	subsection 14(1)
20.	Park truck at dock of cold storage section	subsection 14(1)
21.	Stand truck at dock of cold storage section	subsection 14(1)
22.	Park automobile backed to a dock in buyers' court	subsection 14(3)
23.	Park truck backed to a dock in buyers' court	subsection 14(3)
24.	Park vehicle in buyers' court—not buyer	subsection 14(6)

ITEM	COLUMN 1	COLUMN 2
25.	Park vehicle in buyers' court between 4 p.m. and 7 p.m.	subsection 14(7)
26.	Park vehicle in buyers' court between 4 p.m. Friday and 12 noon Saturday	subsection 14(8)
27.	Park inoperative vehicle outside building in Terminal	subsection 14(9)
28.	Park vehicle not currently registered under Highway Traffic Act outside building in Terminal	subsection 14(9)

Schedule 13

Regulation 952 of Revised Regulations of Ontario, 1990 under the Provincial Parks Act

ITEM	COLUMN 1	COLUMN 2
1.	Park vehicle in area not designated	subsection 10(3)
2.	Fail to display permit on parked vehicle	subsection 16(4)
3.	Park vehicle in position or place that prevents movement of vehicles	clause 20(a)
4.	Park vehicle in position or place likely to prevent movement of vehicles	clause 20(a)
5.	Park vehicle in prohibited area	clause 20(b)
6.	Leave vehicle unattended	subsection 25(1)
7.	Permit vehicle to be left unattended	subsection 25(1)
8.	Leave all-terrain vehicle unattended	subsection 25(1)
9.	Permit all-terrain vehicle to be left unattended	subsection 25(1)

O. Reg. 506/94, s. 1.

Schedule 14

Public Lands Act

ITEM	COLUMN 1	COLUMN 2
1.	Park vehicle on public land contrary to sign	subsection 28(2)

Schedule 15

Regulation 980 of Revised Regulations of Ontario, 1990 under the Public Transportation and Highway Improvement Act

ITEM	COLUMN 1	COLUMN 2
1.	Park on rest area where parking prohibited by sign	section 1
2.	Park on service area where parking prohibited by sign	section 1
3.	Park on area other than rest or service areas where parking prohibited by sign	section (1)
4.	Park in rest area after 9 p.m. and before 5 a.m.	section 2
5.	Park in service area after 9 p.m. and before 5 a.m.	section 2
6.	Park in area other than rest or service areas after 9 p.m. and before 5 a.m.	section 2

Schedule 16

Regulation 1022 of Revised Regulations of Ontario, 1990 under the St. Clair Parkway Commission Act

ITEM	COLUMN 1	COLUMN 2
1.	Park vehicle—area not designated	subsection 11(5)
2.	Park vehicle—area not designated	subsection 21(4)

O. Reg. 47/92, s. 2.

Schedule 17

Regulation 1023 of Revised Regulations of Ontario, 1990 under the St. Lawrence Parks Commission Act

ITEM	COLUMN 1	COLUMN 2
1.	Park heavy vehicle—on parkway	subsection 11(2)
2.	Park vehicle—area not designated	section 15
3.	Park vehicle—area not designated	subsection 22(2)
4.	Place more than one vehicle on camp-site	section 23
5.	Cause to be placed more than one vehicle on camp-site	section 23
6.	Permit motor vehicle to remain in park—after hours	subsection 25(3)

Schedule 18

Regulation 1036 of Revised Regulations of Ontario, 1990 under the Toronto Area Transit Operating Authority Act

ITEM	COLUMN 1	COLUMN 2
1.	Park vehicle not incidental to use of transit system	subsection 10(2)
2.	Park vehicle over 48 hours	subsection 10(3)
3.	Park vehicle—excessive weight	subsection 10(4)
4.	Park vehicle outside designated area	subsection 10(5)
5.	Stand vehicle outside designated area	subsection 10(5)
6.	Stop vehicle outside designated area	subsection 10(5)
6.1	Park vehicle without valid permit	subsection 10(6)
6.2	Park vehicle in designated area without displaying valid disabled person parking permit	subsection 10(9.1)
6.3	Stand vehicle in designated area without displaying valid disabled person parking permit	subsection 10(9.1)
6.4	Stop vehicle in designated area without displaying valid disabled person parking permit	subsection 10(9.1)
7.	Fail to obey sign	subsection 10(10)

O. Reg. 127/91, s. 1; O. Reg. 372/93, s. 1.

Appendix D

Rules of Practice and Procedure
of the
Provincial Offences Court

Rules of the Ontario Court (Provincial Division)
in Provincial Offences Proceedings

R.R.O. 1990, REG. 200 [am. O. Reg. 505/93; O. Reg. 498/94.]

1. In these rules, **"Act"** means the *Provincial Offences Act*.

2. (1) These rules apply to proceedings under the Act and a word or term in the Act has the same meaning in these rules as it has in the Act.

(2) In these rules, any reference to electronic process is a reference to the electronic process in force at the time of the coming into force of the *Provincial Offences Statute Law Amendment Act, 1993*.

O. Reg. 498/94, s. 1.

3. These rules shall be construed liberally so as to obtain as expeditious a conclusion of every proceeding as is consistent with a just determination of the proceeding.

4. The following apply to the calculation of a period of time prescribed by the Act, section 205.7 of the *Highway Traffic Act*, these rules or an order of a court:

1.   The time shall be calculated by excluding the first day and including the last day of the period.

2.   Where a period of less than six days is prescribed, a Saturday or holiday shall not be reckoned.

3.   Where the last day of the period of time falls on a Saturday or a holiday, the day next following that is not a Saturday or a holiday shall be deemed to be the last day of the period.

4.   Where the days are expressed to be clear days or where the term **"at least"** is added, the time shall be calculated by excluding both the first day and the last day of the period.

O. Reg. 498/94, s. 2.

5. A notice or document given or delivered by mail shall, unless the contrary is shown, be deemed to be given or delivered on the seventh day following the day on which it was mailed.

6. For the purpose of proceedings under Part I or II of the Act, the amount of fine set by the court for an offence is such amount as may be set by the Chief Judge of the Ontario Court (Provincial Division).

7. (1) An application provided for by the Act or these rules shall be commenced by notice of application.

(2) A motion provided for by the Act or these rules shall be commenced by notice of motion.

(3) There shall be at least three days between the giving of notice of application or notice of motion and the day for hearing the application or motion.

(4) An applicant or moving party shall file notice of application or notice of motion at least two days before the day for hearing the application or motion.

(5) Evidence on an application or motion may be given,

(a) by affidavit;

(b) with the permission of the court, orally; or

(c) in the form of a transcript of the examination of a witness.

(6) Upon the hearing of an application or motion and whether or not other evidence is given on the application or motion, the justice may receive and base his or her decision upon information the justice considers credible or trust-worthy in the circumstances.

(7) An application or motion may be heard without notice,

(a) on consent; or

(b) where, having regard to the subject-matter or the circumstances of the application or motion, it would not be unjust to hear the application or motion without notice.

(8) Subrules (2) to (5) do not apply in respect of a motion under section 66 of the Act.

8. (1) Where a certificate of parking infraction has been issued in respect of a parking infraction under a municipal by-law without a reference to the number of the by-law that creates the offence, the number of the by-law shall be affixed or appended to the court filing document when the certificate is filed in the office of the court.

(2) Where a certificate of parking infraction has been issued alleging a parking infraction against the defendant as owner of a vehicle, evidence of the ownership of the vehicle shall be affixed or appended to the court filing document when the certificate is filed in the office of the court.

(3) A certificate of parking infraction shall be affixed or appended to the court filing document when the certificate is filed in the office of the court.

(4) Where a defendant delivers a parking infraction notice or notice of impending conviction in respect of an alleged parking infraction under a municipal by-law and gives notice of intention to appear in court for the purpose of entering a plea and having a trial of the matter, the parking infraction notice or notice of impending conviction shall be affixed or appended to the court filing document when the certificate of parking infraction is filed in the office of the court.

(5) Where a defendant files a notice of intention to appear under subsection 17.1(3) or 18.1.1(3) of the Act, the notice of intention to appear shall be affixed or appended to the court filing document when the certificate of parking infraction is filed in the office of the court.

(6) In this rule and subrule 22(2), **"court filing document"** means a document approved by the clerk of the court.

O. Reg. 498/94, s. 3.

9. (1) A provincial offences officer who files a certificate of offence in the office of the court shall file with the certificate of offence a certificate control list, in the form that shall be supplied by the clerk of the court, with the certificate recorded on the list.

(2) A provincial offences officer who files a certificate of parking infraction in the office of the court shall file with it a certificate control list in the form approved by the clerk of the court, with the certificate recorded on the list.

(3) A single certificate control list may be filed with as many certificates of offence as can be accounted for on the certificate control list.

(4) A single certificate control list may be filed with as many certificates of parking infractions as can be accounted for on the certificate control list.

(5) The clerk of the court shall endorse on the certificate control list a receipt for the certificates of offence or certificates of parking infraction filed with the certificate control list.

(6) The clerk of the court shall, on request, give a copy of the receipt to the provincial offences officer who filed the certificate control list.

(7) Subrules (1) to (6) do not apply if a certificate of offence or a certificate of parking infraction is filed in an electronic format.

O. Reg. 498/94, s. 4.

10. A facsimile signature of the person designated by the regulations is sufficient authentication of the certificate requesting a conviction under subsection 18.2(1.1) of the Act.

O. Reg. 505/93, s. 1; O. Reg. 498/94, s. 5.

11. (1) The clerk of the court shall not accept for filing a certificate of offence more than seven days after the day on which the offence notice or summons was served unless the time is extended by the court.

(2) No certificate of offence, certificate of parking infraction or certificate requesting a conviction shall be accepted for filing by direct electronic transmission after the last day prescribed for its filing, unless the time is extended by the court.

O. Reg. 498/94, s. 6.

12. (1) The clerk of the court shall endorse the date of filing on every certificate of offence, certificate of parking infraction or certificate requesting conviction filed in the office of the court, except any such certificate filed in an electronic format.

(2) The clerk of the court shall ensure that the date of filing is indicated on any document filed in an electronic format.

(3) A certificate of offence, certificate of parking infraction or certificate requesting a conviction filed by direct electronic transmission shall be deemed to be filed the day on which the transmission concludes, unless the contrary is shown.

O. Reg. 505/93, s. 2; O. Reg. 498/94, s. 7.

12.1 [Revoked O. Reg. 498/94, s. 8.]

13. (1) On the delivery of an offence notice under section 5 of the Act, a parking infraction notice under subsection 17(1) of the Act or a notice of impending conviction under subsection 18.1(1) of the Act, giving notice of intention to appear in court for the purpose of entering a plea and having a trial of the matter, the clerk of the court shall, where proceedings have been commenced, set a day and time for trial.

(1.1) On the filing of a notice of intention to appear under section 5.1 of the Act, the clerk of the court shall, where proceedings have been commenced, set a day and time for trial.

(2) Where a parking infraction notice issued in respect of an alleged parking infraction under a municipal by-law is received under subsection 17(1) of the Act or a notice of impending conviction for such an infraction is received under subsection 18.1.1(1) of the Act, the clerk of the court shall give notice of the time and place of trial to the defendant and the prosecutor as soon as practicable after the prosecutor has filed the certificate of parking infraction in the office of the court, together with the corresponding parking infraction notice or notice of impending conviction.

(2.1) Where a notice of intention to appear is filed under subsection 17.1(3) or 18.1.1(3) of the Act, the clerk of the court shall give notice of the time and place of trial to the defendant and prosecutor as soon as practicable after the prosecutor has filed the certificate of parking infraction in the office of the court together with the notice of intention to appear.

(3) The clerk of the court shall give notice of the trial to the defendant and prosecutor at least seven days before the day set for trial.

(4) Where a parking infraction is alleged against the defendant as owner of a vehicle, notice of the trial shall be given to the person identified as the holder of the permit, as defined in section 6 of the *Highway Traffic Act*, in the evidence of the ownership of the vehicle affixed or appended to the certificate of parking infraction.

(5) A certificate as to the giving of a notice of trial endorsed on the notice of trial by the clerk of the court shall be received in evidence and, in the absence of evidence to the contrary, is proof of the giving of the notice stated in the certificate.

(6) Where a defendant files a notice of intention to appear under section 5.1 of the Act and it appears that the certificate of offence has not been filed, the clerk of the court shall,

(a) provide the defendant with a receipt for the notice; and

(b) as soon as practicable after the filing of the certificate of offence, set a day and time for trial and issue the notice of trial.

O. Reg. 505/93, s. 4; O. Reg. 498/94, s. 9.

14. (1) A defendant who attends at the time and place specified in an offence notice for the purpose of taking steps under subsection 7(1) of the Act shall give the offence notice to the office of the court specified in the notice.

(2) The court shall give to a defendant a receipt for an offence notice delivered to the court in accordance with subrule (1).

15. (1) The following matters shall be dealt with only in court:

1.   Quashing a proceeding, except under section 9, 18.3 or 18.5 of the Act or under section 205.7 of the *Highway Traffic Act.*

2.   Amending an information, a certificate of offence or a certificate of parking infraction.

(2) A justice may dispose of an application under section 18.3 of the Act on the basis of the parking infraction notice and the form of application presented by the applicant.

(3) A justice may dispose of an application under section 18.5 of the Act on the basis of the form of application presented by the applicant, together with any oral submission the applicant wishes to make or the justice wishes to hear.

(4) A justice may dispose of an application under section 19 of the Act on the basis of the notice of fine and due date and the affidavit of the applicant.

O. Reg. 505/93, s. 5; O. Reg. 498/94, s. 10.

16. A justice shall not quash a proceeding or amend a certificate of offence in respect of a defendant who is appearing before the justice for the purposes of section 7 of the Act.

17. Where a defendant appears before a justice under section 7 of the Act and it appears that the certificate of offence has not been filed in the office of the court, the justice may receive the plea of guilty and submissions of the defendant and specify the amount of fine the justice will impose and the time the justice will allow for payment when the certificate of offence is filed and a conviction is entered.

18. Where a defendant appears before a justice under section 7 of the Act and the justice is of the opinion that the certificate of offence is so defective on its face that it cannot be cured under section 33, 34, 35 or 36 of the Act, the justice shall refuse to accept the plea, shall inform the defendant of the reason for the refusal and shall inform the defendant of the provisions of section 5 or 5.1 of the Act as applicable.

O. Reg. 498/94, s. 11.

19. Money paid to the office of the court by a defendant who was served with an offence notice shall be refunded to the defendant if the certificate of offence is not filed in the office of the court named therein within seven days after the day on which the offence notice was served or within such extension of time as may be granted by the court.

20. Where notice is given to the clerk by the prosecutor that the prosecutor does not intend to file a certificate requesting conviction or a certificate of parking infraction that has been issued in respect of a parking infraction under an Act of the Legislature or under a regulation made under the authority of an Act, the prosecutor shall furnish the clerk with the name and address of the person to whom the parking infraction notice was issued and money paid to the office of the court in respect of the alleged parking infraction shall be refunded to that person.

O. Reg. 505/93, s. 6.

21. Every justice shall keep a daily docket, electronically or in the form supplied by the clerk of the court, and shall record the disposition of every proceeding or matter under Part I or II of the Act dealt with by the justice.

O. Reg. 498/94, s. 12.

22. (1) A justice acting under section 7 of the Act who imposes a fine that is less than the set fine or less than the minimum fine prescribed for the offence by the provision that creates the penalty shall endorse on the certificate of offence or the information, as the case may be, the decision and the reasons for the decision.

(1.1) A justice who quashes a proceeding under section 9 or 9.1 of the Act or under section 205.7 or 205.11 of the *Highway Traffic Act* shall endorse on the certificate of offence or the information, as the case may be, the decision and the reasons for the decision.

(2) A justice who quashes a proceeding under section 18.4 of the Act shall endorse on the court filing document to which the certificate of parking infraction is affixed or appended the decision and the reasons for the decision.

(2.1) A justice who strikes out a conviction under section 18.3 or 18.5 of the Act shall endorse on the form of application the decision and the reasons for the decision.

(3) In addition to recording the decision on a daily docket, a justice referred to in subrule (1) or (1.1) shall complete a separate report, in the form that shall be supplied by the clerk of the court, of the decision and the reasons for the decision.

(4) A completed report mentioned in subrule (3) forms part of and shall be kept with the records of the court maintained by the clerk of the court.

O. Reg. 505/93, s. 7; O. Reg. 498/94, s. 13.

22.1 A justice acting under section 9 of the Act or under section 205.7 of the *Highway Traffic Act* may examine by electronic means a certificate of offence that has been filed in an electronic format and may indicate his or her disposition of the proceeding by electronic means.

O. Reg. 498/94, s. 14.

23. Upon payment of a fine, the administrative officer of the entity receiving the fine shall, upon request, issue to the defendant a receipt for the payment.

O. Reg. 505/93, s. 8.

24. [Revoked O. Reg. 498/94, s. 15.]

25. A justice who issues a warrant of committal under subsection 69 (14) of the Act shall enter the reasons for the warrant in the records of the court.

O. Reg. 498/94, s. 16.

26. Where a person is sentenced to a term of imprisonment and a warrant of committal is issued for custody of the person to commence, under subsection 63(2) of the Act, on a day that is later than the day of sentencing, the clerk of the court, as soon as practicable after the warrant is issued,

(a) shall cause to be given or delivered to the person a notice stating the warrant has been issued and specifying the place where and the time within which the person is to surrender into custody; and

(b) shall deliver the warrant to the individual who is to accept the custody of the person.

27. (1) The following oath is prescribed for the purpose of subsection 84(1) of the Act:

I, ..., do swear (or solemnly affirm) that I am capable of translating and will translate to the best of my skill and ability from .... (name of language) to .... (name of language) from .... (name of language) to .... (name of language) in this proceeding.

SO HELP ME GOD. (Omit this line in an affirmation).

(2) The following oath is prescribed for the purpose of subsection 84(2) of the Act:

I, ..., do swear (or solemnly affirm) that I am capable of translating and will translate to the best of my skill and ability from ....

(name of language) to .... (name of language) and from .... (name of language) to .... (name of language) in proceedings under the *Provincial Offences Act.*

SO HELP ME GOD. (Omit this line in an affirmation).

28. (1) The clerk of the court who receives notice from the clerk of an appeal court that a notice of appeal has been filed shall transmit the order appealed from and transmit or transfer custody of all other material referred to in section 133 of the Act to the clerk of the appeal court within ten days after receiving the notice, to the extent that the clerk of the court receiving notice has the order or the other material in his or her possession.

(1.1) The clerk of the court receiving notice shall direct that any electronic document that has not been previously printed for the purpose of disposing of the charge and that is required as part of an appeal record be printed so as to create an original record, unless the appeal court requests that the document be transmitted to it in an electronic format.

(2) In an appeal from an order made under Part II, if the clerk of the court receiving notice does not have the order or the other material in his or her possession, the clerk may request and the municipality shall provide to the clerk the certificate of parking infraction and proof of ownership of the motor vehicle relating to the prosecution of the matter giving rise to the appeal.

O. Reg. 505/93, s. 9; O. Reg. 498/94, s. 17.

29. Where a transcript of evidence at trial, including reasons for judgment or sentence, is requested from the clerk of the court for the purpose of an appeal, the clerk,

    (a) shall complete and deliver to the person making the request a certificate of preparation of transcript in Form 2 of Regulation 196 of Revised Regulations of Ontario, 1990;

    (b) shall ensure that the transcript is prepared with reasonable diligence;

    (c) shall obtain and attach to the transcript a certificate by the person who prepared the transcript that it is an accurate transcription of the evidence and reasons recorded at trial; and

    (d) shall notify,

        (i) the appellant,

        (ii) the clerk of the court in which the appeal is taken, and

        (iii) if the Crown Attorney is not the appellant or respondent, the Crown Attorney, when the transcript has been completed.

30. The clerk of the court who receives notice of the decision of an appeal court on an appeal from a decision of the court shall give the notice and any written reasons or endorsement included with the notice to the justice whose decision was appealed from.

31. **(1)** Where, upon an appeal, the appeal court has directed a new trial, upon motion by the prosecutor without notice a justice shall issue a summons to the defendant.

(2) Where a justice issues a summons under subrule (1), the clerk of the court shall, as soon as is practicable, give notice to the prosecutor of the time and place of the trial.

(3) Where the appeal court has directed a new trial and sets a date for the trial with the consent of the parties to the appeal, the defendant shall be deemed to have received notice of trial, and subrules (1) and (2) do not apply.

O. Reg. 498/94, s. 18.

32. **(1)** An affidavit of service of an offence notice or summons shall be in Form 101.

(2) An affidavit in support of a request under section 11 or 19 of the Act or section 205.13 of the *Highway Traffic Act* shall be in Form 102.

(3) A certificate under section 11 of the Act or section 205.13 of the *Highway Traffic Act* shall be in Form 103.

(4) A summons under section 22 of the Act shall be in Form 104.

(5) An information under section 23 of the Act shall be in Form 105.

(6) A summons under section 24 of the Act shall be in Form 106.

(7) A warrant for arrest under section 24 of the Act shall be in Form 107.

(8) A notice of cancellation of summons under section 24 of the Act shall be in Form 108.

(9) A summons under section 39 of the Act shall be in Form 109.

(10) A warrant under subsection 40(1) of the Act shall be in Form 110.

(11) A warrant under subsection 40(2) of the Act shall be in Form 111.

(12) A recognizance by witness under section 40 of the Act shall be in Form 112.

(13) A warrant under subsection 40(10) of the Act shall be in Form 113.

(14) An order under subsection 40(6) of the Act shall be in Form 114.

(15) An order under section 41 of the Act shall be in Form 115.

(16) A certificate under section 42 of the Act shall be in Form 116.

(17) An order to attend for examination under section 44 of the Act shall be in Form 117.

(18) A warrant to take a defendant into custody under section 44 of the Act shall be in Form 118.

(19) A certificate of execution of a warrant issued under subsection 44 (6) of the Act shall be in Form 119.

(20) A summons under section 51 of the Act shall be in Form 120.

(21) An order of dismissal under section 53 of the Act shall be in Form 121.

(22) A summons to a defendant under section 54 of the Act shall be in Form 122.

(23) A warrant under section 54 of the Act shall be in Form 123.

(24) A warrant under subsection 63(2) of the Act shall be in Form 124.

(25) A motion under subsection 66(6) of the Act shall be in Form 125.

(26) An order under subsection 66(6) of the Act extending time for payment of a fine shall be in Form 126.

(27) A certificate of default under section 68 of the Act shall be in Form 127.

(28) [Revoked O. Reg. 498/94, s. 19.]

(29) [Revoked O. Reg. 498/94, s. 19.]

(30) [Revoked O. Reg. 498/94, s. 19.]

(31) An undertaking by a defendant to appear shall be in Form 131.

(32) A probation order under section 72 of the Act shall be in form 132.

(33) A summons to a defendant where a new trial is ordered by an appeal court shall be in Form 133.

(34) A recognizance under subsection 149(2) of the Act shall be in Form 134.

(35) A recognizance under section 150 of the Act shall be in Form 135.

(36) An order for detention of a defendant under section 150 of the Act shall be in Form 136.

(37) A warrant under section 155 of the Act for the arrest of a defendant shall be in Form 137.

(38) A certificate of arrest under section 155 of the Act shall be in Form 138.

(39) A certificate under subsection 157(1) of the Act as to failure to comply with a condition of a recognizance shall be in Form 139.

(40) An information to obtain a search warrant under section 158 of the Act shall be in Form 140.

(41) A search warrant under section 158 of the Act shall be in Form 141.

(42) A statement under section 161 of the Act shall be in Form 142.

(43) A warrant remanding,

    (a) a witness under subsection 40(6) of the Act; or

    (b) a defendant under subsection 150(4) of the Act,

shall be in Form 143.

(44) An order for the release of a defendant under subsection 150(2) of the Act shall be in Form 144.

(45) An order for the release of a person in custody under subsection 40(9) of the Act shall be in Form 145.

(46) A warrant of committal the form of which is not otherwise specified in these rules shall be in Form 146.

(47) An order the form of which is not otherwise specified in these rules shall be in Form 147.

(48) A recognizance under subsection 149(3) of the Act shall be in Form 148.

(49) [Revoked O. Reg. 498/94, s. 19.]

(50) An application under section 18.3 of the Act shall be in Form 150.

(51) An application under section 18.5 of the Act shall be in Form 151.

(52) An application under subsection 19 (2) of the Act shall be in Form 152.

(53) An order under subsection 69 (21) of the Act shall be in Form 153.

O. Reg. 505/93, s. 10; O. Reg. 498/94, s. 19.

Appendix E

Appellate Materials

Regulations under the Courts of Justice Act

Rules of the Court of Appeal in Appeals Under the Provincial Offences Act

R.R.O. 1990, REG. 195 [revoked O. Reg. 721/94]

Rules of the Court of Appeal in Appeals Under the Provincial Offences Act

O. Reg. 721/94

Definitions and Interpretation

1. In these rules,

(1) Definitions —

"Act" means the *Provincial Offences Act*; ("Loi")

"appeal court" means the Ontario Court (Provincial Division) or the Ontario Court (General Division), as the case may be, sitting as the appeal court under section 116 or 135 of the Act; ("tribunal d'appel")

"civil rule" means a rule in the Rules of Civil Procedure (Regulation 194 of the Revised Regulations of Ontario, 1990); ("règle civile")

"criminal panel" means any panel of three judges assigned to hear appeals in the week in which a matter is referred to a criminal panel under these rules; ("formation pénale")

"inmate appeal" means an appeal or a motion for leave to appeal by a person who at the timed the notice of appeal or notice of motion for leave to appeal is given is in custody and is not represented by counsel; ("appel d'une personne détenue")

"judge" means the Chief of Justice of Ontario, the Associate Chief Justice of Ontario or a judge of the Court of Appeal; ("juge")

"Registrar" means the Registrar of the Court of Appeal and includes a deputy, associate or assistant Registrar. ("greffier")

(2) Application of rules — These rules apply in respect of appeals under sections 131 and 139 of the Act.

(3) Matters not provided for — Where matters are not provided for in these rules, the practice shall be determined by analogy to them.

Application of Civil Rules

2. (1) Except where otherwise provided by the Act, another statute or these rules, the Rules of Civil Procedure apply, where appropriate and with necessary modifications, to appeals under sections 131 and 139 of the Act.

(2) Civil rules 61.03 (motion for leave to appeal), 61.4 (commencement of appeals), 61.05 (certificate or agreement respecting evidence), 61.07 (cross-appeals), 61.09 (perfecting appeals), 61.10 (appeal book), 61.11 and 61.12 (factums) and 61.13 (dismissal for delay) do not apply to appeals under sections 131 and 139 of the Act.

Special Leave to Appeal

3. (1) Form of notice of motion — A motion for leave to appeal, other than in an inmate appeal or where the moving party is not represented by counsel, shall be made by a notice of motion in Form 1.

(2) Time for service — The notice of motion in Form 1 shall,

(a) be served within 30 days after the date of the order or decision from which leave to appeal is sought;

(b) state the date on which the motion will be heard, being a date not later than 60 days after the date of the order or decision from which leave to appeal is sought;

(c) be filed with proof of service in the office of the Registrar within five days after service.

(3) Idem — The notice of motion in Form 1 shall be served at least three days before the date on which the motion is to be heard.

(4) Form of notice in inmate appeal or appeal by other party unrepresented by counsel — A motion for leave to appeal in an inmate appeal or by another person who is not represented by counsel shall be made by a notice of motion in Form 2.

(5) Time for service — The notice of motion in Form 2 shall,

(a) be served within 30 days after the date of the order of decision from which leave to appeal is sought;

(b) state whether the moving party wishes to present the argument in person or in writing;

(c) where the moving party wishes to present the argument in person, state that the motion will be heard on a date to be fixed by the Registrar.

(6) Service of notice of motion — Service of a notice of motion for leave to appeal shall be affected,

(a) in an inmate appeal, by delivering the notice of motion to the senior official of the institution in which the moving party is in custody;

(b) in an appeal other than an inmate appeal, where the defendant is the moving party, by leaving a copy of the notice of motion with,

(i) the prosecutor; and

(ii) if the prosecutor is not acting on behalf of the Crown, the Crown Law Office (Criminal) of the Ministry of the Attorney General; and

(c) where the prosecutor is the moving party, by leaving a copy of the notice of motion with,

(i) the defendant, and

(ii) if the prosecutor is not acting on behalf of the Crown, the Crown Law Office (Criminal) of the Ministry of the Attorney General.

(7) Motion to be heard by judge — A motion for leave to appeal shall be heard by a judge.

(8) Contents of notice of motion — A notice of motion for leave to appeal shall set out.

(a) the special grounds upon which leave to appeal is sought;

(b) any question of law upon which the appeal is to be founded; and

(c) where the appeal is as to sentence, the basis for the appeal.

(9) Motion record — On a motion for leave to appeal, other than an inmate appeal, the moving party shall serve,

(a) a motion record containing, in consecutively numbered pages arranged in the following order,

(i) a table of contents describing each document,

(ii) a copy of the notice of motion,

(iii) a copy of the proposed notice of appeal,

(iv) a copy of the certificate or information,

(v) a copy of any reasons of the trial court and the appeal court if the reasons are not included in the transcript,

(vi) a copy of any report prepared under the authority of an order made during the course of the proceedings,

(vii) a copy of all affidavits used before the appeal court, and

(viii) a copy of any other material in the court file that is necessary for the hearing of the motion;

(b) relevant transcripts of evidence, if they are not included in the motion record.

(10) Filing — On a motion for leave to appeal under subrule (9), the moving party shall file one copy of the motion record and transcripts, with proof of service, within 30 days after the filing of the notice of motion for leave to appeal.

(11) Responding party's record — On a motion for leave to appeal, the responding party may, where he or she is of the opinion that the moving party's motion record is incomplete, serve a motion record containing, in consecutively numbered pages arranged in the following order.

(a) a table of contents describing each document; and

(b) a copy of any material to be used by the responding party.

(12) Filing — The responding party shall file one copy of the motion record, with proof of service, within five days after service of the moving party's motion record and transcripts.

(13) Tabs may be used — Despite subrules (9) and (11), the parts of the motion record may be divided by numbered tabs provided that the pages within the tabs are consecutively numbered.

(14) Transmittal of inmate notice — The Registrar shall transmit to the Attorney General a copy of a notice of motion for leave to appeal filed by an official of an institution referred to in clause (6)(a).

(15) Inmate motion and motion in writing — A motion for leave to appeal in an inmate appeal or by another person who is not represented by counsel shall be dealt with in accordance with Rule 4.

Inmate Appeals/Appeals in Writing by Unrepresented Defendant — Leave to Appeal

4. (1) Motion for leave to appeal in writing — Where the moving party for leave to appeal is not represented by counsel, the moving party may present the case for leave to appeal and argument in writing, and the motion shall be dealt with in accordance with subrules (2) to (10).

(2) Motion to be dealt with expeditiously — Where the moving party is in custody, the motion for leave to appeal shall be dealt with as expeditiously as possible.

(3) Filing of argument in inmate appeal — In an inmate appeal the written argument shall be filed with the notice of motion or within 15 days of service of the notice of motion by delivering the argument to the senior official of the institution in which the moving party is in custody.

(4) Service and filing of material, unrepresented non-inmate — Where the moving party is not in custody, the moving party shall serve and file the motion record, transcripts and all other material that would be required if the motion for leave to appeal were to be heard with oral argument, within 30 days after the filing of the notice of motion for leave to appeal, and shall file two copies of the written argument with the motion record.

(5) Motion to be considered by judge — The motion for leave to appeal shall be considered by a judge.

(6) Submissions from respondent — If the judge considers that the motion has sufficient merit to require argument from the prosecutor, the judge shall so endorse the file, whereupon the Registrar shall transmit to the prosecutor copies of the notice of motion and the written argument of the moving party, if not included in the notice of motion, together with notification that the submissions of the prosecutor in answer to the motion should be made in writing within seven days of the receipt of the material from the Registrar and that two copies of the submissions should be filed with the Registrar.

(7) Procedure on dismissal of motion — If the judge considers that the motion for leave to appeal does not have sufficient merit to require argument from the prosecutor, the judge shall give written reasons for judgment dismissing the motion.

(8) Respondent's submissions to moving party — Where submissions have been required from the prosecutor, a copy of them shall be transmitted to the moving party together with a notification that he or she may make written submissions in reply within seven days of receiving the submissions of the prosecutor.

(9) Written reasons — When the moving party's submissions in reply have been received, or the time for submitting them has expired, the motion shall be referred for disposition to the judge, who shall give written reasons for judgment, to be dealt with as if the reasons were a reserved judgment.

(10) Time for service, extension — If the notice of motion in Form 2 is not served within the time limited by rule 3, the moving party shall set out in the appropriate place in Form 2 the grounds for seeking an extension of time.

(11) Oral hearing, inmate appeal — Where the moving party is in custody and has given notice that he or she wishes to present the motion in person, and in that event may request the Attorney General to arrange for the attendance of the moving party at the hearing.

Notice of Appeal

5. (1) Time for service — Where leave to appeal is granted, a notice of appeal shall be served in the manner provided in subrule 3 (6) within 10 days after the granting of leave.

(2) Manner of service — Despite subrule (1), the notice of appeal may be served upon the solicitor of record in the manner provided for in rule 16.05 of the Rules of Civil Procedure.

(3) Notice of appeal in inmate appeal — The notice of appeal in an inmate appeal shall be in Form 3.

(4) Notice of appeal in other appeals — The notice of appeal in all other appeals shall be in Form 4.

Order Without Attendance of Counsel

6. Except for an application for release from custody under section 132 of the Act, any order provided for in these rules may be made with the consent in writing of the parties without the attendance of counsel.

Extension or Abridgement of Time

7. (1) General powers of judge — The time for a motion for leave to appeal and to appeal and for doing any other act in connection with an appeal for which a time is prescribed may be extended or abridged by a judge before or after the expiration of the time prescribed.

(2) Notice — Except in an inmate appeal, notice of motion to extend or abridge time shall be given to the opposite party unless otherwise directed by a judge.

(3) Substituted service or dispensing with service — Where, on motion without notice, it appears to a judge that reasonable efforts have been made without success to give or deliver a notice or document in the manner required by these rules or the Act, or that reasonable efforts would not be successful, the judge may make an order for substituted service of the notice or document in such manner as the judge directs or, where necessary in the interests of justice, may dispense with the giving or delivery of the notice or document upon such terms as the judge considers proper in the circumstances.

(4) Extension of time in inmate appeal — An extension of time relating to an inmate appeal may be granted by a judge and the endorsement to that effect shall constitute an order extending the time.

(5) In all cases where the motion for an extension of time in an inmate appeal is served six months or more after the time for serving the notice of motion for leave to appeal, and in any other case where the judge considers it appropriate, the Registrar shall give the respondent notice of the motion.

(6) Within seven days of receiving notice of the motion, the prosecutor shall, if the motion is opposed, file a written response to the motion with the Registrar, and a copy of the response shall be forwarded by the Registrar to the moving party together with a notification that he or she may make written submissions in reply to the response of the prosecutor within seven days after receipt of the response.

(7) If the judge to whom the motion is made under subrule (5), after reviewing the grounds upon which the moving party requests an extension of time and any submissions filed by the moving party or the prosecutor under subrule (6), is of the opinion that an extension of time should be refused, the judge shall give reasons in writing for the refusal.

(8) The reasons given by the judge on the motion shall be sent to the moving party and, where the prosecutor has filed a response, to the prosecutor, and where the motion is granted the prosecutor and the moving party shall be notified by the Registrar.

Transcripts

8. (1) No application to inmate appeals — This rule does not apply to inmate appeals.

(2) Certificate or undertaking — The appellant shall, at the time the notice of appeal is filed with the Registrar, file a certificate of the court reporter stating that copies of transcripts required for the hearing of the appeal have been ordered or file an undertaking in Form 5 that any such transcripts will be filed within 30 days after the filing of the notice of appeal.

(3) Transcripts for the court — Except where otherwise ordered, three copies of the transcript of evidence at the trial and of any evidence received under section 136 of the Act are required for the use of the court.

(4) Contents of transcript — Unless otherwise ordered by a judge, or except as otherwise consented to by the respondent, there shall be omitted from the transcript,

(a) all final argument;

(b) all objections to the admissibility of evidence, except a notation that an objection was made and a brief summary of the nature of that objection and the position of counsel, but the trial judge's ruling and reasons in respect of the objection shall be set out in full in the transcript.

(5) Order for inclusion of additional transcript — A party obtaining an order for the inclusion in the transcript of any portion of the matter referred to in subrule (4) shall furnish the order to the court reporter within five days after the granting of the order, and furnish a copy of the order to the other parties together with confirmation that the order has been sent to the reporter.

(6) Appeal from sentence only — In respect of an appeal as to sentence only,

(a) where there was a plea of guilty at the opening of the trial before any evidence was taken, the transcript shall include the entire hearing before the court, including,

(i) the arraignment,

(ii) the statement of counsel for the prosecution,

(iii) any evidence,

(iv) any submissions of counsel for the prosecution and the defence,

(v) any statement by the defendant prior to the passing of sentence, and

(vi) the trial judge's reasons for sentence;

(b) where the plea was not guilty and was followed by the adducing of evidence, the transcript shall include,

(i) the trial judge's reasons for conviction,

(ii) the verdict,

(iii) any evidence called in respect of sentence,

(iv) any submissions of counsel for the prosecution and for the defence on sentence, and

(v) the trial judge's reasons for sentence.

(7) Agreed statement of facts — Where the plea was not guilty and was followed by the adducing of evidence, then within 30 days of receipt of the transcript referred to in clause (6)(b), counsel for the appellant and for the respondent shall make every effort to agree to a statement of facts which shall be included in the appeal book.

(8) In the event of difficulty in settling the statement of facts, counsel for either party may, on notice, attend upon a judge for directions.

(9) Date of order and completion — The transcript shall include a note of the date the transcript was ordered and the date the ordering party was notified that the transcript was completed.

(10) Completion not to be suspended — After a transcript has been ordered, the completion of the transcript shall not be suspended or the order countermanded without an order of a judge or the Registrar, unless the appeal has been wholly abandoned and the court reporter notified in accordance with subrule 28 (3).

(11) Agreement respecting evidence — Instead of complying with subrule (3), the parties may, within 30 days after service of the notice of appeal, make an agreement respecting the transcript required for the appeal and any such agreement shall be reduced to writing, be signed by the parties, be filed with the Registrar forthwith and form part of the contents of the appeal book under rule 12.

(12) Filing of transcript — Where no transcript is required for the hearing of the appeal other than that filed in the court appealed from, the copies of the transcript shall be filed with the Registrar within 30 days of the filing of the notice of appeal and in all other cases the transcript shall be filed forthwith upon its completion.

Dismissal for Failure to Comply with Rule 8

9. (1) Service of notice to cure default — Where the appellant fails to comply with any of the provisions of rule 8, the Registrar may serve notice on the appellant and counsel for the appellant that the appeal may be placed before the Court of Appeal to be dismissed as an abandoned appeal unless the default is cured within 10 days after service of the notice.

(2) Service of notice that appeal to be dismissed as abandoned — Where the appellant does not cure the default within 10 days after service of the notice, or within such longer period as a judge allows, the Registrar shall serve notice on the appellant and counsel for the appellant of the date on which the appeal will be placed before the Court of Appeal to be dealt with in accordance with subrule (1).

(3) Appellant to be served with copy of order dismissing appeal — The Registrar shall serve the appellant with a copy of an order dismissing the appeal.

(4) Manner of service — Unless a judge otherwise orders, service of a notice on the appellant and counsel under this rule shall be by prepaid registered mail to the addresses as set out in the notice of appeal or as filed with the Registrar.

Processing Appeals

10. Where a notice of motion for leave to appeal has been filed, the Registrar shall transmit a copy of the motion to the registrar of the Ontario Court (General Division) or the court clerk of the Ontario Court (Provincial Division), as the case may be, for the county or district where the proceedings appealed from were held.

Original Papers and Exhibits

11. Upon receipt of a motion for leave to appeal, the registrar of the Ontario Court (General Division) or the court clerk of the Ontario Court (Provincial Division), as the case may be, shall transmit forthwith to the Registrar from the court from which the appeal is taken all the material forming the record, including all documents and exhibits capable of reproduction, unless it is otherwise ordered by a judge.

Appeal Books

12. (1) Contents of appeal book — Except in an inmate appeal, the appeal book shall contain, in consecutively numbered pages arranged in the following order, a copy of,

(a) a table of contents describing each document, including each exhibit, by its nature and date, and, in the case of an exhibit, identified by exhibit number or letter;

(b) the notice of appeal and any supplementary notice of appeal;

(c) the order granting leave to appeal, and any direction or order made with reference to the appeal;

(d) the information or certificate, including all endorsements;

(e) the formal order or decision appealed from, if any, as signed and entered;

(f) the reasons for judgment of the trial court, if not included in the transcript of the trial, together with a further typed or printed copy if the reasons are handwritten;

(g) the reasons for judgment of the appeal court together with a further typed or printed copy if the reasons are handwritten;

(h) any order for release from custody pending appeal and any other order suspending the operation of the sentence;

(i) all documentary exhibits filed at the trial arranged in order by date or, where there are documents having common characteristics, arranged in separate groups in order by date;

(j) all additional documentary exhibits and affidavits used on the hearing of the appeal in the appeal court;

(k) all maps, plans, photographs, drawings and charts that were before the trial judge and are capable of reproduction;

(l) the agreed statement of facts, if any;

(m) where there is an appeal as to sentence, the pre-sentence report, the record of the defendant and any exhibits filed on the sentencing proceedings;

(n) any notice of constitutional question served in accordance with section 109 of the *Courts of Justice Act* and proof of service of the notice upon the Attorney General of Ontario and the Attorney General of Canada; and

(o) a certificate in Form 61H of the Rules of Civil Procedure signed by the appellant's solicitor, or on the solicitor's behalf by someone specifically authorized to do so, stating that the contents of the appeal book are complete and legible.

(2) Material may be omitted from appeal book — Despite subrule (1), with the consent of the respondent or as directed by a judge, some or all of the material referred to in clauses (1)(i) to (k) may be omitted from the appeal book.

(3) Form of appeal book — The appeal book, other than an appeal book prepared by the Attorney General under rule 13 or subrule 23 (3), shall be bound front and back in buff cover stock, and the appeal book prepared by the Attorney General under rule 13 and subrule 23 (3) shall be bound front and back in grey cover stock.

(4) Despite subrule (1), the parts of the appeal book may be divided by numbered tabs provided that the pages within the tabs are consecutively numbered.

(5) The Registrar may refuse to accept an appeal book that does not comply with the rules or is not legible and, in that case, the appeal book shall not be filed without a direction from a judge.

Appeal Book for Unrepresented Appellant

13. Where the appellant is not represented by counsel, the Registrar may require the Attorney General or counsel for the prosecutor to prepare the appeal book.

Factums

14. (1) Heading of factum — Except in inmate appeals, all parties to an appeal and persons who have been granted the right to be heard shall deliver a factum, to be entitled and described on its cover as "Appellant's Factum", "Respondent's Factum" or as the case may be.

(2) Factum to be signed and dated — All factums shall be signed by counsel or on counsel's behalf by someone specifically authorized to do so, or by the appellant or respondent if he or she has no counsel, and the signature shall be followed by the typed name of counsel, if any, and the date.

(3) Contents of appellant's factum — Except in an appeal from sentence only, the appellant's factum shall consist of,

(a) Part I, with the caption "Statement of the Case", containing a statement identifying the appellant, the trial court and the appeal court, the nature of the charge or charges, the result in the trial court and in the appeal court, and whether the appeal is from conviction, conviction and sentence, acquittal or other disposition;

(b) Part II, with the caption "Summary of the Facts", containing a concise summary of the facts relevant to the issues on the appeal, with such reference to the evidence by page and line as is necessary;

(c) Part III, with the caption "Issues and Law", containing a statement of each issue raised, immediately followed by a concise statement of the law and authorities relating to that issue;

(d) Part IV, with the caption "Order Requested", containing a statement of the order that the court will be asked to make;

(e) Schedule A, with the caption "Authorities to be Cited", containing a list of the authorities referred to, with citations, in the order in which they appear in Part III or in alphabetical order; and

(f) Schedule B, with the caption "Relevant Legislative Provisions", setting out the text of all relevant statutes, except where it would be more convenient to separately file an office consolidation from the Queen's Printer for Ontario.

(4) Respondent's factum — The respondent's factum shall consist of,

(a) Part I, with the caption "Respondent's Statement as to Facts", containing a statement of the facts in Part II of the appellant's factum that the respondent accepts as correct or substantially correct and those facts with which the respondent disagrees, and a concise summary of any additional facts relied on, with such reference to the evidence by page and line as is necessary;

(b) Part II, with the caption "Response to Appellant's Issues", containing the position of the respondent with respect to each issue raised by the appellant, immediately followed by a concise statement of the law and the authorities relating to that issue;

(c) Part III, with the caption "Additional Issues", containing a statement of any additional issues raised by the respondent, immediately followed by a concise statement of the law and the authorities relating to that issue;

(d) Part IV, with the caption "Order Requested", containing a statement of the order that the court will be asked to make;

(e) Schedule A, with the caption "Authorities to be Cited", containing a list of the authorities referred to, with citations, in the order in which they appear in Parts II and III or in alphabetical order; and

(f) Schedule B, with the caption "Relevant Legislative Provisions", setting out the text of all relevant statues, except where it would be more convenient to separately file an office consolidation from the Queen's Printer for Ontario.

(5) Length of factum — Unless ordered by the Registrar or a judge, the factum, excluding the Schedules, shall not exceed 30 pages in length.

(6) Form of factum — The appellant's factum shall be bound front and back in blue cover stock, and the respondent's factum shall be bound front and back in green cover stock.

(7) Form of factum — The factum shall be printed on good quality white paper 216 millimetres by 279 millimetres in size and the text shall be printed, type-written, written or reproduced legibly on one side only with double spaces between the lines, except for quotations which may be single spaced, and margins of approximately 40 millimetres on the left-hand side.

(8) Form of factum — The characters used shall be of at least 12 point or 10 pitch size.

(9) Form of factum — Back sheets and covers shall be of 176 g/m^2 cover stock.

(10) Registrar may refuse to accept factum for filing — The Registrar may refuse to accept a factum that does not comply with these rules and, in that case, the factum shall not be filed without a direction from a judge.

Sentence Appeals

15. (1) Sentence appeal factum to be in Form 6 — In an appeal from sentence only, the factum of the appellant, other than the prosecutor, shall be in Form 6.

(2) Where the prosecutor is the appellant, such changes shall be made in the form of the factum as are required.

(3) Time limits for oral argument — On the hearing of an appeal from sentence only, the appellant shall be limited to 15 minutes for the presentation of oral argument and the respondent to 10 minutes.

(4) The appellant shall be allowed five minutes to reply.

(5) In cases of unusual difficulty the panel hearing the appeal may enlarge these time limits as required.

Perfecting the Appeal

16. (1) Service and filing — Except in an inmate appeal, the appellant shall serve on every other party to the appeal and any person entitled by statute or an order of the court to be heard upon the appeal, one copy of an appeal book, one copy of the transcript and one copy of the appellant's factum and immediately thereafter shall file with the Registrar proof of service of the appeal book, the transcript and the factum, and,

    (a) in appeals directed to be heard by five judges, five copies of the appeal book and six copies of the appellant's factum; and

    (b) in all other appeals, three copies of the appeal book and four copies of the appellant's factum.

(2) Certificate of perfection — The appellant shall file with the Registrar two copies of a certificate of perfection stating,

    (a) that the appeal book, transcript and appellant's factum have been served and filed;

    (b) that the transcript is complete;

    (c) the estimated total length of time for oral argument; and

    (d) the name, address and telephone number of the solicitor for each party to the appeal unless the respondent is the Attorney General, and of any person entitled by statute or an order to be heard on the appeal, or where a party or person acts in person, his or her name, address for service and telephone number.

(3) Time for perfection — The appellant shall perfect the appeal by complying with subrules (1) and (2),

(a) where no transcript of evidence other than that filed in the appeal court is required for the appeal, within 60 days after filing the notice of appeal or such longer period as is permitted by a judge or the Registrar;

(b) where a transcript of evidence is required for the appeal, within 30 days after the transcript has been delivered to the Court of Appeal or such longer period as is permitted by a judge or the Registrar; or

(c) where an agreed statement of facts is required pursuant to subrule 8(7), within 60 days after the transcript has been delivered to the Court of Appeal or such longer period as is permitted by a judge or the Registrar.

Motion for Directions

17. The Registrar or any party to the appeal may, on notice, make a motion to a judge for directions in respect of the conduct of the appeal.

Failure to Perfect Appeal

18. (1) Notice of failure to perfect — Where an appellant has not perfected an appeal within the time limits set out in rule 16, the Registrar may serve notice on the appellant and counsel for the appellant that the appeal shall be placed before the Court of Appeal to be dismissed as an abandoned appeal unless the appeal is perfected within 10 days after the service of the notice.

(2) Notice of intent to have appeal dismissed — Where an appellant has not perfected an appeal within the time limits set out in rule 16, the respondent, on notice to the appellant and counsel for the appellant, may request the Registrar to have the appeal placed before the Court of Appeal to be dealt with in accordance with subrule (1), or may move before a judge for directions.

(3) Powers of Court — In considering an appeal referred to it under subrule (1), the Court of Appeal may,

(a) dismiss the appeal as an abandoned appeal;

(b) if the appellant was granted release from custody pending the appeal, revoke the release order and direct that a warrant issue for the arrest of the appellant;

(c) permit the appeal to remain on the list of pending appeals upon such conditions, if any, as the court considers fit, including conditions respecting the time limits for filing the transcript, the appeal book and the factum.

(4) Service of copy of order dismissing appeal — The Registrar shall serve the appellant and the appellant's counsel with a copy of any order or direction made or given under subrule (3).

(5) Manner of service — Unless a judge otherwise orders, service of a notice on the appellant and counsel under this rule shall be by prepaid registered mail to the addresses as set out in the notice of appeal or as filed with the Registrar.

Listing Appeals

19. (1) Notice of date of appeal — Subject to the direction of the Chief Justice of Ontario, the Associate Chief Justice of Ontario or a direction given by a judge as a term of an order made by him or her relating to the conduct of the appeal, the Registrar shall fix the day of the hearing of the appeal and notify counsel, or the party, as the case requires.

(2) Date not to be fixed until appeal perfected — Unless ordered by a judge or the Registrar, an appeal shall be listed for hearing only after being perfected in compliance with rule 16.

(3) Date for filing respondent's factum — The respondent's factum shall be served and filed not later than 10 days before the week in which the appeal is to be heard.

(4) Appeals may be scheduled in afternoon — In scheduling appeals, the Registrar may, where appropriate, prepare separate lists for the morning and for the afternoon.

(5) Duty on appellant to perfect appeal and obtain date — Where the appellant has been granted release from custody pending appeal, the appellant or counsel on his or her behalf shall take all practicable steps to obtain a date for the hearing of the appeal which precedes the date on which the appellant is required to surrender into custody.

Books of Authorities

20. (1) Filing books of authorities — Books of authorities shall be filed no later than Thursday in the week before the week in which the appeal is scheduled to be heard.

(2) Only authorities to be referred to included — The book of authorities shall contain only those authorities intended to be referred to in oral argument.

(3) Marking of authorities — The authorities shall be marked to indicate those passages intended to be referred to in oral argument.

(4) Copies to be legible — The authorities shall be reproduced legibly.

(5) Duplication of authorities to be avoided — A party shall not duplicate authorities already filed with the court by another party.

(6) Colour of cover — The book of authorities shall be bound front and back in coloured stock of the same colour as the party's factum.

Intervention

21. (1) Any person interested in an appeal between other parties may by leave of the Court of Appeal, the Chief Justice of Ontario or the Associate Chief Justice of Ontario, intervene in the appeal upon such terms and conditions and with such rights and privileges as the court, the Chief Justice or the Associate Chief Justice determines.

(2) The factum of the intervenor shall be bound front and back in white coloured stock.

Appeals in Writing (Non-Inmate)

22. (1) Appellant to file appeal books, transcripts and written argument — Where an appellant in an appeal that is not an inmate appeal indicates to the Court of Appeal that he or she desires to present the case on appeal and the argument in writing, the appellant shall file an appeal book, transcripts of evidence, if any, and all other material, except a factum, that would be required if the appeal were to be heard with oral argument, and file the written argument within 30 days after the material has been filed.

(2) Material to be considered initially by single judge — The material in the appeal shall be considered by a judge, who may give directions as to whether the respondent should be requested to file written argument and prescribe the times for doing so and for the filing of any reply in writing by the appellant.

(3) Procedure where judge considers appeal should be dismissed — If the judge considers that no written argument from the respondent is required, the judge shall prepare draft written reasons for dismissing the appeal, and the file shall then be referred to two members of the criminal panel.

(4) If the two members of the criminal panel agree with the judge and sign the reasons for dismissal, the appeal shall be dismissed and the reasons for dismissal shall be dealt with as if the reasons were a reserved judgment.

(5) Procedure where criminal panel requires argument from respondent — If one of the two members of the criminal panel considers that written submissions should be required from the respondent, directions in that respect shall be given in accordance with the provisions of subrule (2).

(6) Where submissions have been required from the respondent, a copy of the submissions shall be transmitted to the appellant together with a notification that he or she may make written submissions in reply within 14 days after receipt of the submissions of the respondent.

(7) When the appellant's submissions in reply have been received, or the time for submitting them has expired, the appeal shall be referred for disposition to a criminal panel, which shall give written reasons for judgment, which shall be dealt with as if the reasons were a reserved judgment.

(8) Criminal panel may require oral submissions — Despite subrule (7), the criminal panel considering the appeal under that subrule may direct that the appeal be listed for hearing and give notice to the appellant that he or she may attend and make oral submissions.

(9) Service — Unless a judge otherwise orders, service of a notice on the appellant under this rule shall be by ordinary mail to the address as set out in the notice of appeal or as filed with the Registrar.

Inmate Appeal — Notice of Appeal and Appeal Books

23. (1) Superintendent to provide inmate notice of appeal — The senior official of a penal or reform institution shall supply to any inmate in his or her custody, upon request, a form of notice of motion in Form 2 and a form of notice of appeal in Form 3.

(2) Superintendent to transmit documents — The senior official shall forthwith transmit to the Registrar any notice of motion and notice of appeal served upon him or her, and shall forthwith deliver to the inmate concerned any documents that may be transmitted to the inmate by the Registrar, and shall inform the Registrar of having done so.

(3) Preparation of appeal book by Attorney General or prosecutor — Where an inmate appeal is directed to be listed for hearing, the Registrar shall request the Attorney General or counsel for the prosecutor to prepare appeal books for the use of the court and the appellant which shall contain,

(a) a table of contents;

(b) the notice of appeal;

(c) the information or certificate;

(d) all exhibits capable of reproduction;

(e) the order granting leave to appeal;

(f) where the appeal is or includes an appeal against sentence, the pre-sentence report, if any, and the record of the defendant, if any;

(g) the transcript of the reasons for judgment in respect of conviction and sentence; and

(h) the reasons for judgment of the appeal court.

(4) Registrar may excuse compliance — The Registrar may, in writing, in an appropriate case, excuse the Attorney General from complying with the requirements of subrule (3), or any of them.

(5) Attorney General to provide copies of appeal books — The Attorney General shall mail one copy of the appeal book to the appellant and file three copies of the appeal book with the Registrar.

Inmate Appeals — Extension of Time

24. If the notice of appeal in Form 3 is not served within the time limited by rule 5, the appellant shall set out in the place provided therefor in Form 3 the grounds for seeking an extension of time.

Inmate Appeals — Presence of Appellant

25. (1) Where the appellant in an inmate appeal has indicated in the notice of appeal that he or she desires to present the appeal in person and the notice of appeal was served within the time limited by rule 5, or an extension of time has been granted, the appeal shall be listed for hearing.

(2) Despite subrule (1), an appellant in an inmate appeal who has indicated that he or she desires to present the appeal in person may request that his or her appeal be dealt with as an appeal in writing, and thereupon a judge may direct that the appeal proceed in accordance with rule 26.

Inmate Appeals — Appeals in Writing

26. (1) Inmate to be given appeal book and time to prepare argument — Where the appellant in an inmate appeal has indicated in the notice of appeal that he or she desires to present the case on appeal and argument in writing and the notice of appeal was served within the time limited by rule 5 or an extension of time has been granted, the Registrar shall notify the appellant that he or she has the right to present further written submissions within 14 days after receipt of the appeal book, unless this has already been done in connection with an application for extension of time for appeal.

(2) Appeal to be considered initially by single judge — The appeal shall be considered by a judge.

(3) If the judge considers that the appeal has sufficient merit to require argument from the respondent, the judge shall so endorse the file, whereupon the Registrar shall transmit to the respondent copies of the notice of appeal, the written submission of the appellant, if not included in the notice of appeal together with notification that the submissions of the respondent in answer to the appeal should be made in writing within 20 days of the receipt of the material from the Registrar and that four copies thereof be filed with the Registrar.

(4) Procedure where judge considers appeal should be dismissed — If the judge considers that the appeal does not have sufficient merit to require argument from the respondent, the judge shall write draft reasons for judgment dismissing the appeal and refer the appeal with the reasons to two members of the criminal panel.

(5) If the two members of the criminal panel agree with the judge and sign the reasons for judgment, the appeal shall be dismissed and the reasons for dismissal dealt with as if the reasons were a reserved judgment.

(6) Procedure where criminal panel requires argument from prosecutor — If one of the two members of the criminal panel considers that written submissions should be required from the respondent, the provisions of subrule (3) where argument is required from the respondent apply.

(7) Where submissions have been required from the respondent, a copy of them shall be transmitted to the appellant by the Registrar together with a notification that he or she may make written submissions in reply within 14 days of receipt of the submissions of the respondent.

(8) When the appellant's submissions in reply have been received, or the time for submitting them has expired, the appeal shall be referred for disposition to the criminal panel, which shall give written reasons for judgment, to be dealt with as if the reasons were a reserved judgment.

(9) Criminal panel may require oral submissions — Despite subrule (8), the criminal panel considering the appeal under that subrule may direct that the appeal be listed for hearing and, in that event, may request the Attorney General to arrange for the attendance of the appellant at the hearing.

Reasons for Judgment

27. (1) In every appeal, the Registrar shall notify the trial judge and the judge of the appeal court of the result of the appeal and where reasons are given in writing or given orally and later reduced to writing, the Registrar shall send a copy of the reasons,

  (a) in an inmate or an appeal where the appellant was not represented by counsel, to the appellant;

  (b) in an appeal conducted by a solicitor, to the solicitor for the appellant;

  (c) to the trial judge and the judge whose order is the subject of the appeal;

  (d) to the Attorney General;

  (e) to the solicitor for the respondent and any person granted intervener status or to the respondent and the intervenor, where not represented by counsel;

  (f) in an appeal from the Ontario Court (General Division), to the Chief Justice of the Ontario Court and the regional senior judge of the region where the trial was conducted;

  (g) in an appeal from the Ontario Court (Provincial Division), to the Chief Judge of the Ontario Court (Provincial Division) and the regional senior judge of the region where the trial was conducted.

(2) Where the reasons in writing or oral reasons reduced to writing are not given, the Registrar shall notify the trial or the judge whose order was the subject of the appeal of the result of the appeal.

Abandonment of Appeals

28. (1) Service of notice of abandonment — Where an appellant desires to abandon the appeal, the appellant shall serve in the manner provided by subrule 3 (6) a notice of abandonment signed by the solicitor of record of the appeal, or by the appellant, in which case the signature shall be verified by affidavit or witnessed by a solicitor or an officer of the institution in which the appellant is confined.

(2) Single judge may dismiss appeal — A judge may thereupon dismiss the appeal as an abandoned appeal, without the attendance of counsel.

(3) Court reporter to be notified — Where an appeal has been abandoned, the appellant shall forthwith notify the court reporter in writing.

Release from Custody Pending Appeal — Contents of Affidavit

29. (1) Contents of applicant's affidavit — Upon an application for release from custody pending appeal, the appellant shall file an affidavit or affidavits, including where practicable the appellant's own affidavit, establishing:

(a) the particulars respecting the conviction;

(b) the judicial interim release status of the appellant pending the appeal from trial decision;

(c) the appellant's places of residence in the three years preceding the conviction, and where the appellant proposes to reside if released;

(d) the appellant's employment prior to conviction, and whether the appellant expects to be employed if released and where;

(e) the appellant's criminal record, if any;

(f) where the appellant proposes entering into a recognizance with sureties, the amount of money or value of other valuable security the appellant proposes should be deposited, and where practicable, the names of the sureties and the amount for which each is to be liable.

(2) Respondent may file affidavit — Where the respondent desires to assert that the detention of the appellant is necessary and to rely on material other than that contained in the material filed by the appellant, the respondent shall file an affidavit setting out the facts upon which the respondent relies.

(3) Parties may cross-examine on affidavits — The appellant and the respondent may cross-examine upon affidavits filed by the opposite party, in accordance with the Rules of Civil Procedure.

(4) Judge may dispense with compliance — A judge may dispense with the filing of the affidavits referred to in subrules (1) and (2) and act upon a statement of facts agreed upon by counsel for the appellant and the prosecutor.

(5) Special meaning of criminal record — For the purposes of clause (1)(e) only, **"criminal record"** includes any record of convictions under the same statute as the conviction sought to be appealed.

Conditions of Release

30. Unless otherwise ordered by the judge hearing the application, all orders for release from custody pending appeal shall contain the conditions,

(a) that the appellant will surrender into custody at the institution from which he or she is released, or such other institution as may be specified in the order, by 6 p.m. on the day prior to the hearing of the appeal or such other date as may be specified in the order;

(b) that the appellant shall advise the Registrar of his or her place of residence.

Variation of Bail

31. (1) Judge may vary order — A judge may, on cause being shown, cancel an order previously made under section 132 of the Act and may make any order that could have been made under that section.

(2) Order may be made without attendance of counsel — An order for a new recognizance or undertaking varying a term may be made by a judge without the attendance of counsel, if the written consent of counsel for the respondent has been filed.

(3) Content of material to be filed — Where the appellant seeks an order under subrule (2) varying a term referred to in clause 30 (a), the material filed in support of the application shall contain a summary of the status of the appeal, an explanation for any failure to comply with rule 8 or 16 and, where applicable, a statement of the earliest feasible date on which the appeal may be heard.

Notice

32. An application referred to in rules 29 and 31 shall be on two clear days notice unless the respondent consents to, and a judge or the Registrar permits, a shorter period of notice.

Transition

33. (1) In this rule, "preceding rules" means the Rules of the Court of Appeal in Appeals under the *Provincial Offences Act* (Regulation 195 of the Revised Regulations of Ontario, 1990) as they existed on the day before these rules come into force.

(2) These rules apply to all appeals, whether commenced before or after the rules come into force, except in respect of steps already taken under the preceding rules.

(3) Despite the repeal of the preceding rules and subrule (2), a judge may make an order that an appeal, or a step in an appeal, be conducted under these rules or the preceding rules or make any other order that is considered just in order to secure the fair and expeditious conduct of the appeal.

Form 1 — Notice of Motion

Court of Appeal for Ontario

BETWEEN:

HER MAJESTY THE QUEEN

(indicate whether applicant or respondent)

— and —

A. B.

(specify name of defendant)

(indicate whether applicant or respondent)

Notice of Motion for Leave to Appeal Pursuant to s. 131 [or 139] of the Provincial Offences Act

TAKE NOTICE that a motion will be made before the presiding judge at Osgoode Hall, 130 Queen Street West, Toronto, Ontario, on (day), (date), at (time) or as soon after that time as this motion can be heard, for an order under s. 131 [or 139] of the *Provincial Offences Act* granting leave to appeal from the judgment of (specify judge appealed from) given on (specify date of judgment appealed from) at (specify place appealed from e.g. the City of Barrie) dismissing (or as the case may be) an appeal from the Applicant, A.B., from the judgment of (specify trial judge, e.g. Her Worship Justice of the Peace C.D.) given on (specify date and place of trial) convicting (or as the case may be) A.B. on the charge of (specify offence e.g. careless driving) contrary to (specify section and statue e.g. s. 130 of the *Highway Traffic Act*, R.S.O. 1990, chap. H.8).

THE SPECIAL GROUNDS FOR LEAVE TO APPEAL ARE:

1. (specify the particular circumstances which make it essential in the public interest or for the due administration of justice that leave be granted).

2.

THE GROUNDS FOR APPEAL ARE:

1. (specify the question of law alone where the appeal is from conviction or acquittal or specify the ground for appeal against sentence).

2.

IN SUPPORT OF THIS MOTION THE APPLICANT RELIES UPON THE FOLLOWING:

1.(set out documents such as transcripts, etc., upon which the Applicant relies, see Rule 4 (9))

THE RELIEF SOUGHT IS:

An Order granting leave to appeal from the judgment of (specify judge appealed from and date of judgment appealed from)

The applicant's address for service is ....

The applicant's address is ....

DATED AT .... this .... day of ....

....

E.F. counsel for the applicant A.B.

To: The Registrar

And to: (respondent)

Form 2 — Notice of Motion for Inmate Appeals and Where Moving Party is Unrepresented

Court of Appeal for Ontario
Motion for Leave to Appeal Under the Provincial Offences Act

To: The Registrar

Name of defendant ....

Place of trial ....

Name of court[1] appealed from ....

Name of judge appealed from ....

Offence(s) of which convicted[2] ....

Statute under which defendant convicted[3] ....

Plea at trial ....

Sentence imposed ....

Date of conviction ....

Date of imposition of sentence ....

Date of disposition of appeal ....

Name and address of place at which appellant is in custody ....

I, the above named defendant, hereby give you notice that I desire to appeal to the Court of Appeal against my[4] .... on the grounds hereinafter set forth on page 3 of this notice.

---

1 Ontario Court (General Division) or Ontario Court (Provincial Division)

2 e.g. careless driving

3 e.g. *Highway Traffic Act*

4 If you wish to appeal against conviction, you must write the word "conviction". If you wish to appeal sentence, you must write the word "sentence". If you wish to appeal both conviction and sentence, you must write the words "conviction and sentence". If you are convicted of more than one offence and wish to appel against some only of the convictions or sentences, you must state clearly the convictions or sentences against which you wish to appeal.

I desire to present my case and argument for leave to appeal,

(a) in person and request that the Registrar fix a date for the hearing of the motion; or

(b) in writing.[5]

Dated this .... day of .... 19..........[6]

Signed(7) * ....

Appellant

I hereby apply for an extension of time within which I may launch my motion for leave to appeal upon the following grounds (here state reasons for delay.)..........

The moving party [strike out inapplicable provisions]

(1) applies under s. 131 [or s. 139] of the *Provincial Offences Act* for leave to appeal conviction upon grounds involving a question of law alone.

(2) applies under s. 131 of the *Provincial Offences Act* for leave to appeal sentence.

(3) applies under s. 139 of the *Provincial Offences Act* for leave to appeal sentence upon grounds involving a question of law alone[7]

Grounds of Appeal

These must be filled in before notice is sent to the Registrar. The moving party must here set out the grounds or reasons he or she alleges why the conviction should be quashed or the sentence reduced. The moving party must also set out the special grounds for granting leave to appeal. Additional pages may be added and you may include your written argument if you do not wish to appear in person..........

Notes

Grounds for leave to appeal

I.

(a) You may apply for leave to appeal to the court of appeal from conviction only upon questions of law alone and only on special grounds which make it essential in the public interest or for the due administration of justice that leave be granted.

(b) You may apply for leave to appeal to the Court of Appeal from sentence only upon special grounds which make it essential in the

---

5 See the notes at the end of this form.

6 This notice must be signed by the defendant. If the defendant cannot write he or she must affix his or her mark in the presence of a witness. The name and address of the witness must be given.

7 You may apply for leave to appeal sentence in proceedings commenced under Part I or Part II of the *Provincial Offences Act* under s. 131 of the Act only on a question of law alone.

public interest or for the due administration of justice that leaves be granted, and in proceedings commenced under Part I or II only on a question of law alone.

Time for serving this notice

II.

(a) Whether your motion for leave to appeal is from conviction, sentence or both, this notice must be served within 30 days of the date of the order or decision from which leave to appeal is sought.

(b) If this notice is served beyond that time when you must apply for an extension of time by completing the application above.

Manner of service of this notice where person in custody

III. If you are in custody this notice of motion must be served by delivering it to the senior official of the institution in which you are confined.

Manner of service of this notice where person not in custody

IV. If you are not in custody you must serve a copy of this notice on the prosecutor and the Crown Law Office (Criminal) of the Ministry of the Attorney General if the prosecutor is not acting on behalf of the Crown. This notice must then be filed in the office of the Registrar of the Court of Appeal, with proof of service, within five days after service.

Filing argument in writing if in custody

V. If you are in custody and desire to submit your case and argument for leave to appeal in writing you may deliver your written argument to the senior official of the institution in which you are confined, with this notice of motion or not later than 15 days from the date that you serve this notice.

Filing argument and motion record if person not in custody

VI. If you are not in custody you must comply with subrule 3 (9) by serving and filing a motion record and transcripts within 30 days of filing of this notice, whether or not you wish to present your argument in writing or in person. The contents of the motion record are described in subrule 3 (9), a copy of which may be obtained from the Registrar's office. If you wish to present your argument in writing, the argument may be included with this notice or filed with the motion record.

Filing notice of appeal

VII. If leave to appeal is granted you will be notified by the Registrar. You will then have 10 days to file a notice of appeal. If you are in custody the notice of appeal must be in Form 3. Copies of Form 3 may be obtained from the officials in the institution or from Legal Aid Duty Counsel. If you are not in custody the notice of appeal must be in Form 4. Copies of Form 4 may be obtained from the Registrar.

If you are in custody you may apply for bail pending your appeal if leave to appeal is granted.

Form 3 — Notice of Appeal for Inmate Appeals

Court of Appeal for Ontario
Notice of Appeal Under the Provincial Offences Act

To:

The Registrar Name of defendant ....

Place of trial ....

Name of court[8] appealed from ....

Name of judge appealed from ....

Offence(s) of which convicted[9] ....

Statute under which defendant convicted[10] ....

Plea at trial ....

Sentence imposed ....

Date of conviction ....

Date of imposition of sentence ....

Date of disposition of appeal ....

Name and address of place at which appellant is in custody ....

I, the above named defendant, hereby give you notice that I appeal to the Court of Appeal against my[11] .... on the grounds hereinafter set forth on page 3 of this notice.

Dated this .... day of .... 19..........

---

8 Ontario Court (General Division) or Ontario Court (Provincial Division)

9 eg. careless driving

10 eg. *Highway Traffic Act*

11 You may appeal to the Court of Appeal from conviction only upon questions of law alone and only after a judge of the Court of Appeal has granted leave to appeal on special grounds. You may appeal to the Court of Appeal from sentence only after a judge of the Court of Appeal has granted leave to appeal on special grounds.

   If you have been granted leave to appeal against conviction, you must write the word "conviction" in this space. If you have been granted leave to appeal sentence, you must write the word "sentence". If you have been granted leave to appeal both conviction and sentence, you must write the words "conviction and sentence". You must state clearly the convictions or sentences against which you have been granted leave to appeal.

Signed[12] ....
Appellant

.....

Note:

(a) This notice must be served within 10 days of the date of order granting leave to appeal.

(b) If this notice is served beyond that time then you must apply for an extension of time by completing the application below.

III. This notice of appeal must be served by delivering it to the senior official of the institution in which you are confined.

.....

I hereby apply for an extension of time within which I may launch my appeal upon the following grounds (here state reasons for delay.)

....

Signed .... Date ....

I desire to present my case and argument,

(a) in person and request that the Registrar fix a date for the hearing of the appeal; or

(b) in writing.[13]

The Appellant [strike out inapplicable provisions]

(a) appeals conviction upon grounds involving a question of law alone.

(2) appeals sentence.

Grounds of Appeal

These must be filled in before notice is sent to the Registrar. The appellant must here set out the grounds or reasons he or she alleges why the conviction should be quashed or the sentence reduced. ....

Form 4 — Notice of Appeal

Court of Appeal for Ontario

BETWEEN:

HER MAJESTY THE QUEEN

(indicate whether appellant or respondent)

---

12 This notice must be signed by the defendant. If the defendant cannot write he or she must affix his or her mark in the presence of a witness. The name and address of the witness must be given.

13 If you wish to present your argument in writing you will be notified by the Registrar of the date for filing that argument or you may include your argument with this Notice of Appeal.

— and —

A.B.

(specify name of defendant)

(indicate whether appellant or respondent)

Notice of Appeal
(Under Section 131 [OR 139] of the Provincial Offences Act)

PARTICULARS OF CONVICTION (or as the case may be)

1. Place of conviction ....

2. Name of trial judge ....

3. Name of appeal court judge ....

4. Offence(s)[14] of which defendant convicted ....

5. Section(s) of statute under which accused convicted ....

6. Plea at trial ....

7. Length of trial ....

8. Sentence imposed ....

9. Date of conviction ....

10. Date of sentence ....

11. Date of disposition of appeal ....

12. Disposition of appeal..........

13. If defendant in custody, place of incarceration ....

The Appellant [use applicable provisions]

(1) appeals against his or her conviction upon grounds involving a question of law alone.

(2) appeals against his or her sentence.

The grounds of appeal are:[15] ....

The relief sought is ....

The Appellant's address for service is ....

The Appellant's address[16] is ....

Dated this .... day of ...., 19..........

_____

14 Note: The notice of appeal must refer to all offences under appeal.

15 Note: If leave to appeal has been granted limited to certain grounds of appeal then it is only those grounds which should be set out here.

16 Note: These rules provide for service upon the appellant of certain material at the address provided in the notice of appeal. If the appellant changes address then the appellant must notify the registrar.

(Name, address and telephone number of appellant's solicitor or (where none)[17] the appellant)

Form 5 — Undertaking

I ....[counsel for the Appellant or, where none, the Appellant] undertake that all transcripts required for the hearing of the appeal in the matter of Her Majesty the Queen and A.B. shall be filed by.......... 19..........

....

(Name, address and telephone number of appellant's solicitor or (where none) the appellant)

Form 6 — Appellant's Factum — Appeal from Sentence Only

Court of Appeal for Ontario

BETWEEN:

HER MAJESTY THE QUEEN

Respondent

— and —

NAME OF APPELLANT

Appellant

Appellant's Factum

Part I — Particulars of the Case

1. Place of Conviction

2. Name of Trial Judge

3. Name of appeal court Judge

4. Offence(s) of which defendant convicted

5. Section(s) of statute under which defendant convicted

6. Plea at trial

7. Length of trial

8. Sentence imposed

9. Date of conviction

10. Date of sentence

11. Date of disposition of appeal

12. Disposition of appeal

13. Present place of incarceration [if applicable]

---

17 Note: The appellant may present the case on appeal and the argument in writing by so indicating to the Court of Appeal. Reference should be made to Rule 22.

14. If defendant released on bail pending appeal, date of release[18]

15. Period spent in pre-trial/pre-sentence incarceration[19]

16. Parole Eligibility date[20]

17. Statutory release date[21]

18. Names of co-defendants and sentences imposed for offences upon which they were convicted[22]

19. Does the defendant have a prior criminal record[23]

20. Present employment[24]

21. Present Marital status[25]

22. Appellant's present age and age at time of offence

23. Was there a pre-sentence report prepared[26]

24. Were there any medical, psychological, psychiatric or similar reports referred to or filed at the sentence proceedings[27]

25. Was there a joint submission and if so what was it[28]

---

18 Note that these Rules require that the Release order be placed in the Appeal Book.

19 Where the incarceration was due to circumstances other than detention on the charges under appeal this should be made clear. Thus if for a portion of the time the defendant was serving sentence on another offence either this period should not be included or there should be a note to this effect.

20 This date is available from the sentence administrator of the institution where the defendant is incarcerated. Where the defendant is serving sentence for other offences other than the offence under appeal this should be made clear in a note.

21 This date is available from the sentence administrator of the institution where the Appellant is incarcerated.

22 Where the defendant relies on disparity as a ground for varying the sentence additional details may be necessary and should be included in Part II of the Factum. These details would include the co-defendant's criminal record, references to the judge's reasons for the sentence imposed on the co-defendants, the involvement of the co-defendant, whether the co-defendant was convicted of other offences so that the totality principle affected the sentence, and any other information which would put the allegation of disparity in its proper context.

23 If the defendant has a prior criminal record it should be set out in detail in Part II of the Factum and should include reference to convictions for offences under the same statute as the offence being appealed.

24 In addition to present employment a fuller history of employment should be set out in Part II of the Factum. If the defendant is in custody then refer to employment at time of conviction or sentence.

25 Where relevant the history of the defendant's marital status should be referred to in Part II of the Factum.

26 If there was a pre-sentence report prepared its contents should be briefly summarized in Part II of the Factum. In addition the entire report must be included in the Appeal Book.

27 Where relevant the contents of such reports should be briefly summarized in Part II of the Factum. In addition the complete report must be included in the Appeal Book, whether or not it was formally marked as an exhibit on the proceedings.

28 A joint submission would include where counsel have agreed on a range of sentences to be submitted to the trial Judge.

26. If no joint submission briefly set out the position of the prosecutor and defence counsel on the sentence proceedings[29]

27. Will there be an application to admit fresh evidence and if so does the Respondent consent to its admission[30]

Part II — Summary of the Facts

The Facts of the Offence[31]

The Background of the Appellant.

Fresh Evidence

> (Here briefly summarize the fresh evidence which on consent has been filed with the court)

Part III — Grounds of Appeal

Part IV — Order Requested

It is respectfully submitted that (*here set out relief requested, e.g. that the appeal from sentence be allowed and the sentence reduced*).

All of which is respectfully submitted ....

Defence Lawyer Counsel for the Appellant

Dated at .... this .... day of ...., 19..........

---

29 The "position" of counsel may simply be that the sentence should take a particular form i.e. incarceration, or may be more specific i.e. a specified term of months or years. If counsel did not make any suggestion as to the type or length of sentence this should be indicated as well.

30 Where the Respondent consents to the admission of fresh evidence on the appeal this evidence may be included in the Appeal Book or filed separately and reference may be made to the evidence in Part II of the Factum. No notice of motion is required, provided that the material is clearly identified as fresh evidence and the Respondent has consented to its admission. Where the Respondent opposes the admission of the fresh evidence then the counsel must prepare a notice of motion returnable on the date of the appeal. The evidence itself should be filed with the notice of motion but in a sealed envelope. There must be sufficient copies for the members of the Court.

31 Where the facts are complicated and somewhat lengthy counsel may wish to include a paragraph containing an overview of facts. In most sentence appeals that paragraph should not be required since these Rules require that this Part of the factum contain a brief summary of the facts.

Rules of the Ontario Court (General Division) and the Ontario Court (Provincial Division) in Appeals Under Section 116 of The Provincial Offences Act

R.R.O. 1990, Reg. 196 [revoked O. Reg. 723/94]

Rules of the Ontario Court (General Division) and the Ontario Court (Provincial Division) in Appeals under Section 116 of the Provincial Offences Act

O. Reg. 723/94

Definitions and Interpretation

1. (1) Definitions — In these rules,

"Act" means the *Provincial Offences Act*; ("Loi")

"appeal court" means the Ontario Court (Provincial Division) sitting as the appeal court under section 135 of the Act; ("tribunal d'appel")

"clerk" means the clerk of the Ontario Court (Provincial Division); ("greffier")

"file" means file with the clerk; ("déposer")

"judge" means a judge of the Ontario Court (Provincial Division) sitting as the appeal court under section 135 of the Act.("juge")

(2) Application of rules — These rules apply in respect of appeals to the Ontario Court (Provincial Division) under section 135 of the Act.

(3) General principle — These rules shall be construed liberally so as to obtain as expeditious a conclusion of every proceeding as is consistent with a just determination of the proceeding.

(4) Matters not provided for — Where matters are not provided for in these rules, the practice shall be determined by analogy to them.

Calculation of Time

2. (1) General — In the calculation of time under these rules or an order of the court, except where a contrary intention appears,

(a) where there is a reference to a number of days between two events, they shall be counted by excluding the day on which the first event happens and including the day on which the second event happens, even if they are described as clear days or the words "at least" are used;

(b) where a period of less than seven days is prescribed, holidays shall not be counted;

(c) where the time for doing an act under these rules expires on a holiday, the act may be done on the next day that is not a holiday; and

(d) service of a document made after 4 p.m. or at any time on a holiday shall be deemed to have been made on the next day that is not a holiday.

(2) Local time — Where a time of day is mentioned in these rules or in any documents in an appeal, the time referred to shall be taken as the time observed locally.

(3) "Holiday" — For the purposes of subsection (1), **"holiday"** means,

(a) any Saturday or Sunday;

(b) New Year's Day;

(c) Good Friday;

(d) Easter Monday;

(e) Victoria Day;

(f) Canada Day;

(g) Civil Holiday;

(h) Labour Day;

(i) Thanksgiving Day;

(j) Remembrance Day;

(k) Christmas Day;

(l) Boxing Day; and

(m) any special holiday proclaimed by the Governor General or the Lieutenant Governor.

(4) Same — Where,

(a) New Year's Day, Canada Day or Remembrance Day falls on a Saturday or Sunday, the following Monday is a holiday;

(b) Christmas Day falls on a Saturday or Sunday, the following Monday and Tuesday are holidays;

(c) Christmas Day falls on a Friday, the following Monday is a holiday.

Notice by Mail

3. A notice or document given or delivered by mail shall, unless the contrary is shown, be deemed to be given or delivered on the seventh day following the day on which it was mailed.

Substituted Service

4. Where, on motion without notice, it appears to a judge that reasonable efforts have been made without success to give or deliver a notice or document in the manner required by these rules or the Act, or that reasonable efforts would not be successful, the judge may make an order for substituted service of the notice or document in such manner as the judge directs or, where necessary in the interests of justice, may dispense with the giving or delivery of the notice or document upon such terms as the judge considers proper in the circumstances.

Service and Filing of Notice of Appeal

5. (1) Notice of appeal — A notice of appeal shall be in Form 1.

(2) Time for service, appeal be defendant — A defendant who appeals shall serve the notice of appeal on the prosecutor and, if the prosecutor is not acting on behalf of the Crown, on the Crown Attorney within 30 days after the date of the decision appealed from.

(3) Time for service, appeal by prosecutor — A prosecutor who appeals shall serve the notice of appeal on the defendant and, if the prosecutor is not acting on behalf of the Crown, on the Crown Attorney within 30 days after the date of the decision appealed from.

(4) Filing — An appellant shall file the notice of appeal with proof of service within five days after service.

(5) Proof of service — Proof of service of the notice of appeal may be made by affidavit.

(6) Admission of service — Where admission of service is endorsed on the notice of appeal, proof
need not be made by affidavit.

Appeal Where Fine Imposed

6. A defendant who appeals from a decision imposing a fine shall file with the notice of appeal a receipt for payment of the fine issued by the clerk of the court that imposed the fine, unless the clerk is satisfied that an order has been made under subsection 111(2) of the Act and a recognizance has been entered into by the defendant in accordance with the order.

Extension or Abridgment of Time

7. (1) Judge's power — A judge may extend or abridge the time for bringing an appeal and for doing any other act in connection with an appeal for which a time is prescribed before or after the expiration of the time prescribed.

(2) Notice — A notice of motion to extend or abridge time shall be given to the opposite party, unless otherwise directed by a judge.

Transcripts

8. (1) Certificate — An appellant shall file with the notice of appeal a certificate of the clerk of the Ontario Court (Provincial Division) as to transcript of evidence in Form 2.

(2) Filing and delivery of transcript — An appellant shall file and deliver to the respondent,

(a) in an appeal against conviction, dismissal, a finding as to ability to conduct a defence or an order under section 161 of the Act, one copy of the transcript of evidence at trial, including reasons for judgment; and

(b) in an appeal against conviction and sentence or sentence only, one copy of the transcript of evidence at trial and submissions on sentencing, including reasons for judgment and sentence, if any.

(3) Transcript to Crown Attorney — Where the Crown Attorney has given notice of intervention after receiving notice of appeal, the appellant shall deliver a copy of the transcript of evidence at trial, including reasons for judgment and sentence, if any, to the Crown Attorney.

(4) Time for filing certificate — An appellant who has been issued a provisional legal aid certificate limited to the filing of a notice of appeal and making a motion for release from custody under the *Legal Aid Act* shall file a certificate in Form 2 within one month of filing the notice of appeal.

(5) Deemed abandonment — An appellant referred to in subrule (4) who does not file the certificate within one month of filing the notice of appeal or within such longer period of time as a judge may permit shall be deemed to have abandoned the appeal.

Recognizances

9. (1) An order for recognizance and recognizance under section 110 of the Act shall be in Form 3.

(2) An order for recognizance and recognizance under section 111 of the Act shall be in Form 4.

Motions Under Act of Rules

10. (1) Notice of motion — A motion provided for by the Act or these rules shall be commenced by a notice of motion.

(2) Time for hearing — There shall be at least three days between service of the notice of motion and the day for hearing the motion.

(3) Time for filing notice — The moving party shall file the notice of motion at least two days before the day for hearing the motion.

(4) Evidence — Evidence on a motion may be given,

(a) by affidavit;

(b) with the permission of the court, orally; or

(c) in the form of a transcript of the examination of a witness.

(5) Power of judge — Upon the hearing of a motion, the justice may receive and base his or her decision on information that the justice considers credible or trustworthy in the circumstances, whether or not other evidence is given.

(6) Hearing where notice not served — A motion may be heard without service of a notice of motion,

(a) on consent;

(b) where the motion is made under section 111 or 112 of the Act; or

(c) where, having regard to the subject-matter or the circumstances of the motion, it would not be unjust to hear the motion without service of a notice of motion.

(7) Appeal by way of new trial — A person making a motion for an order under section 127 of the Act that an appeal be heard and determined by way of a new trial in the court shall give at least seven days notice of the motion to all other parties to the appeal.

Transmission of Material

11. (1) S. 115 notice deemed given — The clerk of the appeal court shall send a copy of the notice of appeal to the clerk of the Ontario Court (Provincial Division) as the notice required by section 115 of the Act.

(2) Time for transmittal of documents — The clerk of the Ontario Court (Provincial Division) shall transmit the order appealed from and transmit or transfer custody of the other material referred to in section 115 of the Act to the clerk of the appeal court within 10 days after receiving the copy of the notice of appeal.

Intervention of Crown Attorney

12. Where a prosecutor is not acting on behalf of the Crown, the Crown Attorney may intervene to act on behalf of the prosecutor or to attend as a party on the appeal.

Listing of Appeal

13. (1) Appeal list — The clerk shall place the appeal on an appeal list for the next sitting of the court at which dates are fixed for hearing appeals as soon as 10 days have elapsed after,

(a) the clerk has received the order appealed from and the other material referred to in section 115 of the Act;

(b) the appellant has filed a copy of the transcript of evidence at trial, including reasons for judgment or sentence, if any; and

(c) any other step required by the Act, these rules or the court has been completed.

(2) Notice period — The clerk shall give at least 14 days notice of the date fixed for the hearing of the appeal to the appellant and the respondent and, where the Crown Attorney has filed a notice of intervention, to the Crown Attorney.

(3) Motion under s. 127 — Where a motion is made under section 127 of the Act for an order that an appeal be heard and determined by way of a new trial in the court, the clerk shall not place the appeal on an appeal list until the motion has been disposed of and 10 days have elapsed since the disposition of the motion.

Directions

14. A party to an appeal may make a motion to the court at any time for directions with respect to the conduct of the appeal.

Factums

15. (1) Where factum not necessary — Unless a judge orders otherwise, a party to an appeal who intends to be present either personally or by counsel at the hearing of the appeal need not file a factum.

(2) Form of factums — Where a factum is required by order of the court or is filed by a party to an appeal, subrules (3) to (7) apply.

(3) Appellant's factum — An appellant shall prepare an "Appellant's Factum" not exceeding 10 pages in length, excluding the Schedule, and shall file, on or before the date specified in the notice of hearing given under rule 13, one copy of the factum, together with proof of service, on all other parties and persons who have been granted the rights to be heard on the appeal.

(4) Same — Except in appeals from sentence only, the appellant's factum shall consist of,

(a) Part I, entitled "Statement of the Case", containing a statement identifying the appellant, the court in which the proceedings arose, the nature of the charge or charges, the result in that court and the nature of each order to which the appeal relates;

(b) Part II, entitled "Summary of the Facts", containing a concise summary of the facts relevant to the issues on the appeal, with such references to the evidence by page and line, or paragraph, as the case may be, as may be necessary;

(c) Part III, entitled "Issues and the Law", containing a statement of each issue raised, immediately followed by a concise statement of the law and any authorities relating to that issue;

(d) Part IV, entitled "Order Requested", containing a statement of the order that the court is being asked to make; and

(e) a Schedule, entitled "Authorities to be Cited", containing a list of the authorities, with citations, to which reference was made in Part III in the order in which they appear in that Part.

(5) Respondent's factum — A respondent shall prepare a "Respondent's Factum" not exceeding 10 pages in length, excluding the Schedule, and shall file, not later than 15 days after receipt of the appellant's factum and not later than 7 days before the date fixed for the hearing of the appeal under rule 13, one copy of the factum, together with proof of service, on all other parties and persons who have been granted the right to be heard on the appeal.

(6) Same — Except in appeals from sentence only, the respondent's factum shall consist of,

(a) Part I, entitled "Respondent's Statement as to Facts", containing a statement of the facts in Part II of the appellant's factum that the respondent accepts as correct and those facts with which the respondent disagrees and a concise summary of any additional facts relied on, with such reference to the transcript evidence by page and line or paragraph, as the case may be, as is necessary;

(b) Part II, entitled "Response to Appellant's Issues", containing the position of the respondent with respect to each issue raised by the appellant immediately followed by a concise statement of the law and the authorities relating to that issue;

(c) Part III, entitled "Additional Issues", containing a statement of any additional issues raised by the respondent, immediately followed by a concise statement of the law and the authorities relating to those issues;

(d) Part IV, entitled "Order Requested", containing a statement of the order that the court will be asked to make; and

(e) a Schedule, entitled "Authorities to be Cited", containing a list of the authorities, with citations, referred to in the order in which they appear in Parts II and III.

(7) Paragraphs — The appellant's and the respondent's factum shall be in paragraphs numbered consecutively throughout.

Appeal in Writing

16. An appellant who intends not to be present in person or by counsel at the hearing of the appeal shall file, prior to the date of the hearing,

(a) a notice in writing of that intention, unless the appellant has already done so in the notice of appeal; and

(b) a statement in writing of the issues and the appellant's arguments on the appeal.

Dismissal of Appeal

17. The court may dismiss an appeal where the appellant,

(a) does not attend in person or by counsel and,

(i) has not indicated in the notice of appeal the appellant's intention not to be present in person or by counsel at the hearing of the appeal,

(ii) has not filed notice in writing of the intention not to be present in person or by counsel at the hearing of the appeal, and

(iii) has not filed a statement in writing of the issues and the appellant's arguments on the appeal;

(b) has filed a notice of abandonment;

(c) has not filed a transcript of evidence at trial, including reasons for judgment or sentence, if any, within 30 days after receiving notice of completion of the transcript from the clerk of the Ontario Court (Provincial Division);

(d) after obtaining an order under subclause 117(1)(b)(ii) of the Act for the examination of a witness, has not filed a transcript of the examination within 30 days after receiving notice of completion of the transcript from the other person before whom the witness was examined; or

(e) has failed to comply with an order of the court in respect of the appeal.

Abandonment of Appeals

18. (1) Notice of abandonment — An appellant who wishes to abandon the appeal may file a notice of abandonment in Form 5.

(2) Signing of notice — The appellant or counsel for the appellant shall sign the notice of abandonment.

(3) Signing by witness — Where the appellant signs the notice of abandonment, the notice must also be signed by another person who witnessed the signing by the appellant.

(4) Affidavit of execution — Where the witness is not counsel for the appellant, the appellant shall file an affidavit of execution by the witness with the notice of abandonment.

(5) Notice to other parties — The clerk shall give a copy of the filed notice of abandonment to each of the other parties to the appeal.

Appeal Respecting Release from Custody

19. (1) Commencing appeal — An appeal under section 152 of the Act in respect of release from custody shall be commenced by a written notice filed and given to all other parties and, if the Crown Attorney is not a party, to the Crown Attorney.

(2) Grounds for release from custody — On the appeal, the court shall order that the defendant be released from custody pending trial if it is satisfied that the defendant will attend in court for trial.

(3) When order for release takes effect — The court shall provide in the order that the order does not take effect until the defendant,

(a) gives an undertaking, either without condition or with such conditions as the court may order, to attend in court for trial; or

(b) enters into a recognizance, with or without sureties, in such amount, with such conditions and before such justice as the court may order, either with or without depositing with the justice money or other valuable security specified by the court.

Official Examinations

20. (1) Definition, "order" — In this rule, **"order"** means an order under subclause 117 (1) (b) (ii) of the Act.

(2) Presence of parties, counsel — Except with the consent of the parties or their counsel, the examination of a witness under an order shall take place in the presence of the parties or their counsel.

(3) Tentative appointment — A party who intends to make a motion for an order for the examination of a witness before an official examiner shall obtain a tentative appointment for the examination before making the motion for the order.

(4) Certificate of official examiner — Upon completion of the examination, the party who made the motion for the order shall file a certificate of the official examiner in Form 6.

(5) Notice of completion of transcript — An official examiner who signs and delivers a certificate in Form 6 shall notify each of the parties to the appeal and the clerk when the transcript of the examination is completed.

Special Commissioner

21. (1) Appointment — Where the court makes an order under clause 117(1)(e) of the Act referring a question to a special commissioner for inquiry and report, the court shall, by order, appoint the special commissioner and fix the date on or before which the inquiry shall be completed and the report filed.

(2) Motion for directions — The special commissioner may make a motion to the court for directions in respect of the inquiry or the report, or both.

(3) Filing of report — Upon completion of the report, the special commissioner,

(a) shall file the report, together with one copy for each party to the appeal; and

(b) shall give notice of the filing of the report to each party to the appeal.

Notice of Decision of Court

22. Immediately after the disposition of an appeal, the clerk shall give notice of the court's decision, including any written reasons and endorsements.

(a) to each party to the appeal who was not present in person or by counsel when the decision was made;

(b) to the clerk of the Ontario Court (Provincial Division); and

(c) to the Crown Attorney, where a prosecutor is not acting on behalf of the Crown.

Transition

23. (1) Definition, "preceding rules" — In this rule, **"preceding rules"** means the Rules of the Ontario Court (General Division) and the Ontario Court (Provincial Division) in Appeals under Section 116 of the *Provincial Offences Act (Regulation 196 of the Revised Regulations of Ontario, 1990) as they read on the day before these rules come into force.*

(2) Application of rules — These rules apply to all appeals, whether commenced before or after these rules come into force, except in respect of steps taken under the preceding rules.

(3) Power of judge — Despite the repeal of the preceding rules and subrule (2), a judge may make an order that an appeal, or a step in the appeal, be conducted under these rules or the preceding rules or make any order that is considered just in order to secure the fair and expeditious conduct of the appeal.

Form 1 — Notice of Appeal Under Section 116
of the Provincial Offences Act

Courts of Justice Act

1. Ontario Court (General Division) or Ontario Court (Provincial Division) at ....

2. Appellant is

   Defendant

   Prosecutor

   Attorney General

3. Name of appellant: ....

   Address for service: ....

4. Counsel for appellant: ....

   Address for service: ....

5. Name of respondent (if known): ....

   Address for service: ....

6. Counsel for respondent (if known): ....

   Address for service: ....

7. Decision of Ontario Court (Provincial Division)(include names of Judge or Justice of Peace appealed from, if known): ....

....

8. Date of decision:

9. The appellant appeals against:

   conviction

   dismissal

   finding as to ability to conduct a defence

   sentence

   order (s. 161 of the *P. O. A.*) by the Ontario Court (Provincial Division) at .... (address of court)

10. If defendant is in custody, place where held:

....

11.

   (a) Description of offence:[32] ....

   ....

   (b) Information Number (if known): ....

---

32 *for example, careless driving*

12. (1) Statute:[33] ....

(2) Section:[34] ....

13. Date of offence: ....

14. Plea at trial: ....

15. The grounds for appeal are: (specify the question of law or issue where the appeal is from conviction or acquittal or finding as to ability to conduct a defence *or* specify the ground for appeal against sentence).

1. ....

2. ....

16. In support of this appeal, the appellant relies upon the following: (set out documents such as transcript, etc. upon which the appellant relies)

1. ....

2. ....

17. The relief sought is: ....

18. The appellant intends:

to be present in person or by counsel and to present the issues and the appellant's arguments orally

to be present in person or by counsel and to present the issues and the appellant's arguments orally

19. Does the appellant intend to make a motion for an order that the appeal be heard by way of a new trial in the appeal court?

( ) Yes ( ) No

20. Date: ....

21. Signature of appellant or counsel: ....

Notes:

1. If appellant's address for service is that of the appellant's counsel, state counsel's full address and add appellant's own full address.

2. Please notify the clerk of the court in writing immediately of any change of address. The court will communicate with you by mail at the address shown by you in this notice unless you notify the court of a change in your address.

3. This notice of appeal must be filed with the local registrar of the Ontario Court (Provincial Division) or Ontario Court (General Division).

---

33 *for example, Highway traffic Act*
34 *section 130*

Form 2 — Certificate of Clerk of Ontario Court (Provincial Division) as to Transcript of Evidence

Courts of Justice Act

1. Ontario Court (General Division) or Ontario Court (Provincial Division)

....

at ....

2. Name of appellant: ....

   Address for appellant: ....

3. Counsel for appellant:

   Name: ....

   Address for service: ....

4. I, ...(name)

certify that: ....(name)

   (1) I am clerk of the Ontario Court (Provincial Division) at ....

   (2) The appellant has ordered copies of the transcript of evidence at the trial including reasons for judgment or sentence recorded at the trial of ....(name of defendant) held at the Ontario Court

   (3) I have accepted the order, will ensure that the transcript is prepared with reasonable diligence and will provide the number of copies ordered.

   (4) When the transcript is completed I will obtain and attach to it a certificate by the person who prepared the transcript as to the accuracy of the transcription.

   (5) When the transcript has been completed, I will notify,

   (a) the appellant;

   (b) the respondent;

   (c) the clerk of the court to which the appeal is being taken; and

   (d) if the Crown Attorney is not the appellant or the respondent, the Crown Attorney.

   Dated at .... on ...., 19......

..........(signature of clerk)

Form 3 — Order for Recognizance and Recognizance Under Section 110 of the Provincial Offences Act

Courts of Justice Act

On motion s. 110 is waived provided that the appellant enter into a recognizance pursuant to s. 110 to appear on the appeal, in the amount of.......... with or without sureties.

.... Judge, Ontario Court (Provincial Division)(General Division)

Be it remembered that on the .... day of, ..., 19......ldr2», the persons named in the following Schedule came before me and jointly and severally acknowledged themselves to owe Her Majesty the Queen the amounts set opposite their names:

		cash deposit	**description of other valuable security**
Surety:	....	$..........	$..
	(name)		(amount)
Address	....		
Surety:	....	$..........	$..
	(name)		(amount)
Address	....		
Surety:	....	$..........	$..
	(name)		(amount)
Address	....		

which may be enforced in the same manner as a judgment of the Ontario Court (General Division) if the appellant fails to comply with the conditions hereunder written.

Taken and acknowledged before me at .... on ...., 19......

Judge/Justice of the Peace

Whereas .... of .... hereinafter called the appellant, was convicted in the Ontario Court (Provincial Division) at .... of the offence of .... contrary to section .... and a sentence of .... was imposed.

And whereas the appellant wishes to appeal that conviction or sentence or both and,

( ) to be released from custody pending the hearing of that appeal

( ) that the application of subsection 111(1) of the *Provincial Offences Act* be waived pending the hearing of the appeal.

Now therefore the condition of this recognizance is that is if the appellant appears on the appeal

(set out any further conditions)

the said recognizance is void, otherwise it is of full force and effect.

..........signature of surety

..........signature of appellant

..........signature of surety

Form 4 — Order for Recognizance and Recognizance Under Section 111

Courts of Justice Act

On motion s. 111(1) is waived provided that the appellant enter into a recognizance pursuant to s. 111(2) to appear on the appeal, in the amount of .... with or without sureties.

..........Judge, Ontario Court (Provincial Division)(General Division)

Recognizance Under Section 111 of the Provincial Offences Act

Be it remembered that on the .... day of ...., 19......, at ...., the persons named in the following Schedule came before me and jointly and severally acknowledged themselves to owe Her Majesty the Queen the amounts set opposite their names, namely:

Surety: .... $......................................(no deposit required)
                 (name)   (amount)
Address   ....

Surety: .... $......................................(no deposit required)
                 (name)   (amount)
Address   ....

Surety: .... $......................................(no deposit required)
                 (name)   (amount)
Address   ....

which may be enforced in the same manner as a judgment of the Ontario Court (General Division) if the appellant fails to comply with the conditions hereunder written.

Taken and acknowledged before me on ...., 19......

.... Judge/Justice of the Peace

Whereas .... of .... hereinafter called the appellant, was convicted in the Ontario Court (Provincial Division) at of the offence(s) of contrary to section .... and a fine of $.......... was imposed.

And whereas the appellant wishes to appeal that conviction or sentence or both and has requested that the application of subsection 111(1) of the *Provincial Offences Act* be waived pending the hearing of the appeal.

Now therefore the condition of this recognizance is that if the appellant appears on the appeal the said recognizance is void, otherwise it is of all force and effect.

This recognizance has been read over and explained to me and I fully understand the same.

..........signature of surety

..........signature of appellant

..........signature of surety

Form 5 — Notice of Abandonment of Appeal

Courts of Justice Act

BETWEEN ....(appellant)

    — AND —

..........(respondent)

Take notice that the appellant has abandoned the appeal in respect of the following matter:

> (describe charge against defendant, state the decision or sentence appealed from and the date of the decision)

Dated at .... on .... 19......

..........(appellant or counsel for appellant)

..........(witness)

Form 6 — Certificate of Official Examiner to Ontario Court (General Division) or Ontario Court (Provincial Division)

Courts of Justice Act

1. Ontario Court (General Division) or Ontario Court (Provincial Division) at ....

2. Name of appellant: ....

    Address for service: ....

3. Counsel for appellant: ....

    Name: ....

    Address for service: ....

4. Name of respondent: ....

    Address for service: ....

5. Counsel for respondent: ....

    Name: ....

    Address for service: ....

6. Name of witness examined: ....

7. Witness was examined by:

    ( ) appellant

    ( ) respondent

    ( ) ....

8. The examination of the witness was completed on the ...., 19......

9. I, ...(name), an official examiner, certify that the,

   ( ) appellant

   ( ) respondent

   ( ) ....

has ordered .... copies of the transcript of this examination, that I have accepted the order, will prepare the transcript with reasonable diligence and will provide the stated number of copies of the transcript.

Dated at ...., on ...., 19......

..........(official examiner)

Rules of the Ontario Court (Provincial Division) in Appeals Under Section 135 of the Provincial Offences Act

R.R.O. 1990, Reg. 198 [am. O. Reg. 504/93; revoked O. Reg. 722/94]

Rules of the Ontario Court (Provincial Division) in Appeals Under Section 135 of the Provincial Offences Act

O. Reg. 722/94

Definitions and Interpretation

1. (1) Definitions — In these rules,

"Act" means the *Provincial Offences Act*; ("Loi")

"appeal court" means the Ontario Court (Provincial Division) sitting as the appeal court under section 135 of the Act; ("tribunal d'appel")

"clerk" means the clerk of the Ontario Court (Provincial Division); ("greffier")

"file" means file with the clerk; ("déposer")

"judge" means a judge of the Ontario Court (Provincial Division) sitting as the appeal court under section 135 of the Act.("juge")

(2) Application of rules — These rules apply in respect of appeals to the Ontario Court (Provincial Division) under section 135 of the Act.

(3) General principle — These rules shall be construed liberally so as to obtain as expeditious a conclusion of every proceeding as is consistent with a just determination of the proceeding.

(4) Matters not provided for — Where matters are not provided for in these rules, the practice shall be determined by analogy to them.

Calculation of Time

2. (1) General — In the calculation of time under these rules or an order of the court, except where a contrary intention appears,

    (a) where there is a reference to a number of days between two events, they shall be counted by excluding the day on which the first event happens and including the day on which the second event happens, even if they are described as clear days or the words "at least" are used;

    (b) where a period of less than seven days is prescribed, holidays shall not be counted;

    (c) where the time for doing an act under these rules expires on a holiday, the act may be done on the next day that is not a holiday; and

    (d) service of a document made after 4 p.m. or at any time on a holiday shall be deemed to have been made on the next day that is not a holiday.

(2) Local time — Where a time of day is mentioned in these rules or in any documents in an appeal, the time referred to shall be taken as the time observed locally.

(3) "Holiday" — For the purposes of subsection (1), **"holiday"** means,

(a) any Saturday or Sunday;

(b) New Year's Day;

(c) Good Friday;

(d) Easter Monday;

(e) Victoria Day;

(f) Canada Day;

(g) Civil Holiday;

(h) Labour Day;

(i) Thanksgiving Day;

(j) Remembrance Day;

(k) Christmas Day;

(l) Boxing Day; and

(m) any special holiday proclaimed by the Governor General or the Lieutenant Governor.

(4) Same — Where,

(a) New Year's Day, Canada Day or Remembrance Day falls on a Saturday or Sunday, the following Monday is a holiday;

(b) Christmas Day falls on a Saturday or Sunday, the following Monday and Tuesday are holidays;

(c) Christmas Day falls on a Friday, the following Monday is a holiday.

Notice by Mail

3. A notice or document given or delivered by mail shall, unless the contrary is shown, be deemed to be given or delivered on the seventh day following the day on which it was mailed.

Substituted Service

4. Where, on motion without notice, it appears to a judge that reasonable efforts have been made without success to give or deliver a notice or document in the manner required by these rules or the Act, or that reasonable efforts would not be successful, the judge may make an order for substituted service of the notice or document in such manner as the judge directs or, where necessary in the interests of justice, may dispense with the giving or delivery of the notice or document upon such terms as the judge considers proper in the circumstances.

Appeal Where Fine Imposed

5. A defendant who appeals from a decision imposing a fine shall file with the notice of appeal a receipt for payment of the fine issued by the clerk of the court that imposed the fine or state in the notice of appeal that the fine has been paid to a municipality responsible for collecting its own parking fines, unless the clerk is satisfied that an order has been made under subsection 111(2) of the Act and a recognizance has been entered into by the defendant in accordance with the order.

Filing of Notice of Appeal

6. (1) Notice of appeal — A notice of appeal shall be in Form 1.

(2) Time and place for hearing — Upon the filing of the notice of appeal, the clerk shall set a time and place for the hearing of the appeal in accordance with section 135 of the Act.

(3) Notice to respondent — The clerk shall give the respondent a copy of the filed notice of appeal and a notice of the time and place of the hearing in Form 2.

(4) Timely notice — Notice of the time and place of the hearing shall be given at least 15 days before the day set for the hearing.

(5) Certificate — A certificate of giving a notice under subrule (3) endorsed on the notice by the clerk shall be received in evidence and, in the absence of evidence to the contrary, is proof that the notice was given.

(6) Interpretation — For the purposes of this rule, where the defendant appeals, the prosecutor is the respondent, and vice-versa.

Notice to Crown Attorney

7. (1) Copies to Crown Attorney — The clerk shall give the Crown Attorney a copy of each notice or document filed with or issued by the clerk in respect of an appeal under these rules.

(2) Intervention of Crown Attorney — Where a prosecutor is not acting on behalf of the Crown, the Crown Attorney may intervene to act on behalf of the prosecutor or to attend as a party on the appeal.

Extension or Abridgment of Time

8. (1) Judge's power — A judge may extend or abridge the time for bringing an appeal and for doing any other act in connection with an appeal for which a time is prescribed before or after the expiration of the time prescribed.

(2) Notice — A notice of motion to extend or abridge time shall be given to the opposite party, unless otherwise directed by a judge.

Transcripts

9. (1) Transcript not required — Unless a judge orders otherwise, a party to an appeal need not provide a transcript of all or any part of the evidence at trial.

(2) Transcripts required — Where the court orders that a transcript of all or any part of the evidence at trial be provided under clause 136(3)(a) of the Act or a party to an appeal files such a transcript, an appellant shall file and deliver to the respondent,

(a) in an appeal against conviction or acquittal, one copy of the transcript of evidence at trial, including reasons for judgment; and

(b) in an appeal against conviction and sentence or sentence only, one copy of the transcript of evidence at trial and submissions on sentencing, including reasons for judgment and sentence, if any.

(3) Transcript to Crown Attorney — Where the Crown Attorney has given notice of intervention after receiving notice of appeal, the appellant shall deliver a copy of the transcript of evidence at trial, including reasons for judgment and sentence, if any, to the Crown Attorney.

Recognizances

10. (1) An order for recognizance and recognizance under section 110 of the Act shall be in Form 3.

(2) An order for recognizance and recognizance under section 111 of the Act shall be in Form 4.

Motions Under Act or Rules

11. (1) Notice of motion — A motion provided for by the Act or these rules shall be commenced by a notice of motion.

(2) Time for hearing — There shall be at least three days between service of the notice of motion and the day for hearing the motion.

(3) Time for filing notice — The moving party shall file notice of motion at least two days before the day for hearing the motion.

(4) Evidence — Evidence on a motion may be given,

(a) by affidavit;

(b) with the permission of the court, orally; or

(c) in the form of a transcript of the examination of a witness.

(5) Power of judge — Upon the hearing of a motion, the judge may receive and base his or her decision on information that he or she considers credible or trustworthy in the circumstances, whether or not other evidence is given.

(6) Hearing where notice not served — A motion may be heard within service of a notice of motion.

(a) on consent;

(b) where the motion is made under section 111 or 112 of the Act; or

(c) where, having regard to the subject-matter or the circumstances of the motion, it would not be unjust to hear the motion without service of a notice of motion.

Directions

12. A party to an appeal may make a motion to the court at any time for directions with respect to the conduct of the appeal.

Dismissal of Appeal

13. The court may dismiss an appeal where the appellant,

(a) does not attend in person or by counsel on the day set by the clerk for the hearing of the appeal;

(b) has filed a notice of abandonment;

(c) has not filed a transcript of evidence at trial, including reasons for judgment or sentence, if any, within 30 days after receiving notice of completion of the transcript from the clerk of the Ontario Court (Provincial Division); or

(d) has failed to comply with an order of the court in respect of the appeal.

Abandonment of Appeals

14. (1) Notice of abandonment — An appellant who wishes to abandon the appeal may file a notice of abandonment in Form 5.

(2) Signing of notice — The appellant or counsel for the appellant shall sign the notice of abandonment.

(3) Signing by witness — Where the appellant signs the notice of abandonment, the notice must also be signed by another person who witnessed the signing by the appellant.

(4) Affidavit of execution — Where the witness is not counsel for the appellant, the appellant shall file an affidavit of execution by the witness with the notice of abandonment.

(5) Notice to other parties — The clerk shall give a copy of the filed notice of abandonment to each of the other parties to the appeal.

Notice of Decision of Court

15. (1) Notice of decision on appeal — Immediately after the disposition of an appeal, the clerk shall give notice of the court's decision, including any written reasons and endorsements,

(a) to each party to the appeal who was not present in person or by counsel when the decision was made;

(b) to the clerk of the Ontario Court (Provincial Division); and

(c) to the Crown Attorney, where a prosecutor is not acting on behalf of the Crown.

(2) Deemed receipt of notice of trial — Where the appeal court directs a new trial and sets a date for the trial with the consent of the parties, the defendant is deemed to have received notice of trial.

Transition

16. (1) Definition, "preceding rules" — In this rule, **"preceding rules"** means the Rules of the Ontario Court (Provincial Division) in Appeals under Section 135 of the *Provincial Offences Act* (Regulation 198 of the Revised Regulations of Ontario, 1990) as they read on the day before these rules come into force.

(2) Application of rules — These rules apply to all appeals, whether commenced before or after these rules come into force, except in respect of steps already taken under the preceding rules.

(3) Power of judge — Despite the repeal of the preceding rules and subrule (2), a judge may make an order that an appeal, or a step in the appeal, be conducted under these rules or the preceding rules or make any order that is considered just in order to secure the fair and expeditious conduct of the appeal.

Form 1 — Notice of Appeal Under Section 135 of the Provincial Offences Act

1. Ontario Court (Provincial Division) at ....

2. Appellant is:

      Defendant

      Prosecutor

      Attorney General

3. Name of appellant: ....

      Address for service: ....

4. Counsel for appellant:

      Name:..........

      Address for service:..........

5. Name of respondent (if known): ....

      Address for service:..........

6. Counsel for respondent (if known): ....

      Address for service:..........

7. Decision of Ontario Court (Provincial Division): (include name of Judge or Justice of the Peace appealed from, if known).........

8. Date of decision: ....

9. The appellant appeals against:

Conviction

Dismissal

Sentence

10. If appellant is in custody, place where held: ....

11.

(a) Description of offence:[35] ....

(b) Certificate Number (if known): ....

12. Statute:[36] ....

13. Date of offence: ....

14. Plea at trial:

The plea entered was: (check off)

guilty

not guilty

not known

15. The appellant wants the appeal court to: (check one)

Find the defendant not guilty

Find the defendant guilty

Order a new trial

Change the sentence

Other: (please specify)

....

16. The grounds of appeal are ....

Complete No. 17 for *Provincial Offences Act*, Part II, Parking Offences where the municipality is collecting its own parking fines.

17. The fine has been paid in full at ....

(municipality) on ....

18. Date: ....

19. Signature of appellant or counsel or agent: ....

---

35 for example, speeding

36 for example, *Highway Traffic Act*

Form 2 — Notice of Time and Place of Hearing of Appeal Under Section 135 of the Provincial Offences Act

Courts of Justice Act

ONTARIO COURT (PROVINCIAL DIVISION)
PROVINCE OF ONTARIO

To:

....

appellant

....

(address)

and

....

respondent

....

(address)

Take notice that the appeal in respect of the .... in the Ontario Court (Provincial Division) on ...., 199......, in respect of the charge that ....(name) of .... on or about ...., 199...... at .... did commit the offence(s) of (set out charges) contrary to .... section .... will be heard in the Ontario Court (Provincial Division) at .... on ...., 199...... at ....

Given at: .... on ...., 199......

....

Clerk

Form 3 — Order for Recognizance and Recognizance Under Section 110 of of the Provincial Offences Act

Courts of Justice Act

On motion s. 110 is waived provided that the appellant enter into a recognizance pursuant to s. 110 to appear on the appeal, in the amount of .... with or without sureties.

....

Judge, Ontario Court (Provincial Division)

Be it remembered that on ...., 19.........., the persons named in the following Schedule came before me and jointly and severally acknowledged themselves to owe Her Majesty the Queen the amounts set opposite their names, namely:

	cash deposit	**description of other valuable security**

Appellant: .... $......... $...
                 (name)   (amount)

Address   ....

Appellant: .... $......... $...
                 (name)   (amount)

Address   ....

Appellant: .... $......... $...
                 (name)   (amount)

Address   ....

which may be enforced in the same manner as a judgment of the Ontario Court (General Division) if the appellant fails to comply with the conditions hereunder written.

Taken and acknowledged before me at .... on ...., 19.........

.... Judge/Justice of the Peace

Whereas .... of .... hereinafter called the appellant, was convicted in the Ontario Court (Provincial Division) at .... of the offence of .... contrary to .... section .... and a sentence of .... was imposed.

And whereas the appellant wishes to appeal that conviction or sentence or both and,

( ) to be released from custody pending the hearing of that appeal

( ) that the application of subsection 111(1) of the *Provincial Offences Act* be waived pending the hearing of the appeal.

Now therefore the condition of this recognizance is that if the appellant appears on the appeal

(set out any further conditions)

the said recognizance is void, otherwise it is of full force and effect.

....

signature of surety

....

signature of appellant

....

signature of surety

Form 4 — Order for Recognizance and Recognizance

Courts of Justice Act

On motion s. 111(1) is waived provided that the appellant enter into a recognizance pursuant to s. 111(2) to appear on the appeal, in the amount of .... with or without sureties.

....

Judge, Ontario Court (Provincial Division)

Recognizance Under Section 111 of the Provincial Offences Act

Be it remembered that on ...., 19.........., at ...., the persons named in the following Schedule came before me and jointly and severally acknowledged themselves to owe Her Majesty the Queen the amounts set opposite their names, namely:

Appellant:	....	$..(no deposit required)
	(name)	(amount)
Address	....	
Appellant:	....	$..(no deposit required)
	(name)	(amount)
Address	....	
Appellant:	....	$..(no deposit required)
	(name)	(amount)
Address	....	

which may be enforced in the same manner as a judgment of the Ontario Court (General Division) if the appellant fails to comply with the conditions hereunder written.

Taken and acknowledged before me at .... on ...., 19..........

.... Judge/Justice of the Peace

Whereas .... of .... hereinafter called the appellant, was convicted of the Ontario Court (Provincial Division) at .... of the offence(s) of .... contrary to section .... and a fine of $.......... was imposed.

And whereas the appellant wishes to appeal that conviction or sentence or both and has requested that the application of subsection 111(1) of the *Provincial Offences Act* be waived pending the hearing of the appeal.

Now therefore the condition of this recognizance is that if the appellant appears on the appeal the said recognizance is void, otherwise it is of all force and effect.

This recognizance has been read over and explained to me and I fully understand the same.

....

signature of surety

....

signature of appellant

....

signature of surety

Form 5 — Notice of Abandonment of Appeal

BETWEEN

.... (appellant)

— AND —

....

(respondent)

Take notice that the appellant has abandoned the appeal in respect of the following matter:

(describe charge against defendant, state the decision or sentence appealed from and the date of the decision)

Dated at .... on ...., 19..........

....

(appellant or counsel for appellant)

....

(witness)

Appendix F

Demerit Point System

Demerit Point System O. Reg. 339/94 [as am. O. Regs. 164/96, 331/97, 538/97]

Interpretation

1. (1) In this Regulation,

"accumulated demerit points" means the total demerit points in a person's record acquired as a result of offences committed within any period of two years, less any points deducted for that period under this Regulation;

"probationary driver" means a person classed as such under section 11.

(2) A reference in this Regulation to a class of driver's licence is a reference to the class of licence as prescribed in Ontario Regulation 340/94.

(3) A reference in this Regulation to "fully licensed driver", "level 1 exit test", "level 2 exit test", "novice driver" and "valid driver's licence" is a reference to those expressions as defined in Ontario Regulation 340/94.

(4) A reference in this Regulation to the surrender of a licence does not include the surrender of the Photo Card portion of the licence.

(5) The short descriptions in Column 3 of the Table to this Regulation indicate, for convenience of reference only, the general nature of the offences under the provisions in Column 1 of the Table and shall not be construed to limit the offences for which demerit points are imposed. O. Reg. 339/94, s. 1.

GENERAL

2. If a person is convicted of an offence under a provision of an Act, regulation or municipal by-law set out in Column 1 of the Table to this Regulation and the penalty imposed by the court for the conviction does not include a period of suspension, the Registrar shall record in respect of the person, as of the date of commission of the offence, the number of demerit points set out opposite thereto in Column 2.

3. (1) If a person is convicted of two or more offences arising out of the same circumstances and the penalty imposed by the court in respect of any of the convictions includes a period of licence suspension, no demerit points shall be recorded.

(2) If a person is convicted of two or more offences arising out of the same circumstances and the penalty imposed by the court in respect of any of the convictions does not include a period of licence suspension, demerit points shall only be recorded for the conviction carrying the greatest number of points and, if that number is the same for two or more convictions, points shall be recorded for one conviction only. O. Reg. 339/94, s. 3.

4. (1) If a resident of Ontario is convicted or forfeits bail in another province or territory of Canada or in one of the states of the United States of America for an offence that, in the opinion of the Registrar, is in substance and effect equivalent to an offence for which demerit points would be recorded upon conviction in Ontario, the Registrar may record the demerit points for the conviction as if the conviction had been entered or the bail forfeited in Ontario for the equivalent offence.

(2) For the purposes of subsection (1), "conviction" includes a plea of guilty or a finding of guilt.

(3) Any accumulated demerit points of a new Ontario resident who becomes a full licensed driver or a novice driver here, including a person classed as a novice driver under subsection 28(6) of Ontario Regulation 340/94 shall be reduced, from the day on which he or she becomes a fully licensed driver or a novice driver,

(a) to seven, if the driver becomes a fully licensed driver and his or her accumulated demerit points total eight or more;

(b) to four, if the driver becomes a novice driver and his or her accumulated demerit points total five or more.

(4) After a reduction under subsection (3), the accumulated demerit points that remain shall be those recorded for the most recently committed offences. O. Reg. 339/94, s. 4.

5. (1) If a person convicted of an offence set out in Column 1 of the Table appeals the conviction and notice of the appeal is served on the Registrar, the conviction and the demerit points related to it shall not be entered on the person's record unless the conviction is sustained on appeal.

(2) If a conviction referred to in subsection (1) and related demerit points have been recorded prior to service of notice of an appeal on the Registrar, the conviction and demerit points shall be removed from the record, and any suspension imposed as a result of the conviction shall be stayed, as of the date notice is served on the Registrar, unless the conviction is sustained on appeal. O. Reg. 339/94, s. 5.

6. (1) The Registrar or the Minister gives sufficient notice of the suspension of a licence to a person to whom such notice must be given under this Regulation if he or she sends it by registered mail to the person's latest address appearing on the records of the Ministry.

(2) The Registrar shall state the effective date of any licence suspension in the notice.

(3) The period of licence suspension is concurrent with the unexpired portion of any other licence suspension under this or any other authority. O. Reg. 339/94, s. 6.

DEMERIT POINTS: FULLY LICENSED DRIVERS

7. (1) If a person who is a fully licensed driver in Ontario in one or more licence classes or a person who is not a resident of Ontario has six, seven or eight accumulated demerit points, the Registrar shall mail a notice setting out the number of points to the person at his or her latest address appearing on the records of the Ministry.

(2) A failure to give notice under subsection (1) does not render any further proceeding under this Regulation ineffective. O. Reg. 339/94, s. 7.

8. (1) If a person who is a fully licensed driver in Ontario in one or more licence classes or a person who is not a resident of Ontario has 9, 10, 11, 12, 13 or 14 accumulated demerit points, the Registrar may require the person to attend an interview before a Ministry official and to provide information or other evidence to show cause why his or her driver's licence should not be suspended.

(2) The Minister may, after giving notice, suspend the person's driver's licence,

(a) if the person fails to attend the required interview; or

(b) if the person does not comply with the Ministry's requirements as a result of the interview; or

(c) if, in the Minister's opinion, the person has not shown cause at the interview why the licence should not be suspended.

(3) A licence suspended under subsection (2) shall not be reinstated until such period as the Minister considers advisable has elapsed from the date the licence was surrendered on account of the suspension or two years have elapsed from the date of the suspension, whichever occurs first. O. Reg. 339/94, s. 8.

9. (1) If a person who is a fully licensed driver in Ontario in one or more licence classes or a person who is not a resident of Ontario has 15 or more accumulated demerit points, the Registrar shall, after giving notice, suspend the person's driver's licence.

(2) A licence suspended under subsection (1) shall not be reinstated until,

(a) in the case of a first suspension, 30 days have elapsed from the date the licence was surrendered on account of the suspension or two years have elapsed from the date of the suspension, whichever occurs first; or

(b) in the case of a subsequent suspension, six months have elapsed from the date the licence was surrendered on account of the suspension or two years have elapsed from the date of the suspension, whichever occurs first.

(3) For the purpose of clause (2)(b), a suspension is a subsequent suspension only if it occurs as a result of a conviction for an offence committed within two years after the expiry of a prior suspension under this section.

(4) If a suspension is imposed on a person who, at the time of the suspension, is a fully licensed driver in Ontario in one or more licence classes or a person who is not a resident of Ontario, the person's accumulated demerit points for convictions for offences that occurred prior to the effective date of the suspension shall be reduced to seven on that date and the remaining points shall be those recorded for the most recently committed offences. O. Reg. 339/94, s. 9.

DEMERIT POINTS: PROBATIONARY DRIVERS

10. (1) Every driver of a motor vehicle on a highway who was classed as a probationary driver in accordance with Regulation 578 of the Revised Regulations of Ontario, 1990, as it read immediately prior to the coming into force of this Regulation, shall remain classed as a probationary driver until he or she satisfies the conditions set out in section 14 or until he or she becomes a fully licensed driver or a novice driver in a class or classes of motor vehicle pursuant to a notice under subsection (2), whichever occurs first.

(2) Within three years of the day this Regulation comes into force, the Minister shall notify each person who is at that time classed as a probationary driver,

(a) of his or her licence status;

(b) of the specific conditions and time limits to be met for converting his or her licence from probationary to fully licensed or novice status; and

(c) of the consequences of not converting his or her driver's licence to fully licensed or novice status within the required time limit.

(3) Despite subsection (1), a person classed as a probationary driver in accordance with Regulation 578 of the Revised Regulations of Ontario, 1990, as it read immediately prior to the coming into force of this Regulation, who resides in Ontario but who has never held an Ontario driver's licence shall be classed as a novice driver on the day this Regulation comes into force. O. Reg. 339/94, s. 10.

11. Any accumulated demerit points of a person who becomes a probationary driver under subsection 14(8) or (10) shall be reduced, from the day on which he or she becomes a probationary driver,

(a) to zero, if they total nine or less; or

(b) by nine, if they total more than nine, and the remaining points shall be those recorded in respect of the most recently committed offences. O. Reg. 339/94, s. 11.

12. (1) When demerit points are recorded on a probationary driver's record for the first time in any probationary period, the Registrar shall mail a notice to the driver at his or her latest address appearing on the records of the Ministry, setting out the number of accumulated demerit points that the driver has and the circumstances under which his or her licence may be suspended.

(2) A failure to give notice under subsection (1) does not render any further proceeding under this Regulation ineffective. O. Reg. 339/94, s. 12.

13. (1) If a person's accumulated demerit points in a period during which he or she was a probationary driver total six or more, the Registrar shall, after giving notice, suspend the person's driver's licence.

(2) A licence suspended under subsection (1) shall not be reinstated until 30 days have elapsed from the date the licence was surrendered on account of the suspension or two years have elapsed from the date of the suspension, whichever occurs first.

(3) If a suspension is imposed on a person who, at the time of the suspension, is a probationary driver, the person's accumulated demerit points for convictions for offences that occurred prior to the effective date of the suspension shall be reduced to zero on that date.

(4) If a suspension is imposed on a person who, at the time of the suspension, is not a probationary driver, the person's accumulated demerit points for convictions for offences that occurred prior to the effective date of the suspension shall be reduced to seven on that date and the remaining points shall be those recorded in respect of the most recently committed offences. O. Reg. 339/94, s. 13.

PROBATIONARY CREDITS

14. (1) A probationary driver ceases to be probationary upon accumulating two probationary credits.

(2) A probationary driver is entitled to one probationary credit for each probationary period during which he or she,

(a) holds, for a total of 12 months, a valid driver's licence, other than a Class L or R driver's licence, issued under the Act; and

(b) does not commit any offence, the conviction for which would result in licence suspension or would have resulted in licence suspension had his or her accumulated demerit points not been reduced by the Registrar under section 9 or 13.

(3) A probationary driver whose licence is suspended during a 12-month probationary period under subsection 9(1), clause 32(12)(b), section 46, section 47 for failure to meet medical standards, or section 198 of the Act,

or under the Motor Vehicle Accident Claims Act or the Compulsory Automobile Insurance Act, does not lose a probationary credit under subsection (2) for the probationary period in which the suspension takes place.

(4) Although, under subsection (3), there is no loss of a probationary credit, the probationary period during which the suspension takes place shall be extended by a length of time equal to the duration of the suspension and entitlement to a probationary credit depends upon compliance with the requirements set out in subsection (2) during the extended period.

(5) If the driver's licence of a probationary driver is suspended for any reason other than a reason set out in subsection (3), a new probationary period shall start on the day after the day the suspension expires.

(6) If a probationary driver with one probationary credit is convicted of an offence committed within the period for which he or she acquired the credit and the conviction results in licence suspension for any reason other than a reason set out in subsection (3), the credit for that period shall be revoked unless the probationary driver meets the requirements set out in subsection (2) during the period from the commission of the offence until the effective date of the suspension.

(7) If a probationary driver with one probationary credit is convicted of an offence committed within the period for which he or she acquired the credit and the conviction would have resulted in licence suspension had his or her accumulated demerit points not been reduced by the Registrar under section 13, the credit for that period shall be revoked unless the probationary driver meets the requirements set out in subsection (2) during the period from the commission of the offence until the effective date of the demerit point reduction.

(8) If a person who has ceased to be a probationary driver under subsection (1) is convicted of an offence committed within a period for which he or she acquired a probationary credit, and the conviction results in licence suspension for any reason other than a reason set out in subsection (3),

(a) the credit for that period shall be revoked;

(b) the person shall again be classed as a probationary driver; and

(c) a new probationary period shall start on the day after the day the suspension expires.

(9) Subsection (8) does not apply if, during the period from the commission of the offence until the effective date of the suspension, excluding any period for which a probationary credit has been awarded, the probationary driver meets the requirements set out in subsection (2).

(10) If a person who has ceased to be a probationary driver under subsection (1) is convicted of an offence committed within a period for which he or she acquired a probationary credit, and the conviction would have

resulted in licence suspension had his or her accumulated demerit points not been reduced by the Registrar under section 9 or 13,

(a) the credit for that period shall be revoked;

(b) the person shall again be classed as a probationary driver; and

(c) a new probationary period shall start on the twelfth day after the day the conviction is registered on the person's record.

(11) Subsection (10) does not apply if, during the period from the commission of the offence until the effective date of the demerit point reduction, excluding any period for which a probationary credit has been awarded, the probationary driver meets the requirements set out in subsection (2).

(12) If subsection (6), (7), (8) or (10) applies, demerit points accumulated as a result of offences committed prior to and including the time of the offence referred to therein shall not be included in determining whether a probationary driver meets the requirements set out in subsection (2) for the period from the commission of the offence until the effective date of the suspension or until the effective date of the demerit point reduction, as the case may be. O. Reg. 339/94, s. 14.

DEMERIT POINTS: NOVICE DRIVERS

15. (1) The Registrar shall mail a notice to a novice driver at his or her latest address on the records of the Ministry setting out the reason for the notice, the circumstances under which his or her licence may be suspended and any other action the Ministry may take if, within any two-year period, the novice driver,

(a) accumulates two, three, four or five demerit points;

(b) has on his or her driver's record two or more convictions for moving violations not arising out of the same circumstances that do not result in an accumulation of demerit points or in a suspension; or

(c) is involved in a collision for which he or she is assessed to be at fault or partially at fault.

(2) A failure to give notice under subsection (1) does not render any further proceeding under this Regulation ineffective.

(3) In this section and in section 16, a "moving violation" is a violation indicated by the letter "M" in the Ministry's Conviction Tables. O. Reg. 339/94, s. 15.

16. (1) The Registrar may require a novice driver to attend an interview before a Ministry official at a designated time and place if, within any two-year period, the novice driver,

(a) accumulates six, seven or eight demerit points;

(b) is involved in two or more collisions for which he or she is assessed to be at fault or partially at fault; or

(c) is involved in a collision for which he or she is assessed to be at fault or partially at fault and has two or more convictions for moving violations not arising out of the same circumstances.

(2) The Minister may, after giving notice, suspend the person's driver's licence,

(a) if the person does not attend the required interview;

(b) if the person does not comply with the Ministry's requirements as a result of the interview; or

(c) if, in the Minister's opinion, the person has not shown cause at the interview why the licence should not be suspended.

(3) A licence suspended under subsection (2) shall not be reinstated until such period as the Registrar considers advisable has elapsed from the date the licence was surrendered on account of the suspension or two years have elapsed from the date of the suspension, whichever occurs first. O. Reg. 339/94, s. 16.

17. (1) If a novice driver has nine or more accumualted demerit points, the Registrar shall, after giving notice, suspend his or her driver's licence.

(2) A licence suspended under subsection (1) shall not be reinstated until,

(a) in the case of a first suspension, 60 days have elapsed from the date the licence was surrendered on account of the suspension or two years have elapsed from the date of the suspension, whichever comes first; or

(b) in the case of a subsequent suspension, six months have elapsed from the date the licence was surrendered on account of the suspension or two years have elapsed from the date of the suspension, whichever occurs first.

(3) For the purpose of clause (2)(b), a suspension is a subsequent suspension only if it occurs as a result of a conviction for an offence committed within two years after the expiry of a prior suspension under this section.

(4) If a suspension is imposed on a person who, at the time of the suspension, is a novice driver, the person's accumulated demerit points for convictions for offences that occurred prior to the effective date of the suspension shall be reduced to four on that date and the remaining points shall be those recorded in respect of the most recently committed offences.

(5) If a suspension is imposed on a person who, at the time of the suspension, if no longer a novice driver, the person's accumulated demerit points for convictions for offences that occurred prior to the effective date of the suspension shall be reduced to seven on that date and the remaining points shall

be those recorded in respect of the most recently committed offences. O. Reg. 339/94, s. 17.

18. (1) Sections 7 to 9 apply, and not sections 15, 16 and 17, to a driver who holds a licence that includes more than one licence class, only one of which is novice class, if he or she is a fully licensed driver in the other licence class or classes.

(2) Sections 12 and 13 apply, and not sections 15, 16 and 17, to a driver who holds a licence that includes more than one licence class, only one of which is novice class, if he or she is a probationary driver in the other licence class or classes.

TABLE

	Column 1	Column 2	Column 3
Item	Provisions for Offences	Number of Demerit Points	Short Description of Offences for Convenience of Reference only
1	Section 200 of the *Highway Traffic Act*	7	*Failing to remain at scene of accident*
2	Section 130 of the *Highway Traffic Act*	6	*Careless driving*
3	Section 172 of the *Highway Traffic Act*	6	*Racing*
4	Section 128 of the *Highway Traffic Act*; subsection 13(3) of Regulation 829 of the Revised Regulations of Ontario, 1990; any provision of the National Capital Commission Traffic and Property Regulations CRC 1978, c. 1044 made under the *National Capital Act* (Canada) fixing maximum rates of speed and any municipal by-law fixing maximum rates of speed where the rate of speed is exceeded by,		
	(a) 50 km/h or more	6	Exceeding speed limit by 50 km/h or more
	(b) 30 km/h or more and less than 50 km/h	4	Exceeding speed limit by 30 to 49 km/h

	COLUMN 1	COLUMN 2	COLUMN 3
Item	Provisions for Offences	Number of Demerit Points	Short Description of Offences for Convenience of Reference only
	(c) more than 15 km/h and less than 30 km/h	3	Exceeding speed limit by 16 to 29 km/h
5	Section 174 of the *Highway Traffic Act*	5	*Driver of bus to stop at railway crossings*
6	Section 164 of the *Highway Traffic Act*	3	*Driving through, around or under railway crossing barrier*
7	Subsections 135(2) and (3), clause 136 3 (1)(b), sub-section 136(2), subsection 138(1), subsection 139(1), subsection 141(5) and sub-sections 144(7), (8) and (21) of the *Highway Traffic Act*	3	*Failing to yield right of way*
8	Clause 136(1)(a), subsec-tions 144(14), (15), (16), (17), (18) and (21), subsec-tions 146(3) and (4) and section 163 of the *Highway Traffic Act*, any municipal by-law requiring a driver to stop for a stop sign or signal light, and the National Capital Commission Traffic and Property Regulations CRC 1978, c. 1044 made under the *National Capital Act* (Canada) requiring a driver to stop for a stop sign	3	Failing to obey a stop sign, signal light or railway crossing signal
9	Section 134(1) of the *Highway Traffic Act*	3	*Failing to obey directions of police constable*
10	Section 134(3) of the *Highway Traffic Act*	3	*Driving or operating a vehicle on a closed highway*
11	Section 199(1) and (1.1) of the *Highway Traffic Act*	3	*Failing to report an accident*

	COLUMN 1	COLUMN 2	COLUMN 3
Item	Provisions for Offences	Number of Demerit Points	Short Description of Offences for Convenience of Reference only
12	Subsection 148(8), sections 149, 150 and 166 of the *Highway Traffic Act*	*3*	*Improper passing*
13	Section 154 of the *Highway Traffic Act*	*3*	*Improper driving where highway divided into lanes*
14	Subsections 175(11) and (12) of the *Highway Traffic Act*	*6*	*Failing to stop for school bus*
15	Section 158 of the *Highway Traffic Act*	*4*	*Following too closely*
16	Section 162 of the *Highway Traffic Act*	*3*	*Crowding driver's seat*
17	Clause 156(1)(a) of the *Highway Traffic Act*	*3*	*Drive wrong way — divided highway*
18	Clause 156(1)(b) of the *Highway Traffic Act*	*3*	*Cross divided highway — no proper crossing provided*
19	Section 153 of the *Highway Traffic Act*	*3*	*Wrong way in one way street or highway*
20	Subsection 157(1) of the *Highway Traffic Act*	*2*	*Backing on highway*
21	Subsections 140(1), (2) and (3) of the *Highway Traffic Act*	*2*	*Pedestrian crossover*
22	Subsections 148(1), (2), (4), (5), (6) and (7) of the *Highway Traffic Act*	*2*	*Failing to share road*
23	Subsections 141(2) and (3) of the *Highway Traffic Act*	*2*	*Improper right turn*
24	Subsections 141(6) and (7) of the *Highway Traffic Act*	*2*	*Improper left turn*
25	Subsections 142(1), (2) and (8) of the *Highway Traffic Act*	*2*	*Failing to signal*

	COLUMN 1	COLUMN 2	COLUMN 3
Item	Provisions for Offences	Number of Demerit Points	Short Description of Offences for Convenience of Reference only
26	Section 132 of the *Highway Traffic Act*	2	*Unnecessary slow driving*
27	Section 168 of the *Highway Traffic Act*	2	*Failing to lower headlamp beam*
28	Section 165 of the *Highway Traffic Act*	2	*Improper opening of vehicle door*
29	Section 143 and subsection 144(9) of the *Highway Traffic Act* and any municipal by-law prohibiting turns	2	Prohibited turns
30	Section 160 of the *Highway Traffic Act*	2	*Towing of persons on toboggans, bicycles, skis, etc., prohibited*
31	Subsection 182(2) of the *Highway Traffic Act*	2	*Failing to obey signs prescribed by regulation under subsection 182(1)*
32	Subsection 106(3) of the *Highway Traffic Act*	2	*Driver failing to wear complete seat belt assembly*
33	Subsection 106(6) of the *Highway Traffic Act*	2	*Driver failing to ensure passenger under 16 years wears complete seat belt assembly*
34	Subsection 106(7) of the *Highway Traffic Act*	2	*Driver failing to ensure child passenger under 23 kilograms occupies position with seat belt assembly*

O. Regs. 339/94, s. 18; 538/97, s. 1; 331/97.

Index